ATLANTIC
OCEAN

Berry
Islands

Spanish Wells
Current
Eleuthera Island
Nicholls'
Town
New Providence
Governor's Harbour
Nassau

Behring
Point

Kemps
Bay

Wemyss
Bight

Arthur's
Town

Cat Island

Little
San Salvador

San Salvador

Cockburn
Town

B A H A M A S

Devil's
Point

Great
Guana
Cay

Rolleville
George
Town

Stella
Maris

Rum Cay

Great
Exuma

Long Island

Samana
Cay

Clarence Town

Crooked Island

Long
Cay

Snug
Corner

Acklins
Island

page 216-7

page 268-9

Cayo
Coco

Ragged Island

La
Madura

juajay

Archipiélago de Camagüey

Cayo Romano

Great
Inagua

abas

nico

Morón

Esmeralda

Cayo
Sabinal

page 280-1

Matthew's
Town

iego de
Ávila

San
Pablo

Nuevitas

Cayos
Ana
Maria

Flo
Camagüey

Puerto
Manatí

Playa
Uvero

San
Antonio

Camalote

Gibara

Guardalavaca

Golfo de
Ana María

Vertientes

Carretera
Central

Macedonio

Puerto
Padre

Banes

Punta
de Mulas

La Lima

Guáimaro

Las
Tunas

Holguín

La Chiva

Reina

La Jagua

Jobabo

Buenaventura

Cueto

Mayari

Sagua de
Tánamo

Moa

Amancio
Rodríguez

Llanura del
Cauto Guacanayabo

1231
Pico del Cristal

1175
Pico del
Toldo

Alturas de Baracoa

Santa Cruz
del Sur

Cauto

Baracoa

Golfo de
Guacanayabo

Manzanillo

Bayamo

Contramaestre

page 298

Guantánamo

Maisí
Punta
de Maisí

Campechuela

Barrancas

Palma
Soriano

Gran
Piedra

Maquelcito

San
Antonio
del Sur

Cajobabo

Niquero

Sierra Maestra

1972
Pico
Turquino

1128
Loma el Jobo

1214

Santiago
de Cuba

Baconao

Cabo
Cruz

Pilón

Windward Passage

Jérémie

Montego
Bay

St Ann's
Bay

Anse
d'Hainault

Les
Cayes

Lucea

JAMAICA

Navassa
(USA)

HAITI

Negril

Jamaica Cha

Port-à-
Piment

Savanna
la Mar

Spanish
Town

Port Antonio

Pointe-
à-Gravois

Mandeville

May
Pen

Kingston

Morant
Point

Portland Point

INSIGHT GUIDES
CUBA

APA PUBLICATIONS

Part of the Langenscheidt Publishing Group

✹ INSIGHT GUIDE

CUBA

Editorial

Project Editor
Alyse Dar
Art Director
Steven Lawrence
Picture Manager
Tom Smyth
Series Manager
Rachel Fox

Distribution

UK & Ireland
GeoCenter International Ltd
Meridian House, Churchill Way West
Basingstoke, Hampshire RG21 6YR
sales@geocenter.co.uk

United States
Ingram Publisher Services
One Ingram Boulevard
PO Box 3006
La Vergne, TN 37086-1986
customer.service@
ingrampublisherservices.com

Australia
Universal Publishers
1 Waterloo Road
Macquarie Park, NSW 2113
sales@universalpublishers.com.au

New Zealand
Hema Maps New Zealand Ltd (HNZ)
Unit 2, 10 Cryers Road
East Tamaki, Auckland 2013
sales.hema@clear.net.nz

Worldwide
**Apa Publications GmbH & Co.
Verlag KG (Singapore branch)**
7030 Ang Mo Kio Avenue 5,
08-65 Northstar @ AMK
Singapore 569880
apasin@signet.com.sg

Printing
CTPS - China

©2011 Apa Publications GmbH & Co.
Verlag KG (Singapore branch)
All Rights Reserved

First Edition 1995
Fifth Edition 2011

CONTACTING THE EDITORS
We would appreciate it if readers
would alert us to errors or outdated information by writing to:
**Insight Guides, PO Box 7910,
London SE1 1WE, England.**
insight@apaguide.co.uk

ABOUT THIS BOOK

The first Insight Guide pioneered the use of creative full-color photography in travel guides in 1970. Since then, we have expanded our range to cater for our readers' need not only for reliable information about their chosen destination but also for a real understanding of the culture and workings of that destination. Now, when the internet can supply inexhaustible (but not always reliable) facts, our books marry text and pictures to provide those much more elusive qualities: knowledge and discernment. To achieve this, they rely heavily on the authority of locally based writers and photographers.

How to use this book

Insight Guide: Cuba is structured to convey an understanding of the country and its people as well as to guide readers through its attractions:

◆ The **Best Of Cuba** section at the front of the book helps you to prioritise what you want to do.

◆ The **Features** section, indicated by a pink bar at the top of each page, covers the political, social, and cultural history of Cuba through illuminating essays on the country's people, beliefs and religions, cuisine, and the arts, music, and sporting scenes.

◆ The main **Places** section, indicated by a blue bar, is a complete guide to all the sights and areas worth visiting. Places of special interest are coordinated by number with the maps. A list of recommended restaurants is included at the end of each chapter in this section.

◆ The **Travel Tips** listings section, with a yellow bar, includes all the practical information you'll need, divided into five sections: transpor-

LEFT: strolling along the Malecón in Havana at sunset.

This version builds on the invaluable work of earlier editors and contributors including **Tony Perrottet**, **Joann Biondi**, **Jane McManus**. Journalist **Danny Aeberhard** wrote the chapter on the future of Cuba in the 21st century. The music feature, "Cuba's Sizzling Sound" was written by **Sue Steward**, an acknowledged expert on Latin American music and author of Salsa: *Musical Heartbeat of South America*.

Other contributors to earlier editions whose work has provided a firm foundation, were **Joby Williams**, **Liz Balmaseda**, **José Antonio Evora**, **Sergio Giral**, **Larry Luxner**, **David Lloyd Marcus**, **Naomi Peck**, **James Rodewalk**, **Alfonso Silva**, **Ned Sublette**, and **Marjory Zimmerman**.

The quote from Colombian author **Gabriel García Marquez** from an article on his friendship with Fidel Castro (reprinted in full in previous editions) is the copyright of Gianni Mina and Ocean Press, and has been reprinted by kind permission of the Talman Company.

The main photographers were **Sylvaine Poitau**, **Anna Mockford**, **Nick Bonetti**, and **Glyn Genin**, who have captured the magic of Cuba. Thanks go to **Janet McCann** for proofreading the guide and also to **Helen Peters** for compiling the index.

Map Legend

—— ·—	International Boundary
—— —— ——	Province Boundary
—— · ——	National Park/Reserve
— — — —	Ferry Route
✈ ✈	Airport: International/ Regional
🚌	Bus Station
❶	Tourist Information
🏛 † ⸸	Church/Ruins
†	Monastery
☾	Mosque
✡	Synagogue
🏰 🏚	Castle/Ruins
∴	Archaeological Site
∩	Cave
⚊	Statue/Monument
★	Place of Interest
⚑	Beach

The main places of interest in the Places section are coordinated by number with a full-color map (eg ❶), and a symbol at the top of every right-hand page tells you where to find the map.

tation, accommodations, activities, an A–Z listing of practical tips, and a handy Spanish language section, with a list of suggestions for further reading.

The contributors

This new edition was commissioned by **Alyse Dar** at Insight Guides' London office. The book was updated and rewritten by **Sarah Cameron** who has spent a lifetime traveling in Latin America and the Caribbean, working first as an economist and then as an author of travel guides. The Caribbean Islands, and Cuba in particular, have become her specialty and she has contributed to many of APA Publications' titles on that region. For this edition, Cameron wrote new essays on Cuban beliefs and religions and the health care system, as well as photo features on birds and diving.

Contents

LEFT: Santiago de Cuba: Cuba's early capital, and the cradle of the Revolution.

Maps

La Habana

Travel Tips

THE BEST OF CUBA: TOP ATTRACTIONS

From wonderful views and heroic sights to colonial architecture and great music venues, here at a glance are Cuba's greatest attractions

△ A magnificent collection of 20th-century Cuban art can be seen at the **Museo Nacional Palacio de Bellas Artes (Arte Cubano)** in Havana, tracing the development of styles from pre- to post-revolutionary painting and sculpture. *See page 163*

△ Imagine the crowds, thousands deep, listening to one of Fidel's eight-hour May Day speeches in the **Plaza de la Revolución**, Havana, standing in the scorching heat on the acres of asphalt overlooked by General Batista's monolithic government buildings. *See page 181*

▷ A Unesco World Heritage Site, **Trinidad** is one of the most beguiling towns in Cuba, a place of great architectural interest, full of atmosphere and color and throbbing with music. *See page 255*

△ Even for non-smokers, a visit to the **Partagás cigar factory** in Havana is an experience, both aromatic and educational, with amazing skills on display. *See page 173*

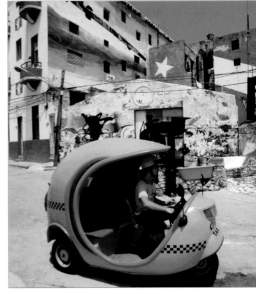

△ When the mists hover over the tobacco fields leaving only the tops of the palm trees and the sheer-sided, limestone *mogotes* on view, the **Valle de Viñales** is one of the most beautiful places on earth. *See page 205*

◁ Construction of the oldest house in Cuba, the **Casa de Velázquez** in Santiago de Cuba, was started in 1516. It is now a fascinating museum. *See page 303*

△ Where exuberant art and music mix, the **Callejón de Hamel** is the place to be on a Sunday afternoon in Havana. *See page 177*

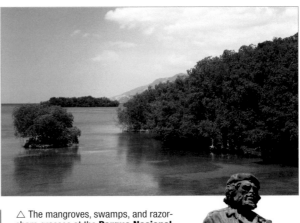

▽ Most of Cuba's famous sons and daughters, including José Martí, are buried in the **Cementerio Santa Ifigenia** in Santiago, where there is an eclectic mix of mausoleums and graves. *See page 305*

△ The mangroves, swamps, and razor-sharp grasses at the **Parque Nacional Desembarco de Granma** still give an idea of how unwelcoming the landing site was for the *guerrilleros* on their arrival from Mexico. *See page 293*

▷ Fans of revolutionary history should make the pilgrimage to the **Monument to Che Guevara**, Santa Clara, with its dramatic statue, the bas-relief of Che's letter to Fidel on leaving Cuba for Bolivia, and the mausoleum where the eternal flame burns for Che and his comrades interred there. *See page 240*

THE BEST OF CUBA: EDITOR'S CHOICE

With its varied natural beauty from mountain top to pristine beach and its troubled history which has spawned dramatic architecture and monuments, Cuba is fascinating, intriguing, and exciting. Here are the editor's top tips for making the most of it

BEST UNSPOILT BEACHES

• **Cayo Levisa**
On the north coast of Pinar del Río province, Cayo Levisa is a small dive resort reached by a short boat trip. *See page 209.*

• **Cayo Sabinal**
A wildlife reserve with deserted, pristine white-sand beaches north of Camagüey. *See page 274.*

• **María La Gorda**
Located in the far west of the island, this lovely beach flanks waters ideal for diving and snorkeling. *See page 210.*

• **Cayo Jutías** A small cay off the north coast of

Pinar del Río, a lovely stretch of white sand and calm, shallow water. *See page 209.*

• **Playa Los Cocos**
Some 8km (5 miles) from the beach resort of Playa Santa Lucía, this is a broad sweep of beach with a fishing village at one end and a few beach bars at the other. *See page 274.*

• **Playa Maguana** Not far from Baracoa, the trees come down to the sweep of white sand in a curved bay where there is just one hotel and beach bar. *See page 323.*

BEST HEROIC SITES

• **Monument to Che, Santa Clara** A dramatic statue overlooks the Plaza de la Revolución while underneath is a museum and a mausoleum where the remains of Che Guevara and some of his fellow fighters are interred. *See page 240.*

• **Monument to Antonio Maceo, Santiago** The impressive monument to the great 19th-century independence fighter dominates the Plaza de la Revolución at the entrance to the town. *See page 299.*

• **Playa Girón** The site of the Bay of Pigs invasion in 1961 is commemorated as "The First Imperialist Defeat in Latin America." *See page 233.*

• **Mausoleum of José Martí, Santiago**
The Father of the Nation lies in a splendid marble mausoleum, where an armed guard is changed every half hour,

accompanied by martial music. *See page 305.*

• **Moncada Barracks, Santiago** The unsuccessful attack on Moncada in 1953 launched the revolution. A museum gives details. *See page 299.*

• **Parque Nacional Desembarco de Granma, Niquero**
On the edge of the Sierra Maestra, this is where the guerrilla war began, in 1956. There is a walkway through the mangroves to the sea. *See page 293.*

ABOVE: the lovely Playa María la Gorda.
ABOVE RIGHT: the dramatic Che Guevara monument, Santa Clara. **RIGHT:** staue of Antonio Maceo, in the Plaza de la Revolución, Santiago.

BEST OUTDOOR ACTIVITIES

Walking in the Valle de Viñales
Take walks with local guides through the breathtakingly beautiful valley. *See page 205.*
● **El Guafe trail** Birds, butterflies, dry tropical forest, and Amerindian ceremonial sites can be seen along the path. *See page 294.*
● **Hiking in the Sierra Maestra**
Great hiking in the national park and up to the highest peak, Pico Turquino, for views of the forest and down to the Caribbean Sea. *See page 291.*
● **Exploring the waterfalls of the Sierra de Escambray** Bracing walks and cooling dips amid pristine scenery. *See page 244.*
● **Scuba diving on the Isla de Juventud** One of the best of Cuba's scuba-diving sites. *See page 327.*

ABOVE: Plaza Vieja in Havana.

BEST PLACES TO HEAR MUSIC

● **Casa de la Cultura de La Habana Vieja**
Performances are held in the theater or in the churchyard. *See page 358.*
● **Casa de la Música Galiano, Havana**
Matinées and late-night performances of salsa, songo, and rock. *See page 358.*
● **La Zorra y el Cuervo, Havana** Famous jazz club on La Rampa. *See page 359.*
● **Casa de la Trova, Santiago** One of the most famous casas in Cuba. *See page 303.*
● **Casa de las Tradiciones, Santiago** An intimate local venue where you will hear authentic music. *See page 359.*
● **Casa de la Música, Trinidad** On La Escalinata, there's music and dancing until the early hours. *See page 359.*

BEST HAVANA PLAZAS

● **Plaza de Armas** Havana's oldest square is lit at night by antique lamps, and is a center of action at all hours. *See page 147.*
● **Plaza de la Catedral** The baroque cathedral and handsome colonial buildings surround the square, where café tables invite you to sit and enjoy a mojito. *See page 149.*
● **Plaza Vieja** The square has been renovated with great care over recent years and is now one of the most gracious in the city. *See page 156.*
● **Plaza de la Revolución** The site of the stark memorial to José Martí and the illuminated mural of Che Guevara. The vast square is not beautiful, but it is impressive. *See page 181.*
● **Parque Central** This leafy square, home to the elegant Hotel Inglaterra, is always buzzing with life, especially in the *esquina caliente*. *See page 161.*

MONEY-SAVING TIPS

● **Stay in *casas particulares***
Rooms in private houses are considerably less expensive than hotels, and offer an opportunity to get to know more about Cuba and the Cuban people. Some are housed in beautiful colonial mansions, but the accommodations and the hospitality can be just as good in more modest homes. They also offer the freshest, tastiest food.
● **Bring everything you need**
Medicines, toiletries, and diapers should all be brought from home. Supplies of these essentials are either limited or nonexistent and not to be relied upon.
● **Travel on long-distance coaches** Cuba's long-distance coaches have comfortable seats, washrooms, and air conditioning, and offer a less expensive alternative to renting a car. They will take you to all the major cities the length of the island – although not to the more out-of-the-way destinations.
● **Bring cash** While credit cards are useful for obtaining cash in an emergency, either through a bank or an ATM, they incur an 11 percent charge. And don't, of course, bring US dollars, as there are additional taxes for exchanging them.

THE ISOLATED ISLAND

Cubans find it difficult to buy soap, yet have the best health-care system in Latin America. It is such contradictions that explode prejudices and make the island such a fascinating place to visit

It is difficult to be unemotional about Cuba. This Caribbean island thrills the senses, befuddles the mind, and tugs at the heart. It is a magical place, full of romantic images: conga drums pounding late into the night; spicy dark rum; baseball, ballet, and dazzling nightclubs; light-hearted street art; quick conversations spiked with sexual innuendo and wicked humor; people who are warm, expressive, and affectionate; music emanating from every window – all enveloped within the aroma of hand-rolled cigars.

There are also more somber images of Cuba: frustrated youths willing to risk their lives in search of a future elsewhere; an outmoded communist system, exacerbated by the privations engendered by a US trade embargo, that is failing its citizens; political repression; crumbling buildings, empty stores, and overcrowded buses. It is a place of great contrasts: immaculately dressed schoolchildren emerge from tumble-down tenements. Political opponents portray it as a dictatorship, yet the people are infectiously exuberant.

Cuba's isolation, however, is becoming a thing of the past. The Ministry of Tourism is eager to reinvent the island as a sophisticated vacation destination, to bring in much-needed income: pristine cays with empty swathes of sand are being transformed into modern beach resorts financed by foreign capital. Colonial mansions are being converted into boutique city hotels. Tourists, however, are shielded from the harsh realities of life on the island. It is a rare traveler who experiences the blackouts, the fuel and water shortages, the inadequate food rations, the long lines, leaky roofs, and heavy-handed bureaucracy that are daily hardships for the average Cuban.

For most visitors, Cuba is a taste of the good life, a tropical retreat, and an exotic escape. Even so, the average tourist will not leave Cuba unaffected. Slowly but surely this Caribbean island gets under your skin and touches your soul. Opinions – often contradictory ones – of the island and its people form quickly. Cuba is an unforgettable experience. ❑

PRECEDING PAGES: delivering a celebration cake by horse and cart in Santiago; a lazy day in Trinidad; Trinidad musicians. **LEFT:** walking to work. **ABOVE LEFT:** musical instruments are everywhere. **ABOVE RIGHT:** a young Cuban.

THE CUBANS

Multiracial and multicultural, the vivacious Cuban people are universally hospitable and friendly. Most appear to support their government, but may not always feel free to express their opinions frankly in public

How do you describe the Cuban character? Words like fun-loving, spontaneous, and warm come to mind (not to mention long-suffering). Regardless of their status in society, Cubans tend to be a generous people. This generous nature, closely linked to the gregarious spirit that characterizes the country, is embedded in the Cuban psyche. For one Cuban to label another stingy is to tag him or her with one of the worst character flaws imaginable. The song written by popular songwriter Juan Formell and sung by his band Los Van Van captures the idea: "My hands are always empty, giving when there's nothing to give. Oh, but what can I do? These are the hands that I have!"

A mestizo people

Barely a trace remains in Cuban culture today of the peoples who were here when Christopher Columbus arrived in 1492. For the most part, Cuba's 11.4 million people are a mixture of European, African, and indigenous ancestry.

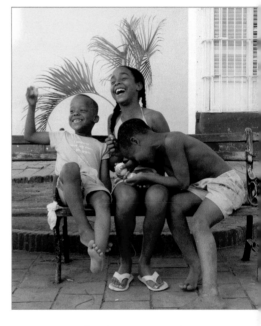

Cirilo Villaverde's famous 19th-century novel Cecilia Valdés o La Loma del Ángel *explores, brilliantly, the theme of the children of white "masters" and their black slaves, and the prejudice they faced.*

The government prefers to emphasize national rather than racial identity, so rarely releases statistics on race, and for a while it deleted all questions about race from the official census.

LEFT: a Baracoa resident relaxing on the doorstep.
RIGHT: sharing a joke in Trinidad.

But some unofficial sources calculate that 70 percent of the population are of mixed race.

With the onset of slavery in the 16th century, many Spanish colonizers satisfied their sexual appetites with their slaves – a practice that was common throughout the Americas. The criollo children born of these unions suffered as much social prejudice as did the black slaves.

From the late 1840s, Chinese immigrants began to form an important segment of the Cuban population. According to historian Juan Pérez de la Riva (author of *Slavery and Capitalism in Cuba*), about 35,000 Chinese were brought from Canton to the island to work as servants in conditions similar to those endured by African slaves. Eventually, more than 100,000 came to Cuba. Though only vestiges remain today, until the 1970s Havana's Chinese neighborhood was one of the city's most prosperous. The so-called *Barrio Chino* in central Havana has been revived over the past few years, and now has a popular market and foodstands attracting both local people and tourists – although it is but a shadow of its former self *(see page 175)*.

Equality for all

Though once common, terms such as *El Chino* (the Chinese man), *El Negrito* (the black one), and *La Mulata* (the mixed-race woman) are rarely

from institutional racism. There are only a handful of black people in the upper echelons of the government, and only about a quarter of Cuba's Communist Party are black or mulatto; and there's evidence that black people have not benefitted proportionately from employment in the lucrative tourism industry during the recent boom. According to Carlos Moore, a black Cuban exile scholar, the color of power in Cuba has not changed at all.

The Catholic Church

The Catholic Church was officially separated from the Cuban Government with the birth

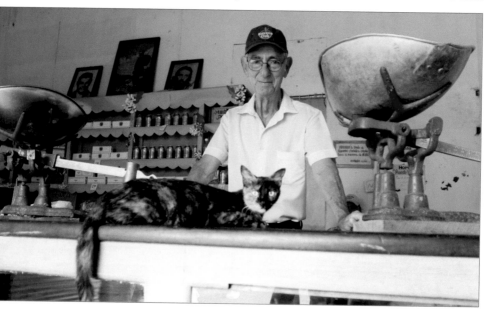

used today – even mentioning racial distinctions is a social taboo (although Chino, as a nickname, does still exist). In the 1950s, skin color was a divisive issue. Black people had very little access to good jobs or professions, and were not allowed to join certain clubs or attend private schools.

With its promise of "equality for all," the revolutionary government has gone a long way toward diminishing the effects of racial discrimination. Today, Cubans of all races and ethnic backgrounds are born in the same hospitals, attend the same schools, and are buried in the same cemeteries. But some sociologists argue that, although opportunities for black people advanced quite dramatically after Fidel Castro took power, the country still suffers

In leafy Parque Vidal, the main square of Santa Clara, the double sidewalks that once provided separate walkways for black and white people are still visible.

of the republic in 1902. Until the revolution, though, the government considered the Catholic Church its natural ideological ally. As in most Latin American cultures, it served as the foundation of an ordered society. But with the pronouncement of the socialist government in 1961, organized religion was condemned to disappear, and Catholic dogma was replaced by that of Marxism-Leninism. The church was not outlawed, but the government viewed it as a dangerous rival and a focus for dissent.

For many years practicing Catholics were punished by limited access to schools and job opportunities. To attend Mass was to "lapse into the past," and the "past" was regarded by revolutionaries as a Bad Thing. But religious observation continued in private, and after the break-up of the eastern bloc, reappeared in public again.

The papal visit

A landmark event occurred in January 1998, when Pope John Paul II visited the island – the

exploit the fact that the Pope had publicly opposed the US embargo, so as to isolate the position of the US Government and the Miami exile community.

The Cuban state's position on religion has altered somewhat in recent years. Practicing Catholics are allowed to join the Communist Party, and the state is now officially described as "secular" rather than "atheist." There seems to be far greater tolerance of religious observance than there was before, and while the number of people attending Catholic services is not high, neither is it negligible, especially among elderly people.

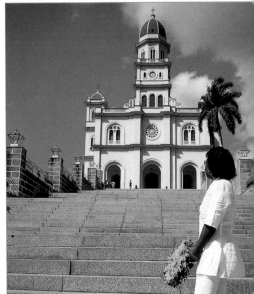

last place in Latin America that he had not toured. The paradox was not lost on observers: that a Pope who had spent much of his papacy fighting communism should meet a Marxist like Fidel, who had completely relegated the role of the Catholic Church and institutional religion under his regime.

The Pope was keen to advance the cause of religious freedom and human rights in Cuba; whereas Castro hoped to benefit from the international prestige of the event (demonstrating that his regime had nothing to hide), and to

LEFT: shopkeeper and companion in Sancti Spíritus.
ABOVE: open-air service outside a Methodist church, Santiago. **RIGHT:** Catholicism is still strong in Cuba.

The power of Santería

Although all forms of religious devotion were proscribed for many years, Santería has survived. It is a mixture of Catholicism and traditional West African beliefs brought here by slaves in colonial times. Although it began as a religion of Cuba's black population, Santería followers now come from all walks of life. It is estimated that at least 90 percent of Cubans have participated in some form of Santería ritual, despite the fact that for many years it, too, was discouraged by the state.

As in Catholicism, Santería priests, called the *babalawos*, offer guidance and counsel, but the source of their divine wisdom differs. Instead of consulting one supreme being, *babalawos* use various instruments to interpret the wishes of the *orishas* or gods. Each sign carries many myths and stories which the priest will interpret for his client. A *babalawo* might advise a patient to sprinkle Catholic holy water around their home in order to chase away evil spirits. If the problem is caused by the spiritual presence of a dead loved one, they might instruct the patient to "steal a mass." To do this, the patient would attend a Catholic Mass where the souls of the dead are being prayed for, and when the priest mentions the names of the dead who are being honored, they would whisper the name of their loved one. The annoying spirit then

but it has by no means dissolved the island's deep-rooted *machismo* spirit. Far from liberating them socially, the government's goal of incorporating women into the workforce has actually led to their having two jobs: one at the workplace and the other in the home, doing most of the cooking, shopping, cleaning, and child-minding. However, this is not so different from what happens in the US and many European countries.

Raúl Castro's wife, Vilma Espín, who died in June 2007, championed women's rights and lobbied for men to do more in the home and, especially, with raising children. She founded

floats away and leaves the person in peace. *(See pages 82–5 for more on Afro-Cuban religions.)*

Women's rights

Women walking alone on the street are often bombarded with overt sexual comments from men. These *piropos* (flirtatious remarks) range from a courteous compliment to a blatant invitation for sex. Many Cuban women, however, accustomed to this from an early age, are capable of giving just as good as they get. *Cubanas* may be victims of *machismo* in some areas of life, but they appear remarkably self-confident.

Many years of official policy designed to achieve the "equality of women" have undoubtedly improved the lot of women in Cuba,

the Federación de Mujeres Cubanas (the Federation of Cuban Women) in 1960, and in 1975 drew up the Family Code, which obliged men to share housework and childcare. While this is obviously difficult to enforce, it was a move in the right direction.

Through education, women are now involved in all aspects of the economy and the community. However, there are still very few women in the higher echelons of government and those with most prominence are family. Celia Sánchez, like Vilma Espín, was linked with the Castro brothers in the Sierra Maestra, and was hugely influential, but she too is now dead. Of the next generation, only Dr Aleida Guevara (daughter of Che) and Mariela Castro Espín (daughter of Raúl and Vilma) are given world-wide political exposure in addition to their jobs in pediatrics and sex education. As in many Western countries, women are a small minority in the Council of Ministers and in the Armed Forces high command where real power lies.

A negative side effect of the revolution has been the increasing divorce rate. According to government statistics, about 5 percent of marriages ended in divorce in 1953. It is now estimated that, among Cubans aged from 25 to 40, a remarkable 60 percent of marriages fail. One reason for this is the lack of independent living space for newlyweds, who are forced to

Homophobia and gay rights

Born of two essentially patriarchal cultures, Cubans are largely *machista*, and tradition-ally homophobic. Although official statistics estimate Cuba's homosexual population to be between 4 and 6 percent, the real figure is likely to be much higher since many gay people maintain public heterosexual relationships in order to avoid harassment. Since the early 1960s, thousands of gay people have fled the island, including a large contingent that left during the Mariel boatlift of 1980 *(see page 87)*.

However, there is more official tolerance of gay people these days. Homosexuality was

live in cramped apartments with their families. The decline of the influence of the Catholic Church has also been a factor, though another reason for the rise is the fact that the revolu-tionary government has made it much easier to obtain a divorce: all it takes is a few hours and about half a month's salary. Again, this should be seen in relation to the situation elsewhere: the US has the highest divorce rate in the West-ern world (44 percent), followed by the UK and Canada. Not as high as in Cuba, but indicative of a growing trend.

LEFT: Santería practitioner dressed all in white.
ABOVE: female factory workers in Baracoa.
RIGHT: Vilma Espín, who championed women's rights.

legalized in 1979, and generally discrimination is less institutionalized today, although police harassment, for example, still exists. The movie *Fresa y Chocolate (Strawberry and Chocolate)*, about a gay intellectual who falls in love with a straight Communist Party militant, brought the gay issue to the forefront in the early 1990s; it played to full houses in Havana and won several international awards.

Groups of gay men and women have begun to form associations and to meet formally to discuss gay rights – a move that even a few years ago would have raised quite a storm. Also, many believe that a great deal depends on where

The generation gap

Members of the older generation, who remember the time before the Revolution, are now enjoying the fruits of their labors. The ones who made the choice to remain in the country after the exodus of the early 1960s are now benefitting from the state health service, from old people's homes and pensions. Their income may be meager, but at least they have a roof over their heads.

Their children, now in their 40s, have been brought up on revolutionary dogma. They have learned how to work the system and many families know how to exploit the state to maximum

gay people work. Intellectuals and university students are far more tolerant than are blue-collar workers or farmers of individual sexual preferences – but this is the same the whole world over.

Mariela Castro, director of the National Center for Sex Education and an activist for LGBT rights, was instrumental in getting a law passed in 2008 allowing sex change operations. She also campaigns for effective Aids prevention and is an executive member of the World Association for Sexual Health. She has produced a prolific academic output and has had a considerable impact on the acceptance of the human rights of transvestites, homosexuals, and bisexuals in Cuba.

A girl's 15th birthday, her "quinceañera," is a milestone, requiring extensive celebrations. Those who can afford it assemble a photo album, with the girl posing in a number of gowns, including a frothy wedding dress.

advantage. There may be a bureaucrat, who can get round rules and regulations, a farmer, who can keep them supplied with food, someone who works in tourism to bring in hard currency, an academic who can access the internet, and a relative in Miami who can send funds. The family works together as a unit to maximum advantage.

The younger generation, however, is potentially a pressure cooker waiting to explode. They see the material benefits their contemporaries are enjoying in Miami and around the world and they yearn for the clothes with designer labels, the iPods, the Blackberries, and the laptops, none of which is available to them. Teenage rebellion, subversive music, even something as simple as leaving home and living independently, are all impossible dreams. The state controls where they live, their careers, their income, and their entertainment. It is no wonder that some still risk the shark-infested sea to reach the promised land.

and mend" has been essential since the Special Period of economic hardship after the fall of the Soviet Union.

Nothing is thrown away in Cuba. Plastic bags are washed and used over and over again. Men make a living out of refilling disposable cigarette lighters. "*Poncheros*," puncture repair men, are constantly in demand. Housewives spend all morning going round the "*agropecuarios*" and black markets until they have secured enough food to feed their families that day.

"*No hay,*" "There isn't any," is a phrase frequently heard in shops

Make do and mend

"*No es fácil*" is an expression that is frequently heard, meaning "Life's not easy." The daily grind to make ends meet is referred to as "*la lucha,*" the struggle. Trying to make a peso salary worth the equivalent of US$20 last until the end of the month is an uphill struggle even with subsidies that mean housing, health care, and education are all paid for. Tourists marvel at the old American cars still on the road, held together with the apocryphal elastic band, and the unspoilt houses stuffed with antiques, but "make do

LEFT: Guantánamo schoolgirls. **ABOVE:** Reinaldo Arenas, who went into exile in 1981. **RIGHT:** a *ponchero* at work on a Bayamo street.

Support or discretion?

It is difficult for an outsider to know exactly how Cubans feel about their government and society. If they are critical, they are unlikely to express it openly. On the one hand, people talk with apparent sincerity about the "triumph of the revolution," and appear supportive of Castro. On the other hand, there are those who find the system insupportable, and who make their feelings known by leaving – or trying to. Most people would like some of the consumer goods and freedoms that tourists take for granted, but tend to blame shortages and hardships on the *bloqueo*, as they call the US embargo, while they wait, no doubt with mixed feelings, to see what changes are in store.   ❑

DECISIVE DATES

PRE-COLUMBIAN PERIOD (6000 BC–AD 1492)

c.6000–3000 BC
First waves of native American settlers, pre-ceramic hunter-gatherer groups, known as the Guanahatabeys, the ancestors of the Ciboneyes.

c.AD 600
Arawak-speaking Taínos reach Cuba, arriving in hollowed-out tree-trunk canoes. They dominate eastern and central Cuba, although Ciboney groups are never entirely dis-

placed. Taínos bring a more settled, agricultural way of life.

c.1490
Native population estimated at over 100,000.

SPANISH SETTLEMENT (1492–1762)

1492
Columbus sights Cuba.

1508
Sebastián de Ocampo circumnavigates the island.

1509
Diego de Velázquez's first expedition.

1511–15
Velázquez returns to found Baracoa, followed by six other initial settlements (villas) around Cuba.

1512
Cacique Hatuey, the great Taíno chief, is burnt at the stake. Indigenous resistance crumbles. Subsequently most of the indigenous people are massacred, die of disease, or become forced laborers under the encomienda system.

1515
Santiago de Cuba becomes the capital.

1519
Havana is moved from the south coast to its present position on the north coast.

1523
The first African slaves are brought to work in the mines and on plantations.

1537
First slave revolt crushed.

1546
French pirates plunder the eastern town of Baracoa.

1555
French forces sack Havana. By order of Felipe II (1527–98) fortresses are built to protect Havana and Santiago.

c.1560
Fewer than 3,000 indigenous people remain.

1607
Havana named official capital.

1869
Rebels issue Constitution of Guáimaro.

1871
José Martí, independence fighter, poet and journalist, is exiled to Spain; he later settles in New York.

1873
Céspedes replaced as rebel leader.

1878
Peace treaty signed. Rebel factions split.

1879–1880
The "Little War" breaks out.

1886
Spain abolishes all slavery.

1892
José Martí founds the Cuban Revolutionary Party from exile in the US.

1895
The Second War of Independence, led by Martí, who dies in the first battle at Dos Ríos.

1896
Antonio Maceo, who took over the independence leadership role, is killed in western Cuba.

1668
English expedition under Henry Morgan sails to Puerto Príncipe (modern Camagüey) and sacks the town.

1682
The Inquisition comes to Cuba, and strikes first in Remedios, which is torched after a Spanish priest discovers "devils."

1717
Tobacco trade declared a Crown monopoly.

THE BRITISH OCCUPATION (1762–3)

1762
Havana falls to a massive British invasion force. The port is opened up to international trade, breaking the monopoly of the Spanish Crown.

1763
Havana is returned to Spanish rule as Britain swaps Havana for Florida (the Treaty of Paris).

PRECEDING PAGES: Guantánamo schoolchildren. FAR LEFT TOP: replica of a Taíno sculpture, Bariay Bay. LEFT MIDDLE: Christopher Columbus. LEFT: El Morro fortress, Havana. ABOVE: 19th-century wood engraving of slaves harvesting sugar cane in Cuba. RIGHT: independence fighter, José Martí.

SUGAR BOOM AND SLAVERY (1774–1840)

c.1790s
Sugar replaces tobacco as Cuba's most valuable export. African slaves are imported in huge numbers to work on the plantations.

1795
French Haitian landowners flee the slave revolution and settle in Oriente (Cuba's eastern province).

Early 1800s
The price of sugar and land soars. Beginnings of independence movements in Cuba. Simón Bolívar leads anti-colonial revolts across Latin America.

1837
Latin America's first railroad in operation between Bejucal and Havana.

TWO WARS OF INDEPENDENCE (1868–98)

1868
Carlos Manuel de Céspedes liberates his slaves near Manzanillo and issues call to arms against Spanish overlords, sparking the Ten Years' War.

Máximo Gómez returns from exile and continues the struggle. Spanish forces initiate a "scorched-earth" policy in the countryside.

1898

Battleship USS *Maine* sunk in Havana's harbor after an explosion, which prompts the US to enter the conflict. Spanish forces defeated at the Battle of San Juan Hill. Spain signs a peace treaty ceding control of Cuba to the US.

CORRUPTION AND COUPS (1901–59)

1901

The Platt Amendment adopted: Guantánamo naval base ceded to the US, which claims the right to intervene in Cuban affairs. Provokes

widespread Cuban anger.

1902

Tomás Estrada Palma is inaugurated as president.

1906–9

Marines invade to protect US interests.

1912

Afro-Cuban Black Uprising is savagely repressed.

1924–33

General Machado's presidency prone to venality and violence. General strike forces him to flee.

1934

Fulgencio Batista stages a coup. Puppet president installed under army control. Abrogation of Platt Amendment, but Guantánamo left in US control.

1940–4

First Batista presidency after national vote.

1952

Batista seizes power and cancels elections.

1956

Fidel Castro's guerrilla force sails from Mexico in the

Granma. Hideout established in Sierra Maestra.

1958

Guevara opens second front in Sierra del Escambray. Batista flees.

THE REVOLUTIONARY YEARS (1959–90)

1959

Castro enters Havana. First land reform introduced; literacy and public-health campaigns launched.

1960

Nationalization of major companies.

1961

US-backed invasion results in Bay of Pigs fiasco. Castro declares socialist nature of revolution.

1962

Cuban Missile Crisis brings world to brink of nuclear war. Cuba brought further into Soviet orbit. US economic blockade begins in earnest.

1964

Castro pays first visit to USSR.

1965

Che Guevara resigns posts and leaves for Africa.

1967

Guevara killed in Bolivia.

1970
Failure of 10 million-ton sugar harvest target.

1976
Right-wing terrorist group bombs plane, killing all 73 Cuban athletes on board.

1980
Mariel Boatlift: 120,000 leave Cuba – legally – for Miami.

1989
Execution of General Ochoa for alleged drug smuggling and corruption.

THE SPECIAL PERIOD AND RECOVERY (POST-1990)

1991
Russian economic aid axed after end of the Soviet Union; food and fuel shortages begin.

1993
Dollar legalized; limited forms of private enterprise allowed. Economic privations continue.

1994
Crisis of the boat people: 35,000 Cubans try to flee to Miami. US tightens immigration controls.

1996
Draconian Helms-Burton legislation passed by US Congress tightens the embargo's stranglehold.

1997
Che Guevara's remains are returned from Bolivia.

FAR LEFT TOP: American postcard from 1898 whipping up interventionist feeling. LEFT MIDDLE: trophy from the Bay of Pigs invasion, Museo de Girón. LEFT: Antonio Maceo. ABOVE: the flag of Cuba. RIGHT: Raul Castro on a visit to the Guantanamo Bay area.

1998
The Pope visits Cuba and criticizes the US embargo.

1999
Five-year-old Elián González survives a rafting accident en route to the US. Despite fierce protests in Miami, Elián is returned to his Cuban father.

2002
Nearly half the sugar mills close; 100,000 workers lose jobs. Two hurricanes strike western Cuba; 350,000 people evacuated.

2003
75 dissidents sentenced to jail terms of up to 28 years. Worldwide condemnation.

2004
The UN's Human Rights Commission votes to press for human-rights inspections. US tightens sanctions again, restricting visits by US Cubans and their remittances home. Castro retaliates by banning transactions in dollars.

2006
Castro hospitalized in July; temporarily hands over power to his brother, Raúl.

2008
Raúl Castro confirmed as president. Fidel remains party leader and continues to be a strong presence.

2009
Raúl Castro removes Fidelistas from Council of Ministers, appointing army and Communist Party officials to run the economy.

2010
The Roman Catholic Church negotiates the release of the remaining 52 of the 75 political prisoners arrested in 2003, most of whom leave for Spain.

CONQUISTADORES AND PIRATES

Long before Columbus arrived in Cuba the island had been populated by groups of indigenous people, who were to be subjugated to the European conquistadores. The island's early colonial history was a turbulent one as booms and busts in gold and sugar changed its fortunes

The first European to glimpse the coast of Cuba was Christopher Columbus, who on his initial voyage in 1492 pronounced it the most beautiful land "that eyes had ever set upon." This beautiful land had, of course, been discovered several thousand years beforehand by peoples Columbus assumed were Indians – a misnomer that has stuck.

The first groups of indigenous people to colonize Cuba were pre-agricultural hunter-gatherers. Quite how and when they first arrived is not known for certain, but it seems that they arrived in different waves of migration from about 6,000 years ago, from the Orinoco delta of modern-day Venezuela, from Central America, and possibly also from Florida and the Mississippi basin.

Historians have attempted to classify these indigenous peoples with different names at different times. Once known as Guanahatabey, they are more commonly referred to as Ciboney, but they all shared a common pre-agricultural,

> Some Taíno finds can be seen in the Museum of Anthropology in Vedado (Havana), and in the little Archeological Museum in Baracoa, close to the spot where a famous Taíno tobacco idol was found.

pre-ceramic heritage. Their cultures were characterized by the use of shell implements, and they lived in caves or basic settlements across the island.

LEFT: a statue of the Taíno warrior Hatuey.
RIGHT: a depiction of Columbus's arrival in Cuba.

From about AD 600 onward these hunter-gatherer groups were displaced gradually in some parts of Cuba by waves of new immigrants – the Arawak-speaking Taíno peoples. The Taínos had followed the arc of the Antilles islands in their hollowed-out tree-trunk canoes, arriving from the region of the Orinoco delta. The Taínos brought with them a more settled, agricultural way of life, and they were the dominant group of peoples when Columbus arrived, although some earlier indigenous groups still survived.

The Taínos lived in communities of palm-thatched homes, described by Columbus as looking like large tents, scattered randomly around as if in a camp. For food, they combined fishing and hunting with agriculture – growing staple crops like cassava, peppers, beans, and sweet potatoes, and fruits such as guavas and pineapples.

Their society had a hierarchical structure, at the apex of which were hereditary chiefs *(caciques)* and shamans *(behiques)*. The shamans presided over curative rituals, linked to the worship of a pantheon of gods and ancestor spirits. Taínos believed in an afterlife, and revered idols, called *cemíes*, lovingly carved out of hardwoods, stone, or coral, which they kept in special shrines.

Spanish conquest

The Spanish first settled on the island of Hispaniola (present-day Dominican Republic and Haiti), where they enslaved and brutalized the indigenous population. Soon they started to look west, hoping to find gold in Cuba.

However, their reputation preceded them, and some *caciques* were determined to resist. The most famous of these was the great warrior Hatuey, who had witnessed Spanish massacres in Hispaniola and fled to eastern Cuba. When the conquistador Diego Velázquez landed in Baracoa in 1511 at the head of an expedition to settle the island, Hatuey fought back.

Columbus's very first contacts with the island's native peoples were marked by mutual curiosity and, it seems, a certain respect, even if this wasn't to last for long. Columbus made sure his sailors took nothing from the first dwellings they entered, but no doubt this was partly because he was more interested in gold and pearls than in the fishing nets, spun cotton, silent dogs, and tame wild birds that they encountered.

Columbus noted, "They very willingly traded everything they had, but they seemed to me a people short of everything." However, he admired their happiness and generosity. His sailors brought back to Europe tobacco, syphilis, and news of a world ripe for conquest.

SPEAKING WITH THE GODS

The Jeronymite friar, Ramón Pané, recorded Taíno customs in his *Account of the Antiquities of the Indies* in the late 15th century. Of their ceremonies he writes: "To purge themselves, they take a certain powder, called *cohoba*, snorting it up the nose, which intoxicates them in a way that they don't know what they're doing; and in this way they say many incoherent things, in which they affirm that they are speaking with the idols." Once thought to be tobacco, *cohoba* is now believed to be the crushed seeds of an acacia-like tree – *Anadenanthera peregrina*, still used today by some Venezuelan indigenous groups, and known as *yopo*.

But despite a long game of hide-and-seek in the caves and mountains of the east, Hatuey and his followers were eventually captured and put to the stake in 1512. When offered baptism at his execution, the chieftain asked if there were any Christians in heaven; when told that there were, he proclaimed that he preferred to burn as a pagan.

Between 1512 and 1514, Velázquez and his men founded the seven original "villas" of Cuba – Baracoa, Santiago, Bayamo, Camagüey, Trinidad, Sancti Spíritus, and Havana. The Spanish then set about rounding up the indigenous population for use as forced labor. Resistance

gold. But rather than be subjected to such an existence, many committed suicide by hanging themselves or by drinking poisonous untreated cassava juice. The Spanish perceived this as evidence of the Taínos' inherent laziness.

Those who survived the initial brutality were in large part wiped out by European diseases

> The island's name derives from a native term for the island, Cubanacán, and not, as some believe, the Spanish for barrel (cuba), after the barrel-shaped hills seen by the first sailors.

continued sporadically for the next couple of decades, but the outlook was bleak.

A Caribbean genocide

Thousands of Cuba's indigenous peoples were killed in the initial phase of conquest, either in skirmishes, or in massacres conducted by the more brutal of the early conquistadores. Some fled to the mountains, where they would be hunted down with muskets and dogs. Many more were forced to work as slaves, to grow food for the Spanish, or to dig for copper and

FAR LEFT: a Taíno figure, Baracoa. LEFT: a pre-Columbian idol, Banes Museum. ABOVE: Bartolomé de las Casas at the execution of an Indian chieftan.

against which they had no resistance – diseases like smallpox, measles, tuberculosis, and even the common cold.

Champion of the people

Only a few brave Spaniards dared to speak out against what they were seeing. The most famous champion of the native peoples was Bartolomé de las Casas, the so-called "Protector of the Indians." As one of the first settlers in Cuba in 1513, he had exploited indigenous slaves in the mines and on his estate, but he turned against this system when a Dominican priest refused him absolution. On becoming a Dominican friar he campaigned passionately for the just treatment of native peoples, but he failed in his goal of abolishing the harsh *encomienda* system, which granted Spanish conquistadores land and the right to use the inhabitants of that land as forced labor.

Although gold made some of the first settlers astonishingly rich, the supply quickly petered out. The conquistadores soon found other, more tantalizing, rewards: Hernán Cortés set off to conquer Aztec Mexico, and soon afterward Francisco Pizarro toppled Inca Peru. Plundered gold and mined silver began streaming into the Spanish coffers, and soon Cuba was reduced to the status of supply post for the more lucrative plundering of South and Central America.

While the ports of Panama overflowed with riches, and soldiers shod their horses with silver, the island's seven settlements remained little more than wretched provincial villages.

Cuba's strategic position, however, saved it from oblivion. Treasure from the New World still had to be brought back safely to Spain via the Caribbean Sea, which was becoming infested with foreign pirates. A system of fortresses was established on the orders of Spanish king Felipe II, so that treasure could be conveyed in short hops from port to port.

Havana was moved from the south to its current spot on the north coast, and acquired

BARTOLOMEU O PORTUGUÊS

Bartolomeu de la Cueva, nicknamed "o Português," has the dubious honor of being credited with establishing the "Pirates' Code," the set of rules by which pirates governed themselves. During the 1660s he lived with buccaneers on Hispaniola for several years before moving his operations to attack shipping off Campeche, southeast Mexico. Then, with his crew of 30 men and a small ship carrying just four guns, he managed to capture off the coast of Cuba a 20-gun man-o'-war that was carrying 70,000 pieces of eight and a large cargo of cacao beans.

He set sail with his booty for Port Royal, the notorious pirate haven on Jamaica, but strong winds pushed him back to the west of Cuba. Rounding Cabo de San Antonio,

he ran into three Spanish warships, which relieved him of his cargo. He then sailed to Campeche, where he was captured but escaped, eventually getting back to Port Royal. There he assembled another crew, and returned to Campeche to recapture "his" ship. Sailing it round the south of Cuba en route to Port Royal he ran aground off the Isla de la Juventud, losing everything. After that he joined Henry Morgan's pirate gang, but died in Cuba, probably in 1672.

As the French writer Alexandre Exquemelin noted in *Buccaneers of America*, he "made many violent attacks on the Spaniards without gaining much profit from marauding, for I saw him dying in the greatest wretchedness in the world." Obviously, piracy did not always pay.

massive new walls and fortifications which took more than 40 years to build *(see page 165)*. It became the key point in Spain's whole transportation system: fleets from Cartagena in Colombia, San Juan in Puerto Rico, and Panama City converged here for resupplying, while Latin America's first shipyard turned out merchant and warships. At the eastern end of the island, Santiago de Cuba was fortified as a secondary port.

First signs of wealth

These military accouterments, however, did not make life in the towns any less squalid. On the

today. Like colonial overlords everywhere, the Spaniards trapped in this remote backwater tried desperately to hang on to their heritage: *caballeros* (gentlemen) would wear finery and frills despite the tropical heat, keep in touch with the latest in the arts in their European homeland, and host lavish dinner dances in the midst of plagues of malaria and yellow fever.

As one traveler to Cuba remarked: "The palaces of the nobles in Havana, the residence of the governor, the convents, the cathedral, are a reproduction of Burgos or Valladolid, as if by some Aladdin's lamp a Castilian city had been taken up and set down again unaltered on the

contrary, the constant parade of seamen and desperate adventurers did the reverse, turning both Havana and Santiago into warrens of taverns, brothels, and muddy, narrow streets. Even so, some of the wealth rubbed off, and merchants could make modest fortunes loading up the galleons with provisions for the long journey to Spain.

With the proceeds of these sales, Cuba attracted a rudimentary upper class who constructed some magnificent stone buildings – a smattering of which still survive in Old Havana

shore of the Caribbean Sea. And they carried with them their laws, their habits, their institutions and their creed, their religious orders, their bishops and their Inquisition."

Pirates on the rampage

Despite Spain's best efforts, the uninhabited swamps of Florida and the island maze of the Bahamas became havens for freebooters and buccaneers of every nationality, ready to pounce on any ship passing along Cuba's coast. The more brazen found the cays and islands off Cuba's south coast to be perfect bases for their activities.

The most famous (or infamous) names in the history of piracy all touched on the island's

LEFT: a 16th-century engraving depicting Cortés sailing to Cuba. **ABOVE:** Havana's port was heavily fortified. **RIGHT:** the infamous Henry Morgan.

coast, and many became embroiled, over the years, in the shifting patterns of war between Spain and more recent interlopers in the Caribbean, the English, the French, and the Dutch.

Drake and Morgan

It was England's Francis Drake (1540–96), a favorite of Queen Elizabeth I, who started the habit of calling in at Cabo de San Antonio, Cuba's westernmost point, for fresh water and turtle eggs on the way to and from raids on Cartagena and Panama.

The most ruthless and successful buccaneer of all arrived in the following century. This

prisoners, whom they permitted to starve in the churches. In the meanwhile they did not cease to torment them daily after an inhuman manner, thereby to make them confess where they had hid their goods and money, though little or nothing was left them. They punished also the women and little children." Morgan then went on to sack Panama City, and after retiring to London was appointed Governor of Jamaica.

In 1715, the biggest Spanish treasure fleet ever gathered started off from Havana loaded with nearly 7 million "pieces of eight," and thousands of bars of silver. This time, it was nature rather than piracy that was to prove the

was Henry Morgan, son of a well-to-do Welsh farmer, who was hired by the English Government in 1668 to seek intelligence on Spanish activities in Cuba.

Morgan took this as a license to sail his 750 men the 80km (50 miles) inland to Puerto Príncipe (modern Camagüey) and attack it. The Spanish governor got wind of his plan and had a force drawn up to meet Morgan, but, he reported, "the pirates were very dextrous." The Spaniards were defeated and the town forced to surrender. Morgan locked the inhabitants in the churches, and set about sacking the town.

According to chronicles, Morgan's men "fell to banqueting … and making great cheer after their customary way, without remembering the poor

THE INQUISITION STRIKES

The Inquisition descended most famously on the town of Remedios in 1682, when the parish priest declared that the village had been invaded by 800,000 devils (more than 1,000 devils per inhabitant – which is quite a lot). After burning the odd, possessed victim, soldiers torched the settlement, ordering the villagers to move to relatively useless land, where the town of Santa Clara was being established. This could be Cuba's first real-estate scam: the property was owned by the parish priest who had "discovered" the devils, and who hoped to rent it out at a tidy profit. The villagers, however, defied pressure and decided to rebuild their town.

venture's undoing. Though the fleet waited until after the hurricane season, it ran straight into a storm in the Gulf of Florida. Nearly 1,000 of the 2,500 passengers lost their lives, and wreckage littered the entire Florida coast, where it was picked off by passing buccaneers.

The tyranny of "white gold"

Dramatic as these events were, Cuba's real future was being shaped in its first sugar fields. When Columbus first landed in the Americas, sugar was one of the most valuable commodities in Europe, imported for a fortune from the Orient and weighed out by the tablespoon. He

sugar-cane plantations, while boatloads of slaves were transported from Africa to work on them. The first African slaves were brought to Cuba as domestic servants, but before long they were being forced to work in the mines and on sugar or tobacco plantations. With the indigenous population wiped out, the Spanish needed an alternative source of labor and Africans were deemed more robust and resilient. Even Fray Bartolomé de Las Casas *(see pages 35–6)* had spoken out in favor of the African slave trade, as a way of protecting his beloved "Indians" from rapacious exploitation. And before long, a second phase of brutalization had begun.

quickly realized the Caribbean's potential, and on his second voyage he brought the first sugar-cane roots from the Canary Islands and planted them in what is today the Dominican Republic. Within a century, the cultivation of sugar cane had spread across the Caribbean islands and to the coast of Brazil.

Cuba started off as a comparatively minor sugar producer – cattle ranching and then tobacco were more important initially – but gradually more and more lush forests of mahogany and ceiba were uprooted to make way for

LEFT: an 18th-century engraving of Havana harbor with chain across the entrance.
ABOVE: African slaves in the sugar fields.

Until the late 18th century, the slave trade was run under license from the Spanish Crown, although a sizable illegal slave-smuggling trade existed too. And although the trade was initially on a far smaller scale than it was to become in the 19th century, nevertheless thousands of peoples from across Africa – from countries like Senegal, Mali, and Sierra Leone; Yoruba-speaking peoples from present-day Nigeria; Bantú peoples from the Congo and Angola; and even from as far away as Mozambique – were hauled across the ocean, all bringing different cultural traditions and languages. With the slaves came African gods, myths, and rituals, which the Christian priests could not eradicate despite their zeal.

Life on the plantations was terribly harsh – thousands died from overwork, disease, and poor nutrition, and beatings were common. There was a severe dearth of women, as slavers preferred importing young men, who were stronger and therefore represented better value. Women were often raped by their overseers; and slave families could be broken up by selling their children.

Desperate measures

There were uprisings throughout the colonial period, one of the first ones taking place as early as 1537, when slaves rose up and joined in an

,assault by French pirates on the city of Havana. And the Spanish lived in constant fear of slave rebellion. Some slaves, termed *cimarrones*, chose to escape, fleeing to the mountains where they sometimes developed small communities (*palenques*), possibly joining too with remnant indigenous communities, but they always lived under the fear of recapture by slave-hunters and their savage dogs.

Just outside Santiago stands a monument to slaves who fled from the harsh conditions of forced labor in the copper mine, El Cobre, in the 18th century. Other slaves, in desperation, even chose to commit mass suicides – many believing that after death they would be resurrected in Africa.

The Last Supper

Just how bizarre Cuban rural society had become by the end of the 18th century can be seen by the events that took place near Santa María del Rosario, a village southeast of Havana. The account comes from historian Manuel Moreno Fraginals (1920–2001), a leading authority on plantation slavery in Cuba, and was captured in the classic Cuban film *La Última Cena – The Last Supper –* made in 1976 by Cuban director Tomás Gutiérrez Alea.

In a fit of religious fervor, the Count de Casa Bayona (whose former home now houses the Colonial Art Museum in Havana) invited a dozen of his slaves to a feast on Maundy Thursday (the day before Good Friday). Acting out the role of Jesus Christ, he washed the feet of each slave personally. When the overseer refused to give the slaves a holiday on Easter Sunday, as had been promised by the count, because the Bible teaches that Sunday should be a day of rest, they rose up in rebellion, burning the plantation to the ground.

Hearing the news, the count arrived with armed horsemen to supress the uprising. Horrified at what he perceived to be the ingratitude of the 12 slaves who had feasted with him, he ordered that they should be hunted down and executed. Their heads were placed on pikes in the cane fields as a warning to their fellow-workers that, whatever the Bible might say, all men were not created equal in Cuba. ❏

THE CORNISH IN EL COBRE

El Cobre copper mine has a link with the English county of Cornwall, a prominent tin-mining area. The Spanish abandoned the mine in the early 19th century, and a visiting English businessman, finding there were still rich copper deposits, founded the Cobre Mining Company, and imported steam engines and labor from Cornwall. Thousands came in the 1830s, but harsh conditions, and mosquito-borne yellow fever, resulted in a high death rate, and the number of workers dwindled. By 1870 the enterprise was over: the seam was becoming exhausted, and the destruction caused by the uprising against the Spanish *(see page 46)* was the final straw.

LEFT: the film *La Última Cena* was based on a real, and horrific, event.
RIGHT: an idealized depiction of slave life.

THE STRUGGLE AGAINST COLONIALISM

Cuba was one step behind the liberal changes that spread through other Latin American colonies in the 19th century. But Spain's "Ever Faithful Isle" did eventually fight to gain independence from Spain. Inevitably that meant it came within the sphere of influence of the USA

In the early 1800s, every Spanish possession in the New World successfully rose up against colonial rule – except Cuba and Puerto Rico. In Havana, barely a voice was raised in support of the romantic liberation movements being led by heroes such as Simón Bolívar and José de San Martín, much to the embarrassment of modern Cuban historians. On the contrary, Cuba became Spain's military springboard for the many attempts to reconquer her tattered empire, which dragged on for decades and left much of South and Central America in ruins. A short-lived movement for Cuban independence was quelled by Spain in 1823 and relative calm returned.

By 1825 the Spanish had reluctantly given up on the New World and retreated to its two loyal Caribbean possessions – the more valued of which, for the next 40 years, would remain Cuba – referred to in Madrid as "the Ever Faithful Isle."

The Cafetal La Isabelica near Santiago, now under Unesco protection, was the plantation house of a coffee estate belonging to a family of French descent, who had fled from Haiti's slave rebellion.

Predictions of ruin

Cuban Creoles, masters of a slave society, were in fact desperate to avoid independence. They had been kept in a state of constant terror since the bloody slave rebellion in neighboring Haiti

in the 1790s: French refugees had landed on the beaches around Santiago, starving, desperate, telling wild tales of race slaughter, laced with lurid images of voodoo and throbbing African drums. Napoleon's army was defeated on the shores of the new black republic, and white Cubans were worried that their island might follow suit. "There is no country on earth where a revolutionary movement is more dangerous than Cuba," declared one planter, predicting "the complete ruin of the Cuban race."

Even so, greed was stronger than fear. The expansion of the slave population during the later 18th and early 19th centuries was unparalleled, for two main reasons. First, in 1762, the

LEFT: 1901 cartoon satirizing US involvement in Cuba.
RIGHT: Carlos Manuel de Céspedes.

British had captured the heavily fortified city of Havana, after storming the main forts guarding the harbor. This was simply a consequence of a wider war Britain was waging against France and her ally, Spain. They then trained the very guns that were meant to protect the city against its own walls, forcing its capitulation in just two weeks. The Governor of Havana was sent back to Spain in disgrace, but the heroic resistance of the captain commanding El Morro fortress, Don Luís de Velasco, earned him a posthumous ennoblement from his king.

The British divided up the tremendous spoils of the city's public monies and warehouses, and then endured sickness and disease, until Havana was returned to Spain a mere seven months later. Spain regained possession of her beloved colonial city only by handing Florida over to the British. However, an important legacy of the occupation was that the British had allowed Havana to trade freely with other nations, thus breaking the monopoly that Spain had enjoyed since the 16th century, and this liberalization vastly increased the trade in slaves. Once broken, this monopoly could not realistically be reimposed by the returning Spanish. Freed from this economic straitjacket, the Cuban economy boomed, and there were real

HUMAN LIFE DEVALUED

German naturalist Alexander von Humboldt, visiting Cuba in 1800, witnessed life on the sugar plantations. He was appalled by the attitude of Cuban slave owners: "I have heard discussed with the greatest coolness whether it was better for the proprietor not to overwork his slaves, and consequently have to replace them with less frequency, or whether he should get all he could out of them in a few years, and then have to purchase newly imported Africans."

incentives to increase production of its chief commodity: sugar.

Secondly, the Haitian rebellion destroyed the sugar plantations there, pushing sugar prices sky-high, and many of the refugees who resettled in Cuba brought with them expertise and improved production techniques. Cuba soon became the world's biggest producer of "white gold." It was a new era of fabulous wealth and sudden fortunes.

Dependence on sugar and slaves

Nothing could stop sugar cane consuming the countryside – citrus fields were replanted, the last forests uprooted, even tobacco plantations were plowed over (growth of the crop being restricted to the narrower fields of the province of Pinar del Río). A steadily increasing supply of slaves was needed for the plantations, especially as workers survived for an average of only seven years. The number of slaves in Cuba stood at 40,000 in 1774, but by 1867 when the last known slave ship landed its cargo, an estimated 600,000 Africans had been imported.

Africans were bought and sold in newspaper classifieds, next to advertisements for horses and farm implements. In a rare gesture of leniency, some planters allowed their slaves to dance at night to drums, praying they were not communicating news of rebellion. Uprisings did occur, and were brutally repressed. By the mid-1820s blacks outnumbered whites on the island.

A new "sugarocracy" arose in Cuba: the sugar center of Trinidad sprouted resplendent palaces with names like Hope, Gamble, and Confidence. Their owners could afford to take shopping trips to Europe, bringing back Persian carpets, Italian paintings, and French chandeliers. Sumptuous mansions transformed Havana from a "large village," in foreigners' eyes, to Spain's "jewel of the Caribbean," a city of elegant iron grilles (rejas), gracious curlicues, and beautiful stained glass. The streets were paved with granite imported from New England, and trade with the United States boomed – the beginning of a relationship that would dominate much of Cuba's modern history.

The wind of change

The 19th century brought with it new ideas of liberation, independence, and emancipation, which swept through empires and their colonies. The slave revolution in Haiti, US independence from Britain, and Latin American countries' independence from Spain, all led to changes in outlook. Cuba was not immune, though modernization came late as a result of entrenched economic interests. A few criollos (Cuban-born Spaniards) began to sympathize both with the abolition of slavery and independence from the corrupt and inflexible Spanish administration, but their power was limited.

Their liberal views should be seen in the context of the European (principally British) push to abolish slavery, with some of the more

enlightened Cubans recognizing the beginning of the end of enforced labor. In 1811, Spain abolished slavery at home and in all its colonies except Cuba, Puerto Rico, and Santo Domingo. Under British pressure, Spain signed treaties to ban the Atlantic slave trade in 1817 (even receiving £400,000 from Britain for doing

> When in 1848 President Polk offered US$100 million to buy Cuba, Spain's foreign minister commented that his country "would rather see it sunk into the ocean."

so) and 1835, but this was completely ignored in Cuba and the trade continued covertly until the 1860s. In neighboring Jamaica, slaves were emancipated in 1833, but they would have to wait until 1886 in Cuba, a delay that caused more than a few rumblings of discontent among the oppressed, and understandable fear among the landowning, slave-owning class, whose economic interests were at stake.

Cubans started to seek reforms and greater autonomy from Spain. Politically, they fell into three groups: those who favored annexation to the US; those who favored complete independence from Spain together with the abolition of slavery; and those who wanted to remain part of Spain but with a separate constitution and

LEFT: slaves' lives were hard and short, and owners began to fear rebellions. **RIGHT:** souvenir lithograph from the Grand Cuban-American Fair 1896, New York City.

greater autonomy. There were three attempts at annexation, supported by slave-holding southern states, but all failed because the North and the abolitionist South were vehemently against annexing another slave-holding country.

The push for freedom

By the 1860s, Cuba was producing about a third of the world's sugar and was heavily dependent upon slaves and indentured laborers from China to do so. Spain was intransigent in refusing to allow political reforms to give the colony more autonomy within the empire and it came to the point when many Cubans were at last ready to

Latin America's first railroad was built in 1837 from the Güines sugar fields to Havana, using the labor of African slaves, Chinese workers, and indentured Irishmen. Thirteen workers perished for every kilometer of track laid.

end Spanish colonial rule. In 1868, a small-plantation owner, Carlos Manuel de Céspedes, freed the slaves at one of his plantations near Manzanillo, and declared Cuba independent, sparking off the Ten Years' War with Spain. The revolutionaries realized that they would only win against Spain if all Cubans, including free blacks and slaves, presented a united front. Free and runa-

way slaves swelled the Liberation Army's ranks. Known as *mambís* – a word that meant "rebel" in the African Congo – they often fought with machetes for lack of guns, and went barefoot and near-naked for want of boots and uniforms.

Antonio Maceo, the "Bronze Titan," was a black soldier who rose from the ranks to become major-general and one of the most popular leaders in the struggle. Like a character in a García Márquez novel, he is said to have survived innumerable assassination attempts, fought in 900 battles, been wounded 25 times, and lost his father and nine of his 13 brothers in the war. Many pro-Spanish whites were afraid that he would attempt to become president, and gathered under the slogan: "Cuba, better Spanish than African!"

Adventurers came from around the world to join the struggle against Spain. One was former American Union army officer Henry Reeve, who was captured and shot by a Spanish firing squad. Left for dead, he survived and became a leading general and anti-slavery voice, remembered as *El Inglesito*, "the little Englishman." But the war ground on for a decade, took 200,000 lives, and ended in stalemate. The Moret Law, passed in 1870, freed all children of slaves born after 1868 and any slave lucky enough to live to be over 60, but slavery itself was untouched. The Zanjón Convention, which brought the war to an end, enabled a limited number of Cubans to elect representatives to the Spanish *Cortés* (parliament), but there was no autonomy. The war left the economy crippled, and, with land prices at a level lower than they had been in years, US companies began to invest heavily in Cuban real estate, developing a significant financial interest in the country's future. They bought up many sugar plantations and sugar mills and, as sugar beet started to dominate the European market, Cuba became ever more dependent on the US to buy its main crop.

Finally, in 1880, the *Cortés* approved the law of abolition, although this amounted to little in the way of freedom. The law introduced an eight-year *patronato* (tutelage) for all slaves, whereby they had to continue working for their owners with no pay. It took a royal decree in 1886 to make the *patronato* illegal, and finally abolish slavery in Cuba. It probably had as much to do with the changing working conditions as it did with morality. Free and contract workers, together with more efficient processing techniques, allowed economies of scale.

The fighting starts again

The end of the Ten Years' War solved nothing, and Cuba was like a volcano waiting to erupt. There were other, unsuccessful attempts at rebellion, but the most successful was fostered in the US. In 1895, the carnage began again with the Second War of Independence, this time led by the great Cuban theorist José Martí *(see page 51)*. A lawyer, poet, and journalist, Martí's writings, and his organizational activities among Cubans living in the US in the 1870s and 1880s, had infused the independence movement with ideas of social justice: the goal was not just a free Cuba, but a Cuba without its vast inequalities of wealth and racial

Spanish forces started a scorched-earth policy in the Cuban countryside, executing *guajiros* (farmers), burning farms, and putting the survivors into labor camps. The strategy failed; by 1898, the Spaniards were exhausted and at the point of withdrawing. But another colonial power had been watching the conflict with increasing interest: the United States of America.

Enter the United States

As long as a century before, North American thinkers had decided that Cuba was crucial to their country's strategic interests. Throughout the 1800s, there were calls for outright

divisions. Unfortunately, he was killed in his first battle in 1895. However, the seemingly indestructible Antonio Maceo was still around to keep the flame of revolution burning, until he too was killed in a skirmish with Spanish troops on the border of Havana and Pinar del Río provinces, at the end of 1896. The tragedy left the Cuban cause in the hands of another stalwart veteran of the earlier war, General Máximo Gómez, who had been persuaded by Martí to return from exile to help lead the independence struggle.

Unable to engage the elusive rebels directly,

LEFT: a United States version of the Battle of San Juan Hill.
ABOVE: a Spanish depiction of the same battle.

AN ENGLISH VIEW

In 1895 the young English officer Winston Churchill took his winter leave in Cuba as war correspondent for the London *Daily Graphic.* The jaunt was "awfully jolly," young Winston found, especially as he was able to celebrate his 21st birthday in a war zone. Churchill had his first experience of being fired upon while having breakfast, but the guerrillas melted into the countryside and he spent most of his visit "wandering round and round in this endless humid jungle." He had begun his trip sympathizing with the rebels, but began to feel sorry for the Spanish losing their "Pearl of the Antilles." "They felt about Cuba just as we felt about Ireland," he wrote.

annexation, and several filibustering expeditions set out from Florida to the Cuban shores, hoping to provoke a popular revolt that would cause Cuba to fall "like a ripening plum into the lap of the Union" (in the happy phrase of John Quincy Adams). Four US presidents even offered to buy Cuba from the Spanish during the first half of the 19th century, seeing the island as part of the natural orbit of their increasingly powerful and expansionist country. With more than US$100 million invested by 1898, there were many in Washington who worried that radicals would take over an independent Cuba.

in Havana harbor, killing 260 people. Hearst and Pulitzer both claimed that the explosion on the *Maine* was caused by a Spanish mine (it was Hearst who coined the immortal, and very catchy, slogan, "Remember the Maine, to hell with Spain!"), and though some Cubans today subscribe to the belief that it might have been a deliberate explosion caused by the US itself to precipitate their involvement in the war, the evidence points to an accidental munitions explosion in the hold. Today there is a monument to the *Maine* in Havana on the Malecón.

Within a month, President McKinley had declared war; three months after that, the US

American emotions had already been whipped up by the press. Newspaper barons William Randolph Hearst (Orson Welles's model for *Citizen Kane*) and Joseph Pulitzer (who would give his name to America's greatest journalism prize) competed to offer the most lurid and heart-rending tales of the Spanish troops' cruelty: images of Cuban streets awash with blood, bayoneted babies, and deflowered virgins became daily fare for millions from Kansas to New York.

"Remember the Maine!"

The pretext for intervention came on February 15, when the USS *Maine* – a battleship sent to protect US interests – mysteriously blew up

Navy had blockaded the Spanish Navy in the harbor of Santiago de Cuba, at the eastern end of the island. A huge American expeditionary force landed north of the city. It was led by an obese veteran of the Indian wars, General William Shafter (1835–1906), and accompanied by a boatload of eager, albeit diarrhea-ridden, journalists.

Although the US Congress passed an amendment stating that they were not claiming sovereignty in Cuba, nationalists quickly had cause to doubt the benefits of US assistance. Shafter and his men took one look at the ragged Cuban Army and refused to allow them into battle – publicly blaming their lack of shoes and poor weapons, in private appalled that so many of them were black and mulatto (mixed race) – the reporter Stephen Crane called them "real tropic savages." Shafter suggested that the Cubans keep up the rear, digging trenches and latrines. Unsurprisingly, the commanding general, Calixto García, refused to cooperate.

The Spanish Army had very little fight left in it, but a showdown of sorts came at the Battle of San Juan Hill, on the outskirts of Santiago. The American Rough Riders were led in a famous charge by Edward Roosevelt, a short-sighted weakling as a child who had taken up *machista* pursuits from tiger hunting to soldiering in compensation. The Spanish were defeated, although

eral Shafter arranged a victory march through the streets of Santiago, but the Cuban forces were barred from participating.

The highjacked revolution

The US set up a military government to administer the country. After 30 years of fighting, Cubans had, in fact, traded one set of colonial masters for another. In 1901, US Congress agreed to withdraw its troops in exchange for guarantees that the country would remain an American protectorate. The so-called Platt Amendment – composed in Washington to be included verbatim in the Cuban Constitution – allowed the

the Americans took heavy casualties. Roosevelt's first missive to the US President was sheepish, but the national press hailed it as an extraordinary military achievement. Roosevelt rode the wave of popularity on to the governorship of New York and, in 1901, the presidency. Two days after San Juan, the Spanish Navy made a quixotic sally from Santiago only to suffer a rapid defeat.

It had been a "splendid little war," as one US official noted, giving the Americans an instant empire (Puerto Rico, Guam, and the Philippines were snapped up at the same time). Gen-

LEFT: Afro-Cuban soldiers found that peace did not bring prosperity. **ABOVE:** the 1898 Currier and Ives lithograph *Our Victorious Fleets in Cuban Waters.*

UP WITH THE USA

Not everything the US did during its military occupation was repressive. Positive developments included setting up state education, eliminating a famine, improving sanitation, and eradicating yellow fever on the basis of the discoveries of Cuban scientist, Carlos J. Finlay. The economy was restored to relative health, and sugar exports were encouraged under an import preference system. Public administration and the judiciary were reformed and an electoral system introduced. This led to the election of a constituent assembly which in 1901 approved a liberal constitution that separated Church and State and introduced universal adult male suffrage.

United States to intervene in Cuban internal affairs: it forced Cuba to lease them naval bases at Río Hondo and Guantánamo Bay, and gave the US the right to veto Cuba's trade or loan pacts with third countries. Understandably, news of the legislation caused rioting around Cuba,

> Not all Americans were caught up in the jingoism of the US defeat of Spain in 1898: the vitriolic Mark Twain wrote that the Stars and Stripes should be replaced with a Skull and Crossbones.

can investment in Cuba rocketed. United States companies snapped up land at bargain prices, and even set up mini "colonies" for American immigrants in places such as Isla de la Juventud.

The final tragedy of Cuba's false freedom was the "Black Uprising" of 1912. Afro-Cubans – many of whom had fought courageously in the Wars of Independence – were disgusted to find that the new republic was happy to leave them in effective serfdom. They formed their own political party, the Partido Independiente de Color, only to have it banned.

Finally, open rebellion spread throughout the country. Cuban forces led by General

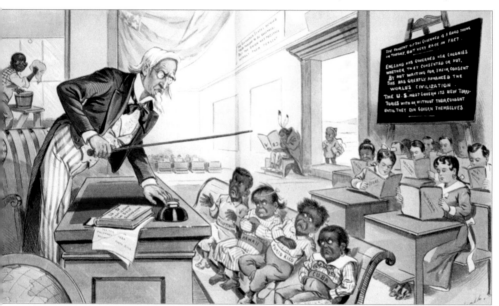

but the US military governor made it clear to the constitutional convention in Havana that the *yanquis* would not be leaving on any other terms. Tomás Estrada Palma, Cuba's first president, reluctantly signed the amendment.

The independence that wasn't

The Stars and Stripes came down in May, 1902, and Cuba began its stunted, compromised freedom. In the coming years, US Congress sent in the Marines on a regular basis to protect American interests, and even reinstated US military rule entirely from 1906 to 1909. None of the social reforms envisaged by José Martí was enacted; elections were held, but were usually fraudulent, and corruption was rife. At the same time, Ameri-

Monteagudo crushed the uprising with the help of US Marines and, more viciously, local Creoles, who took revenge on the Afro-Cubans in retaliation for a century and a half of fear.

"It is impossible to tell the number of dead," the general soon reported, "because it has degenerated into widespread butchery in the hills." One contemporary writer stated that "entire families were machine-gunned in their *bohíos* [huts]." Some 3,000 Afro-Cubans are estimated to have been massacred in two months. The "black fear" had been wiped out with blood, and Cuban racism was more brutally ingrained than ever. ❑

ABOVE: Uncle Sam lectures four "children," including Cuba in this 19th-century political cartoon.

José Martí

From the tiniest Cuban village to cities across Latin America are images of this romantic visionary whose greatness is undisputed

Born in 1853, Martí began his career as an independence fighter at 15, when he helped start an anti-colonial newspaper, *The Free Fatherland*, in Havana and denounced a fellow student for marching in a Spanish procession. He was charged with treason and sentenced to hard labor in a stone quarry. A frail youth, the experience ruined his eyesight, gave him a hernia and permanent scars on his ankles from the shackles he wore (in later life, he always wore a ring made from these shackles). After six months, Martí was sent into exile in Spain – the beginning of a journey that took him to France, England, Mexico, Guatemala, back secretly to Cuba, to exile again in Spain, escape to France, then to the US and south to Venezuela.

In 1881 Martí finally settled with his family in New York City, a center for Cuban exiles, and was initially intoxicated with the United States ("One can breathe freely," he wrote. "For here, freedom is the foundation, the shield, the essence of life.")

The enthusiasm was short-lived, however, and Martí soon saw the United States as the greatest threat to Latin American independence. He viewed as crucial the prevention of "the annexation of the peoples of our America by the turbulent and brutal North which despises them... I have lived within the monster and I know its entrails – and my sling is the sling of David."

For 15 years in the United States Martí kept up a punishing routine of political organizing, lecturing, purchasing weapons, and writing firebrand speeches, newspaper columns, essays, and exquisite, avant-garde poetry (his *Versos Sencillos* were married to the music of *Guajira Guantanamera* in the 1960s in what became the unofficial Cuban national anthem). He ate little, slept only in snatches, but glowed with nervous energy. Traveling to Florida – always in a heavy black suit and bow tie, his pointed moustache neatly clipped – Martí visited cigar factories to recruit Cuban exiles to his cause. Cuba would not be truly free, he argued, without economic, racial, and sexual equality – thus adding an inspiring social element to the potent rhetoric of nationalism.

Martí, though, was not content to remain an intellectual. In 1892, he founded the Cuban Revolutionary Party. Three years later, plans were made to rekindle the independence struggle: a message, hidden in a Havana cigar, was sent to General Antonio Maceo in Cuba.

Martí and Máximo Gómez landed secretly on the southeast coast, in a tiny boat that was nearly dashed to pieces in the middle of a storm. Escaping to the sierra of the Oriente, they were joined by hundreds of supporters. But life as a guerrilla was

harsh: Martí's emaciated frame was weighed down by a heavy coat, pack, and rifle, and he often fell on the mountain trails.

On May 19, 1895, near Bayamo, Martí went into his first day of battle carrying a picture of his daughter over his heart. He was shot dead almost immediately as he charged toward the enemy, without ever having drawn his gun. A martyr to the cause, he has been worshiped by Cubans ever since and only Che Guevara is as instantly recognizable and revered. Today, José Martí's words have been appropriated by both sides of the political divide: Fidel Castro views him as the home-grown ideologue of the Revolution, while right-wing Miami Cubans named their anti-Castro broadcast stations Radio Martí and TV Martí. ❏

RIGHT: José Martí, an undisputed hero.

THE AGE OF DECADENCE

From the 1920s to the 1950s, Havana was a playground for wealthy Americans seeking guilt-free sex, cheap alcohol, and gambling. The mafia and corrupt Cuban politicians joined forces to preside over this hedonistic era

At the height of Prohibition in the United States, which lasted from 1920 to 1933, "personal liberty" became the euphemistic reason for thousands of US tourists to take the short boat ride to Cuba from Florida, to drink and have the sort of fun they wouldn't have at home. Havana became a symbol of decadent pleasure, and the flow of Americans visiting for sun, sex, and alcohol turned into a flood after World War II.

Havana quickly became the prostitution capital of the Western hemisphere. Businessmen could choose their mulatta for the weekend from photos at the airport; the notorious Casa Marina specialized in 13-year-old girls and boys from the provinces (with only a minor surcharge for virgins). Lovely, long-legged mulattas trod the boards of the Tropicana, while the more adventurous visitors headed for live sex acts in seedier surroundings; a regular showtime favorite was Superman, who measured his spectacular erection by lining up 12 silver dollars side by side. Stars like Errol Flynn and Gary Cooper visited every winter in their luxury yachts. George Raft, who specialized as a film-star gangster, was full-time host of the Red Room at the Hotel Capri.

And the whole, rum-soaked party went on to the fabulous rhythms of mamba, rumba, and *son*. Cuba's 12-piece bands, musicians all decked out in white tuxedos, were in demand from Manhattan to the Parisian Left Bank, though the big money in Havana went to American jazz bands and front-liners like Nat King Cole.

Strong-man government

Gerardo Machado was elected President in 1924. A populist, he invested in public works projects

and tried to diversify the economy, helped by the rise in tourism. However, the Great Depression after the US stock-market crash in 1929 and a sudden fall in sugar prices in the late 1920s left him faced with strikes and demonstrations. Students, the middle classes and trades unions were united in opposition, but all rebellion was met with violence. Troops were regularly called out to break strikes; demonstrators were gunned down; hired thugs, called *porros*, abducted and tortured enemies of the regime, who then "disappeared." The US considered intervening again to prevent civil war and its ambassador began negotiations in 1933, but this interference was the last straw for the nationalists, who called a general strike. Machado hopped on a plane to

Miami, supposedly carrying five revolvers and as many bags of gold bullion. The new government was equally incapable of restoring peace, facing more strikes, mob attacks, and occupations of factories. In the ensuing chaos, the figure who took control was a young army sergeant, a mulatto of humble social origins called Fulgencio Batista, part of a revolt of non-commissioned officers. In quick succession he took the rank of colonel, then gained full control of the army and became a general. Before long, he emerged as the major player in Cuban politics, managing the government through a string of puppet presidents. The "Batista Era" had begun.

fare legislation, and by public works, housing construction, and other job creation projects. In 1940 he introduced a new Constitution which included universal suffrage, a minimum wage, pensions, social insurance, and an eight-hour day. It was never fully implemented. Batista remained unpopular, however, opposed by students and radical nationalists who felt the full force of

> During Prohibition, refined Havana nightclubs raged all night and the casinos rivaled those of Las Vegas.

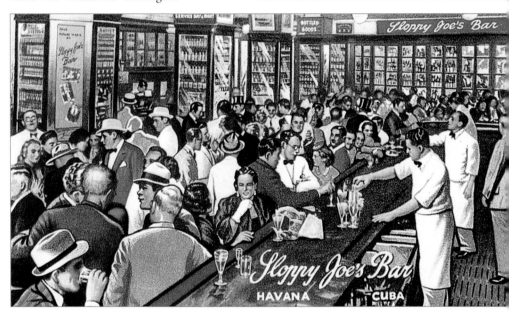

In 1934, the US Government, perhaps confident that its interests were secure, repealed the Platt Amendment that guaranteed its power of intervention – although the Americans retained their lease on the naval base at Guantánamo. By 1940, Batista had wearied of running Cuba through others and ran for president himself, winning an apparently fair election.

Batista's government, supported by the armed forces, and US and Cuban business interests, was nationalist, populist, corrupt, and violent. He pacified trades unions by passing social welfare legislation.

political violence. In 1944 he lost the elections to their candidate, Dr Ramón Grau San Martín, of the Partido Revolucionario Cubana-Auténtico, who was followed in 1948 by his protégé, Carlos Prío Socarrás. High sugar prices kept them afloat, but neither president did anything to stem the rampant corruption nor the grinding poverty in the countryside, social inequalities, unemployment, illiteracy, and minimal health care.

In 1952, Batista staged a coup, suspended constitutional and democratic government, and began a harshly repressive dictatorship.

Havana and the Mob

In a city where fabulous sums could be made from booze, drugs, gambling, and prostitution,

---

LEFT: grand hotels, like the Sevilla-Biltmore (now the Mercure Sevilla), sprang up during Havana's heyday.
ABOVE: Sloppy Joe's, a famous Havana bar.

it is not surprising that the American Mafia was not far behind. The Mob gained a foothold during the Prohibition years, using Cuba as a base for running rum to the Florida Keys. A far more lucrative opening came in 1938, when Batista invited Meyer Lansky to take over the operation of two crooked casinos and a racetrack. Known as "the Jewish godfather," Lansky was the brains behind the US's national crime syndicate, formed by uniting the various warring families in the 1930s.

Lansky soon had the places "reformed." The establishments flourished, and more casinos soon followed – with regular kickbacks to Batista, brokered by Lansky. What was better, as far as the Mafia was concerned, was that the whole thing was perfectly legal.

In 1953, Batista appointed Meyer Lansky his personal adviser on gambling reform, to clean up Havana. Games were regularized, and the secret police employed to arrest and deport card sharps. The irony was not lost on many people. When he was asked why American gangsters were so welcome in Cuba, the US Ambassador replied: "It's strange, but it seems to be the only way to get honest casinos." The Batista dictatorship was the climax of Cuba's age of decadence, a time when corruption reached mythic proportions. The revi-

PARADISE FOUND

The Spanish poet Federico García Lorca came here in 1930 and stayed for three months. "This island is a paradise," he rhapsodized in a letter to his parents. "If I ever get lost, they should look for me either in Andalucía or Cuba." Already a recognized poet, Lorca was befriended by a string of habanero bohemians and took full advantage of Cuba's pleasures. The atmosphere of sexual liberation apparently made García Lorca more overt about his own homosexuality than he had been in his own country: it was in Cuba that he wrote *The Public*, the first Spanish work to feature male lovers, although only two scenes were ever published during his lifetime.

talized casino industry was part of a massive push to promote tourism: a new airline opened, visas were waived for visiting Americans, and all new hotels were granted tax-free status. The number of hotel rooms in Havana nearly doubled in six years. Oiling the gears was a Byzantine system of bribes – Meyer Lansky is said to have deposited more than US\$3 million in Batista's personal bank account in Switzerland, and according to one observer, they were "like brothers."

Meanwhile, the secret police became less secret and more savage in hunting down opposition figures. Corpses of tortured dissidents were strung from lamp-posts as a warning to anyone who dared to speak out against the roulette wheels and poker machines in Havana.

The lure of the tropic

Cuba's combination of unlimited sensual pleasures, lawlessness, and corruption – along with the *frisson* of danger – exerted an almost irresistible fascination for the many writers and artists who passed through Havana.

Ernest Hemingway visited throughout the 1930s for marlin fishing, and then moved to Cuba permanently. Although he regularly drank himself into a stupor, and could become aggressive, Hemingway's streak of midwestern puritanism was strong enough for him to remain largely innocent of the seedier side of Havana life.

Last days of the frenzy

For many, the disparity between Cuba's fun-loving image and brutal reality was becoming too great. Many Cubans were disgusted with the levels of corruption into which their country had sunk, and the spectacle of the opulent, Mafia-run casinos alongside Cubans sleeping on the sidewalks and in burned-out cars. Even some foreigners felt moral qualms. As the Cuban-American writer Enrique Fernández-Más put it: "On the road to pleasure, your driver could turn around at a stop light and show you photos of bodies bloodied with bullets and young faces ripped apart by tortures so

No such qualms restrained the English writer Graham Greene. During a brief visit in 1957, Greene explored romantic, decadent Cuba and immortalized it in his novel *Our Man in Havana*. Greene found the Cuban capital a place "where every vice was permissible and every trade possible," and lapped up "the brothel life, the roulette in every hotel, the fruit machines spilling out jackpots of silver dollars, the Shanghai Theater where for one dollar twenty-five cents one could see a nude cabaret of extreme obscenity with the bluest of blue films in the intervals."

savage – vividly described by the *revolucionario* driver – that the daiquirís, the sweet roast pork, the yummy yams, the fine Havanas, the hot sex, nothing tasted good any more."

But not everyone noticed the changing of the winds. In 1957, Lansky opened his own hotel, the Riviera, on the Malecón. It was the largest in Havana. Ginger Rogers performed in the hotel's Copa Room on opening night; Seemingly oblivious to what was going on in Cuban politics, Meyer Lansky stayed put. This time the consummate gambler got it wrong. He gambled everything on Havana – and, as he later put it, "I crapped out." After the revolution, the casinos were closed, the Mob's properties nationalized. Havana's age of decadence was at an end.   ❑

FAR LEFT: Federico García Lorca. **LEFT:** Fulgencio Batista. **ABOVE:** high times in a Havana nightclub, 1946.

THE REVOLUTION

The 1959 Revolution was one of the 20th century's most distinctive political triumphs for the underdog. It ended the blatant corruption and inequality of the Batista years, but conflict with the USA, and support from the USSR, brought the world to the brink of nuclear war

As the age of decadence flourished in Havana, the roots of a revolution were beginning to take hold in the countryside. Under Batista's rule, a small elite enjoyed a grand lifestyle, while the majority of the rural population endured appalling poverty. Few had running water, electricity, or access to health care or education. A quarter of all Cubans were unable to read or write, and a quarter of adult males were unemployed. The country was rife with corruption, oppression, and inequality.

The Moncada attack

One year after Batista began his second term in office, a brazen young lawyer named Fidel Castro concluded that an armed uprising was the only way to end the dictator's reign. This was not Castro's first attempt at power. A year earlier he had tried to run for a seat in Congress but, in a Machiavellian move by Batista, the elections were surreptitiously canceled.

You may still see slogans – especially in and around Santiago – declaring "Es Siempre el 26" (It is always the 26th), a reference to the 26th July Movement and the attack on the Moncada barracks in Santiago.

Hoping to spark a mass uprising, on July 26, 1953, Castro and 128 of his fellow anti-Batistas mounted an attack on the Moncada army barracks in Santiago. But as the music of Carnival blared in the background, the young revolu-

tionaries were brutally defeated. Despite being a total failure, the coup marked the beginning of the Cuban revolution. Six rebels died in the attack, and 55 more were later killed by the police. Those who escaped, including Castro, took refuge in the Sierra Maestra mountains, but soon afterward were rounded up and jailed. Fortunately for Castro, the arresting officer was sympathetic to the cause, and took him to a local jail rather than the government prison where he would surely have been killed.

History will absolve me

For Batista, having Castro executed in secret would have solved many problems, but

LEFT: Fidel and his brother Raúl (to his right) in 1957.
RIGHT: time runs out for Fulgencio Batista.

Castro's capture had become public knowledge, so any such attempt would have fomented further anti-government sentiment, so he had to put the rebel on trial. Acting as his own lawyer, Castro delivered a five-hour speech that would sink deeply into the minds of the Cuban underclass when eventually smuggled out of jail. He called Batista the worst dictator in Cuban history, and described in detail the sorry living conditions of the majority of the Cuban people. He also called for universal education, agrarian reform, and a total restructuring of the government, then delivered his famous words: "Condemn me if you will. History will absolve me."

July Movement (M-26), named for the attack at Moncada in 1953. M-26, which had roots in Cuba's 19th-century struggles, was the philosophical foundation that became synonymous with Castro's revolution. Castro traveled to New York and Miami to raise money for the impend-

> The yacht, Granma, on which Fidel's revolutionaries sailed to Cuba, was named by its first (English-speaking) owner for his grandmother. Later, Granma became the name of Cuba's newspaper, and a whole province.

Time to reflect

Sentenced to 15 years, Castro was imprisoned on the Isle of Pines (now the Isle of Youth). While there, he read the works of Marx and studied successful peasant uprisings. He also lectured to fellow inmates and plotted the revolution that would bring him to power. After serving less than two years, he was released under a government amnesty on Mother's Day in May 1955 (El Día de La Madre is a major event in Cuba) – a decision that Batista would later regret.

Soon after his release, Fidel Castro and his comrades went into exile in Mexico. There, he met a young Argentine doctor, Ernesto "Che" Guevara, and together they created the 26th of

ing revolt, gathered guns and ammunition, and campaigned for support from abroad.

In November 1956, Castro, Che, and 80 other revolutionaries left Mexico and sailed to Cuba. After several days floundering in stormy seas, they landed on December 2 at Playa Las Coloradas, about 160km (100 miles) west of Santiago. The plan had been to arrive in Santiago at the end of November, to assist a potential uprising led by M-26 member Frank País, but the delayed arrival of Castro and his men meant that this uprising was crushed in just a few hours. A few days after they disembarked from their boat they were ambushed by Batista's troops who captured and killed most of the crew.

Among the dozen survivors were Castro, his

younger brother Raúl, and Che. Joined by a group of peasants and a few fellow revolutionaries, the ragged band quickly slipped away into the Sierra Maestra where they founded the Rebel Army. One of those who joined them was a wealthy and spirited revolutionary named Vilma Espín, who became Raúl Castro's wife, founded the Federation of Cuban Women, and remained active in politics until her death in June 2007 *(see pages 22-3)*.

Guerrillas in the mountains

Entrenched in the mountains, the Rebel Army saw themselves as warriors of the common *New York Times*, into their mountain camp for a clandestine interview with Castro. Swayed by the boisterous bravado of Fidel and his men, Matthews' account praised the Rebel Army and gave the world a romantic first impression of the dashing young revolutionary. Batista insisted that Matthews' story was fabricated, and Castro was actually dead. Days later, the *New York Times* responded with irrefutable evidence: a photograph of Matthews and Castro smoking cigars together in the mountains.

With his name and face now known the world over, public support for Castro in Cuba multiplied. In March 1957, students stormed the

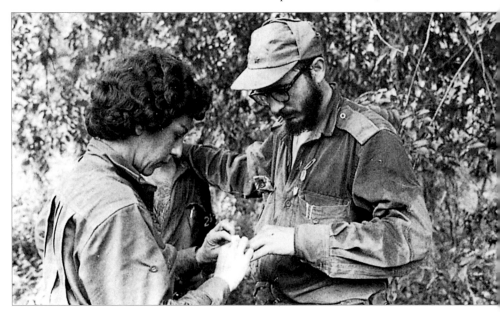

people, and set out to spread their revolutionary ideas. During the next few years, they set up an informal government, drew up a manifesto, organized schools and hospitals in rural areas, and established their own radio station, Radio Rebelde, to campaign for a democratic Cuba. Needing the support of the underground movements in Havana, they aligned themselves with the Students' Revolutionary Directorate and the Civic Resistance Movement.

In a clever public-relations coup, the rebels smuggled Herbert Matthews, a reporter for the

LEFT: Raúl Castro and Che Guevara in the mountains.
ABOVE: Fidel Castro with his long-time companion, Celia Sánchez.

Presidential Palace in an attempt to kill Batista, while another group took over a radio station and falsely announced his death. The following year a general strike was called in support of the Rebel Army, and disgruntled naval officers tried to stage a rebellion in the port of Cienfuegos.

The turning point of the revolution came in July 1958, when a battalion of Batista's forces surrendered to Castro's troops after a 10-day siege. The Rebel Army, which by this time was about 50,000 strong, charged ahead.

Followed by troops, Castro advanced into Santiago, Raúl into northern Oriente, and, in the most decisive move of all, Che Guevara into Santa Clara. By December 1958, the rebels had shattered Batista's army, which retreated in

Che

Decades after his death, "Che" Guevara is a Marxist hero, an icon by government decree, and model for Cuba's ideal socialist man

Guevara is known throughout Cuba simply as Che, an affectionate Argentine expression equivalent to "mate," "pal", or "buddy." Each morning, Cuban schoolchildren recite the patriotic slogan: "Pioneers of communism, we shall

be like Che." Throughout the country, posters of his handsome face hang on thousands of living-room walls and women swoon as if he were a movie star. When the bio-bic Che (Steven Sodebergh, 2008) was screened at the Latin America Film Festival in Havana, the actor Benicio del Toro got a standing ovation for his portrayal of their favorite hero.

Born in Argentina in 1928, Guevara came from a left-leaning, middle-class family. As a child he developed severe asthma that later brought about his decision to become a doctor. As a medical student he traveled through South America on a motorbike and after graduation in 1953 he took off again to travel through South and Central America, seeking political adventure.

After witnessing the CIA-inspired overthrow of the socialist Árbenz government in Guatemala in 1954, Guevara moved to Mexico, where he met the then exiled Fidel Castro. Soon afterward, he joined the 26th of July Movement and was later to command the decisive guerrilla attack in Santa Clara that led Batista to flee Cuba. He also became Castro's principal ideological counselor and closest friend.

Once the government was established, he supervized the appeals and firing squads of opponents and Batista officials. As Minister for Industry he instituted agrarian reform, and as president of the National Bank of Cuba, he negotiated trade agreements with Eastern-Bloc countries. In 1960 he wrote a book called *Guerrilla Warfare* that became a manual for revolutionary strategies in the Developing World. In it, he advocated the use of guerrilla tactics to defeat imperialism; moral rather than material incentives for work; and working-class solidarity.

During the 1960s, an entire generation of radical youths idolized his purist Marxist beliefs, selfless devotion, and relentless work ethic, and his dramatic image blessed protest movements in Paris, London, Washington, Montreal, Tokyo, Bombay, and Baghdad.

A member of the macho world of brave guerrilla fighters, Guevara was impetuous, daring, and reckless. He was also a brilliant intellectual who spoke French, wrote poetry, and represented Cuba in international chess competitions. In 1965 he resigned from his posts (some say he'd fallen out with Castro over the growing influence of the Soviet Union in Cuban affairs) and, after a brief spell fighting in the Congo, he attempted to foster revolution in the Bolivian highlands. The campaign proved a disaster and Guevara was captured and killed by the CIA-backed Bolivian Army in 1967.

Castro declared three days of national mourning, then spent years creating a Guevara cult. After the collapse of the Soviet Union, Castro tried to rekindle some revolutionary passion by implementing a nationwide "Let's Be Like Che" campaign. Then, in 1997, Che's mortal remains were discovered in Bolivia and returned to Cuba *(see page 234)*.

Che Guevara remains Latin America's most celebrated modern revolutionary. The French philosopher Jean-Paul Sartre described him as "the most complete human being of our age," and *Time* magazine listed him as one of the 100 most influential people of the 20th century. ❏

Left: Che Guevara, iconic revolutionary.

defeat. A terrified Batista fled the country to the Dominican Republic. The following morning, people all over the island rejoiced. Ebullient revelers danced in the streets, applauding Batista's downfall. In Havana, throngs of peasants stormed into the casinos, which had been off-limits to them for years. Some vandalized the slot machines, while others brought their pigs in to have a look.

After announcing the triumph of the revolution from the balcony of Santiago's town hall on January 2, 1959, the handsome 32-year-old Castro took off with his guerrillas for a victory drive to Havana. Euphoric crowds cheered as they passed through the countryside. When they arrived in the capital a week later, tens of thousands of supporters welcomed them.

At the Riviera Hotel, workers walked out of their jobs. Meyer Lansky, the boss, found himself in the kitchen cooking dinner for guests as his wife waited tables. For Lansky and his cronies, the good life was over. Words from Castro's speech echoed in his head: "We are ready not only to deport the gangsters, but to shoot them." Lansky knew he meant it. He moved his gambling business to the nearby Bahamas, and offered a large bounty for Fidel Castro's head.

A new Cuba

Cubans in New York and Miami celebrated the fall of Batista and made plans to return to the island. The revolution was praised worldwide as a true victory for the Cuban people, and even the US Government was initially optimistic about the changes taking place.

In the spring of 1959, a victorious Castro declared himself the prime minister of Cuba, and Che Guevara was appointed president of the National Bank. Hundreds of Batista supporters were jailed, many of them executed, and by the following year sweeping political changes were taking place across the country.

The new government passed an agrarian reform act which limited private land ownership; under Batista, 70 percent of the land had been owned by a mere 8 percent of the population. Fidel's regime also confiscated foreign-owned industries in an effort to end US control of the island (North Americans owned more

RIGHT: a revolutionary poster (now in Havana's Museum of the Revolution) invites Batista to flee the country.

than 165 major companies including 90 percent of the public services and 40 percent of the sugar industry).

Farms, plantations, oil refineries, and communications systems were nationalized. The government also outlawed racial discrimina-

> As Castro delivered a victory speech, a flock of white doves was released into the air and one of the birds landed on his shoulder. This was taken by followers of Santería as an omen that he had been chosen to deliver them from oppression.

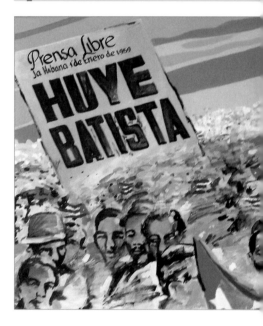

tion, created a low-income housing program, made free health care and education available to all, and implemented new policies for farming, sports, music, the arts, and defense.

The redistribution of wealth meant instant rewards for the peasant class, but just as quickly, the middle and upper classes were stripped of the privileges they had enjoyed. Already having had their homes confiscated, many feared what might come next, and fled to Miami. Forbidden to take any possessions with them, most left with nothing more than the clothes on their backs. Women sewed their wedding rings into the hems of their dresses to smuggle them out. Once in Miami they established a vocal anti-Castro community of exiles that criticized the new government, and looked forward to the day they could return to their homes.

In 1960, Fidel Castro delivered his first speech to the United Nations and was introduced to Soviet Premier Nikita Khrushchev. While in New York, he also met the radical American Black Power leader Malcolm X.

At about that time, the US began to see Castro as a threat to its national security, and mysterious things started happening. A French ship, *La Coubre*, delivering Belgian armaments, inexplicably exploded in Havana harbor as unidentified low-flying planes flew over the city. The US was the prime suspect.

In response, Castro took an aggressive stance. In January 1961, he expelled 11 US diplomats. Soon afterward, the two countries severed diplomatic relations, and the US began an economic embargo that brought the import of American goods to a halt. It further isolated the island by persuading all but two Western-hemisphere nations (Canada and Mexico) to cut trade and diplomatic ties with Cuba.

The Bay of Pigs

In April 1961, a CIA-trained brigade of 1,500 mercenaries, mostly Cuban exiles from Miami, landed at Playa Girón in the Bahía de Cochi-

FIDEL THE SURVIVOR

The Cuban leader estimates that there have been 20 CIA-inspired attempts on his life; one agency director, William Colby, expressed surprise, saying he was aware of only five. The ingenious (if ineffective) ways of attempting to assassinate Castro (apart from simply shooting him), included:
• contaminating his cigars with botulism.
• giving him a toxic dose of LSD.
• lacing a chocolate milkshake with cyanide.
• smearing his wet suit with tuberculosis spores.
Cuban exiles in Miami and the mafia were the CIA's two natural partners in crime, but their plots never worked.

nos (Bay of Pigs), hoping to instigate an anti-Castro coup. The invasion was a complete fiasco. The element of surprise was lost because US bombers attacked Cuban airfields days beforehand; the raids failed to destroy the Cuban airforce, leaving the attackers open to assault from the air. The counter-revolutionaries were no match for Cuba's military, led by Castro; and local people, whom it was hoped would be sympathetic to the exiles' cause, were strongly pro-Castro.

Within 72 hours the US brigade was defeated. A few men were killed, the rest taken prisoner. For their release, the US traded $50-million worth of medicines that Cuba had been unable to buy due to the embargo. Castro emerged as the clear victor, while US President Kennedy was humiliated. The invasion was seen by Cubans as a blatant imperialist stunt, and relations between the two countries worsened still further. The incident also garnered support for Castro throughout Latin America, and rendered him fearful of a US military invasion. The United States did little to alleviate those fears, instigating covert activities including plots to assassinate Castro (*see panel, left*).

By the end of 1961, Castro's platform for a freely elected democratic government had changed. Following the Bay of Pigs invasion he had shocked the world by pronouncing Cuba's

in October 1962, the Soviet Union and the United States came face to face with the reality of nuclear war, over what has gone down in history as the Cuban Missile Crisis.

The US demanded that the Soviets remove the missiles, and threatened to bomb Cuba if they refused. The world watched in horror as the possibility of war came uncomfortably close. The Soviets eventually relented and an uneasy peace was restored.

Despite the fact that an agreement was reached, the US was not happy with the outcome. In 1963, President Kennedy relegated relations with Cuba to fall under the US Trad-

revolution to be a "socialist revolution." Some believe his conversion to Marxism was merely a pragmatic move to gain favor with the Russians, without whom the island did not stand a chance of surviving the US embargo.

On the brink of war

In order to support socialist Cuba, the USSR supplied economic aid, as Castro had anticipated, and shipped nuclear missiles to Cuba to defend the island. The threat of nuclear weapons stationed just 140km (90 miles) away was too much for the US Government, and

ing with the Enemy Act, which tightened the embargo and prohibited all commercial and personal contact between the two nations. The US became the only country in the world to forbid its citizens to travel to Cuba; the political impasse became even more intractable.

Castro was incensed that he had not been consulted during the talks between the two superpowers, but the reality was that he had thrown in his lot with the Soviets and was powerless to prevent them from dictating terms. He had to content himself with an unwritten assurance that the US would not sponsor a further invasion of Cuba, and with the fact that, for the briefest of periods, he'd managed to turn the tables on his enemy in the insecurity stakes. ❏

LEFT: victorious Cuban soldiers at the Bay of Pigs.
ABOVE: Khrushchev welcomes Fidel to Moscow.

SOCIALISM OR DEATH

During the 1960s and 1970s, Cuba played a role in world affairs out of all proportion to its size. Since then, progress has been curtailed by crippling domestic problems, taxing even Fidel Castro's ingenuity

Although resolved diplomatically, the Cuban Missile Crisis *(see page 63)* provoked even more Cold War hostility from the United States, and pushed Castro firmly into the Soviet camp. In addition, it helped to turn the country into an audacious socialist experiment and a feisty Third World power.

Cuba's Communist Party was restructured in 1965, and the following year, despite Soviet disapproval, Castro was determined to export his revolutionary ideals. In 1966 he claimed that the Andes would become the next Sierra Maestra. But the Soviet Union (which provided money and arms) pressed Castro to pursue a less independent foreign policy. It seems that Che Guevara was determined to carry out a policy of directly fomenting revolution, with or without Soviet support, and left Cuba to fight first in Africa and then Bolivia.

Friends and foes

With the death of Guevara in Bolivia in 1967, Castro realized he had to take a different path to global influence. In 1968 he personally endorsed the Soviet invasion of Czechoslovakia, and cemented the bond with his powerful ally. Castro then directed his energy inward. To lessen Cuba's dependence on the sugar industry, he tried to diversify the economy through industrialization. But thousands of educated Cubans had fled and the country lacked skilled labor. The US embargo limiting the import of industrial equipment was another hindrance, and the industrialization plan failed. Sugar, once again, became the main force of the economy.

LEFT: a 1970s May Day parade in Havana.
RIGHT: Fidel Castro speaking in Havana, 1965.

NEIGHBORHOOD WATCH

To help dissuade counter-revolutionary activities, Castro created neighborhood-watch groups known as Committees for the Defense of the Revolution (CDRs). The CDRs organized labor and implemented health and education programs, but also served as vigilantes and as the Big Brother of the revolution. Members monitored their neighbors and reported all non-conformist behavior to the government. Still in operation today, there are more than 100,000 CDRs on the island, comprising about 75 percent of the population. Membership is voluntary, but belonging to a CDR brings a guarantee of social benefits, while not belonging may possibly bring trouble.

Big Brother is watching

In the name of the revolution, the 1960s marked the beginning of decades of political repression. Anyone seen as non-supportive of the government was deemed "socially unacceptable," and thousands of these "dissidents" were jailed.

Police sealed off the bohemian neighborhoods of Havana and interrogated artists, writers, and intellectuals. Non-supportive poets were silenced. Education and cultural policies became more severe, trades unions were disbanded, and the media fell under absolute government control. By the late 1960s, an ideological straitjacket had smothered the country.

than-red" communist-obsessed US continued covert activities against Cuba, including more CIA-backed assassination attempts on Castro. In addition, several of Cuba's trade missions in Europe were bombed by anti-Castro terrorists.

As a result, the Soviet Union beefed up its military and economic support to Cuba. Eastern-bloc technicians were sent to the island while Cuban students were invited to study in Moscow. Financial aid steadily increased and was measured in billions of dollars. At the time, Cuba was receiving generous shipments of oil priced far below standard OPEC rates, while its sugar crop was bought at inflated prices. About

After poor sugar harvests in 1963–4, Castro called upon the whole nation to meet a target of 10 million tonnes of sugar by 1970. Everyone spent time working in the fields but the goal was never met.

one-half of all Soviet aid to the Developing World poured into Cuba. Boosted by Soviet weapons and fighter planes, Cuba's defense system developed into the most powerful military force in Latin America, much larger than those of Brazil or Mexico.

The heady 1970s

Practicing Catholics, Protestants, Jews, and Santeros were persecuted – any religious affiliation was deemed anti-revolutionary. Prostitutes were sent to vocational schools for rehabilitation, homosexuals were imprisoned in labor camps, and all remnants of bourgeois society were eliminated throughout the island.

Throughout the 1960s, the "better-dead-

For most Cubans, the 1970s are remembered fondly as the heady days of the revolution. With the utmost confidence, Castro became the international spokesman for Developing World causes, traveling to South America, China, Vietnam, and Africa. In 1974 the Soviet premier Leonid Brezhnev visited Cuba and publicly endorsed his Caribbean comrade. In front of enraptured crowds, the two men predicted that communism would some day triumph throughout the world. The next year, the Organization of American States lifted its sanctions against Cuba and many Latin American nations resumed ties with the country.

Economically, Cuba advanced, and the gains of the revolution were indisputable. Unheard of in most Developing World countries, Cuba's health-care system eliminated infectious diseases, drastically lowered the infant mortality rate, and curtailed population growth. The number of doctors grew from 6,000 to more than 25,000. The government also paved roads

he aligned himself with left-wing revolutionary movements. In 1975 he flexed his military muscles by sending 200,000 soldiers to Angola. Cuban troops fought on the side of the Marxist SWAPO government, following South Africa's decision to assist Angolan UNITA rebels. This conflict continued a tradition of Cuban assistance with what Castro saw as anti-imperialist movements in Africa, which went back to the days of Che Guevara. In 1978 he did the same for Ethiopia.

But Angola was Cuba's greatest triumph – as attested to by Nelson Mandela, who says the defeat of South African troops there helped

throughout the countryside, built low-rent apartment buildings, and eradicated illiteracy. Cubans felt proud.

International involvement

Although Cuba's political system was redesigned to mimic the Soviet model, Castro remained very much his own man. This was especially so when it came to foreign policy. He saw Cuba as part of the non-aligned movement, but nevertheless got heavily involved in Africa. Capitalizing on Cuba's Afro-Cuban heritage,

LEFT: Cuba's literacy campaign created the most literate population in Latin America.
ABOVE: Cuban soldiers in Angola.

precipitate the downfall of the apartheid state in his own country.

Back on his own side of the world, Castro befriended left-leaning leaders in nearby Jamaica and Grenada and, in 1979, hosted the annual conference of the non-aligned nations. That same year Cuba also supported the Soviet invasion of Afghanistan, and the socialist revolution in Nicaragua which brought the Sandinistas to power.

In 1976, the Cuban Communist Party finally approved its new Marxist-Leninist constitution. This constitution redrew provincial boundaries, creating 14 provinces and the federal district of Havana. It also created the assemblies of People's Power (*Poder Popular*), governing bodies of elected officials who delegate power at municipal, provincial, and national levels. The National Assembly elected Fidel Castro president of the Council of State and Raúl Castro first vice president.

Socialismo o Muerte

At the beginning of the 1980s, Cuba was still a Latin American symbol of independence from US imperialism, but the quality of life in the country was beginning to decline. Productivity dropped off, and health care, education, and social services deteriorated. Castro blamed the country's problems on the "workers who do not work and the students who do not study," and then fired numerous government economists.

Many of Cuba's economic problems, however, were caused not by lazy workers or students but by blatant mismanagement. The government had appointed Communist Party members to professional positions for which they were not qualified, destroyed the plantation system, and refused to develop the tourism industry. And a political system designed for the Soviet Union did not translate well to Cuba.

In 1980 public protests escalated to the point that the government permitted anyone who wanted to leave to do so – including, it is said,

REJUVENATING SLOGANS

By the late 1980s, Cuba was billions of dollars in debt to the USSR, and was forced to cut food rations. In an attempt to rejuvenate the revolutionary spirit, Castro revised the *¡Patria o Muerte!* (Fatherland or Death) slogan used to punctuate his lengthy speeches in the 1960s – *¡Socialismo o Muerte!* became the new slogan. Another motivational motto was "100 percent Cubano." Both were plastered on billboards throughout Cuba.

many criminals who were freed from prison in order for them to leave. That year, 125,000 Cubans fled to the US in the so-called Mariel boatlift *(see page 87)*, adding to the several hundred thousand who had left in the early years of the revolution.

In 1985, the Cubans in Miami set up Radio Martí, an anti-Castro propaganda station aimed directly at Cuba. The station's reports of how great life was in the US stirred up even more discontent, although Castro limited this by jamming its frequency.

Criticisms and scandals

On the international level, Cuba received harsh criticisms for its human-rights violations.

A report filed by Amnesty International condemned the country for its abuse of political prisoners, and the beatings, psychological torture, and solitary confinement taking place in Cuba's prisons became a thorny issue.

In 1989, more public disgrace fell on the country. General Arnaldo Ochoa, a much-decorated military figure, and six other military officials, were charged with corruption and drug trafficking. Found guilty of pocketing millions of dollars and allowing Colombian cocaine smugglers to use Cuba as a way-station en route to the US, the officers were put before a firing squad.

living in our home with another man's wife."

Members of Cuba's Communist Party agreed with their leader. For them, *perestroika* and Gorbachev's other main goal – *glasnost* (transparency and freedom from censorship) – were dirty words. Untouched by the looming crisis, party members were a privileged class in Cuba. With access to food, cars, gas, travel abroad, and imported goods, they bitterly resisted change.

When the USSR finally fell apart in 1991, the impact on Cuba was devastating. At a stroke, the country lost annual subsidies of US$6 billion in economic aid, $1 billion in military assistance, 10 million tons of oil, and $6 billion worth of

The Eastern Bloc crumbles

As the Ochoa scandal shook the country, communist dominoes in Eastern Europe were beginning to tumble. When Mikhail Gorbachev assumed power in Moscow and put forth his *perestroika* economic reforms, many predicted that Soviet money would flow less freely, causing chaos for the Cuban Government. But Castro made it quite clear that he had no interest in multiparty governments or a free-market system. Ever ready with a well-honed phrase, he said: "For us to adopt *perestroika* would be like

LEFT: family slogan painted on a wall in Baracoa.
ABOVE: Fidel Castro and Mikhail Gorbachev during an official visit to Cuba in 1989.

imported goods. It also now had to sell its sugar at market value. The scarcity of available oil paralyzed Cuban industry and transport. Adding to the turmoil, Cuba's sugar harvest was the lowest in 30 years.

The "Special Period"

Beset by economic crises, but unwilling to adopt either *perestroika* or *glasnost*-style reforms, the government implemented a belt-tightening survival strategy known as the "Special Period in Time of Peace." In order to compensate for the loss of Soviet subsidies, Castro told the Cuban people to work harder and be patient. He then demanded sacrifices like none they had ever known before.

Energy consumption was drastically reduced, oxen replaced tractors in the fields, and food rations were slashed to a minimum survival level. Government-produced television programs instructed citizens on how to grow their own vegetables, make their own candles and soap, and turn dried banana skins into sandals. Horse-drawn buggies were put back in service, and cheap, low-grade oil was substituted to fire electric plants, causing a pall of dirty smoke over Havana.

In addition, the government imported a million Chinese bicycles and ordered the people to start pedaling. Encouraging Cubans to adopt cycling, Fidel Castro told them: "Expanding the use of the bicycle is an indicator of cultural advancement." But for the millions of secretaries, teachers, and factory workers who had to spend hours a day riding to work, it was more like pedaling back in time.

The "Special Period" – which only officially ended in 2005 – meant that life for the average Cuban citizen was bleak. People watched in dismay as the crowded apartments in which they lived slipped even further into disrepair. Electric wires dangled precariously in the streets, telephones rarely worked, and elevators were often out of order.

LIVING ON THE *LIBRETA*

The ration book *(libreta)* was introduced in 1962, initially as a temporary measure in the face of the US embargo, but generations of Cubans have now grown up knowing no other system. The principal of providing every Cuban with the basic staples, with a balanced diet of proteins, fats, and carbohydrates, is no longer affordable and the government wants to reduce subsidies. What is available on the *libreta* has been whittled down and now provides less than a third of the daily calories needed per person. Free lunches have been eliminated from the canteens of state companies and Cubans see the end of the *libreta* in sight.

To increase the supply of food to the markets, the government has now started to transfer more land to private farmers. "The land is there to be tilled," said Raúl, "and we must offer producers adequate incentives."

However, although fruit, vegetables, cereals, and pulses are now available in free farmers' markets *(agropecuarios)*, they are expensive relative to the price paid for goods listed in the *libreta*, and beyond the reach of many.

Potatoes and peas were removed from the *libreta* in 2009. Before that, Cubans were entitled to buy up to 4lbs of potatoes and 10oz of peas a month, each costing around 1 centavo per lb, but now they cost 5 and 17 centavos respectively, a huge increase for Cuban families who spend 60–70 percent of their household budget on food, a proportion which is likely to rise.

Times get tougher

Hungry, frustrated Cubans soon grew tired of waiting in long lines for pitiful goods. Sugar, coffee, and rum – the backbone of the Cuban economy – became a luxury for most people. And while Cubans had lived with the *libreta* or ration book since the early 1960s *(see panel on previous page)*, fewer and fewer goods seemed to be actually available.

Patients had to get used to bringing their own sheets to hospitals, and surgeons were allotted only one bar of soap a month with which to wash their hands. Herbal remedies replaced drugs, and hemp was used for sutures.

Capitalist tinkerings

Faced with rousing discontent, Castro made some compromises that in the past were non-negotiable. In 1991, he eased travel restrictions abroad, released some political prisoners, permitted more free speech than ever before, and granted autonomy to farmers, who were now permitted to sell a proportion of their surplus produce on the open market, often at cripplingly high prices.

It was a sign of just how serious the crisis had become when, in 1993, Fidel Castro swallowed his pride and legalized the use of the American dollar, to which previously only a few privileged

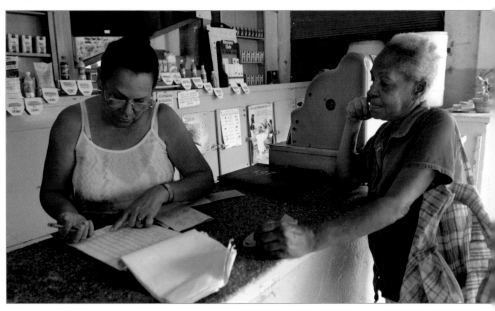

In schools, textbooks were shared among several children, and work in exercise books written in pencil so it could be erased and the books passed on to the next class. Factories sat idle, there were no fertilizers for crops, and harvests rotted in the fields for want of methods of distribution. Newspapers and magazines shut down for want of paper. Toilet tissue, toothpaste, shampoo, and aspirin became luxury items. Cubans had to buy in what were then dollar shops – but first they had to get access to dollars.

citizens (including high-ranking members of the Communist Party) had had access.

In the same year Castro permitted people to go into business for themselves by offering licenses in more than 100 categories, including mechanics, fishermen, farmers, taxi drivers, hairdressers, and restaurateurs. The self-employed had to pay a small fortune for a trading license and in income tax, thus putting a sharp brake on both private enterprise and dollar investments from Miami Cubans.

Meanwhile, to make up for the loss of Soviet subsidies and to combat the United States embargo, Cuba began to woo new investors – notably Canada, Mexico, and members of the European Union – in what are commonly

FAR LEFT: queuing at the butcher shop. **LEFT:** buying produce at a farmers' market. **ABOVE:** typical Old Havana neighborhood grocery store.

known as "joint ventures." These countries pumped hundreds of millions of dollars into the economy, above all into tourism, but also in the fields of nickel mining, oil exploration, and the pharmaceutical industry.

Tightening the noose

During the 1990s, Castro alluded to a reconciliation with the US – something that proved a phantom hope, even in the more relaxed atmosphere of the post-Cold-War era. In 1992, the powerful Cuban-American lobby in the US helped ensure the passing of the so-called Torricelli Act, which sought to tighten sanctions in

an effort to bring down the struggling Cuban regime. It prohibited subsidiaries of US companies from trading with Cuba, and linked any repeal of sanctions to Cuba hosting free and fair elections.

Sanctions were ratcheted up again in 1996, when the then US president, Bill Clinton, gave way to pressure from Cuban Americans and approved the Helms-Burton legislation *(see panel below)*, named after its sponsors in the US Congress. Among other provisions, the Helms-Burton legislation raised the threat of suing any company worldwide that did business with Cuba involving assets on the island that

THE CESSNAS INCIDENT

In February 1996, Cuban MiGs (Russian-built fighter planes) shot down two unarmed Cessnas piloted by members of the Brothers to the Rescue organization *(see page 88)*, on the lookout for rafters crossing to Miami. The Cessnas had crossed into Cuban airspace in defiance of a warning issued by the Cuban authorities, who viewed these flights as violations of an agreement with the US to clamp down on those encouraging emigration from Cuba. The Cessnas' four Miami Cuban crewmen were killed, and the subsequent outcry in the US helped smooth the passage of the Helms-Burton legislation, which President Clinton had previously opposed.

had been confiscated by the Castro regime in the 1960s. Consequently, relations between the US and countries that were investing in Cuba – especially Canada and some members of the European Union – came under strain.

The legislation also helped to polarize the debate on sanctions within the United States – some powerful business and humanitarian interests spoke up against the continuation of sanctions, which they believed had failed in their primary objective of bringing down the Castro regime, and which sections of the business community thought were denying US companies valuable investment opportunities. Some, too, believed that the influential Cuban-American lobby had overreached itself.

The *bloqueo*

The US embargo (called the *bloqueo* in Cuba) also attracted international disapproval. In 1997, 143 countries in the UN General Assembly voted against the embargo, with just three in favor (the US, Uzbekistan, and Israel). The figures for the same resolution in 1992 were 59 in favor, 3 against, and 71 abstentions.

Cuba's regime was also given a shot in the arm by the much-publicized visit of Pope John Paul II in January 1998. Castro agreed to release some 300 political prisoners ahead of the papal visit; the Pope, for his part, criticized Cuba on human-rights issues, but he also spoke out lip service to egalitarianism. The island essentially became divided into two classes – those with dollars, and those without. Dollars could be acquired through fair means or foul: on the one hand they might be sent by relatives living abroad, or earned through a thriving business; on the other hand, they could be gained from black-market dealing or prostitution. Many Cubans also converted their hard-earned pesos into dollars at government exchange bureaux known as *cadecas*, but they got a miserable return – with an average monthly salary worth less than US$10.

For those with dollars, life improved beyond

indirectly against US sanctions, calling any such embargo "deplorable." This saw the US Government relax the embargo slightly: direct flights between Miami and Havana resumed in July 1998, and more North American politicians and businessmen began visiting Cuba, though under tight restrictions.

Dollars or death

However, Cuban society was showing the strain. Decriminalizing the dollar had a devastating effect on a society brought up at least to pay

LEFT: Pope John Paul II with Castro during an official visit in 1998. **ABOVE:** counting freshly printed Cuban convertible peso notes.

measure, hence the booming, clandestine economy. Fear that the dollar sector was getting out of control – that some people were becoming "too rich" – led to a seesaw economic policy: shop openings were followed by sudden closures, and laws were passed and repealed without notice. Police would appear at the door at 6am to close "illegal" businesses – the dispossessed businessman only discovering in that morning's edition of *Granma* that some new law had been enacted, making his business illegal. Such tactics, together with high taxation, fines, and overwhelming bureaucratic control, created tremendous insecurity and unease in a population that felt it must earn dollars in order to survive. ❏

CUBA IN THE 21ST CENTURY

Raúl Castro has succeeded his brother, but Fidel remains a strong presence. Early changes appear to be predictable, and most believe Cuba's immediate future will still be controlled from within the state

As Cuba moved into the 21st century, the Revolution was already four decades old, and in many ways the island seemed to be stuck in a time warp. But change was on the way. The demise of Cuba's great *caudillo*, Fidel Castro, has been predicted for decades, and in July 2006, when he underwent urgent intestinal surgery, he handed over supreme power "temporarily," to his younger brother Raúl, the head of the Revolutionary Armed Forces. This marked the effective beginning of the post-Fidel phase, and a further step was taken in February 2008, when Raúl was inaugurated as president by a newly formed National Assembly. Fidel remains head of the Communist Party, however, and Raúl promised that his brother would be consulted on matters of national importance. This confirmed that, at least in the near future, things would remain the same.

However, Raúl is introducing some economic changes, although the early post-Fidel phase has so far been uncontroversial. The state still has great control over its population through

> "The commander in chief of the Cuban revolution is unique," Raúl said, after being unanimously confirmed as president. "Fidel is Fidel; as we all know, he is irreplaceable."

organizations like the neighborhood CDRs (*see box, page 65*); and the army is firmly wedded to the state, benefiting as it does from a network of companies, most visible of which is the tour-

ism enterprise, Gaviota, as well as ministerial appointments for senior officers.

A rosier future

In November 2004, in response to tighter US sanctions, Castro banned commercial transactions in dollars, which would have to be exchanged for *pesos convertibles* (CUC). But Cuba's economic future appeared to be picking up – so much so that in 2005, the authorities declared the end of the "Special Period" that had been in place since the fall of the USSR. However, the world economic slowdown and three hurricanes in 2008 forced the government to demand new sacrifices of its citizens.

LEFT: attending a protest in Havana.
RIGHT: a food market stall holder, Baracoa.

The economy has been helped by Cuba's continued tourism growth, along with the shift away from older mainstays. In 2002, the government finally recognized that the sugar industry was no longer sustainable. It closed nearly half the processing plants, and in 2007 the harvest was the leanest in a century. Nowadays, exports like nickel are far more valuable than sugar.

International agreements

Agreements with China and, above all, Venezuela, have helped Cuba thwart US attempts to isolate it diplomatically and economically. President Hugo Chávez of Venezuela, a firm admirer and ally of Fidel, agreed massive oil deals on favorable fixed terms, which have alleviated Cuba's energy crisis. In return, Cuba exported some 30,000 doctors and health-care workers to Venezuela. This is the most obvious example of a strategy of "health diplomacy," which sees Cuban doctors working in other Latin American countries and also in West Africa, although many Cubans complain that their own health service has suffered as a consequence.

Options for change

For decades, many observers outside Cuba presumed that the regime would collapse after its

NEW LEADERS JOIN THE OLD GUARD

The Bush administration in the US refused to deal with a Cuban government that contains Raúl Castro or any members of the old guard, but a number of these men are still prominent in the Council of State. Cuba's leader, and his vice president José Ramón Machado, both fought alongside Fidel, as did Ricardo Alarcón, the head of the National Assembly. Most of the younger generation of technocrats groomed by Fidel have been removed by Raúl. There were rumors that their personal ambitions were counter-revolutionary and they were replaced by old guard members of the armed forces. The Council has got older rather than younger.

charismatic leader was removed from power, died, or was incapacitated. This scenario envisaged a flood of dollar-rich Cuban exiles from Miami and New Jersey sweeping into the island on a tide of capitalist counter-revolution, with Cuba turning into a type of Puerto Rico. But the reality seems different; Cuba appears unlikely to undergo either this type of radical transformation or the one that occurred in Europe's former Eastern Bloc countries.

Other options include a move to a more capitalist model, as seen in China, where there is still a totalitarian type of control. This was an economic model that Fidel refused to adopt in the 1990s, but in July 2007, Raúl said that Cuba might have to turn to foreign investment.

Whether this will happen is uncertain, as Fidel is still a force to be reckoned with, but Raúl has acknowledged that "structural and conceptual changes" are needed.

The major initial change has been a move to transfer land to private individuals, to stimulate agricultural production – an acknowledgment that state-controlled agriculture was inefficient and could not feed the population. The government has also allowed the legal purchase of a variety of consumer goods – computers, cell phones, and DVD players – which is good for those who can afford them, but a computer costs three times the average annual wage.

A challenging time

In the meantime, the challenges facing the administration are legion. Wages and state pensions have been increased slightly, but they are still minimal by Western standards. The administration has the difficult task of trying to keep the generation of young Cubans – born well after the Revolution – from wanting to leave the island, while at the same time maintaining social provisions in health and education.

One of these battlegrounds is likely to be over access to information technology – for the time being the authorities are maintaining strict controls on Cubans accessing the full World Wide Web, allowing access only to a country-wide intranet. Then there are continuing challenges, such as reinvesting in outdated infrastructure and industries, and fighting corruption. And there will be new ones, too, like preventing power struggles in an age when there is no clear, charismatic leader who carries with him the legitimacy of the original Revolution.

However, the chances of violent upheaval in Cuba seem to have receded, although they may still happen after Fidel's death. The years ahead will bring change and transition, but it seems likely to be largely peaceful, and controlled by internal authorities rather than from abroad.

Cuba's internal political opposition is weak – and although the US seeks to fund opposition groups, many dissidents choose to retain their independence. In 2002, the so-called Varela Project was organized by one prominent dissident, Oswaldo Payá, calling for a number of political and economic reforms. The petition gained 11,000 signatures, but came to naught, and the following year, a crackdown saw 75 opposition figures imprisoned. This led to widespread international condemnation (Amnesty International declared the activists prisoners of conscience). In 2010, one of those prisoners, Orlando Zapata Tamayo, died after a hunger strike of 80 days, sparking renewed outcries in the USA and Europe.

The role of the United States

Of course, the position of the United States has a significant role to play in future developments

in Cuba. Relations between the two are still stuck in a time warp. There is an ongoing debate in the US about the merits of sanctions – some groups believe US policy has been hijacked by the influential Cuban-American lobby. But the United States' official foreign policy is still resolutely anti-Castro. It was hoped that when Obama took office he would remove travel restrictions and allow ordinary Americans to visit Cuba, but this has not happened.

The US refuses to deal with what it considers a "succession" government rather than a "transitional" one, and states that it will only end sanctions once Cuba is committed to free and fair multiparty elections, and all political prisoners are released. ❑

LEFT: socialist posters adorn walls and billboards throughout Cuba. **RIGHT:** Raúl Castro, his brother's heir.

Fidel Castro

He was a major player on the world stage for five decades, but will he go down in history as a megalomaniac dictator or unique statesman?

Fidel Alejandro Castro Ruz was born in Birán in Oriente in 1926. His father, Ángel Castro y Argiz, was a Galician immigrant who made his money out of sugar and investments. His mother, Lina Ruz González, who had been a servant in his

father's home, bore Fidel, his two brothers, Ramón and Raúl, and his four sisters, Angelita, Juanita, Enma, and Agustina, all out of wedlock. The couple only married after Ángel's first wife died, when Fidel was 15 years old. With a farm employing 300 people, the Castros were wealthy, but not of the cultured class.

Prone to temper tantrums, the young Castro was a troublesome child, maybe because of his illegitimacy and being raised in foster homes. Sent to a Jesuit boarding school in Santiago de Cuba, he was initially teased about his crude manners, but he proved an able student, both intellectually and in sport.

Later, he attended Belén College in the capital, before going on to obtain a law degree from the University of Havana, where he frequently instigated student protests. It was during this period that he honed his skills in oratory.

After graduation, Castro briefly practiced law, but since he refused to accept money from his impoverished clients, he had to survive on the largesse of his family. In 1948 he traveled to Colombia where he was arrested for inciting anti-imperialist demonstrations.

That same year he married Mirta Díaz-Balart, a wealthy philosophy student with family ties to Batista. The couple honeymooned in Miami and New York, and received US$1,000 from Batista as a wedding gift. In 1949 their son, Fidelito, was born, but five years later they divorced. Mirta remarried and left Cuba, and has never spoken publicly about her ex-husband.

In 1959, Castro swept into the limelight with his Christ-like demeanor and outlaw charisma, and seized control of Cuba. As an international statesman and icon of the radical left, he mesmerized cheering crowds in cities all over the world, from Baghdad to Hanoi and Prague. For many years, he was the self-proclaimed leader of the developing world. He saw eight US presidents come and go, and passed from being the world's youngest political leader to being the longest-serving head of state.

A determined grip

Castro set about ruling his island with absolute power, surrounding himself with an entourage of yes-men who would cater to his ego and bathe him in adulation. His national security apparatus, embedded in every crevice of the island, helped maintain total authority. Anyone opposing him was labeled subversive and harassed or jailed. However, unlike most dictators, there is no street named after him, his birthplace is difficult to get to and not promoted. There is no personality cult.

Many have deserted him – his children, Alina and Fidelito, now live abroad, and Alina attacked him in a book published after she fled to the US in the 1990s. Others, the *fidelistas*, revere him as the man who brought them cradle-to-grave health care, free education, and social security benefits. He has many names, including El Comandante and El Jefe Máximo (The Maximum Leader).

Castro's personal life

If Castro the politician is hard to understand, Castro the man is even more elusive. Although a public figure, he gained a reputation as a very private person and a master of self-concealment. Fiercely intelligent and strictly disciplined, he will never admit defeat. When working, he rarely got a good night's sleep, for to sleep is to be off-guard. Instead of going to bed, he would take short naps at his office. Though believed to be fluent in English, he does not speak it in public. In his spare time he reads voraciously, but he stopped puffing on his trademark cigars in the 1980s, as part of a public no-smoking campaign. Although the true nature of his abdominal surgery in 2006 has been kept secret, his illness has no doubt curtailed many of his hobbies – gardening, swimming, fishing, and driving his Jeep, although playing chess is

Gabriel García Márquez, the Nobel Prize-winning Colombian author, is a long-standing friend of Fidel's – the two men first met in 1959, and the writer was one of the first people outside Castro's inner circle to see him after his illness. He greatly admires Castro, and has said: "He has the nearly mystical conviction that the greatest achievement of the human being is the proper formation of conscience, and that moral incentives, rather than material ones, are capable of changing the world and moving history forward. I think he has been one of the greatest idealists of our time and this, perhaps, may be his greatest virtue, although it has also been his greatest danger."

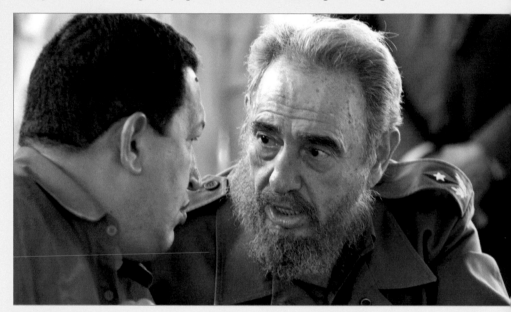

something he can probably still do as well as ever.

Rumors abound, stating that Castro had hundreds of romantic encounters and fathered dozens of children. But following his divorce, he was linked publicly to only one woman, Celia Sánchez. A vivacious upper-middle-class *cubana* and devoted companion during the rebel campaign, Sánchez was the love of his life. A champion of social causes, she was always popular with the Cuban people, and also held substantial power in the government. Celia's death from cancer in 1980 reputedly hit the Cuban leader hard.

LEFT: a youthful Castro released from jail in 1955.
ABOVE: Castro with his friend and supporter, Hugo Chávez, president of Venezuela, in 2006.

Taking a back seat

Castro is still an icon for some, especially on the Latin American left – above all, Venezuelan President Hugo Chávez, who is in many ways his political heir on the international stage. At home, Castro named his younger brother Raúl as his successor in 1997, some nine years before illness forced him to take a back seat, and in February 2008 Raúl was inaugurated as president. "I am not eternal," Fidel has said. "Suddenly, one discovers that almost everything is behind and that life has its limits." However, he is also reported to have said, "I am a revolutionary and revolutionaries do not retire." He remains leader of the Communist Party and he still writes *Granma* editorials, under the by-line Comrade Fidel. ❑

BELIEFS AND RELIGIONS

The mixture of African and Hispanic cultures in Cuba is nowhere more apparent than in religion where African spiritual beliefs blend comfortably with Catholicism

S panish Catholic priests working in Cuba were always seen to be politically conservative in colonial times, siding with the white, upper-class elite, first against the native Taínos and later against the imported African slaves. They opposed independence from Spain in the 19th century and opposed the Revolution in the 1950s. Church and State were separated under the new constitution approved in 1901 under the influence of the USA, and the US occupation allowed Protestantism to get a foot in the door, but compared with other Latin American countries religion was not a major part of people's lives. Although there are some magnificent cathedrals and churches in the cities, few villages had a church and most Cubans rarely went to Mass. Fidel Castro was educated by Jesuits, but the Church received no favors from him after the Revolution, and most priests headed for Miami. Practicing Catholics were banned from joining the Communist Party, effectively keeping them out of any position of authority.

Resolving conflict

Eventually, however, Castro mellowed and the regime became more tolerant on issues of race, sex, and religion. He stated that there was no conflict between Marxism and Christianity and was particularly supportive of liberation theologists and their quest for a just society. The Pope condemned the US trade embargo in the late 1970s, prompting Castro to invite him to visit Cuba. During the 1980s, Castro allowed the import of Bibles, permitted the issue of visas to priests and missionaries, and authorized the construction of new churches. In the 1990s a new Cardinal was appointed

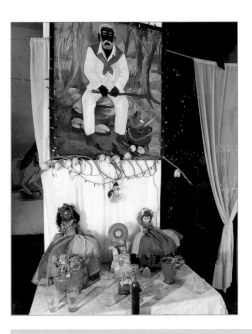

Christmas was abolished in the 1960s because it interfered with the sugar harvest. By the time it was reinstated in 1997 a whole generation had grown up not knowing what it was all about.

after a gap of more than 30 years. Communist Party membership was opened to religious believers, congregations rose, and baptisms soared.

In 1996 Castro took off his fatigues, donned a suit and tie, and went to visit Pope John Paul II at the Vatican. The Pope reciprocated in 1998, Cuba being the only Latin American country he had not visited by that time. He criticized free market ideology, which he saw as promoting excessive individualism and undermining the role of society. The two men clearly found common ground on the need for social justice despite disagreeing on such fundamental matters as abortion and contraception.

Huge crowds greeted the Pope at the open-air Masses held all over the country, and there is a bust outside the Basílica del Cobre near Santiago commemorating his visit. At the Pope's request, Castro reinstated Christmas Day as a public holiday, but more major reforms on human rights and political prisoners were ignored.

such as animal sacrifice, communication with the deities via trance, and sacred drumming, became the basis of the syncretic Regla de Ocha cult, or Santería (the "Way of the Saints").

Slaves were not allowed to practice their native religion and were ostensibly converted to Catholicism, but many Spanish masters chose not to notice that when their slaves observed a saint's day they were really celebrating their own *orishas*. It was because of this that the *lucumí* syncretized, or merged, the Spanish saints with their own *orishas*, many of whom shared similar characteristics. The term Santería was originally used derisively by the Spanish to

Santería

From the mid-16th century until the end of the slave trade, hundreds of thousands of Africans were forcibly removed from their cultures and brought to Cuba. Although there were many nations affected, speaking hundreds of different languages, the most numerous were the Yoruba-speaking peoples from Nigeria, Dahomey, and Togo, who were collectively known as *lucumí*. They brought with them their deities, or *orishas*, which together with their legends and customs,

PRECEDING PAGES: a *quinceañera* celebration for 15-year-old girls. **LEFT:** a *boveda*, or spirit altar. **ABOVE:** an *orisha* offers counsel through the body of a human host at a *bembé* (drumming party).

THE COLOR OF LOVE

St Valentine's Day is special in Cuba, when women dress up and step out with their boyfriends or husbands and families. Havana's Malecón is thronged with couples late into the night, restaurants and bars have long lines outside, and sellers of fabric roses encased in plastic bubbles and little heart pins do a brisk business. The color of love in Cuba is yellow or gold, and women frequently wear it on this day. Oshún, the goddess of rivers, beauty, and love, is always dressed in yellow or gold. Her shrine at the Basílica del Cobre outside Santiago is filled with fragrant white mariposa flowers, while outside flower sellers offer yellow sunflowers in her honor.

mock the Africans' seeming over-devotion to the saints but later became a generally recognized term to describe the religion. Over the years the number of deities has dwindled and now only about two dozen regularly receive tribute at the rites known as *toques de santo*. However, the number of believers is thought to be equal to that of Catholicism and includes prominent Communist Party members. The vast majority of *santeros* consider themselves also to be Catholics, have been baptized, and often require initiates to be baptized too.

Every *orisha* has his or her rules and regulations, including a code of conduct, dress, decoration, and diet which believers must follow, together with specific chants and rhythms to be beaten on the sacred *batá* drums.

Each *toque de santo* begins and ends by calling upon Elegguá, guardian of roads and doors who stands at the crossroads of the human and the divine, and controls our destiny. Nothing should be done without his permission. Elegguá is dressed in red and black, and in the Christian calendar he is equivalent to the Holy Child of Atocha, caring for travelers and pilgrims.

Olofi or Olorun (syncretized with both the Father and the Holy Spirit) is the supreme creator of all things but he is believed to have

THE SECRET SECT OF ABAKUÁ

Abakuá, or ñañiguismo, is a secret, closed sect, rather than a religion, and has been compared to freemasonry. It is only open to men, has a distinctly macho outlook, and embraces the fraternal aims of mutual assistance. "Friendship is one thing and the Abakuá another" is a phrase used to describe this loyalty. Members follow seven secret commandments, have secret signs, and perform arcane ceremonies wearing special vestments. The sect originated among slaves from the Calabar or Cross River region of southeastern Nigeria and southwestern Cameroon and was first noted in the first half of the 19th century, although no one is quite sure when it started. It is found principally in Havana, particularly around Guanabacoa, Regla, and Marianao, but also in

Matanzas, Cárdenas, and Cienfuegos. Membership is high among dock workers in those ports.

Ñañigos are also called *diablitos,* or little devils, when they dress in their ceremonial outfit of a multicolored checkerboard dress with a conical headpiece topped with tassels for their Carnival dances. Their rhythmic dance music contributed to the development of the rumba, and it is believed that Ñañigos invented the *guaguancó,* a type of rumba. They have, however, been involved in most forms of Cuban popular music, and many commercial recordings have been made in their secret language, the musicians being aware that their chants could only be interpreted by fellow Ñañigos.

handed over care of the world to Obatalá (Our Lady of Mercy), who is dressed entirely in white and is the god of peace, truth, wisdom, and justice. His son is Orula or Ifá (syncretized with St Francis of Assisi among others), the lord of divination who communicates only with

Anybody dressed all in white is likely to be an Iyawó – someone recently initiated into Santería, and undergoing a year of communion with the orishas. The necklaces are sacred: each one represents one of the orishas.

Yemayá's sister, Oshún (Virgin of Charity, and Cuba's patron saint), the sensual dancing goddess of rivers, beauty, and love. Oyá (St Teresa of Avila) is the goddess of winds and lightning and the queen of the cemetery. Babalú Ayé (syncretized with St Lazarus) dresses in purple but is covered in sores and limps on crutches, being the god of leprosy, venereal disease, and a number of skin diseases and problems.

Palo Monte

Regla Conga, or Regla de Palo Monte, is a cult that was brought to Cuba by slaves from the Bantu-speaking regions of the Congo basin.

his *babalawo*, or priest; the latter predicts the future by casting eight pieces of coconut or turtle shell, known as the *ékuele*.

The most powerful *orisha* is Changó (syncretized with St Barbara), lord of fire, thunder, war, drums, and virility, and dressed in red. He is the son of Yemayá (Virgin of Regla, the patron saint of Havana Bay), who is mistress of the seas and goddess of motherhood and is dressed in blue and white. Her other son, Oggún (St Peter), is also a war god and patron saint of blacksmiths. Both of them compete for the affections of

Palo Monte is found mostly in the provinces of Havana and Matanzas but is more fragmented than Regla de Ocha, with which it co-exists harmoniously as they are both non-sectarian and non-proselytizing. It is divided into several different sects, the most well known being the *mayomberos, kisimberos,* and *briyumberos.*

Ceremonies involving rum and tobacco (and sometimes gunpowder) are used to predict the future, using the forces of nature to perform good or evil magic. Its main supernatural spirit is *nganga*, who lives in an iron container or earthenware pot along with the *mpungus*, or saints. As with the other religious cults, Palo Monte's ceremonies utilize drum rhythms that are exciting and energizing. ❏

LEFT: the guardian of roads and doors, Elegguá stands at the crossroads of the human and the devine.
ABOVE: a Ñañigo and initiate during an Abakuá ceremony.

DREAMING OF MIAMI

Over the decades thousands of Cubans have fled to Miami as political or economic refugees. Ironically, the remittances they sent back to their families helped keep the Cuban economy afloat during its most difficult period

I n 1959–62, hundreds of thousands of wealthy Cubans left the island in the aftermath of the revolution, either in fear because they had supported the Batista regime, or because of the increasingly evident socialist slant of Castro's policies.

Landless peasants and poor farmers then came from the countryside and took over the vacated mansions. Their children grew up in cities living lives very different from their own, some becoming doctors, professors, and engineers. Yet many Cubans still wished to emigrate to Miami.

In 1980, after a week-long crisis in which thousands of Cubans sought asylum in Havana's foreign embassies (11,000 in the Peruvian embassy alone), Castro announced that anyone who wanted to leave could do so. Around 125,000 promptly did, aided by small craft from Miami, in what became known as the Mariel Boatlift.

For the Castro regime, these people were traitors or "worms" *(gusanos)*, and were denounced by the state media as *escoria* (scum). Castro ensured that thousands of criminals were disgorged from Cuban prisons to join the exodus. But the refugees turned out to be mostly respectable, hard-working people: doctors, teachers, academics, and members of Castro's new educated class. In other words, people who owed their status to the revolution they had rejected.

What had gone wrong? Why, after 20 years of a revolution marked by great social changes, of

a revolution that was still popular in some sectors and that was marked by a vehement anti-Americanism, did so many Cubans still yearn for a life in the United States?

Opportunity stifled

Most of the people who seek to leave Cuba say the revolution has failed because it denies two freedoms. Political freedom, and also, especially for young people, economic freedom. They complain bitterly about the lack of opportunity to "get on" in the world. Those who have trained to be professionals often can't afford a house – many married couples live with their children in a single room at their parents' house. Doctors

---

LEFT: inner tubes, once a means of floating to Miami, are now used for fishing. **RIGHT:** diving from the rocks in front of the Malecón, Havana.

earn less in a month than a waiter or taxi driver can make in convertible peso (CUC) tips from tourists in a day.

As one young émigré – an agricultural engineer – said, "In the United States I will have the chance to live my life. I may fail – there's always a risk. But at least I will have had the chance. Here, if you do not conform, if you are not a revolutionary man, you have no chance to succeed. None at all."

Home away from home

These emigrants have settled in different Cuban-American communities across the

Little Havana (the coffee is not the real thing, of course – federal politics ensures that no goods from the island ever reach the United States).

Escaping the "Special Period"

The obsession with Miami reached a peak in the early 1990s, when Cuba faced crippling hardships after the fall of the Soviet Union, and people were so desperate to leave that they were willing to risk their lives on a fragile raft. Many had no idea of the difficulties they faced. A distance that seemed small on a map took many days, even weeks, to reach. All too often, empty rafts would wash up on the Florida Keys. The

United States, but most Cubans make the tropical city of Miami their home – near enough to Cuba to keep alive their dreams of a successful return or of counter-revolution.

José Martí was there in the 19th century, plotting the overthrow of Spanish colonial rule. Cubans fled there in the 1930s during the brutal dictatorship of Machado. Castro visited exiled Cubans there in 1955 when seeking funds for the overthrow of Batista. After more than a hundred years, Miami has taken on a strong Cuban flavor – the city is essentially Spanish-speaking, largely because of its dominant Cuban community; restaurants and stores sell American-made replicas of Cuban brands, and the scent of strong, sweet "Cuban" coffee fills the air of

horror stories did not deter those determined to leave, usually sailing with a large painted banner to catch the attention of the Brothers to the Rescue, an exile organization that launched planes from Miami to search for rafters.

Between 1989 and 1994, more than 10,000 rafters made it to Miami. The Cuban coast-guard stopped a further 37,800. Castro claimed that the US precipitated the crisis by refusing to grant sufficient entry visas, and said he would no longer prevent Cubans from leaving, sparking a mass exodus – between August and September 1994, around 2,000 rafters a week set sail. The US authorities feared the consequences of a mass migration like that of the Mariel Boatlift, and started to ship those picked up at sea to internment camps at its Guantánamo military base. In the weeks following the start of the "rafters crisis" during the summer of 1994, people in Havana began to get used to the sight of bodies washing up in the bay – many of them chewed up by sharks. Although about 40,000 Cubans made it to the United States that year, it is estimated that between five and nine thousand died in the attempt.

The crisis led to talks between the United States and Cuba, whereby the Cuban authorities agreed to clamp down on the would-be refugees, rafters picked up at sea would be returned home, and the US would grant 20,000 but ending up disillusioned by the rampant consumerism, the widespread waste of resources, the long hours of work needed to maintain the coveted lifestyle, the threat of unemployment, and the difficulties of being confronted with large medical bills and tussles with insurance companies.

These days, a significant proportion of illegal Cuban emigrants who still risk the crossing travel with professional immigrant smugglers. It's a multimillion-dollar industry. Cubans, usually funded by their relatives in Miami, pay up to US$10,000 per person. And in Cuba there are – despite massive security measures – still

visas a year by lottery to Cubans seeking to leave the island. This lottery proved popular – each year the numbers applying for US visas doubled until 1999 when the US State Department claimed it had received as many applications as there were families living in Cuba.

An ongoing exodus

To this day, Cubans still try to make the sea crossing, although not in the numbers seen during previous crises. Some are put off by reports – true or not – of Cubans going to Miami

LEFT: makeshift raft crossing the Florida Straits.
ABOVE: young refugees at Guantánamo. **RIGHT:** baseball is equally popular in Cuba and the US.

CUBAN MULES

Many seats on the flights from Miami and Los Angeles are bought by Cubans with a US visa and a green card. Resident in the US, they supplement their income by traveling back and forth, shopping to order. Spare parts for old cars, computer equipment, and other specialized goods are delivered personally to Cuban customers after "negotiations" with customs officers. Many things that are unobtainable in Cuban shops are brought in surreptitiously by these "mules," who are ostensibly visiting their families. Every so often there is a crackdown and goods are confiscated if a mule is deemed to have come into the country too frequently.

attempts to hijack boats and planes. You will see a heavy police presence at places like the ferry that crosses Havana bay to Regla; and in April 2003, three alleged ferry hijackers were put to death by Castro's courts. The security checks for domestic flights are often more stringent than for international ones; and in May 2007, a gun battle in Havana's airport thwarted another unsuccessful attempted hijacking.

The grass is always greener

While those in Cuba dream of life in Miami, the old guard there still dreams of returning to Havana. Veterans of Batista's time and the Bay of Pigs still gather in Miami's Little Havana to plot and scheme over cups of coffee at the Café Versailles. Old men now, they still cling to their dream that the Castros will be overthrown and they will return home. Miami-based terrorist organizations such as Alpha 66 and Omega 7 have carried out several unsuccessful incursions into Cuban territory. Exile leaders admit that the bombs that exploded in Havana's hotels in the summer of 1997, killing an Italian tourist, were organized and paid for in Miami.

These desperate acts, though, are the work of the older generation. Cuban-Americans born in the USA, or those who have arrived since the

INTERNATIONAL BATTLE

One of the most dramatic immigration cases took place in 1999. Five-year-old Elián González was one of a handful of people who survived when the small craft he had been traveling in overturned. His mother and nine others drowned. His father (divorced from his mother) called for Elián's return to Cuba, and the boy became the subject of a fierce international custody battle between relatives in Miami (backed by Cuban-American organizations) and the US Government, backing Elián's father in rare agreement with the Cuban regime. Elián did return home, to the jubilation of thousands of Cubans who had demanded his return at government-organized rallies.

Mariel Boatlift, have a different way of taking on the regime, using their prosperity to fund businesses in Cuba. Most of Cuba's *paladares* (family-run restaurants) started up using Miami money, either as a loan or by direct investment. Many Cubans who left on rafts returned as tourists or entrepreneurs, helping friends and family set up new businesses that have changed the once moribund face of Havana.

Cubans without Miami connections resent this: they see the families of exiles able to live well while they suffer on a monthly ration that barely lasts a week. Havana's shopping malls have been fueled by the spending power of those who receive money from abroad. Ironically, some argue that remittances sent by the exile community helped prevent economic collapse during the "Special Period."

Not all Miami Cubans feel the same about remittances – some people complain that their families back home are too demanding, seeing them as cash cows to be milked at every oppor-

> The "Christmas Laws" passed after the revolution to confiscate émigrés' property remain in force today. Anyone who emigrates legally still forfeits their possessions and their inheritance rights.

economic rather than political reasons, are not at all troubled by the idea of taking vacations in Cuba. The Miami Cuban community no longer has a monolithic approach to the Cuban state. The majority remain anti-regime, but most now back calls for dialog rather than confrontation with the Cuban Government.

Journeys "home" increased after the resumption of direct flights from Miami to Havana in 1998, but the policy swung back six years later, when President George W. Bush tightened travel restrictions. Then, US-based Cubans were only allowed to visit "close family," and only once every three years, for no longer than two weeks.

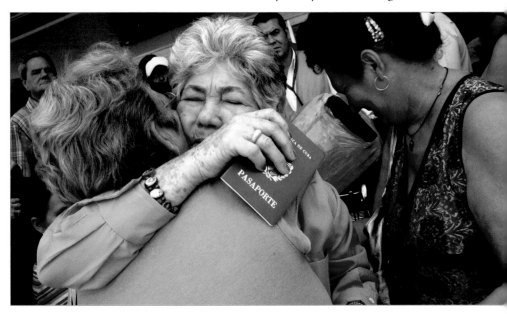

tunity. Many are working-class people with mortgages and heavy financial commitments who can find the burden of helping families in Cuba too much for them.

Room for dialog

These days, too, there is more contact between the two communities than there was in the aftermath of the revolution, when political refugees vowed not to return until Castro had been ousted. Subsequent refugee groups like the *marielitos* and the rafters, having left Cuba for

The election of Barack Obama and a Democrat administration in the White House in 2009 saw the end of travel restrictions for Cuban -Americans (although not for all Americans) and unrestricted family visits are now allowed. There is still a limited number of flights from Florida and Los Angeles, which are insufficient to meet demand, and there is a steady flow of visitors. In March 2008, Raúl Castro similarly made some cosmetic changes and allowed Cubans to stay in hotels previously restricted to foreign guests, and to rent cars at state-run agencies. Few Cubans can afford a beach holiday in Cayo Coco, but at least they are now allowed to accompany their Miami relatives if the latter are paying. ❑

LEFT: demonstration in Miami in favor of keeping Elián González in the US. **ABOVE:** woman embraces a relative at Jose Martí airport in Havana.

CUBA'S ARCANE TRANSPORTATION SYSTEM

Fascinating, exotic, frustrating, and divisive, depending on your standpoint, the beleaguered transportation system is a visible microcosm of Cuba's economic woes

In the late 1980s, oil supplies from the Eastern Bloc that had provided the island with 90 percent of its fuel began to dry up as the Cuban-sugar-for-Soviet-oil deal came to an end. Scarcity of fuel meant that outside the main cities motorized transportation virtually vanished, a situation that has changed little today. Roads are all but deserted, oxen pull plows that till the fields, and horses and carts ply the streets of provincial towns in place of buses.

But, most noticeably, bicycles are everywhere – more than 1 million were imported from China in the early 1990s, and in this make-do-and-mend society many of them are still going strong. It's as if the clock has been turned back to a pre-industrial age. Cycling has become part of the fabric of everyday life, with special parking lots for bicycles and tire-repair shops everywhere. Bicycle taxis – bici-taxis – vary in design from town to town, depending on when and where they were imported from China.

The island's current tribulations and its decades of isolation from the Western world have resulted in other memorable forms of transport. Wonderful old Cadillacs get top billing, but also look for veteran motorcycles with sidecars or bicycles with sidecars carrying the whole family, and on the railroads anything from magnificent steam trains to wheel-less buses that can run along the tracks.

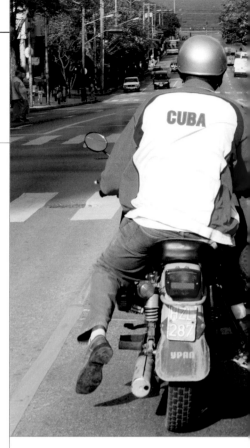

ABOVE: a motorcycle is a precious commodity, tirelessly maintained despite the chronic shortage of spare parts for models obsolete in the rest of the world.

BELOW: *coches*, or horses and carts, serve as buses and taxis all over the island. An average ride will cost just a few pesos.

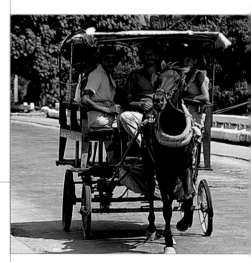

LEFT: coco-taxis: these are a fun way to get around Havana and some other cities, as long as you don't have luggage. They use less fuel than conventional taxis and are therefore cheaper.

THE STRUGGLE TO GET AROUND

The recent purchase of many new buses (called *guaguas*) means fewer lines and less overcrowding than in the "Special Period," but things still get bad at peak times and cancellations are common. Cubans still need to book in advance for a seat on a crowded long-distance Astro bus – tourists have to use Víazul, the dedicated convertible peso service *(see Transportation in the Travel Tips section, page 338).*

Hitchhiking *(la botella)* is a way of life for Cubans of all ages, but definitely not for tourists, as anyone who was kind enough to pick you up would risk a fine. This is not any old hitchhiking: state officials, called *amarillos*, because they wear yellow jackets, supervise crowds of hitchers at designated places, usually on the edge of towns and cities. Officials wear blue jackets in towns and are known as *azules*. State vehicles are obliged to stop, and *los amarillos* will allocate people to each vehicle on a first-come, first-served basis. Pregnant women and children get priority.

ABOVE: Cubans say these two-humped giant "camel" buses, now relegated to the provinces, are like the Saturday movie on TV: they always contain sex, violence, and swearing.

ABOVE: queuing for buses in Havana may look haphazard but everyone knows their place in the line.
LEFT: the ubiquitous bicycle, usually made in China, is the family vehicle throughout Cuba.
BELOW: spacious old cars from the 1940s and 1950s are still used as route taxis for Habaneros.

TOURISM: SALVATION OR SELLOUT?

Post-revolutionary Cuba viewed the tourist industry with disdain, but nowadays it has no option but to embrace it to prop up the economy

Revolutionary Cuba, a land of socialist ideals and egalitarian values, once said "never again" to tourism. Back in the decadent 1950s, Havana, with its sophisticated hotels, clubs, and casinos, catered to the whims of wealthy Americans, and had a worldwide reputation for gambling, drugs, prostitution, pornographic films, and live sex shows. But although the industry was lucrative, much of the infrastructure was foreign-controlled, leaving few in Cuba who actually benefitted from the profits.

Rejecting excess

Part of Fidel Castro's struggle against Batista stemmed from his revulsion at the excesses of tourism, and the neo-colonialism it represented. Castro denounced tourism as a vulgar example of the dichotomy between the haves and the have-nots. After he took power, he promised Cuba would never again be a playground for the rich and beautiful. Instead it would rely on

> There is an old and rather cynical Cuban joke: an adult asks a child the classic question: "What do you want to be when you grow up?" The child answers: "A tourist."

the sugar industry and other natural resources to fuel its economy.

The new government immediately set about closing casinos and nightclubs, the prostitutes were rounded up and sent to learn useful

LEFT AND RIGHT: Cuba's coastal areas are idyllic playgrounds for foreign visitors.

trades, and the hotels were put to use as vacation retreats for local workers. During the 1960s and 1970s, many of the foreign visitors to Cuba were either journalists or people wanting to express solidarity with the revolution. Others were Eastern Bloc communists on government-paid Cuban vacations.

The government promoted "social tourism," whereby sympathetic visitors from around the world were invited to the island to visit model communities, hospitals, schools, and other places where the achievements of socialism were put on display. But between 1963 and 1975, the island received only about 3,000 foreign visitors a year.

However, when the economy began to show signs of strain in the early 1980s, the government had to reconsider its policy toward tourism, and "health tourism" became the new trend. Foreigners were invited to Cuba for a first-rate face-lift or a coronary bypass at a much lower cost than they could have found at home. But by the mid-1980s, the government realized that "health tourism" was not going to provide the economic boost and foreign exchange the island needed, and it launched an international campaign to promote pleasure tourism. After the collapse of the Soviet Union, this campaign became much more aggressive.

year, bringing more than US$2 billion into the Cuban economy. It is estimated that if the US were to lift the travel ban for all Americans, more than 1 million would immediately book holidays in Cuba.

A pact with the devil

Having come full circle, the tourism industry has created embarrassing ideological problems for the government. Tourism employs more than 80,000 people, but this represents only about 2 percent of the overall workforce. Tourism jobs are highly sought-after because they offer access to tips in foreign currencies or convertible pesos

Tourism is gold

"In the past we feared that tourism would defile us," Castro told his compatriots, "but tourism is gold." So began the push to make tourism the new business frontier of the island – one that saw investors from places like Europe, Mexico, and Canada being offered extremely non-socialist incentives that would allow them to operate in Cuba for at least 10 years without paying taxes on their income.

Progress came quickly. In 1995, tourism became, for the first time, the island's biggest source of hard currency. In 1984, fewer than 200,000 foreign tourists visited Cuba; by 1998 there were more than a million – nowadays, well over 2 million visitors come to Cuba each

DANGEROUS LIAISONS

More often than not, the sex scene these days revolves around bars and clubs, either through none-too-subtle flirtation that in some places can border on harassment or through young pimps. These days, few *jineteras* are prepared to offer their services for the sake of a dress or a meal – many make more money in a week than a government minister earns in a year. Western men should also know that the age of consent in Cuba is 18 and picking up a young girl is likely to be a blackmail trap. There are also the parallel, though much smaller, types of sex tourism: Western women with young Cuban men, and same sex-liaisons.

(CUCs). Many teachers, doctors, and engineers leave their professions to work in more lucrative jobs as waiters or bellhops. Tourism has also bred corruption. Cubans wishing to work in a foreign currency/CUC enterprise often have to bribe managers for the privilege of doing so.

Nicolás Guillén wrote Tengo (I Have) *in the 1960s to celebrate the Cuban people's renewed access to the beaches and hotels. The poem seems ironic today, when tourists once again have privileged access to these areas.*

rassed into action by the scale of this sex trade, and the all-too-evident parallels that could be drawn with the sordid side of tourism in pre-revolutionary Cuba. Many *jineteras* were arrested and sent to "re-education" camps in the countryside. However, everything is still available for both genders, straight and gay, and the market is very active.

Tourism apartheid

The most distasteful aspect of Cuba's tourism industry is the division it has created between local people and tourists. Isolated from the public, most beach resorts are enclaves operating a

The superb colonial architecture, impressive scuba diving, fishing, and fine flora and fauna attract a certain number of high-spending tourists, but many more are deterred by the dilapidated infrastructure and the relatively poor standard of service.

Sex tourism flourishes undercover, despite crackdowns. One such crackdown, in the summer of 1999, targeted the hordes of scantily clad girls (called *jineteras* after the Spanish word for jockey) who used to hang around tourist hotels. The authorities had probably been embar-

system of "tourism apartheid." Cubans are now permitted to stay at hotels, but only if they can afford to pay in CUCs, which eliminates all but the fortunate few.

Although the electricity grid is now being improved after years of neglect, the authorities will still prioritize fuel supplies for the hotels while private homes suffer regular blackouts (*apagones*). Tourists can easily buy gas for their rental cars, while local people must ride bicycles or squeeze into overcrowded buses. And beautiful beaches, which were once the domain of the islanders themselves, are being gobbled up by developers. In theory, there are no private beaches in Cuba, but in many resorts they might as well be. ❏

LEFT: a fleet of Transtur tourist buses along the Malecón. **ABOVE:** selling souvenirs brings some income.

CUBA'S SIZZLING SOUND

There's nowhere else like it: for "Cuba," read "Rhythm."
Here you will find a depth of musical talent that is,
perhaps, unequaled anywhere in the world

Music and Cuba have been synonymous for well over a century; in no other communist country have music and revolution marched so closely, hand in hand. Even during the final build-up to the 1959 revolution, at the dramatic closure of that legendary era when Havana was a fantasy island playground for American tourists, the bands played on and visitors rushed to the city's casinos, bars, hotels, glitzy nightclubs, and beaches.

Revolution never quashed the music: film footage of Castro's guerrillas moving toward Havana shows Che Guevara with a guitar on his back. All through the "Special Period," the state still supported musicians, and the music began to launch a new flush of tourism.

The beat goes on

Today, music is the state tourist board's golden egg; millions of visitors flock to Cuba for the same reasons the Americans once did: the rum, sun, sex, music, and dancing (no gambling,

Many people were introduced to Cuban music by the Buena Vista Social Club, liked what they heard, and went on to discover much more about the island's rhythms, its musical history, and changing styles.

however, which is strictly counter-revolutionary). Ironically, they often travel in the same, now patched-up, Oldsmobile taxis to the same still glitzy nightclubs, bars, and hotels built by

LEFT: sweet sounds on the Malecón. **RIGHT:** a dancer in Havana's Callejón de Hamel.

the Americans and abandoned in 1959. The Hotel Nacional, where Sinatra sang and American high society (and gangsters) partied, is still hugely impressive; the breathtaking Tropicana nightclub still sees dancers in towering headdresses parade across galleries between the palm trees, and singers today perform on the same stage that shook to the voice of the future Queen of Salsa, Celia Cruz, and the delights of Nat King Cole. Hotel Rivera's elegant nightclub is now the Palacio de Salsa (Salsa Palace).

The ruffle-sleeved shirts survive yet the decadence is gone. But most hotels and restaurants provide some kind of live music, and salsa venues in the capital include the prestigious Casa de la Música, and small rooftop bars like the Pico Blanco in Hotel St John's, a must for smoochy boleros. Compay Segundo's old haunt, the beer garden El Tropical, is today a landmark venue for the raunchy Cuban salsa called *timba (see box, page 104)*, and the narrow alley, the Callejón de Hamel, in the Vedado district hosts rumba drumming, dancing, and singing on Sundays.

Music wherever you go

Visitors today are never far from music, with *timba* trombones ricocheting around the narrow streets, scorching jazz drumming rising the trailblazing band, Irakere), who is a regular at the rooftop Jazz Café, playing with his scat-singing sister, Mayra, or his own small group.

Breaking it down

Many tourists visit Cuba for the salsa dancing, often on special packages, and the chances are that leading salsa bands like Los Van Van *(see pages 104 and 105)* will provide music for their classes back home, and the live soundtrack to their vacation. To navigate the overwhelming range of music, the local radio stations Taíno (bilingual and for tourists) and Rebelde (mixing news, interviews, and music, in Spanish)

from basement bars, and sweet guitar melodies in Buena Vista style, drifting from pavement cafés in Old Havana. The 70-year-old song *Guantanamera* is as ubiquitous as images of Che Guevara, and the evocative *Chan Chan* is a reminder of the impact the *Buena Vista Social Club* movie and album has had on the surge of tourism since the late 1990s.

While tourist hotels worldwide offer cheesy stereotyped shows, Cuba's conservatoire-trained musicians treat tourists to music that is often of a spectacularly high standard (although they trot out plenty of *Guantanamera*s, as well) and they are often internationally acclaimed, even Grammy-winning artists, such as the Afro-Cuban jazz pianist, Chucho Valdés (founder of are more useful than the solitary newspaper, *Granma*, and Cuban TV presents home-grown bands live and on video.

While Havana is the epicenter of Cuban music, it doesn't hold the monopoly on variety or excitement. Santiago, in the eastern state of Oriente, is equally rich in traditional and modern music, and its Carnival (held in late July) beats Havana's hands down.

Santiago is a heavily African city with its own musical identity. The dance music conga sensation, Sur Caribe, is an upbeat salsa-rap big band, influenced by the winning combination of violins and trombones pioneered by Los Van Van but also involving traditional Santiago carnival instruments – the raucous *corneta china*

(Chinese cornet) and portable drums made world-famous in the 1930s by Desi Arnaz, and still alive and kicking in conga bands today. Led by Ricardo Leyva, the *orquesta* has a string of albums under its belt and regularly tours abroad. In contrast, Septeto Típico de Tivoli is a neo-traditional *son* band, the *corneta* replacing the conventional trumpet.

Trova

Santiago is a focus for the trova song style, supported around Cuba in *casas de la trova*. Santiago's is a celebrated meeting place, where singers, composers, guitarists, and friends met

who perform internationally. Their songs are almost as familiar as those of their international contemporaries, and their successors, including Carlos Varela and Amaury Pérez, have moved closer to rock's singer-songwriter tradition.

One of Havana's celebrated *trova* hang-outs is the Bodeguita del Medio, a small bar in Old Havana where writers, poets, and musicians rehearsed new works and debated revolution. Today, tourists crowd the bar, and crane their necks to read their autographs, most famously that of Hemingway, with whom the bar is most closely associated. *Trova* musicians' repertoires roam through guitar-based styles, and include

to drink rum, smoke cigars, and be transported by the guitar melodies, vocal harmonies, sensual rhythms, and lyrics inspired by the country life and work, patriotic or revolutionary themes.

Some guitarists once lived a troubadour's life, playing *trova* songs alongside soldiers during the 19th-century Independence War with Spain, and during Castro's guerrilla war. The latter spawned a *nueva* (new) *trova* movement linked to Latin America's 1960s revolutions, and key figures, Pablo Milanés and Silvio Rodríguez, are now superstar elder statesmen

LEFT: Cuba is a great place to salsa. **ABOVE:** Ibrahim Ferrer, vocalist with the Buena Vista Social Club, who died in 2005.

THE BUENA VISTA SOCIAL CLUB

The 1990s brought an upsurge of interest in traditional Cuban music with the release of the *Buena Vista Social Club* movie and album. Pride of place among the elderly stars "rediscovered" by American guitarist, composer, and singer Ry Cooder went to Compay Segundo, half of the superb 1950s duo, Los Compadres, who came out of retirement and recorded a Grammy-winning CD in 1998. He was still touring the world in his nineties, but died in 2003. Sadly, most of the other 1950s greats have since died, too: pianist Rubén González in 2003, and vocalists Ibrahim Ferrer in 2005, and Pío Leyva in 2006. Only Omara Portuondo is still going strong.

the ubiquitous *son*, which is at the root of most popular Cuban music, including salsa.

Son

Son became universally familiar through the Buena Vista Social Club phenomenon. Its origins lie in Oriente province, against a backdrop of late 19th-century coffee and sugar plantations. By the 1920s, it had reached Havana, and rapidly adapted to an urban style. *Son* is both truly African and truly Cuban, built around call-and-response singing, rough, often high-pitched lead voices, ands repetitive guitar riffs working in percussive harmonies with the hand

Although known as rumba, his popularized *son* differs from the Afro-Cuban rumba that originated in slave communities and involves drumming, dancing, and chant-singing.

Rumba

Rumba is thought to have emerged among the Congolese dock workers in the late 1800s in the port of Matanzas, following the abolition of slavery. The original drums were boxes taken from the docks, but are now polished, finely tuned instruments, often played in multiple, differently tuned "nests." The word "nest" describes both the music and the parties at

percussion. Most crucial are the two hard-wood blocks *(claves)* clacking out the *clave* rhythm, which underlies Cuban popular music. *Clave*'s syncopated beat forces dancers into action, and musicians into the basic rhythm around which they can improvise.

In 1920s Havana, country migrants initially busked on the streets and in cafés, but their infectious sweetness and catchy rhythms seduced wider audiences, and trios expanded to more sophisticated sextets and septets, boosted with bongos, double bass, and trumpets. In salons and dancehalls the guitars would be replaced by pianos. Don Azpiazu's big-band recording of *El Manicero (The Peanut Vendor)* in 1931 ignited an international rumba craze.

which it is played. Master conga drummers have played key roles in the development of original new styles, including the imaginative percussionist Chanquito's role in Los Van Van, and that of the late Angá Diaz, who developed a symphonic sound.

Matanzas still has some of the most brilliant *rumberos* in Cuba: Los Muñequitos de Matanzas (The Little Dolls) and Clave y Guaguancó both perform at international festivals and the city's squares. Of the scores of varieties of rumba, three main types are preserved: *guaguancó, yambú,* and Columbia, each with specific drums, rhythms, and dance styles. One of Cuba's most famous singers, the late Lázaro Ros, who died in 2005, could sing in around

800 different African languages, and his rumba group, Olorun, worked with rock groups that blended Afro-Cuban religious music with modern styles. A true rumba is a profound experience which can be shared in street sessions in Matanzas, near the Teatro Sauto, and at Rumba Saturdays in Havana's Vedado district.

Country music: *guajira*

Cuba's country music, *música guajira*, is rooted in Andalusia in southern Spain, descended from the Spanish peasants who came to the island two centuries ago, but blends influences from the African cultures of fellow workers. It was originally a form of after-work escapism for exhausted Spanish farmers and cattle herders, and for African workers in the sugar-cane plantations, tobacco fields, and factories. Like country workers elsewhere, they would pull out a guitar and sing, with family and friends joining in, adding touches of their own.

Its gorgeous melodies are carried on lilting acoustic guitars or *laoud* (a version of the Arabic *oud*) with verses in the poetic song tradition, praising landscapes, detailing everyday lives and loves, and adding improvised gossip.

Many *guajira* singers, including Compay Segundo, were known for harmonizing duets. Compay's Buena Vista companion, Eliades Ochoa, is a quintessential *guajiro* with his cowboy hat, nimble-fingered guitar playing, and high-pitched, soaring voice, but it was the late Polo Montañez's raw countryman's voice that reignited the traditional sound in two great albums, *Guitara Mía* and *Guajiro Natural*. ("Discovered" relatively late in life, Montañez died, far too young, in a car accident in 2002.)

Taking country music to town

Musicians who rose beyond the family porch left the land to busk or play in town bars and cafés, and, if lucky, to perform on the radio. Most significant composers and performers ended up in the cities; the early 20th-century composer Guillermo Portabales recorded songs whose sensual lilting melodies, accompanying images of ox-cart drivers and untouched landscapes, have resonated with economic migrants everywhere.

LEFT: music fills the air in Santiago. **RIGHT**: Polo Montañez, the much-loved *guajiro* singer, died in a car crash at 47.

In 1950s Havana, the country duo, Celina y Reutilio, performed romantic, upbeat songs heavily African-influenced and delivered in harmonies led by Celina's powerfully expressive voice. Celina González became an ardent defender of the New Cuba through her long-running country-music radio show.

It was the 1930s radio singer, Joseíto Fernán-

> Guajira *music still inspires national pride today, and was central to the Buena Vista Social Club's repertoire, and its success.*

dez, who launched the classic *La Guajira Guantanamera* onto the world. The song, about a girl from Guantánamo, became popular through a 1935 radio soap opera, but had lyrics based on a poem by independence hero and poet José Martí. It is now heard in every tourist niche in Cuba. *Guajira* music still inspires national pride today.

Danzón to cha-cha-chá

A small but significant French element in the Cuban mix is traceable to the late 18th-century arrival in Oriente (eastern Cuba) of French colonizers' families and slaves escaping the Haitian revolution. They brought the *contredanse*, a variation of the English country dance, played by trios on piano, violin, and flute, and this laid the foundations for the elegant dances called *danzón*. Expanded into orchestras called *charangas*, they gradually incorporated a mild African syncopation, which extended its popularity. The most significant Havana *charanga* was run by flautist Antonio Arcano, and featured the double-bass player Israel "Cachao" López and his brother, the pianist Orestes. In the late 1930s, they invented a mutant version with a syncopated ending they called mambo, which was declared devil's music for some years. But the 1940s hit records by the brilliantly eccentric Cuban pianist Pérez Prado spread mambo's popularity to the US, and from there, around the world in a sanitized, softened guise by the band leader Xavier Cugat. Mambo was the dance craze in 1950s Manhattan, and laid the trail to salsa.

Another offshoot of the *danzón*, the cha-chachá, had fewer African qualities than mambo, and was deliberately tailored by its creator Enrique Jorrín (director of Orquesta América) for American tourists and dancers. The first chacha-chá, *La Engañadora*, in 1953, ignited a fever that overwhelmed mambo's popularity around the world. The greatest *charangas* remained in Cuba – Orquesta Riverside, and the sensational Orquesta Aragón, still playing today.

TIMBA SALSA

Salsa comes in scores of varieties all over Latin America, but in Cuba, the dancers' soundtrack is a sizzling mutation called *timba*. The trail to *timba* was laid by young musicians creating music for the post-revolutionary era. Chucho Valdés' Afro-Cuban big band Irakere transformed jazz, and Juan Formell's Los Van Van reinvented dance music through the brassy, swinging *songo* rhythms. *Songo* is a feast of conversations between violins and trombones, and the jagged rhythms that backed hit songs packed with gossip and catch phrases. Irakere's ex-flautist, José Luís Cortés, founded NG (New Generation) La Banda in the 1980s and crystalized the *timba* sound with brass choruses, funk-bass lines, and risqué slang. NG was a university for *timba* stars including the brilliant Issac Delgado, who took it into America's salsa charts, and the heart-throb, Paulito F.G.

The 1990s opened to David Calzado's outrageous Charanga Habanera, whose compellingly edgy songs caused fan hysteria, official panic, and a ban. The acrobatic breakdancing female singers left to found the stunning Azucar Negra. Manolin "El Medico" de la Salsa and Manolito y su Trabuco continue a more conventional line, but Los Van Van's dreadlocked vocalist, Mayito, remains frontman for the still-dynamic band. Today's leaders include the electronic-acoustic orchestra, Chispa y los Complices, which is infecting the new *timba* dancers around the world.

Son montuno to timba salsa

As the *danzón* was being modified into the cha-cha-chá, a blind Cuban musician of Congolese descent, Arsenio Rodríguez, updated the *son* by extending the repetitive instrumental section to create *son montuno*. The master *tres* guitarist manipulated the slackly strung, resonating strings to create a searing, unmistakably Cuban sound, which has been extensively imitated by modern groups, including Sierra Maestra.

Throughout the 1940s and 1950s, La Sonora Matancera occupied an important place in the story. Formed in Matanzas in the 1920s, it moved to Havana in the late 1940s, and introduced a

The Cuban variety of salsa is called *timba* (*see panel, previous page*), and was a product of experimentation by the dazzling Los Van Van, and its founder and bass player, Juan Formell, with the original *songo* rhythm created for the band by conga player Changuito, which brought some of the power and drama of rock and funk into Cuban music. Formell's exchanges between violins and trombones were the sensation of the 1980s and 1990s, and Los Van Van remains the premier dance group on the island. Their albums are hugely popular and their songs, full of wry observations and street slang, capture the mood of their audience in any decade.

fireball singer named Celia Cruz who became everybody's favorite. Cruz's male counterpart was Beny Moré, a sensational dancer, singer, and arranger who spent the 1940s in Mexico City, performing mambos and boleros (made for his searingly expressive high voice) and appearing in Mexican movies. Back in Havana, "El Bárbaro del Ritmo" (the Barbarian of Rhythm) launched his horn-driven Banda Gigante (Big Band), noted for its up-tempo arrangements of brass, percussion, and interlocking piano, whose influence continued into salsa.

LEFT: Los Van Van reinvented dance music with swinging *songo* rhythms. **ABOVE**: Chucho Valdés and his band, Irakere.

Timba is the soundtrack to 21st-century Cuba, through its propulsive, edgy rhythms, braying trombone choruses, and driving funk bass lines. Contemporaries of Cortés, including the popular idol Issac Delgado, followed a more traditional singer/band route, but he broke the rules by recording a hit in New York with leading 1980s salsa producer, Ralph Mercado. The popular singer, Adalberto Alvarez, has shifted toward a more pan-Caribbean beat, but remains 100 percent Cuban, while the trombone band Dan Den, founded by the pianist Juan Carlos Alfonso, became popular for its modern, electronic sound. Other key salsa bands include Yumurí y Sus Hermanos and the Vocal Sampling. This six-piece a-capella group reproduces perfectly the sound of an entire salsa band, using only their mouths, cupped hands, and slapped bodies, and are an international phenomenon. The radical Bamboleo introduced shaven heads, break dancing, and sexual routines to the musical scene, but the wildest 1990s bunch, David Calzado's Charanga Habanera, once banned from performing live because of their "lewdness," inspired the new wave of rap-based acts that are popular today.

The jazz thing

From the 19th century onward, the sea links between Havana and New Orleans enabled important musical interchanges: Afro-Cuban rumba became a basic part of New Orleans' jazz musical vocabulary, and African-American jazz came to Havana almost at birth.

Modern Cuban musicians understand both European-style musical theory and Afro-Cuban traditions and those skills have been exploited particularly in the new jazz. Pioneering the move, Cachao López made a series of legendary recordings of *descargas* (jam sessions) in the 1950s with leading soloists from the dance bands, expanding the ad-lib solo slots in popular music to become the entire piece. *Descargas* is still an inspirational best-selling CD, as fresh today as in 1959.

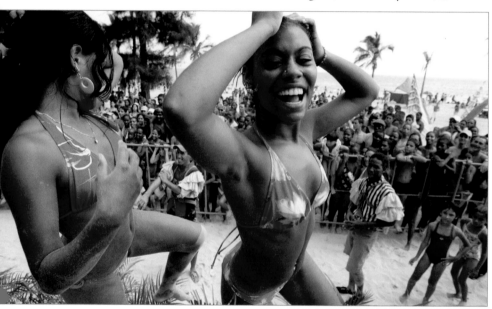

CUBAN HIP-HOP

The lyrics of Cuba's 500-plus approved hip-hoppers concentrate on social issues, criticism, and humor, and their electronic beats vie with "live" brass, guitars, and percussion. Following the first Havana Hip-hop Festival (1995), Castro legitimized the underground, and encouraged newcomers like Obsesión and Amenaza – who re-formed in Paris as the Grammy-winning Orishas and put Cuba on the rap map. Subsequent compilation albums including *Hora de Abrir los Ojos* (Time to Open Your Eyes) and *Cuban HipHop All-Stars* exposed the scene, and the international DM Ahora! label showcases the rap big band Interactivo, and rap-poet sensation, Telmary.

Jazz is central to Cuban music, though many exponents are easier to catch live during foreign tours. Irakere, the 15-piece group founded in 1970 by pianist Chucho Valdés, fused North American jazz idioms, and has operated as a university for young soloists, including *timba* pioneer, José Luís Cortés. Two original members, Paquito D'Rivera and Arturo Sandoval, are now international stars based in the US, and Valdés is an elder in Cuban music, professor at the University of Havana, and a multi-Grammy-winning solo artist who occasionally still rejoins Irakere. His recent reunion concerts and recordings with his father, Bebo Valdés, who has lived outside Cuba since 1960, produced some marvelous, moving musical conversations.

The electronic invasion

The 1990s international explosion of hip-hop slowly but inevitably penetrated the Cuban scene, via illicit American radio and TV, which, of course, captivated the imagination of Cuban youth. The pioneering Orishas emerged in Cuba as a popular rap duo but transferred to Paris and sprang a future Grammy-winning album, *A lo Cubano* (In the Cuban style), on the market. Its fusion of electronic and "live" Cuban rhythms, rapped and sung vocals, influenced today's thriving Cuban hip-hop scene.

This scene is officially endorsed by the government, and showcased annually at the Havana Hip-hop Festival, held every August, and for which the state provides the sound system. Early on, Fidel Castro apparently performed alongside rappers Doble Filo at a baseball game, and today, the state supports more than 500 hip-hop artists, many with international reputations.

There is also a thriving underground music scene, not approved by the government. Much of it, like reggaeton, is influenced by US trends and also other Latin music, but with a Cuban feel. Young Cubans record it in makeshift studios and distribute it on home-made CDs and memory sticks. A fusion of reggae, rap, Latin and electronic rhythms, reggaeton has swept the dance floors with its sensual beat and raunchy lyrics, despite the lack of government support.

Cultural interchange with US Latin artists and Latin American performers is increasing and, as Cuban music has become more widely known, so has international music become more influential in Cuba. In addition to the Latin styles this also includes rock music, originally the pariah of the revolution for its "foreign, noisy, and scandalous beats." It was only in 2007, with the creation of the Agencia Cubana de Rock, that official approval was eventually given, on the basis that "if you can't beat 'em, join 'em." Forever fearful of youthful rebellion, the government chose to entertain and control, renovating an old theater, Maxim Rock, with state-of-the-art technology for performances. One of the leading metal/Latin/thrash bands is Tendencia, from Pinar del Río, which fuses hard rock with Afro-Cuban rhythms, using the *batá* drum. Led by singer Kiko Mederos, a high-school teacher and director of the

town's Casa del Joven Creador, they have toured abroad and have a fan base in Spain.

New generation

Groups like AfroCuba, Cuarto Espacio, and Perspectiva continue the musical explora-

> *Metaleros listen to heavy metal; Repas are salsa and reggaeton fans from Havana's poorer suburbs; Mikis are into techno and crave all the latest electronic gadgets, like iPods, cell phones, and MP3 players.*

tions. Prominent among a new generation that emerged from the Buena Vista Social Club project is pianist Roberto Fonseca, who made his name with the singer Ibrahim Ferrer, and mesmerizes with sparkling, inventive performances that betray his early experience as a drummer. In 2007, his album *Zamazu* was released to international accclaim. Composer and pianist Omar Sosa is another who blends Cuban, African, and European music with jazz, to great effect. This restless search for new music has characterized the story of Cuban music for centuries, and shows no sign of diminishing. Whatever your musical taste, you will find much to please you in Cuba, in clubs and bars, at high-profile festivals, or simply in the city streets. ❑

LEFT: a reggaeton dance competition at a Union of Young Communists beach party. **RIGHT:** member of a local rock band rehearsing in Cienfuegos.

THE ARTS

Elitist and derivative art of colonial times was replaced in the 20th century by a creative, inclusive, home-grown tradition in painting and architecture. Literature, dance, and cinema have all flourished, too, although censorship has inevitably taken its toll

Cuba has one of the most vibrant artistic histories in the Caribbean, largely owing to its location and cross-cultural history. Forming a maritime crossroads between Europe, Africa, and the Americas, it has long fed off a cultural exchange across the Atlantic Ocean.

Although the island was originally inhabited by various indigenous groups *(see page 33)*, relatively few pre-Columbian artifacts have been discovered in Cuba, especially when compared with the marvels that have been unearthed in Peru or Mexico, for example. However, a few beautiful Taíno pieces have survived – stone and wooden idols, and wooden ceremonial seats.

With the rapid extermination of the indigenous population, whatever else there may have been of the non-material side of native culture died out too, leaving an almost blank cultural slate. The culture of the Spanish invaders was tempered by the influx of African slaves, French plantation owners escaping from the Haitian revolution in 1790, and Chinese indentured laborers in the second half of the 19th century. America's intercession in Cuba's war against Spain in 1898 added yet another cultural outlook – best exemplified in the grandiose Capitolio building in Havana, which closely resembles the Capitol in Washington, DC.

Art in the 20th century

During the colonial period, the pictorial arts were dull and staid – stiff portraits of wealthy ladies and tepid landscapes tended to decorate aristocratic homes and offices, mimicking

the high-society tastes of Europe. In the 20th century, however, things began to change. The rise in nationalism in the political arena was reflected in the arts, with writers and artists getting inspiration from Afro-Cuban images and culture. The generation of painters of 1927–50 is known as La Vanguardia. They were influenced by the modernism of post-Impressionist European artists as well as the vibrant landscapes and people they saw around them in Cuba. From 1900 to the end of the 1950s, Cuban art gained international acclaim and, thanks to the many foreign artists visiting the island, Havana became one of the most celebrated cultural centers in Latin America.

LEFT: Alicia Alonso with the late Marcel Marceau.
RIGHT: frescoed ceiling in the Teatro de la Caridad.

Cuba's most prominent artists from this era include René Portocarrero (1912–85), who created fantastic versions of Havana and beautiful Creole women; and Wifredo Lam (1902–82), who incorporated the mystical dimensions of his Afro-Cuban heritage with erotic and magical symbolism. Lam spent much of his life in Madrid and Paris, and was greatly influenced by Picasso's cubist legacy. Other major artists were Leopoldo Romanach (1862–1951), with his robust country people and gloomy interiors; Fidelio Ponce (1895–1949), who painted young women, children, and saints in faint monochromes; Mariano Rodríguez (1912–90), who famously incorporated roosters into all his vivid, powerful paintings; Amelia Peláez (1897–1968), who evoked the Cuban spirit in her tropical still-lifes; Servando Cabrera (1923–81), who painted robust countrymen and some impressive nudes; and Antonia Eiriz (1929–95), who fascinated the art world with her Goya-esque monsters and ghostly nightmares.

The work of all these artists has been displayed in galleries in Europe and the United States, but the best place to see a wide selection of their works is in the Arte Cubano section of the Museo Nacional Palacio de Bellas Artes in Havana (*see page 163*).

REVOLUTION AND THE ARTS

Castro introduced an aggressive program of cultural reforms that tried to enhance artistic expression. In 1959, one of the first acts of the new government was the creation of the Instituto Cubano del Arte e Industria Cinematográficos (Cuban Film Institute; ICAIC) and the Consejo Nacional de Cultura (National Cultural Council; CNC). The Escuela Nacional de Arte (National School for Art; ENA), founded in 1962, served as the cradle for new artists and teachers in painting, music, dance, and drama.

State sponsorship opened the door to many artists but compromised their freedom of expression. In 1962 Castro defined his policy toward artists and intellectuals: "Within the revolution, everything; outside the revolution, nothing."

During the mid-1960s, those who had differing opinions about the cultural program, as well as those who were non-committal, were removed. Many liberal artists were condemned to silence, others sought asylum, some were persecuted as "anti-social elitists," or exposed as homosexual. The most unfortunate were despatched to prison or to one of Cuba's new labor camps. Directors and writers became more cautious as they were forced to fulfill the artistic and cultural requirements. Socialist ideology began to dominate. The Education and Cultural Congress introduced further reforms designed to increase censorship. Hundreds of actors, writers, and directors lost their jobs in the early 1970s as the totalitarian ring tightened.

Post-Revolutionary art

Painting is a field in which Cuban artists have managed to retain a fairly healthy degree of freedom of expression, in spite of the difficulties involved. Surviving the sclerosis of socialist realism, the contemporary generation of Cuban artists has developed diverse styles, many with strongly anti-establishment undertones, through their often abstract art.

Afro-Cuban mythology and folklore are more apparent in Cuban art than ever before, as seen in the works of Manuel Mendive (b. 1944), one of Cuba's most famous contemporary artists. An initiate in Santería and Palo Monte, he has

expressive work outdoors, away from the official galleries where their paintings could be censored. The streets of Havana became a living exhibition where painters not only displayed their canvases, but also turned the streets into studios in which they created their work. Because of its dissident style, this rejection of

> Víctor Manuel's (1897–1969) stunning 1924 painting Gitana Tropical (Tropical Gypsy), with its echoes of Cézanne and Gauguin, symbolizes the beginning of modernism in Cuban art.

cultivated an intricate, primitivist style laden with Afro-Cuban symbolism, and his work is appreciated worldwide. You can see his paintings in the Arte Cubano section of Havana's Museo Nacional de Bellas Artes. Look out, also, for the work of Flora Fong (b. 1941), of Cuban-Chinese descent, who combines Caribbean colors with a light touch that hints at her ethnicity. She also works with ceramics, stained glass, and textiles.

Artecalle, or street art, developed in the 1980s, whereby young artists displayed their highly

official art was finally suppressed. Some exponents were harassed by the police and most of their work was confiscated. Many young artists left Cuba, although some established their names abroad without breaking their ties with the government. Many of these artists, who trained in the 1980s and were part of a movement where everything was questioned and deconstructed, are still based in Cuba, while exhibiting regularly around the world.

Carlos Garaicoa (b. 1967) studied thermodynamics before enrolling at the Instituto Superior de Arte in 1989–94. He uses a multidisciplinary approach including architectural models, drawings, photographs, and videos to portray the failure of modernism as a catalyst for social change.

LEFT: René Portocarrero's *The Evening Meal.*
ABOVE AND RIGHT: paintings by Mariano Rodríguez and Eduardo Abela, both from 1938.

Tania Bruguera (b. 1968), an installation and performance artist, divides her time between Havana and Chicago, creating, teaching, and exhibiting, while her work is held in collections ranging from the Wifredo Lam Center in Havana to the Museum of Modern Art in New York. Much of her work concerns issues of power and control. Controversially, in 2009 at a gallery in Havana, she told the audience that for one minute they could say whatever they liked into the microphone. Several chose to ask for freedom and democracy – the government denounced it as "an anti-cultural event of shameless opportunism."

ART IN CAMAGÜEY

Not all artists gravitate to Havana. Camagüey is surprisingly wellendowed with artists, whose studios are usually open to visitors (see www.pprincipe.cult.cu). Nazario Salazar Martínez is known for his ceramics, paintings, and graphic design. Orestes Larios Zaak is a painter but you can see other artists at his workshop working on ceramics, ironwork, and paintings. Lorenzo Linares Duque is known for his landscapes and paintings of cockerels. Martha Jiménez Pérez is a painter and sculptor, whose work can be seen in the Plaza del Carmen. Ileana Sánchez Hing is a Naïve painter whose recent work includes a series of colorful paintings of gay and lesbian couples.

José Angel Toirac (b. 1966) came to public attention with his 1996 *Tiempos Nuevos* series in which he portrayed Castro in well-known advertisements, such as Marlboro and Calvin Klein, interpreted to illustrate the way in which Cubans are caught between two rival systems.

Theater

The 19th century was a golden age for Cuban theatre, as philanthropists financed the construction of magnificent auditoriums, and going to the theatre became an increasingly popular pastime. Notable playwrights emerged, such as Gertrudis Gómez de Avellaneda, José Jacinto Milanés, José María de Heredia, and Joaquín Lorenzo Luaces, whose work is still appreciated today. However, the beginning of the 20th century saw the decline of drama. The government was indifferent, playwrights struggled and audiences dropped off. By the middle of the 20th century playwrights were lucky to get their work staged and performances usually lasted for one night only.

In the 1950s ten *salitas*, "pocket theaters," were opened in Havana, attracting regular audiences. New playwrights emerged, some of whom became the greats of the 20th century. The most important were Virgilio Piñera (1912–79), Carlos Felipe (1911–75), and Rolando Ferrer (1925–76). There was an eclectic mix of Spanish melodramas, romantic comedies, British and Broadway hits, and European avant-garde, as well as Cuban dramas. The success of the pocket theaters allowed plays to be staged in larger venues and to run for several weeks instead of days, increasing quality and professionalism. The government took an interest and playwrights were paid for their works, and received copyright.

The momentum continued after the revolution. In 1959, 48 Cuban plays were produced, more than the total shown in 1952–8, while in the 1960s almost 400 Cuban plays were premiered. Drama was divided more or less between realistic and experimental. From 1965–70 the theater reflected the artistic and ideological struggles going on in the country; few theater companies traveled abroad and few foreign companies visited, leaving Cuban theater isolated and xenophobic.

The 1970s were the dark ages. In 1971 the first national Congress of Education and Culture approved repressive measures relating to art and culture, including removing homosexuals from positions of contact with youth. Many actors, directors, designers, and playwrights lost their jobs; a list was made of forbidden plays and authors; theater groups were disbanded and others created, including the Bertolt

> Two of Cuba's best playwrights, Eduardo Manet and José Triana, went to live in Paris. Manet's Las Monjas (The Nuns) has been translated into over 30 languages. Triana's Worlds Apart premiered in Stratford-upon-Avon.

a less dogmatic period followed in the 1980s. Some of the previously banned theater workers were allowed back in and playwrights' work was published. It was too late for some, who had either died or fled the country, but some playwrights who suffered in the 1970s, such as Tomás González and Eugenio Hernández Espinosa, were rehabilitated. In the 1990s many of the works of the 1950s and 1960s were rediscovered, while among new authors were Abilio Estévez, Alberto Pedro Torriente, Joel Cano, Ricardo Muñoz, Reinaldo Montero, and Raúl Alfonso. Ideological debate is now tolerated, and many of the issues currently under discussion in society are

Brecht Political Theater. Audiences voted with their feet. Subsequently, the 1970s saw the creation of Teatro Nuevo, a grass-roots movement with state support whose best example was the Grupo de Teatro Escambray. Living in a rural community, so as to understand the lives of the people, they worked collectively. Alibio Paz, a member of the group, became a notable playwright, concentrating on contemporary themes and debate in the context of rural traditions and cultural attitudes.

Gradually, although nothing was said officially,

being aired on the stage. There is a wide range of theater companies, from conventional to experimental, street theater, rural, provincial, political or works for children, interpreting a wide range of foreign and national plays.

Dance

Although touring companies visited, including the great Romantic ballerina Fanny Elssler in 1842 and Anna Pavlova in 1917, there was no home-grown ballet in Cuba until the Sociedad Pro-Arte Música started ballet evenings in 1931. Its conservatory produced Alicia Alonso, the most influential Cuban dancer and ballet director ever, and the two Alonso brothers, Alberto (dancer and choreographer) and

LEFT: contemporary ceramic art at Martha Jiménez Pérez' studio in Camagüey. ABOVE: Havana street theater performance by psychiatric hospital patients.

Fernando (dancer, ballet director, and husband of Alicia). Born Alicia Ernestina de la Caridad del Cobre Martínez Hoyo on December 21, 1920, she trained with the School of American Ballet in New York before becoming a professional ballerina. A detached retina forced periods of inactivity, but she continued to dance, working with many of the leading choreographers such as Anthony Tudor. She was known for her classical style and flawless technique, and her interpretation of *Giselle* is a benchmark against which all others are judged.

In 1948 Alicia and her husband returned to Havana to set up her own company, Ballet Ali-

let school and funding to maintain a company. She got it. Her company was converted into the Ballet Nacional de Cuba and the National Ballet School was created. State funding provides free ballet education to anyone in Cuba selected on the basis of talent. The company has won international acclaim for its repertoire, which includes classical and modern works, many by Cuban choreographers. When not touring abroad, the company performs mainly in Havana's Gran Teatro or Teatro Nacional. Despite no peripheral vision and increasing blindness, Alonso still directs the company, having memorized all the major works.

Carlos Acosta is acknowledged as one of the greatest dancers ever, on a par with Rudolf Nureyev and Mikhail Baryshnikov. His soaring leaps have earned him the nicknames of "the flying Cuban" or "Air Acosta."

cia Alonso, and two years later came a school. She continued to perform abroad, using her earnings to fund her Cuban enterprises. When Castro was fighting in the Sierra Maestra she sent him a message appealing for support. He did not forget and soon after the revolution he came knocking on her door. He asked what she needed to create a ballet and she requested a bal-

The world-famous ballet star, Carlos Acosta, owes his training to the National Ballet School and is a protégé of Alicia Alonso. He currently dances with the Royal Ballet in London and in 2009 he helped to organize a visit by the company to Cuba, the first time for over 30 years that an international dance company had been to the island. Spectacularly popular, thousands watched the classical and avant-garde dances on outdoor screens when tickets sold out. In 2010, Alicia Alonso, aged 89 and blind, took the Ballet Nacional de Cuba to tour the UK in sell-out performances.

The Camagüey Ballet, founded shortly after the Revolution, once had an impressive reputation, but has lost some of its best dancers to the bright lights of the capital. Contemporary dance is also flourishing. Danza Contemporánea de Cuba, under Miguel Iglesias, grew out of Conjunto Nacional de Danza Modernas, begun by Ramiro Guerra in the early post-revolutionary years. Another company, Ballet Rakatan, fuses contemporary and traditional dance styles with flamenco and Afro-Cuban rhythms. The Ballet Folklórico Cutumba, based in Santiago de Cuba, performs vibrant ritual dances and chants from the Afro-Cuban cultures, and there are many amateur dance groups across the country who dedicate their efforts to maintaining elements of African culture.

Before the Revolution, many Cuban writers had gone abroad, and several returned during a period of literary renaissance in the early 1960s, when they received preferential access to housing and a guaranteed income. Writers like the poet Nicolás Guillén were given official patronage by the revolutionary government, and some were even sent overseas as cultural attachés.

Nicolás Guillén (1902–89) was a lifelong communist and after the revolution enjoyed the prestige of being Cuba's National Poet.

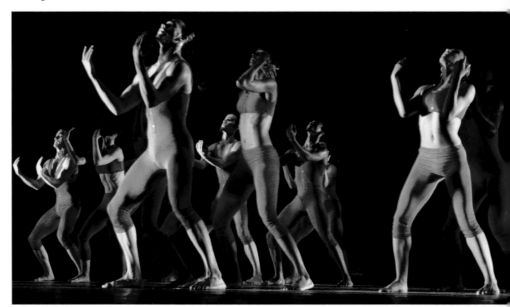

Literature

Cuba has produced some outstanding writers, some of whom have an international reputation: Guillermo Cabrera Infante *(see page 116)*; Alejo Carpentier (1904–80), who moved to Paris in 1966 where he served as Cuban Ambassador; poet, playwright, and critic Severo Sarduy (1937–93); and poet and novelist José Lezama Lima (1910–76), are leading lights of Latin American literature. Backtracking to the 19th century, Cuba's brightest star was poet and revolutionary, José Martí *(see page 51)*.

LEFT: members of UK's Royal Ballet pay tribute to Alicia Alonso at García Lorca Theatre, Havana. **ABOVE:** performance by Danza Contemporánea de Cuba.

However, the international literary scandal known as the Padilla Affair changed all that. In 1968, Herberto Padilla (who died in Alabama in 2000) won an award for his book *Fuero del Juego (Out of the Game)*, a collection of poems that discredited the myths of revolutionary society. Though the award was given by a prestigious international jury, the book was banned in Cuba, and Padilla was arrested. This caused an outcry among intellectuals abroad, including writers like Gabriel García Márquez and Jean-Paul Sartre, who had until then been supportive of Castro's regime.

After this, a large number of writers were marginalized and their books taken out of circulation. The era of limited toleration of literary dissent had ended. Many writers left, including Guillermo Cabrera Infante, winner of the 1997 Cervantes Prize, the most prestigious Spanish-language literature award, who is often described as Cuba's greatest 20th-century author. He lived in London from 1965 until his death 40 years later, and remained highly critical of Castro and his regime.

In 1987, the Cuban leadership re-evaluated the issue of artistic censorship, and in the 1990s, because of the massive exodus of writers and artists, the government took a more lenient attitude toward literary taboos.

In addition to the writers mentioned above,

novels published over a number of years.

Cuban writers now find it easier to express their ideas without heavy censorship, and many poets and novelists feel they are carrying on where literature left off in the 1960s. Popular authors such as Pedro Juan Gutiérrez and Leonardo Padura Fuentes write about the difficulties of making a living in Havana and are openly critical of the sacrifices demanded by the state.

Cinema

Film is the most favored of the arts. Cuban cinema kicked off with the arrival of Castro and the Cuban Institute of Cinematography (ICAIC). A

other Cuban writers well worth reading – both those who stayed and those who left – are anthropologist Miguel Barnet (b. 1940), whose best-known work is *Biografía de un Cimarrón (The Autobiography of a Runaway Slave)*, published in 1967; Lydia Cabrera – famous for her studies into Afro-Cuban religions – who died in 1991; Lisandro Otero González (b. 1932), whose most recent work, *Charada*, was published in Havana in 2004; and Reinaldo Arenas, whose openly gay lifestyle led to his imprisonment, and who left for Miami in the Mariel Boatlift. He committed suicide in New York in 1990. His autobiography, *Before Night Falls*, was made into a highly acclaimed movie in 2000 (*see page 25*). His major work was *Pentagonia*, a series of five

FILM FESTIVALS

The New Latin American Film Festival, founded in 1979 and held in Havana every December, may not be as well known in Europe as the festivals in Cannes and Venice, but it attracts film-makers and actors from all over the world. Its prestigious Coral prizes are the Latin American equivalent of the Oscars. The International Low-Budget Film Festival, founded in 2003 by the late film-maker Humberto Solás, is held in Gibara in Holguín province in April every year, showcasing films which have cost less than US$300,000 to make. There are categories for documentaries, short feature films, and experimental video projects.

militant cinema industry set about promoting the advantages of the socialist system. Cuban documentaries were shown in the most remote corners of the island. Inspired by this movement, other Latin American film-makers created political documentaries that became a vehicle for left-wing liberation movements around the world.

In 1986 one of the best film schools in the world was founded in San Antonio de los Baños (*see page 192*) by Colombian novelist Gabriel García Márquez, Argentine poet and film-maker, Fernando Pirri, and Cuban film-maker, Julio García Espinosa. Thousands of students from Asia, Africa, and Latin America have studied there, and it is relatively free from following the constraints of the official party line.

The leading light among Cuba's film directors was Tomás Gutiérrez Alea (1928–96). His 1969 movie *Memorias del Subdesarrollo (Memories of Underdevelopment)*, about a middle-class Cuban who refuses to leave for Miami in the early 1960s but is unable to fit into revolutionary society, is a modern classic. His 1966 comedy *La Muerte de un Burócrata (Death of a Bureaucrat)* is also well worth seeing; and *Fresa y Chocolate* (1994), co-directed by Juan Carlos Tabío, created a stir inside and outside Cuba.

Although Cuba is full of creative energy, most cultural institutions felt the crunch of economic crisis during the "Special Period" in the 1990s. The film industry was all but shut down and most new movies were made with foreign money. Book publishing was badly hit, too. Writers, artists, actors, and film-makers struggled to survive. Fortunately, things are picking up again now.

Economic woes also saw a return to a harsher government attitude, and it seemed that the period of relative tolerance had been a false dawn. Movies such as the well-received 1995 comedy *Guantanamera* and Oscar-nominated *Fresa y Chocolate* (both directed by Gutiérrez Alea and Juan Carlos Tabío) were severely criticized by Castro in a speech in 1997, arousing fears among the artistic community – and those who simply enjoyed cinema – of a return to the dark days of total censorship.

The head of ICAIC, Alfredo Guevara (a lifelong communist and friend of Castro), gave an emotional press conference defending the movies. But after a flurry of resignations and a meeting between Castro and leading artists, the official position prevailed, and Guevara stated that artistic "mistakes" had been made, and that the artistic community must be careful not to damage public morale or values.

Contemporary Cuba in film

Recent movies depicting contemporary Cuba include *Suite Habana* (2003), directed by Fernando Pérez Valdés. A documentary without dialog, chronicling a day in the life of several real people in the city, it has been widely praised.

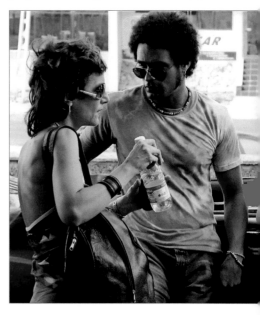

It can be interpreted as critical and subversive or as a tribute to the resilience of people supporting the revolution. *Habana Blues* (2005) is a Spanish-Cuban co-operative effort, directed by Benito Zambrano, a Spaniard who studied at the San Antonio de Baños film school and who has described the movie as his homage to Havana. *El Cuerno de la Abundancia (Horn of Plenty*, 2008), directed by Juan Carlos Tabío, is an affectionate comedy based on a true story of a family in a small town who hear they may have inherited a fortune in London. It follows their hopes and dreams, their struggles against bureaucracy, their greed and their fights, until they discover that the inheritance has gone to a branch of the family in Miami. ❑

FAR LEFT: Guillermo Cabrera Infante. **LEFT:** poster for the groundbreaking film, *Fresa y Chocolate*. **RIGHT:** a still from the 2005 movie *Habana Blues*.

THE ESSENCE OF CUBAN FOOD

The items on Cuban menus may all seem pretty similar, but there is good-quality food to be found, although not always in the obvious places, along with some delicious fresh fruit – not to mention the cocktails

Most Cuban food is simple. It is the fare of *el campo* (the countryside), which reflects local harvests and earthy suggestions of its Spanish and African roots. It allows, for instance, a dish of Galician inspiration to be served together with African-style accompaniments. Cuban cooking isn't fancy, but Cubans love food.

The Cuban staples

If Cuban creole *(criollo)* cuisine had a national dish, it would, without question, be roast pork *(puerco* or *cerdo)* served with black beans *(frijoles)*, white rice *(arroz)*, and plantains *(plátanos)*, which is what people eat at New Year celebrations. Rice and beans are traditionally prepared in two forms: kidney beans with rice, known as *moros y cristianos* (Moors and Christians), or black beans with rice *(congrí)*. A delicious soupy stew of black beans *(potaje)* is sometimes served alongside plain white rice.

> Food gets into the music. The island's most famous singer, Beny Moré, teased the marranito, *the little pig: "We're going to make you* jamón *(ham) and* chicharrón *(pork scratchings").*

Root vegetables are also popular accompaniments, particularly *yuca* (also called cassava, a starchy tuber), *malanga*, and *boniato*. *Malanga* is not unlike yuca, and *boniato* is a tasty kind of sweet potato.

LEFT: fruit stall at the Camagüey farmers' market.
RIGHT: black beans – a Cuban creole staple ingredient.

Chicken *(pollo)* appears on many menus – invariably fried. Fish *(pescado)* is usually *pargo* (snapper) or any plain steak of white fish that is simply called *pescado*.

The ingredients, herbs, and spices most used in traditional Cuban cooking are cumin, oregano, parsley, sour oranges, and *ajo* – garlic. *Sofrito*, a paste of chopped onion, garlic, and green pepper sizzled in oil, is the basis of many dishes. In these days of scarce ingredients, a popular seasoning for vegetables and meat is a tasty mixture of sour orange, garlic, and oil, called *mojo* *(see recipe on page 122)*. You won't often find meat stews on a menu, but look out for the *ajiaco*, a classic infusion of meat and vegetables.

Although you can see piles of seasonal vegetables in markets, you don't often find them in restaurants. Salad often means a heap of grated white cabbage slightly pickled with a vinegar dressing. However, when you do get fresh produce – tomatoes, for example – they can be deli-

> Sugar is the basis of Cuba's fine rum, but also for one of its favorite non-alcoholic drinks, guarapo, *which is the cloudy, sweet juice of raw, pressed sugar cane. You will see it being sold from carts in the street.*

its quota, and you will find a wide range of goods on sale, from fresh vegetables to meat, eggs, and honey. The food you eat in *paladares* will have come from an *agropecuario*. Unfortunately these products are relatively expensive and most local people can't afford them.

Some things, such as beef and lobster, can only be sold by the state, but there is, of course, a black market. If you stay in a *casa particular (see page 340)* and order dinner (in some towns your *casa* may be the best place to eat), your host may ask you if you would like *pollo de mar* (sea chicken), as if the word lobster should not even be mentioned. But if you want it, it will be available.

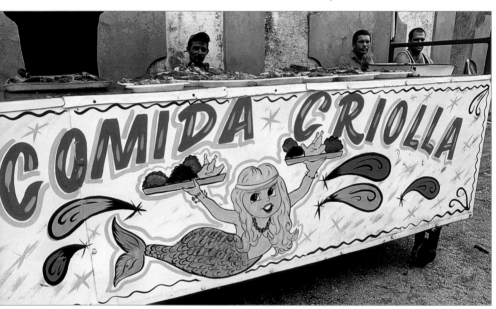

cious, full of flavor, and invariably organic.

During the "Special Period," the tough years after the collapse of the Soviet Union when there were shortages of absolutely everything, Cuba became the land of "no hay" – which means, "there isn't any," and people had to learn to cook with whatever was available. Lean times forced a new kind of cuisine upon the Cuban people, who became masters of improvisation, stretching and enhancing rice with whatever was available, planning vegetarian meals in a culinary culture obsessed with meat.

The opening of farmers' markets *(agropecuarios)* in 1994 made a wider choice of ingredients available. These are markets where farmers sell their surplus produce, after the state has bought

THE VERSATILE PLANTAIN

Cuban cooking exalts lowly ingredients. Take, for instance, the plantain, *el plátano*. You can fry it ripe *(maduro)* in slices, or green *(verde)* in paper-thin chips *(chicharitas)*. You can fry thicker wedges of green plantain, squash them, and fry them again for *tostones.* You can boil plantain chunks, ripe or green, mash them with a fork, drizzle with olive oil, and sprinkle with crunchy fried pork rinds for *fu fú* – a dish of west African origin and something of an acquired taste. You can fill mashed plantains with *picadillo*, minced meat, and melted white cheese to make a *pastel de plátano*. In fact, you can do just about anything except eat them uncooked.

Fruit

Fruit in Cuba is a delight, and so are the juices made from it. Everything is harvested in season, when it is at its peak: sweet, juicy pineapples, grapefruits that need no sugar, mangos like you've never tasted before, and bananas – the small, chunky ones are the best. Avocados, too, are at their perfect, creamy best when picked straight from the tree. Unless you buy it in markets you are most likely to come across fruit on the breakfast table of a *casa particular* or the breakfast buffet in a hotel. Despite being plentiful and cheap it is rarely offered as a dessert. Freshly squeezed fruit juices can be found in

will see special versions of these cakes being handed out of bakers' storefronts to waiting crowds and, everywhere you go, notice people carrying them home, often one in each hand, or balancing them on bicycle handlebars.

In the east of the island, try the *cucuruchu* for the ultimate in sweetness. This is grated coconut, sometimes flavored with fruit juice and (mostly) sugar and sold in ingeniously fashioned banana-leaf wrappings.

Cuban rum

The first thing that comes to mind when one thinks of drinking in Cuba is rum. Along with

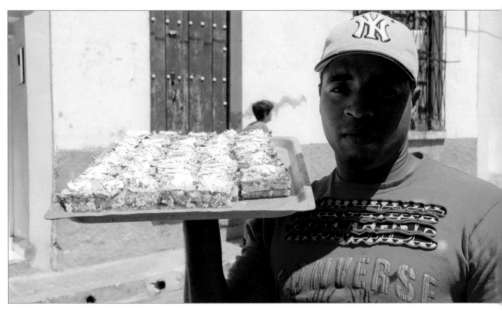

many bars, in whatever variety is most available – ask for *jugo natural* to get the real thing.

Sweet treats

The role of dessert on Cuban menus is usually played by ice cream (and it is generally very good, too) or the ubiquitous *flan*, a caramel custard. Cubans do, on the whole, have a sweet tooth – you just need to look in a bakery window at the fluffy pink and baby-blue iced confections to realize that. If you are in Cuba for Mother's Day (the second Sunday in May) you

---

LEFT: *comida criolla* for sale on a street stall.
ABOVE: cakes in Cuba – often thickly iced in bright colors and ultra-sweet.

cigars, this is Cuba's best-known product. Rum, of course, is a sugar-based alcohol, and Cuba has always had plenty of sugar. The best-known and biggest brand is Havana Club. There are various types, but you will most often find Añejo 3 Años, Añejo Reserva, and Añejo 7 Años, of which the latter is the best. There is also a white rum, Añejo Blanco. Although Bacardi rum originated in Cuba (in Santiago) it is no longer made or sold here. The Bacardi family, fiercely opposed to Castro, had their business appropriated and left the island after the Revolution. Bacardi is now made in Puerto Rico.

A good, aged rum (*ron* in Spanish) can be drunk neat, like a brandy or whisky (ask for *ron de siete años*), but white or three-year-old rum is used as the basis of Cuba's famous cocktails: the *mojito* (rum, lime, mint, and soda water), the *daiquirí* (rum, lime juice, sugar, and crushed ice), the *piña colada* (rum with pineapple juice and coconut), and the Cuba Libre. The latter – which means Free Cuba – originated at the end of the 1898 War of Independence and was made with rum and Coca-Cola.

Beer and wine

As well as rum, Cubans are also very fond of beer, which is hardly surprising in this hot climate. Cristal, a light beer made by the Mayabe Brewery, can be found all over the island. The same brewery makes Mayabe, ordinary and extra, which has more flavour. Hatuey beer is made in Havana but is not always easy to find. Bucanero is made in Holguín and found mostly in the east, while Tínimo, made in Camagüey, can be difficult to obtain outside that city.

You can buy wine in some places, certainly in the better hotels and restaurants, but don't expect to find it everywhere. There is small-scale wine production in Pinar del Río province *(see page 199)*, sold under the Soroa label, but most of the available wine comes from Chile or Argentina.

MOJO CRIOLLO

The classic sauce for pork, but it is also used to add flavor to vegetables, such as *malanga*.

For four people:

8 garlic cloves, chopped, 1 tsp salt

1 tsp ground oregano (optional)

½ tsp ground cumin (optional)

½ cup sour orange juice

½ cup olive oil

Mash the garlic and salt to form a paste. Blend in the spices. Add the sour orange juice and leave for 30 minutes; stir in the olive oil. Sour orange juice appears in many Cuban recipes but you can substitute sweet orange juice and lime or lemon juice.

Home-grown coffee

Cuba produces and consumes some excellent coffee, mainly Arabica, the majority of which is grown in the Sierra Maestra region where the mountainous climate is ideal. Ask for a *café con leche* if you want coffee with hot milk – this is normally drunk at breakfast time. A *café cubano* or *cafecito* (little coffee) is small and strong like an espresso, except that it will come ready sweetened unless you ask for it "*sin azúcar*," although many Cubans, known for liking sweet things, think this is a little bit odd. ❏

ABOVE: Havana Club white rum is usually used for cocktails such as the *mojito*; the dark version can be drunk neat.

Eating out

A good *paladar* or a meal in a *casa particular* will introduce you to Cuban food at its best, far removed from a soulless state restaurant

State-owned restaurants can be identified by the credit card stickers on the door. A few are good, particularly in Havana, but most are boring, offering poor, quality food and even worse service. They will invariably charge you in CUC$. They do, however, offer some variety in cuisine, with Italian, Spanish, or Chinese the most common. Resort hotels usually have buffet and à la carte restaurants where you can find something you like, although the food often appears recycled or reheated. At the cheaper end of the state sector are fast-food joints, burger bars, or fried chicken places for a greasy snack. Bars and cafés have snacks and light meals for lunch but sandwiches are usually cheese, ham, or cheese and ham, with stodgy white bread.

In Santiago and other towns in the east of the island, the government is opening new restaurants which charge in pesos Cubanos. They are designed to appeal to Cubans and offer them affordable dining to improve their social wellbeing, but there is nothing to stop tourists eating there too, at a fraction of the cost of a CUC establishment. There are some teething problems but many are worth trying. Street stalls also charge in pesos, selling lunch-time sandwiches and stodgy pizza, but check these carefully if you are concerned about hygiene. Most are best avoided.

For many years after the 1959 revolution, family-run restaurants were illegal, as was virtually every kind of private enterprise. They operated clandestinely, yet everyone knew where they were; even policemen and party members could be seen eating in them. Then, in 1994, the law was changed and these establishments, called *paladares*, could start doing business more openly. Cuba was suddenly full of *paladares* offering cheap home cooking – usually serving the traditional menu of pork, beans, and rice.

But in 1996, the government realized that it had created a highly successful, profitable sector of the economy that was making some people too wealthy. Consequently, *paladares* were obliged to register with the state, meet strict public-health standards, and pay both a license fee and devastatingly high taxes – as much as US$1,000 a month in Havana, regardless of how many meals were served. The result was that many *paladares* were driven out of business.

The days of the cheap meal eaten in the family sitting room are not entirely over, however. These *paladares* have simply moved back underground. Refusing to register and paying no taxes, they come and go, but, as in the old days, everyone in the neighborhood knows where they are. All you have to do is to ask around: any local person will

be able to tell you the addresses of two or three that are open.

The alternative to eating out is to eat in your *casa particular*. This may lack the atmosphere of a good *paladar*, but has the advantage of allowing you to order exactly what you want, when you want it. You can be sure that the food will be bought and cooked fresh that day and any special dietary requirements can be catered for.

Vegetarians often find that this is by far the best option, and many *casa* owners have become quite skilled at providing meat-free meals. You may need to check, however, that beans are not cooked with the traditional lard, and some vegetarians prefer to travel with their own cooking oil, which they lend to their hosts. ❑

ABOVE: international dishes are often on the menu at top hotels and resorts such as Havana's Hotel Nacional.

SPORT

One irrefutable triumph of the revolution has been in the domain of athletics. Cuban sportsmen and women regularly dominate world-class opposition, and sporting opportunities for all are regarded as a right

In 1944, the young Fidel Castro was voted athlete of the year at Belén College in Havana, where baseball was his specialty. "If I hadn't been an athlete, I wouldn't have been a guerrilla," Castro has said. He was once offered a professional contract to pitch for a US team but, by his own admission, he was not major-league material. Had Castro's arm been better, he might never have taken up arms against Batista, and the world would have been a very different place. Cuba might still be a playground for wealthy Americans, and it is extremely unlikely that there would have been a large sign displayed outside the Cuban national sports training center, proclaiming *"Fidel: Atleta Número Uno."*

The right of the people

Less than a month after taking power, Castro addressed Cuba's assembled sports organizations and declared: "It is a shame that sport has been so undervalued. Less than 10 percent of our youth participate in sports. We must promote them at all costs. We must inundate every corner of the island with sports equipment. We should strive to improve our athletes rapidly."

Another Castro quotation is plastered around sports arenas: "Sport is the right of the people." With the creation of the National Institute of Sports, Physical Education and Recreation (INDER) in 1961, Cuba began to fulfill this pledge. Today, nearly half the population has participated in organized sports.

The base of Cuba's sporting pyramid is its 80,000 elementary school children. Every year

students compete in the School Sports Games. Those that excel are invited to be tested for admission to the Schools for Sports Initiation (EIDE), whose students range in age from 11 to 16. EIDE students attend regular classes, but they are also given advanced coaching and face high-level competition. Those who perform best graduate to one of the Schools of Higher Athletic Performance (ESPA) where students hope to be noticed by a coach from the national ESPA in Havana.

Incentives

It took more than a decade for this system to make an impact on the sports world, but when

LEFT: Yargelis Savigne, world champion triple jumper.
RIGHT: baseball is a national obsession.

it did, it did so with a bang. Teófilo Stevenson, a heavyweight boxer from eastern Cuba, won a gold medal at the 1972 Olympics in Munich. Stevenson won another gold at the 1976 Games in Montreal, where another great Cuban athlete, Alberto Juantorena, won gold medals in the 400- and 800-meter races – the first man ever to win both events in one Olympic Games. Stevenson won a third gold medal in Moscow in 1980. Both Stevenson and Juantorena now hold posts in INDER. They are two illustrations of another Cuban sports philosophy: "The greatest incentive that can be given to an athlete," Castro said in 1959, "is security in their retirement and a proper reward for champions."

> *Sport in revolutionary Cuba is seen as an integral part of one's physical and moral education. In the words of Castro himself, "Sport is an antidote to vice."*

International events

Overall, Cuba has performed very well at international sporting events for a nation of its size. In the Pan-American Games, Cuba stands second behind the US in the overall medals table.

ONE TO WATCH - YARGELIS SAVIGNE

Born in 1984 in the town of Niceto Pérez, "Yayi" as she is known in Cuba is a prime example of the success of the Cuban sports education system, having attended the Rafael Freyre EIDE Sports School on the outskirts of Guantánamo. Benefitting from professional coaching, she progressed through the National School Games to the National Junior Championships until she made the national junior team in 2001. At her international debut she won the 2002 CAC Junior crown for the long jump in Barbados. As a senior, she joined the Cuban team for their European tour in 2005, competing in the triple jump as well as the long jump.

That year was her breakthrough: she won silver in the triple jump at the World Championships in Helsinki and bronze at the World Athletics Final in Monaco. By 2007 Savigne was a world champion triple jumper, winning gold at the World Championships, Osaka, the Pan-American Games, Rio de Janeiro, and the World Athletics Final in Stuttgart. In 2008 she took the gold at the World Indoor Championships in Valencia with a personal best of 15.05 meters. She matched the distance at the Olympics but had to content herself with fifth place. In 2009 she won gold at the World Championships in Berlin and followed that with silver at the World Indoor Championships in Doha in 2010. She is coached by Milán Matos and the Olympic long jump champion Iván Pedroso and is managed by high jump champion, Javier Sotomayor *(see page 129)*.

Its greatest success in these games came in 1991, when it played host to the event. Cuba had staked significant prestige on the outcome, managing to stage the games despite the financial strictures caused by the collapse of the Soviet Union and the subsequent loss of Soviet subsidies. The risk paid off, with Cuba becoming only the second nation ever to displace the US at the top of the tree – an obvious reason for national pride.

The nation has likewise punched above its weight at the Olympics, although it seems to be slipping slightly in the table of nations. At the 1992 Olympics in Barcelona, Cuba was the fifth-highest medal winner with 31, surpassing

"To beat an American is the most important thing," said one Cuban boxer. "Knocking out an American is better than knocking out a better boxer. It's transcendent."

Baseball

Another Cuban passion is baseball, which came to the island at the end of the 19th century, when the North American influence was starting to outweigh that of Spain. The first games were played in around 1865 between Cuban dock workers and US sailors. Spanish authorities associated the game with the cause of Cuban independence – and revenues from

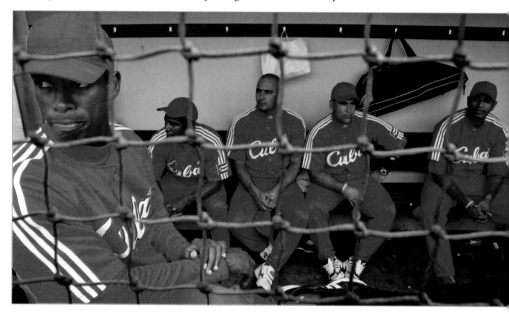

larger countries such as France and Britain. In Atlanta in 1996, they came eighth with 25 medals; in Sydney in 2000 they came ninth in the overall table (one above the UK); in Athens in 2004 they came 11th, winning 27 medals, including nine golds; and in Beijing in 2008 they came 12th, winning 24 medals (two gold, 11 silver, 11 bronze).

Although it has a good record in athletics and some martial arts like judo and taekwondo, the real mainstay in terms of medal-winning is in boxing – one of the island's sporting passions.

baseball games did, indeed, support José Martí's independence movement. As a result, the game was banned in parts of the country in 1895.

Repeated visits from US Marines after independence heightened baseball's popularity, as did the increasing numbers of North American players seeking Caribbean warmth and winter paychecks. Though the sport was originally the realm of Cuba's economic elite, it quickly caught on among all classes of society.

All over Cuba you will see evidence of the game's popularity. Even the smallest community has a baseball pitch, and in city streets you will see small boys practicing shots – even when they only have a stick, and perhaps a tin can for a ball.

LEFT: brothers training in a makeshift gym at the back of their home. **ABOVE:** the Cuban national baseball team wait for play in the dugout.

Major-league riches

The island has totally dominated baseball since it was made a full Olympic sport in Barcelona in 1992, winning three of the five golds awarded since then. The only blemishes came in 2000 in Sydney, when they were beaten into silver-medal position by the US, and in 2008 in Beijing when they were beaten by South Korea. Cuban players assert that they play for the love of the game and their country, and are not interested in the millions of dollars they could earn in major leagues.

Defections, however, have become increasingly common, and some of the island's finest players have abandoned Cuba for multimillion-dollar contracts and the chance to play in prestigious United States major leagues. Dozens of Cuban baseball players have defected since the early 1990s, but not all of them elect to stay in the United States – many go on to a third coun-

> Star baseball pitcher Yadel Marti and outfielder Yasser Gomez were thrown out of the top league team in 2008 for an unspecified reason, believed to have been linked to an attempted defection.

try to negotiate a lucrative contract which is free of US baseball's rules on exclusive rights.

The legal way

Cuba does export some of its athletic talent through official channels, and INDER takes half the earnings of coaches and athletes who go abroad legally to work and compete. Cuban sports personnel work in some 40 different countries and, in 2002, the authorities came to an agreement with Japan's professional baseball leagues for Olympic stars like slugger Orestes Kindelán and third-baseman Omar "El Niño" Linares to play there. But when it comes to the United States, that avenue is firmly closed. INDER refuses to sanction players leaving for the US, and the US does not permit the wages of professional players to go back to Cuba.

In the footsteps of the greats

Two of Cuba's outstanding athletes of the 1990s were the runner, Ana Fidelia Quirot, who triumphed in the 800-meter race at the World Championships in 1997 – having made a remarkable comeback from a severe burns accident – and the phenomenal high jumper, Javier Sotomayor (who enjoys the additional prestige of having been a deputy in Cuba's National Assembly). Sotomayor can rightfully lay claim to the title of greatest high jumper of all time. At the age of 16

Cubans reacted angrily, accusing the United States of doctoring the tests in order to tarnish Cuba's sporting reputation. Castro launched a campaign to try and clear Sotomayor's name and Cuba refused to suspend him. After his ban was reduced from two years to one, Sotomayor came back to win a silver medal in high jump in Sydney in 2000.

After more than 20 years in the limelight, and after testing positive in another drug test, this time for an anabolic steroid (an allegation he strongly denied), Sotomayor retired in October 2001, just before his 34th birthday, which is a grand old age for a high jumper. ❑

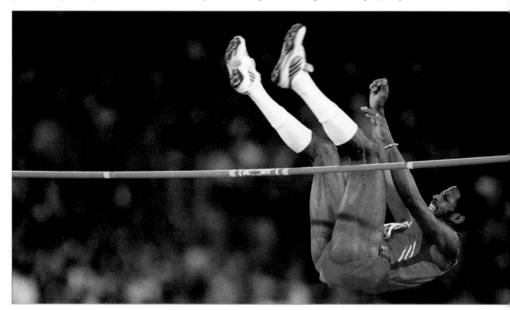

he set a new record for that age group by clearing 2.33 meters. He frequently broke the world record (pushing the mark up to 2.45 meters in 1993 – a record that still stands); claimed Olympic gold in 1992 (Cuban boycotts meant he missed the 1984 and 1988 Games); and won World Championship golds in 1995 and 1997.

Sporting controversy

However, Sotomayor was stripped of the gold medal he won at the 1999 Pan-American Games in Winnipeg, Canada, when he allegedly tested positive for cocaine. The

LEFT: training on the beach at Trinidad. **ABOVE:** world champion Javier Sotomayer.

OPEN TO ALL – BIG AND SMALL

In Havana, top budding gymnasts train at the Provincial School for Gymnastics, in an ornate colonial building on the Prado. While they practice their world-class routines, on the other side of the building a group of five-year-olds might be working on cartwheels. Despite the disparity between these extremes of talent and experience, there is an air of accessibility to the elite athletes that meshes nicely with the irony of this formerly exclusive club being put to popular use. It is difficult to imagine a top-level national athlete in any other country training alongside primary-school kids, but, like so many of Cuba's apparent contradictions, it seems to work.

PLACES

A detailed guide to the entire archipelago
of Cuba, with principal sites clearly
cross-referenced by number to the maps

Most visitors to Cuba spend at least a few days in Havana, one of the most exciting capital cities in the world, despite being a relatively young one. Havana is where five centuries of Cuban history coalesce with the merging of peoples from Europe, Africa, China, and, of course, the Americas, a city saturated with romance, nostalgia, and intrigue. Although sadly dilapidated in parts, it should not be missed, as there is nowhere else like it in Latin America for architecture and culture. A visit here can easily be combined with one of the many beach resorts that have been developed along the north coast, from the well-established Varadero to the luxury now found on the cays, formerly the lonely preserve of fishermen and birds.

However, the "real Cuba" lies out in the provinces. With a judicious combination of short domestic flights, organized tours, comfortable long-distance buses, taxi rides, and rental cars, you will be able to penetrate the less-frequently visited hinterland.

For a pure taste of rural life, to the west of Havana lies the province of Pinar del Río, the tobacco-growing region that is one of the lushest and most spectacular parts of the island. A journey to the central south coast should include visits to Playa Girón on the Bay of Pigs, the wildlife-filled Zapata peninsula, the port of Cienfuegos, and Cuba's colonial jewel, Trinidad. Inland, Santa Clara provides the last resting place of Che Guevara, a Mecca for students of the revolution. Offshore, Cayo Largo is the favored beach resort, while the Isle of Youth is a major diving center.

The rural heartland is the slowest and least-visited part of Cuba, where cities such as Camagüey and Holguín are interesting stopover points, steeped in history and with thriving beach resorts within easy reach. The east has its own thriving identity and traditions. Santiago, Cuba's second city, is often a few steps ahead of Havana in culture and music. The little colonial town of Baracoa is a delight, and exploring the highways, remote beaches, and craggy mountains of the Oriente remains one of Cuba's great adventures. ❑

PRECEDING PAGES: view of Trinidad from the Museo Romántico; Viñales valley; Old Havana street leading to Capitolio; **LEFT:** a trusty old car in Trinidad. **ABOVE:** a proud fisherman and a watchful youth.

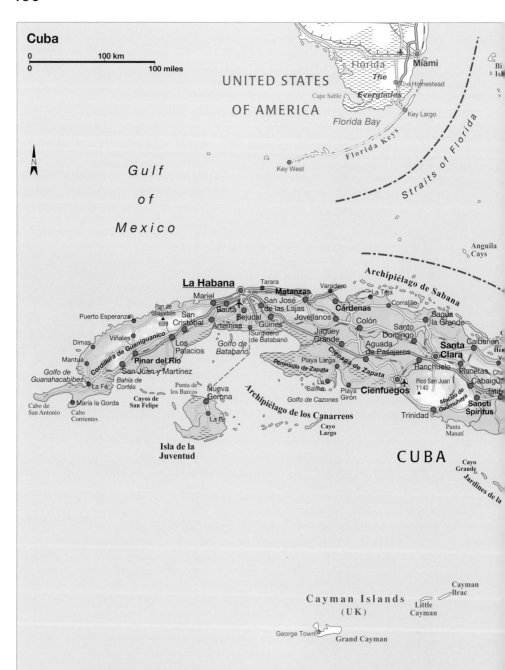

Cuba

0 ___ 100 km
0 ___ 100 miles

N

INTRODUCING HAVANA

A city of more than 2 million inhabitants,
Cuba's capital offers far more than
just its astonishing colonial core

Seen from a distance, Havana looks spectacular. Waves crash over the city's famous promenade, the **Malecón**, where lovers stroll past pastel-colored buildings. Stone fortresses turn golden in the Caribbean light, recalling the days when Havana was the jewel in the Spanish Crown, its harbor full of galleons loaded with South American silver.

For many years after the Revolution turned its attentions to the impoverished countryside, the city didn't see a lick of paint, but serious attempts have now been made to stem the tropical decay. The partly Unesco-funded renovation of 17th-century Old Havana started the ball rolling in the mid-1990s, and now numerous colonial buildings have been restored to their former splendor – many of them housing museums and galleries. In 1998, work began on the salt-pitted Malecón. In the early 21st century many parts of the badly decaying Central Havana (which borders Old Havana to the west) and Vedado districts are receiving long-overdue attention.

There are two areas, linked on the sea side by the Malecón, on which most visitors will concentrate. First, **La Habana Vieja** (Old Havana), a mixture of beautifully renovated squares and buildings, and narrow, noisy streets where Cubans live in cramped conditions. Second, **Vedado**, which was modeled on Miami; most of its tallest buildings are the hotels originally financed by the US mafia in the 1940s and 1950s. Here and in the other main western suburb, Miramar, farther afield, the pre-revolutionary mansions of the rich are today occupied either by Cuban families – whose homes crumble splendidly amid lush foliage – or by a number of embassy officials, foreign investors, and Cuban bureaucrats.

Havana is exhilarating, exhausting, with a neurotic, anxious edge to life. It is one of the most fascinating places on earth – a city of great paradox and tremendous presence. As well as Cuba's political and economic center, it is also the focus of Cuba's artistic life, its youth culture, and its aspirations for the future. ❑

LEFT: twilight on the Malecón. **ABOVE RIGHT:** models of Cuba's famous old cars make popular souvenirs. **ABOVE LEFT:** drums can be heard on any street corner.

Monumento a Calixto García
Malecón
Swiss Embassy
US Interests Section
PARQUE JOSE MARTI (SPORTS GROUND)
18 Casa de las Américas
Calle 3
Calle 7
Calle 5
Calle 9
Calle 11
Calle 13
Avenida Washington
Hotel Riviera, Miramar, Playa, Siboney
Estrech
Hotel Presidente
Calle 7 (Calzada)
Linea
Edificio Focsa 8
Monumento al Maine 7
Museo de la Danza
Calle 15
Avenida O
Avenida L
6 Hotel Nacional
Iglesia del Sagrado Corazón de Jesús
Calle 13
Calle 17
Hotel Victoria
Avenida M
Hotel Capri
Malecón
Calle 23
Humboldt
Linea
Calle 11
Avenida de Los Presidentes (G)
Avenida K
Avenida J
Calle 21
COPPELIA Ice Cream Park 11
Hotel St John
10
Museo Casa de Abel Santamaría 9
Hornos
Torre San Lá
Museo de Artes Decorativas 17
Avenida F
Calle 17
Calle 19
Avenida I
Avenida H
Hotel Habana Libre
Calle 25
Hotel Vedado
Príncipe
Vapor
Jovellar
Calle 15
Avenida E
Calle 27
San Lázaro
Avenida A
Parque John Lennon
Calle 15
Avenida D
Calle 17
Avenida C
(Rampa)
Universidad de La Habana 12
Julio Antonio Mella
Calzada de Infanta
Hamel 5
Concordia
19
Casa de la Amistad
VEDADO
Museo Antropológico Montané
13 Museo Napoleónico
San Francisco
Neptuno
Aramburu
San Miguel
Calle 19
Mariana Grajales
Espada
San Rafael
Calle 21
La Tropicana
Calle 23
Calle 25
Calle 27
Hospital
San Martín (San José
Paseo
Avenida B
Estadio Juan Abrahantes
Valle
CENTI (CENT
Zanja
Salud
Avenida A
Calle 29
Castillo del Príncipe
Allenda
Castillejo
Soledad
Jesús Peregrino
Calle 2
Paseo
Calzada de Zapata
Quinta de los Molinos 14
Avenida Salvador Allende (Carlos III)
Pocito
Casa de Cu de Centro H
Calle 4
Calle 6
ESTADIO RAMON FONST
Lugareño
Bruzón
Enrique Barnet (Estrella)
Xrife
Plasencia
Árbol Seco
Retiro
Subirana
Franco
Oquendo
Calle 31
CEMENTERIO DE COLÓN 20
Calle 32
Calle 35
Terminal de Omnibuses Astro
Desagüe
Peñalver
Desagüe
Teatro Nacional
Ministerio del Interior
19 de Mayo
Benjumeda
Benjumeda
C. Protestantes
Calle 47
Aranguren
Santo Tomás
Julia Borges
Calle 6
Plaza de la Revolución
15
Paseo
Legado Cultural Hispánico
Clavel
Santa Marta
Calle 39
Calle 41
16 Monumento José Martí
P. Vidal
(Zaldo)
Arroyo (Avenida Manglar)
Avenida de Colón
Avenida Carlos M. de Céspedes
Palacio de la Revolución
Territorial
Calzada de Ayestarán
Ave. 20 de Mayo
M. Abreu
San Martín
Calzada de Infanta
Pedroso
Bellavista
Panorama
Hidalgo
San Pedro
Avenida Rancho Boyeros
Ermita
Panchito Gómez
Masón
General E. Núñez
L. Ferrocarril
Amenidad
Estéve
Santa R
Lombillo
Estancia
Marino
Avenida de la Independencia
San Pedro
Auditor
San Pablo
Pedro Pérez
Universidad Campos
Estévez
Fernandú
Estación de Ferrocarriles 19 de Noviembre
Este
Factor
Estancia
Marino
Tulipán
Lombillo
Ermita
Tulipán
La Rosa
3ra
2da
1ra
Claver
San Pedro
Mariano
Pie. Vista Hermosa
CERRO
Pedroso
Patria
Estadio Latinoamericano
Cádiz
Zequeira
Romay
San Joaquín
Connill
José Martí Airport
Ayuntamiento
Unión y Ahorro
Borrego

OLD HAVANA

Restored grandeur reveals the might of Spain's most precious colonial city, but Old Havana is more than a living museum. Life on the streets is vibrant and noisy, and just as interesting as the fine architecture

La Habana Vieja, **Old Havana**, is the city's vibrant beating heart, and this is where most visitors to Cuba spend the first day or two of their visit – a tremendous place to begin any vacation.

The compact grid of narrow colonial streets, graceful squares, and aristocratic mansions that make up Old Havana was, for some 350 years, the entire city. It was only in the 1860s that the massive city walls were knocked down and *habaneros* began distinguishing the district as "old." For many years, the area was allowed to languish – which was a blessing in disguise, since it meant Havana escaped the Disneyland-style restoration of some other colonial Caribbean cities. Castro's government prioritized putting money into developing the impoverished countryside, and left the capital untouched.

In spite of the decay, evident everywhere after such chronic neglect, the 1959 revolution saved Old Havana. The Batista regime had had the area scheduled for demolition: cars could not easily pass down the narrow streets, and more land was needed to satisfy the fever for high-rise hotels, casinos, and nightclubs.

Since the old city was placed on the Unesco World Heritage List in 1982, and with the added incentive of turning it into a major tourist attraction,

the authorities, under the directorship of the indefatigable Dr Eusebio Leal Spengler, the city historian, have embarked on an ambitious process of restoration. This has rescued sections of the city from decay, and restored many buildings to their former glory, but in other areas, buildings continue to collapse after bad weather. Still, some 150 of Havana's remaining buildings date back to the 16th and 17th centuries, 200 from the 18th, and 460 from the 19th, which makes it the best-preserved colonial city in the Americas.

Main attractions
PLAZA DE ARMAS
PLAZA DE LA CATEDRAL
MUSEO DE ARTE COLONIAL
CASA DE LA OBRA PÍA
PLAZA VIEJA
CAPITOLIO
MUSEO NACIONAL PALACIO DE BELLAS ARTES
MUSEO DE LA REVOLUCIÓN
EL MORRO
CASTILLO DE SAN CARLOS

LEFT: Havana's capitol building.
RIGHT: fishing from the Malecón wall.

Castillo de San Salvador de la Punta **30**

31 El Morro

Tunnel

32 Castillo de San Carlos de la Cabaña

Estudiantes de Medicina

29 Monumento de Máximo Gómez

Malecón

San Lázaro

Cárcel

Morro

Genios

Refugio

Crespo

Colón

Consulado

Industria

Trocadero

Paseo de Martí (Prado)

Ánimas

Virtues

Hotel Mercure Sevilla

Fábrica de Tabacos La Corona

Museo de la Revolución

Granma

28

Agramonte

27 Museo Nacional Palacio de Bellas Artes: Arte Cubano

Edificio Bacardí

Hotel Plaza

Neptuno

Hotel Inglaterra

24

Sa Rafael

PARQUE CENTRAL

Gran Teatro de la Habana

23

San Martín

San Rafael

25 Museo Nacional Palacio de Bellas Artes: Arte Universal

El Floridita

26

Agramonte (Zulueta)

Avenida de Bélgica (Monserrate)

Bernaza

Cristo

Villegas

Aguacate

22 Capitolio

Dragones

PARQUE DE LA FRATERNIDAD

Máximo Gómez (Monte)

Corrales

Apodaca

Gloria

Aponte

Cienfuegos

Cárdenas

Factoría

Misión

Somerūelos

Suárez

Diaria

Estación Central de Ferrocarril

Mercado Agropecuario

Egido (Av. de Bélgica)

Curazao

Picota

Museo Nacional de la Música

Palacio de la Artesanía

Peña Pobre

Cuarteles

Avenida de las Misiones

Iglesia del Santo Angel Custodio

Chacón

Tejadillo

Habana

Aguiar

Empedrado

PARK CERVANRWS

San Juan de Dios (Progreso)

O'REILLY

LA

HABANA

VIEJA

Obrapía

Lamparilla

Amargura

Brasil (Teniente Rey)

Muralla

Compostela

Sol

Porvenir

Luz

Anfiteatro de La Habana

PARQUE INFANTIL

Avenida del Puerto (Carlos Manuel Céspedes)

PARQUE LUZ Y CABALLERO

Tacón

Cuba

Centro Wifredo Lam

La Bodeguita del Medio

6

Plaza de la Catedral

7

Museo Alejo Carpentier

5 Museo de Arte Colonial

4 Catedral de La Habana

Museo de Arqueología

3 Castillo de la Real Fuerza

Casa de Lombillo

Palacio del Segundo Cabo

2 El Templete

Palacio de los Capitanes Generales

1

Plaza de Armas

Hotel Santa Isabel

Museo de Ciencias Naturales

Palacio de Turismo

Hotel Ambos Mundos

8

Obispo

CADECA

Casa de la Obra Pía

12

9 Casa de los Árabes

Museo Numismático

Depósito de los Automóviles

10

Iglesia y Convento de Santa Teresa

Casa de África **11**

Casa Guayasamín

Baratillo

Lonja del Comercio

(OLD

HAVANA)

Iglesia de Santo Cristo del Buen Viaje

Casa de la Cultura

Museo Histórico de las Ciencias Carlos J. Finlay **17**

15

Museo de Arte Religioso **13**

Plaza de San Francisco

Convento de San Francisco de Asís

Mercaderes

Oficios

Churruca

Centro de Desarrollo de las Artes Visuales

Plaza Vieja **16**

Cámara Oscura (Edificio Gómez Villa)

La Casona

San Ignacio

14 Museo de Ron

Santa Clara

Inquisidor

San Pedro

Regla

Iglesia y Convento de Belén

Convento de Santa Clara **18**

Acosta

Jesús María

Merced

Iglesia Parroquial del Espíritu Santo **19**

Iglesia de la Merced **20**

Damas

21 Casa Natal de José Martí

Conde

Leonor Pérez (Paula)

San Isidro

Velazco

Antigua Iglesia de San Francisco de Paula

Desamparado

Estación de La Coubre

Fundición

★ Muralla de La Habana

Canal de Entrada

Casablanca

N

Old Havana

0   200 m

0   200 yds

The restoration of the island's most historical site resulted in demographic changes in what was once one of the liveliest *barrios* (neighborhoods) in the city. People were moved out of Old Havana in their thousands, their homes becoming cafés, restaurants, hotels, and museums. Most were re-housed in the less picturesque (but far more comfortable) projects of Alamar that disfigure the city vista east of El Morro. As a result, the well-kept and well-policed streets and squares have lost much of their appeal, becoming unnaturally quiet, especially at night. However, current thinking has become more sensitive to social change, and there are now attempts to allow people to remain in or return to the renovated buildings.

Vestiges of the life that filled Old Havana can still be seen in the grid of largely unrestored streets between Calle Brasíl (Teniente Rey) and the train station, where hundreds of families inhabit waterless, crumbling mansions. Music blares from every window, washing hangs from balconies, boys practice baseball shots, scraggy dogs scavenge for food, and life is lived outdoors to escape the heat of crowded rooms in which air conditioning is not an option. Catch it while you can – it may soon be gone.

The heart of the Old City

The **Plaza de Armas** is Havana's oldest square, and the best place to begin any walking tour of the city. In the evening, it is lit by antique filigree lamps, and on many nights an orchestra plays in the open air. It is the focus for much of the street life of the restored city, and is surrounded by cafés, bars, and restaurants, such as the Café La Mina. In the center of the leafy square is a statue of Carlos Manuel de Céspedes, rebel president and leader of the first War of Independence in the 1860s. A second-hand book market, which sells revolutionary literature in various languages, is held here (Wed–Sat 9am–6pm); and you will often see costumed troupes

of entertainers – stilt-walkers, dancers, and drummers – performing here.

The majestic building on the west side of the plaza is the **Palacio de los Capitanes Generales ❶** (Palace of the Captain-Generals), perhaps the finest example of Baroque architecture in Havana. Completed in 1780, this was home to the Spanish Governor until independence, and of the US Military Governor for the few years thereafter. Cuban presidents lived here until 1917, when they moved to the Capitolio and this became the mayor's office.

Today the palace houses the **Museo de la Ciudad** (City Museum, Tacón 1, between Obispo and O'Reilly; tel: 7-861-5779; daily 9am–7.30pm, last tour 5pm; charge), which has by far the most lavish of Havana's many collections of colonial artifacts. You can visit independently but you get to see more if you take the guided tour. Keep an eye out for the machete of independence fighter General Antonio Maceo, and the dining room with 400 plates hanging on the walls. The King of Spain's Hall was kept constantly ready in case His Majesty ever decided to inspect

La Giraldilla on the Castillo de la Real Fuerza is a symbol of Havana.

BELOW: entertainers take a break in the Plaza de Armas.

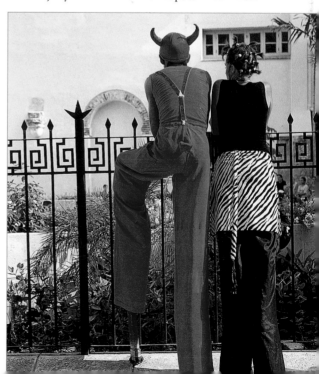

Havana, though no monarch ever did so. The courtyard garden is delightful, hung with vines and bougainvillea, with a statue of Christopher Columbus at its center.

Nearby, on the south side of the Plaza de Armas, is the **Museo de Ciencias Naturales** (Museum of Natural History; Obispo 61 between Baratillo and Oficios; tel: 7-863-2687; Tue–Fri 9.30am–5.30pm, Sat–Sun 9.30am–4.30pm; charge). Working with the American Museum of Natural History in New York, it has become far more user-friendly of late. Among its wide collection of flora and fauna is a beautiful exhibition of Cuban snails.

At the plaza's northeast corner is **El Templete ❷**, a Doric-style temple with three large paintings by French artist Jean-Baptiste Vermay inside (Baratillo 1 between O'Reilly and Narciso López). One canvas is said to be the first in Cuba to portray black and white people in close company. A column marks the spot where the city was refounded in 1519 as "La Villa de San Cristóbal de la Habana," with a Mass being said under the sacred ceiba tree.

The original tree was uprooted by a hurricane in 1828 and replacements have been planted several times. The current descendant is still credited with magical powers, partly because ceibas are considered sacred to the Yoruba religion (on which Santería is based). During an annual festival on November 16, *habaneros* celebrate that first Mass: thousands of people fill the square, and often wait many hours to fulfill a ritual – circling the tree three times and placing coins at its roots to bring good luck in the coming year. Visitors to the temple are encouraged to do the same.

Nearby stands the beautiful **Hotel Santa Isabel**, which was originally built in the 18th century as the Palacio del Conde de Santovenia; a ruin for many years, it has now been restored to five-star status (*see page 341*), and is one of the nicest in the city.

Across the street from El Templete is the **Castillo de la Real Fuerza ❸** (Tue–Sun 9.30am–5pm; charge), the oldest building in Havana. This powerful fortress, complete with drawbridges, iron cannon, and murky green moat, was built on the orders of Felipe II after the city was sacked by pirates, and was completed in 1577.

Topping its tower is the city's symbol, the bronze figure of **La Giraldilla de la Habana** (a replica, in fact – the original is in the Museo de la Ciudad). Called Iñez de Bobadilla, she was the wife of conquistador Hernando de Soto, who left Cuba to search Florida for the fountain of youth. Instead, he found only miserable death. La Giraldilla spent every afternoon for four years in the tower, watching for his return. From the roof there are good views of the harbor.

The impressive Baroque building on the northwest side of the square is the **Palacio del Segundo Cabo**, which was the headquarters of the Spanish vice-governor in colonial times. It has a beautiful courtyard, and houses the Instituto del Cubano del Libro, and a small bookstore.

Plaza de la Catedral

Two blocks north is the **Plaza de la Catedral**. This beautiful square was once a rather seedy place, known as Plazuela de la Ciénaga (Little Swamp Square). It was the place where the city's rainwater drained, and was once dominated by the 16th-century Zanja Real or "Royal Ditch" *(see page 156)*. The site of a fish market before construction began in the 18th century, it was the last square to be built in Old Havana.

It is named for the Baroque **Catedral de La Habana ❹** (Empedrado corner of San Ignacio; tel: 7-861-7771; Mon–Fri 10am–3pm, Sat 11am–2pm, Sun Mass 9.30am–noon; free, but small charge to go up the tower), which dominates the square and forms part of the most harmonious collection of buildings in the city.

Officially termed the Catedral de la Virgen María de la Concepción Inmaculada, but better known as the church of Havana's patron saint, San Cristóbal, the building was finally finished in 1777, after several setbacks. It was begun as a church by the Jesuits in 1748, but was halted when King Carlos III ordered them out of Cuba in 1767, and gained cathedral status only in 1793. There are bells in both of the towers: the shorter tower has a bell from the Cuban city of Matanzas; the taller one, a bell from Spain. At midnight on New Year's Eve, the cathedral bells ring and crowds gather to rap at the great timber doors for luck in the new year. The interior holds an altar of Carrara marble inlaid with gold, silver, and onyx.

For many years the cathedral held the supposed ashes of Columbus, though most people now believe they were those of his son, Diego. Brought from Santo Domingo in 1796, they were returned to Spain after Cuba won independence in 1899.

Colonial homes

On the east side of the square is the **Casa de Lombillo**, built in 1741. The former mansion of a Cuban slave trader, it housed Cuba's first post office, and is now the headquarters of Dr Eusebio Leal Spengler, the city historian. Beside the Casa de Lombillo is

Ornate knocker on the door of Havana's cathedral.

BELOW: Havana's 18th-century cathedral.

Sign at the entrance to the Museo de Arte Colonial.

BELOW: marble statue of a sleeping boy at the Museo de Arte Colonial.

the **Casa del Marqués de Arcos**, built in 1742 for Cuba's royal treasurer and now an art gallery.

Directly opposite the cathedral is another beautifully restored colonial building, the **Palacio de los Condes de Casa Bayona**. Constructed in 1720 for Governor General Chacón, it houses the **Museo de Arte Colonial** ❺ (San Ignacio 22, corner Empedrado; tel: 7-862-6440; daily 9.30am–5pm; charge), which is packed with a variety of artifacts from four centuries of colonial rule. Most of the rooms, centered on a blue-and-yellow colonial courtyard shaded by a huge palm tree, are open to the public, and are furnished to give an idea of the lifestyle of a wealthy Havana family in the 19th century.

There is one room dedicated to the city's famous *vitrales*, the stained-glass windows and panels that are a Cuban specialty, including the distinctive swing doors known as *mámparas*. Note also the superb wooden **Mudéjar** (Arab-inspired) ceilings upstairs, known as *alfarjes (see pages 170–1)*.

Just off the southwest corner of the square is the **Callejón de Chorro**, a tiny cul-de-sac where a wonderfully restored Art Nouveau building houses the **Taller Experimental de Gráfica** (Experimental Workshop of Graphic Arts). Here you will find good-quality silk screening and printing for sale, and you can often watch local artists at work in the studios.

Next around the square is the **Casa de Baños** (Bathhouse), rebuilt in 1909 over a 19th-century original; the water was fed directly into the baths from the Zanja Real water ditch. A plaque marks the spot. Today, the building houses the **Galería Manuel** which sells excellent art, clothes, and Tiffany-style lamps. Next door, taking up most of the west of the square, is **El Patio** restaurant. This beautiful colonial building was formerly the **Casa de los Marqueses de Aguas Claras**, the 16th-century former home of Governor General Gonzalo Pérez de Ángulo. Outside, a talented house salsa band plays sets for those sipping cool *mojitos* on the terrace or at tables and chairs set in the floodlit square. Inside, the palm-filled courtyard is the setting for a formal

Restoration

Visitors to Old Havana should bear in mind that the huge amount of restoration work going on in the city may mean that some of the sights they wish to see are closed for renovation – a process that may be short-lived or may take several years to complete. Similarly, some of the places under restoration at the time of writing may once again be open. The process is a fascinating one, as buildings that were under wraps and encased in scaffolding, billowing building dust, emerge in a pristine state. A splendid book about the restoration program, highly illustrated with photographs showing buildings before and after they were rescued from collapse, can be found in the bookstore in the Palacio del Segundo Cabo in the Plaza de Armas, and the one in Calle Obispo, just off the same plaza.

and somewhat overpriced restaurant, where you may be serenaded with music from the grand piano if there's no competition from the salsa band.

Art and artesanía

Farther along, next to the cathedral, in a pretty, pinkish building, is the **Centro Wifredo Lam ❻** (San Ignacio 22, corner Empedrado; tel: 7-861-2096; Mon–Fri 10am–5pm; free), a cultural center dedicated to one of Cuba's most famous 20th-century artists (1902–82). It exhibits the works of artists from Cuba and the rest of the world, and is one of the venues for the Havana Arts Biennial, which has been running since 1984.

Calle Empedrado

Leading off the Plaza de la Catedral to the east along Calle Empedrado, you come to the **Museo de Arqueología** (Tacón 12 between Empedrado and O'Reilly; tel: 7-861-4469; Tue–Sat 9am–5pm, Sun 9.30am–1pm; charge), in a mansion once owned in the 18th century by a freed slave, Juana Carvajal, who inherited it from her owner,

Lorenza Carvajal. The museum contains both Cuban and Peruvian archeological finds, while outside, on the corner of Tacón, Empedrado, and Oficios, you can see an archeological dig with remnants of the old sea wall and the Boquete fish market.

West of the cathedral, Calle Empedrado's first main sight is the famous bar and restaurant, best known for its Hemingway connections, **La Bodeguita del Medio ❼**, which started life in 1942 as a grocery store. The story is that poets and writers from a nearby print shop used to drop by to check their galleys here, so the owner first offered a few drinks, then lunch. Gradually, more and more tables were set up, until the place became the epicenter of Havana's bohemian life, frequented by talented writers such as Alejo Carpentier and Nicolás Guillén. Cuba's national drink, the *mojito*, was perfected here.

Today, La Bodeguita is still informal and atmospheric, although the only Cuban bohemians here are likely to be working as waiters. Photos and memorabilia from famous diners clutter the

BELOW: Restaurant El Patio in the Plaza de la Catedral.

Many of Havana's buses are school vehicles, obtained from other countries when they went out of service. You will notice that many still have the words "Escoliers" or "Schulbus" on the front.

walls, which have been tattooed with so many signatures that they are almost black. A sign over the bottles in the front bar was supposedly written and signed by regular customer Ernest Hemingway: "*My Mojito in La Bodeguita, My Daiquirí in El Floridita.*" Not perhaps, his most profound statement, but typically pithy, and a whole lot less banal than some other people's contributions to the great graffiti debate that plasters the bar's walls. According to Tom Miller in *Trading With the Enemy (see page 375)*, it was a hoax anyway, made up by Papa's drinking pal Fernando Campoamor to attract customers. If so, it has certainly worked: from morning to closing, the barman can't pour out *mojitos* fast enough. Errol Flynn was another frequent visitor, but nowadays the mix is mainly camera-toting tourists and *jineteros* (hustlers).

Further along on the same side of the street is the lovely **Museo Alejo Carpentier** (Empedrado 215 between Cuba and San Ignacio; tel: 7-861-3667; Mon–Fri 8.30am–4.30pm; free), dedicated to the Cuban writer (1904–80). The house, also called the Casa de la Condesa de la Reunión, built in 1870, has a lovely central courtyard and contains many interesting artifacts. The house and contents were donated by Carpentier's widow (along with the rights to all his royalties), to be used as a museum run by a non-governmental, non-profit organization.

One block south along Calle Cuba is **Calle O'Reilly**, named after a Spaniard with Irish ancestry, Alejandro O'Reilly, who was the first Spanish governor after the island was handed back by the British in 1763. A plaque on the corner of Tacón reads "Cuba and Ireland: Two island peoples in the same seas of struggle and hope."

Opulent Calle Obispo

Calle Obispo is one of the best-known and most pleasant streets in Old Havana: it was the first street in the old city to be pedestrianized and restored. It is also one of the busiest, and contains a number of places visitors will find useful (*see margin tip*). One classic 1920 guidebook to Havana likens Obispo's open-air stores to caves, with windows full of "diamonds and Panama hats, tortoise shells, Canary Island embroidery and perfumery." Café windows were stacked with chocolate and almond cakes, wine stores offered Russian liqueurs in miniature glass bears.

Things have changed a lot since the 1920s, but though Havana is still far from being a consumer paradise, many expensive-looking stores have opened, all selling goods for *pesos convertibles* (known as CUCs), at prices well out of the reach of all but a handful of Cubans – even those who have access to convertible currency. They stock everything from designer clothes to bed linen and smart sunglasses, although there are still a few, but dwindling, Cuban peso stores with almost nothing for sale. You can also see, and buy, the work of local artists displayed in small upstairs rooms or the spaces they rent at the front of private houses.

The famous pharmacy, **Drogería Johnson** (on the corner of Aguiar), suf-

BELOW: lots of artists have studios in Calle Obispo and the surrounding streets.

fered a serious fire, and is now being refurbished, a process that looks set to take some time. No doubt it will eventually look as good as before, with polished mahogany benches and ceramic medicine jars. **Farmacia Taquechel** (Obispo 155 between Mercaderes and San Ignacio) dates back to 1896 and has already been restored, with its floor-to-ceiling mahogany shelves supporting beautiful porcelain jars containing herbal remedies and potions.

Another wonderful old pharmacy, **Sarrá**, on the corner of Compostela and Brasil (also called Teniente Rey), has also been refurbished and returned to its original state, as part of the city restoration program.

Another Hemingway haunt

Heading back down Obispo toward Plaza de Armas, you pass the **Hotel Ambos Mundos** ❽ (No. 153). For CUC$2 you can visit room 511 where Ernest Hemingway wrote *For Whom the Bell Tolls*: the room is tidily kept, with an antique typewriter (though not Ernesto's) and several copies of 1930s US magazines. The rooftop bar

is a regular stop on the tour-group trail. The hotel has been extensively refurbished and has a wonderful piano bar in the lobby. Opposite the hotel hangs a bell marking the original site of the University of Havana, founded here in January 1728. This bell originally tolled to signal the beginning of students' classes.

South along Calle Oficios

The next, cobbled section of Obispo leads back to the Plaza de Armas. South out of the plaza on Calle Oficios, is the **Casa de los Árabes** ❾ (Oficios 16 between Obispo and Obrapía; Tue–Sat 9am–5pm, Sun 9am–1pm; free). A surprising number of Cubans are of Middle Eastern origin and this beautiful colonial mansion celebrates Arab culture. On the first floor is a small museum of costumes, tiles, and carpets. Upstairs is a beautiful, tiled fountain, where worshipers wash before attending prayers in the adjoining one-room mosque. A knowledgable and friendly curator will unlock the upstairs rooms and take you in. His little tour is given free, but a donation is much appre-

WHERE

On Obispo you will find an Infotur office (between Bernaza and Villegas) and an Infotur kiosk (corner of San Ignacio), as well as the Etecsa office (corner of Habana) with phone kiosks and internet access; and a branch of Cadeca (between Aguiar and Habana) for exchange facilities and ATMs. For more details on all of these, see the A–Z section.

BELOW: there are plenty of public phones, but making a call isn't always easy.

Stained-glass mediopuntos are one of the loveliest features of Havana architecture.

ciated. Next door is a restaurant, Al Medina, in which you can eat *tabbouleh* and *hummous* and other eastern dishes in a pretty courtyard *(see page 167)*.

Across the street is the **Depósito de los Automóviles** ❿ (Car Museum; Oficios 13 corner Justiz; tel: 7-863-9942; Tue–Sun 9am–7pm; charge) – although just about any street in Havana could claim this title. Here resides a fabulous collection of venerable roadsters and limos, including vehicles in which revolutionary young bloods like Camilo Cienfuegos and Celia Sánchez would tour around Havana on affairs of state.

On the corner of Oficios and Obrapía is the **Hostal Valencia**, the first colonial home in Old Havana to be converted into a hotel. Its rooms are grouped around a vine-draped courtyard with a pleasant bar and a restaurant. While a lovely place to stay, the hotel is regularly invaded by sightseers during the day.

Around Obrapía

BELOW: Art Deco ornamentation on the Barardí building.

Turn right into Calle Obrapía and you pass the **Casa de Oswaldo Guayasamín** (Obrapía 111 between Mercaderes and Oficios; tel: 7-861-3843; Tue–Sat 9am–4.45pm, Sun 9am–1pm; free), the house of one of Latin America's foremost 20th-century artists. Though Ecuadorean by nationality, Guayasamín (1919–99) always had a close affinity with Cuba, and belonged to the left-leaning artistic community that found inspiration here. There are a few original paintings in the house, which mainly stages temporary exhibitions. The third of four portraits Guayasamín painted of his friend, Fidel Castro, can be seen in the Fundación La Naturaleza y el Hombre in Miramar *(see page 189)*.

Farther along Obrapía is the **Casa de Africa** ⓫ (Obrapía 157; tel: 7-861-5798; Tue–Sat 9am–5pm, Sun 9am–1pm; charge), with an impressive display of African artifacts, many of them donated by the city's African embassies. The third floor is dedicated to the Afro-Cuban religions of Santería, Abakuá, and Palo Monte *(see pages 82–5)*.

Opposite, at No. 158, is the delightful lemon-yellow **Casa de la Obra**

Art Deco

While Old Havana is famous for its colonial architecture, there are some remarkable examples of the Art Deco style, worth seeking out during a tour of the old city. On Avenida de las Misiones stands the beautiful Edificio Bacardí, an extravagant confection topped with the statue of a giant bat, which was the Bacardí family emblem. Formerly the headquarters of the Bacardí Rum Company, which was based in Cuba until the family fled the island in the early 1960s, the building, dating from 1929, is a strange mixture of Swedish granite, Cuban limestone, tiles and terracotta, resembling a giant three-dimensional mosaic. You can get a great view of this landmark building from the roof terrace of the Hotel Plaza on the northeast corner of the Parque Central.

Pía ⓬ (tel: 7-861-3097; temporarily closed for renovation), once the home of the Calvo de la Puerta family. The *obra pía* (pious act) commemorates Martín Calvo de la Puerta's action in providing dowries for five orphan girls every year. The imposing doorway leads into a creeper-strewn courtyard and one of Old Havana's finest colonial mansions. Built in 1665 and enlarged in the 1700s, the building's best rooms are upstairs.

Highlights include the rare *cenefas* – painted floral borders – on the staircase, and the elegant, open-sided dining room. On the roof are the small rooms where the family's slaves were housed. A room on the first floor is dedicated to Alejo Carpentier, housing some of his photographs and personal effects, and his car, a Volkswagen Beetle.

A waterfront square

Walking in the rest of the Old City can be pleasant in any direction. Returning to the Hostal Valencia and walking south along Oficios brings you to another historic square, the **Plaza de San Francisco**. At its center is the Fuente de los Leones (Lion Fountain), built in 1836, and on one side the immense and refurbished business center in a former commodities market, the **Lonja del Comercio**. The main landmark here, however, is the **Convento de San Francisco de Asís ⓭** (daily 9am–6pm; charge).

First built in 1608 and rebuilt in 1737, San Francisco has a 40-meter (130ft) bell tower that is one of the tallest on the continent and was once Havana's best lookout for pirates. The building was taken over by the British in 1762–3 and, as it had been used for Protestant services, Catholic *habaneros* would never again worship in it. Since the 1840s, it has been a customs office, a post office, and a warehouse. Its two cloisters house a **Museo de Arte Religioso** (Museum of Religious Art). One of the strangest exhibits is the pickled remains of Teodoro, a Franciscan monk, in jars set into the left side

of the church. The beautiful cloisters are perhaps more interesting than the items on display. The Basílica Menor is now a venue for classical recitals, often held in the early evening.

If you continue a short way south along the waterfront you will reach the **Museo de Ron ⓮** (Av. del Puerto 262 between Sol and Muralla; tel: 7-861-8051; Mon–Thur 9am–5pm, Fri–Sun 9am–4pm; guided tours; charge), one of the most fascinating museums in the city. The tour takes you through the whole process of rum production and ends with sampling and an opportunity to buy. The highlight for many people is the extensive model railway running around a model of a sugar refinery. The adjoining Havana Club bar is wood paneled and appealing, and sometimes has live music. There is also an art gallery exhibiting contemporary Cuban artists' work.

Calle Mercaderes

Stretching away from Plaza de San Francisco on all sides are newly restored cobbled roads and freshly painted mansions, many of them now

WHERE

Running from the northern end of Plaza de San Francisco is Calle Baratillo where there is a sculpture garden founded in memory of Diana, Princess of Wales. Behind the Convento de San Francisco there is another garden, this one in honor of Mother Teresa of Calcutta.

BELOW:
Plaza de San Francisco flower girls.

This historic square takes its name from the adjacent 16th-century Convento de San Francisco de Asís.

BELOW RIGHT:
bronze statue of El Caballero de Paris.

cafés, stores, or art galleries. Walking west along Calle Brasil (Teniente Rey) where you can see excavated parts of the old watercourse, the Zanja Real, you reach the Plaza Vieja, and off to the right runs the traffic-free **Calle Mercaderes** ⓯, one of the prettiest and best-restored streets in the old city.

Mercaderes houses the **Museo de Chocolate** – really a café with displays related to chocolate making and consumption, which serves cups of delicious, thick, pure chocolate. Lining up in temperatures of 35°C (95°F) to drink cups of hot chocolate in an air-conditioned interior may seem odd, but it's worth it.

At No. 117, you'll find one of the many elegant stores springing up in Old Havana – the **Tienda de Los Navegantes**, beautifully fitted out in polished wood, which sells maps and navigation charts, both old and new. The **Casa del Tabaco** (Tue–Sat 10am–5pm; free) is a fascinating little museum, well worth a quick visit. Many of the exhibits were donated by the world's most famous ex-smoker, Fidel Castro himself. Notice the cigar box in the shape of the house where Castro was born. You can also buy cigars fresh from a large humidor. Then there is the **Maqueta de la Habana Vieja** – a scale model of the old city; a little garden with a statue of Simón Bolívar, and the **Casa de Simón Bolívar**, funded by the Venezuelan Government, where music is played in a blue-and-white courtyard.

Plaza Vieja

Back now to **Plaza Vieja** ⓰ (Old Plaza), built in the 1500s to create a space for bullfights and fiestas, and once one of Old Havana's principal squares. A famous fountain with four dolphins once stood here, but it fell victim to 1930s "modernization." For decades an underground parking lot ruined any chance the square had of being picturesque, while the surrounding buildings crumbled. But this has all changed and, with the exception of one building, where work is still in progress, the renovations are now complete. The plaza is again one of the most beautiful in Havana, and a place where children are brought to play ball games.

El Caballero de Paris

Outside the Convento de San Francisco is a statue of a man nicknamed El Caballero de Paris (The Gentleman of Paris). There are many stories attached to this figure, but the most commonly accepted is that he was a man who became insane while in prison in the 1920s, falsely accused of theft. (In other versions he was incarcerated simply because he *was* insane – something that used to happen under General Machado's regime.) On his release he wandered the streets of Havana, wearing a flowing cloak even in the hottest weather, never begging even when destitute, and distributing flowers and feathers to passers-by. He became a much-loved figure in the city, which erected this monument in his memory. You will often see people stroking the statue's prominent beard, which is said to bring good luck. The beard has been rubbed to a shiny gold, as has one of the elegant fingers on his left hand.

There are also a number of explanations given for his unusual name: while it is agreed that he did not come from Paris, theories range from one that his French wife-to-be died in a shipwreck while on her way from France to Cuba, to the more mundane explanation that he had worked in a Havana restaurant called the Paris.

El Caballero died in a psychiatric hospital in 1985, at the age of 86, and is buried within the church.

On the northeast corner, on the roof of a yellow-and-white wedding cake of a building, is the **Cámara Oscura** (Teniente Rey corner Mercaderes; tel: 7-866-4461; daily 9am–5.20pm; charge). An elevator takes you to the eighth floor, where there are amazing views over the city, and the camera obscura hones in on details of nearby buildings as well as the general vista.

On the southeastern corner of the plaza, the amazing Art Nouveau **Hotel Palacio Viena**, built in 1906, was for a long time a *solar* – a residential hotel where many families lived cheek by jowl – but is currently undergoing much-needed restoration.

To the south of the square is the former home of the Conde de Ricla, a Spanish captain general, now an art gallery known as **La Casona** (Muralla 107 corner San Ignacio; tel: 7-861-8544; www.galeriascubanas.com; Tue–Sat 10am–5.30pm). This fine 18th-century colonial house has various galleries of contemporary art and glasswork, and some rare murals on the stairway. Its trio of *mediopuntos* is among the best examples of stained-glass windows in Havana. The building also houses the **Galería Plaza Vieja**, which specializes in Afro-Cuban works.

On the southwestern corner of the square is a restaurant-bar, the **Cervecería Taberna de la Muralla**, with its own organic microbrewery, very popular after a hot day sightseeing around the city. On the western side, in the colonial Casa de las Hermanas Cárdenas, is the **Centro de Desarrollo de las Artes Visuales** (San Ignacio 352, between Teniente Rey and Muralla; tel: 7-862-9295; Tue–Sat 10am–5pm; charge), which focuses on contemporary works by Cuban and other Latin American artists.

Just to the northeast of the plaza is the **Museo Histórico de las Ciencias Carlos J. Finlay** ⑰ (Calle Cuba 460 between Amargura and Brasil; tel: 7-863-4824; currently closed for renovation), a museum dedicated to the history of science in Cuba, named after the doctor who discovered the vector for yellow fever, once a massive killer, but something that has now been eradicated. The museum includes an elegant neoclassical lecture theater

The broad expanse of the Plaza Vieja has become a playground for children.

BELOW: the Plaza Vieja has been returned to its former glory.

Architectural detail of one of the city's colonial churches.

(where Albert Einstein once gave a lecture) and an atmospheric 19th-century pharmacy.

A trio of churches

Heading south down San Ignacio and turning right on Santa Clara you come to the recently renovated **Convento de Santa Clara** ⓲ (Cuba 610 between Luz and Sol; tel: 7-861-3335; Mon–Fri 8.30am–5pm; charge), an enormous 18th-century former convent that was renowned as a refuge for dowerless girls. It contains a vast, tree-filled main courtyard, the Clarisa nuns' cells, and lovely cloisters.

There is a small *hostal*, used mainly by educational groups, and still partially under renovation. The convent now houses a conservation institute where all the restoration techniques being utilized in the renovation of Old Havana are honed – including carpentry, the restoration of old tiles, and the making of new ones. All the works in the old town have been undertaken using, wherever possible, the same materials and techniques as used by the original craftsmen.

South of here, on Calle Acosta, is the delightful **Iglesia Parroquial del Espíritu Santo** ⓳ (Mon–Sat 8am–noon, 3–6pm, Sun 9am–noon), one of Havana's oldest churches. Built in the 1670s as a religious retreat for "free negroes," this fully renovated gem displays Moorish influence on its facade and the cedar ceiling, and features catacombs whose roofs are supported by tree trunks. The chapel vault has a mural (sadly almost erased by the passage of time) depicting the Dance of Death.

A little farther down Calle Cuba you will reach the lavish **Iglesia de la Merced** ⓴ (Mon–Sat 8am–noon, 3–5pm, Sun 8am–noon), dating from 1746. This is one of Havana's most famous churches as it is dedicated to Santa Mercedes, who becomes Obatalá in the Santería faith. On September 24, hundreds of worshipers – often wearing white (white is Obatalá's color) or carrying white flowers – congregate here to pay tribute. And at any time of the year, you may see white-clad Santería devotees worshiping here. Note the flower sellers all around, for flowers are a common gift of thanks for requests granted by the saints. The church itself is dark and ornate with wonderful trompe l'œil frescoes and a peaceful, leafy cloister.

Along the waterside

The atmosphere changes as you hit the busier streets on the fringes of Old Havana. This is not an area that attracts many visitors, but there are a few sights worth seeing if you have time to spare.

By the harbor, where Calle San Ignacio meets the dock road (here called Desamparado), is a pretty little former church, now beautifully renovated, the **Antigua Iglesia de San Francisco de Paula** (Mon–Fri 9am–5pm, Sat 9am–1pm). It has an interesting collection of modern art with a Christian theme and some fine stained glass. A variety of classical concerts is held here on some evenings, and it is also the base for the musical group called Ars Longa.

BELOW: Iglesia Parroquial del Espíritu Santo.

Farther along the waterfront you come to some interesting remnants of the old city walls, the **Cortina de La Habana**. Slaves worked for 23 years to build these walls, which were 1.5 meters (5ft) thick and more than 10 meters (30ft) tall. The first walls were begun in 1674, but were altered and expanded up until the late 18th century. They ringed the old city until 1863, when they were torn down to allow for expansion.

Nearby stands a stark, dramatic monument to the Belgian ship *La Coubre*. Carrying armaments for the Cuban Army, it blew up on March 4, 1960, killing 72 sailors and dock workers: was it an accident or – as the Castro government has always maintained – the work of the CIA?

Three blocks north up Avenida de Bélgica (Egido), on Leonor Pérez (confusingly also called Leonor Paula), is the house where Cuba's most revered figure was born. The **Casa Natal de José Martí** ㉑ (Leonor Pérez 314 between Picota and Egido; tel: 7-861-3778; Tue–Sat 9.30am–5pm, Sun 9.30am–1pm; charge) is a small, simple

house, painted yellow and blue in typical Havana style. Martí was born here in 1853 and it was his home until he was five years old.

The house contains letters, first editions, manuscripts, photos, even locks of his hair. There is sometimes a line to get in as the house is a popular place for school visits. It is worth seeing simply because Martí is such an iconic figure *(see page 51)*.

Around the corner stands the Moorish-Victorian **Estación Central de Ferrocarriles** (Central Train Station) – unmissable with its soaring twin towers.

Capital projects

Officially, the sights that follow belong in Central Havana, but they are so closely integrated with Habana Vieja that we have included them in this chapter.

From the station, follow Avenida de Bélgica (Egido) northward. This is a broad, busy street with a number of CUC stores that sell soap, shampoo, and the like to local people who have access to *convertibles*. It follows the

Serving coffee in the Café de Paris.

BELOW:
Havana girls on their way home from school.

Vintage 1950s American cab waiting for customers in front of Capitolio.

line of the old city walls north past a small farmers' market – an *agropecuario*. Turn left along Dragones to the enormous, grandiose **Capitolio** ㉒ (Paseo de Martí between San Martín and Dragones; tel: 7-861-0261, 7-863-7861; www.capitolio.cu; daily 9am–6pm; charge), which dominates the skyline all around.

Built in the 1920s as the new presidential and governmental palace, it closely resembles the design of the Capitol in Washington DC, continuing the process of Americanization begun in 1902 when the United States effectively took over from Spain as Cuba's colonial master. Before the revolution it was the home of the National Congress, but it now houses the Cuban Academy of Sciences. Guided tours run through its proud interior into the former presidential offices and halls of congress, but you can also go round on your own.

The huge bronze doors and marble floor of the domed entrance hall are impressive, as are the broad staircases, but it's a rather soulless place. There are some interesting photographs on

BELOW: view of Capitolio's impressive dome.

the walls showing the various phases of its construction.

The diamond set in the floor of the entrance hall is point zero, from which all measurements are taken in Cuba. Outside, at the foot of the grand flight of stairs, many old American cars wait to offer visitors a taxi ride, as do horse-drawn carriages and coco-taxis.

Standing next door to the Capitolio is the flamboyant **Gran Teatro de la Habana** ㉓ (Paseo de Martí 458; tel: 7-861-3077/5873), completed in 1837, and housing El Teatro García Lorca, where the Cuban National Ballet performs. It contains several auditoriums – the gold auditorium is grand, if surprisingly small inside, with plush red seats and a bewitching painted ceiling. The Baroque theater building also houses cultural institutions. Ballet dancers, opera singers, and theater companies rehearse here, and tours are sometimes offered. There are regular performances by the national ballet and opera companies, usually at weekends. It is well worth getting a ticket if you can.

Sightseeing in Style

Outside the Capitolio there are always a number of 1950s limousines – Buicks, Chevrolets, Packards, Chryslers. But unlike the many beat-up models you see traveling slowly and noisily around town or stopped with their hoods open while the driver works wonders with a screwdriver, these have shiny bodywork and gleaming hubcaps. They belong to Grancar, a state-owned company that specializes in taking visitors for tours around the city – or as far afield as they want to go. Driving through Havana in one of these limos is a great experience, and not as expensive as you might think, as all rates are strictly controlled. You do, however, usually get a better deal if you ring the company office (tel: 7-648-7338) rather than making an arrangement with a driver on the street.

Parque Central

The Gran Teatro occupies part of one side of the **Parque Central**, which, with its stately royal palms (many bearing tourist graffiti from the 1940s and 1950s), always seems to be buzzing with activity from early morning until midnight. In the center is a white marble statue of José Martí. The corner of the park nearest the Capitolio is called the Esquina Caliente or "Hot Corner" where men gather and debate (hotly), mainly about baseball.

Next door to the Gran Teatro is the splendid, neo-Baroque facade of the **Hotel Inglaterra** ㉔, so named because it was popular with early travelers from England. The sidewalk outside its doorways, nicknamed "the Louvre Sidewalk," has been one of the busiest spots in Havana for generations. The covered café here is a great place for people-watching, but you will get plenty of hassle from the street.

Initially, in the mid-19th century there was a two-story building here called Café y Salones de Escauriza, subsequently renamed El Louvre. This was a popular place for pro-independence

conspirators to speak, and one such occasion in 1869 prompted Spanish soldiers to open fire. Not all Spaniards were so ruthless: an officer protesting the execution of eight Cuban students in 1871 broke his sword against the door, and a plaque commemorates his bold, humanitarian gesture. The building opened as a hotel in 1875, was given a third floor in 1886, and a fourth in 1914, when it became one of the most opulent places to stay in the Americas. The Arab-influenced dining room off the lobby is still impressive.

Artistic corner

On the east side of the Parque Central is the *Arte Universal* section of the **Museo Nacional Palacio de Bellas Artes** ㉕ (San Rafael between Zulueta y Monserrate; tel: 7-861-5777; www.museonacional.cult.cu; Tue–Sat 10am–6pm, Sun 10am–2pm; charge; combined ticket available for this and the *Arte Cubano* section, *see page 163*). Housed in the old Asturian cultural center on Calle San Rafael, it contains Latin America's largest collection of antiquities, as well as works by Goya, Rubens, Velázquez,

TIP

A statistic that your Capitolio tour guide will tell you is that the bronze statue symbolizing the republic in the entrance hall is 17 meters (56ft) high, weighs nearly 50 tonnes, and is said to be the third-largest indoor statue in the world.

BELOW:
Hotel Inglaterra overlooking Parque Central.

TIP

You have to check your bags in when you go into either the Museo de la Revolución or the Bellas Artes. You are allowed to take a camera with you into the former, but they are forbidden in the latter.

Turner, Gainsborough, and Canaletto, many of which were left behind by Batista's family and cronies when they fled after the revolution.

Hemingway's bar

Just southeast of the Palacio de Bellas Artes is **El Floridita** N, made famous as Ernest Hemingway's favorite haunt (it features in his novel *Islands in the Stream*). It was frequented by the Hollywood set who came to Havana in the 1950s – Errol Flynn, Frank Sinatra, Ava Gardner, Gary Cooper, and Marlene Dietrich were all regulars. *Esquire* magazine in 1953 ranked it with the 21 Club in New York, the Ritz in Paris ,and Raffles in Singapore as one of the best bars in the world. It is claimed that the daiquirí cocktail was perfected here, though it was probably originally invented in Santiago province as an anti-malarial potion for miners. Certainly it was at El Floridita that the drink became famous, and Hemingway even invented his own version, the "daiquirí special," which is still served.

Not much else is the same as in Hemingway's day, when it was an informal, old-fashioned place, with ceiling fans and a three-piece band. Today it has been renovated and polished up into one of the most expensive restaurants in Cuba, with a life-size bronze statue of Hemingway near his favorite seat, on the far left of the original wooden bar. It still serves the best, if overpriced, daiquirís in town but, although friendly, the bar lacks the atmosphere of the Bodeguita del Medio (*see page 151*), and it is, of course, another blatant tourist trap.

The faded glory of the Prado

Running north from the Parque Central is the **Prado** (officially known as the **Paseo de Martí**), the historic, popular promenade lined with trees and lion statues, that stretches all the way to the Malecón. The Prado officially divides Central Havana from Old Havana, and forms an easy landmark in the transition between the touristy Old Town and the real city of working *habaneros*. This boulevard, with its raised walkway set with colored marble and stone, has seen better days. Construction began

BELOW RIGHT: white weddings are still as popular as ever.

Sealing Deals and Tying Knots

The Prado is important territory. The area between Colón and Refugio has become widely known as an unofficial property market. Cubans are not permitted to sell property – only to exchange it. "*Se permuta*" signs pinned to doors and balconies around the city mean the residents want to exchange their house either with another in a different area, or, more commonly, because family pressure means they want two small houses for one large one. These are more difficult to fix since almost everyone has one large house and wants two smaller ones. This means money as well as property changes hands, illegally, so people gather on the Prado to make deals. Sometimes the equivalent of thousands of dollars changes hands, in a country where the average wage translates at around US$20 a month.

At Prado No. 306, on the corner of Calle Animas, is the **Palacio de Matrimonios** (Wedding Palace), where on Monday, Wednesday, Friday and Saturday you can see wedding parties in hired tuxedos and frothy white dresses make their grand entrances and exits. Take a look inside, too, at the gilded, chandeliered luxury of this former aristocrat's palace. The non-religious ceremony has a strong socialist feel – the man promises to help his wife with housework and childcare (though few Cuban men ever do).

in the late 1700s, to build a promenade outside the old city walls, and continued until 1852 (by which time the walls had collapsed), and its buildings were once home to Havana's richest, most aristocratic families. Some of them are extraordinarily beautiful – and extraordinarily dilapidated. Renovation work is proceeding, but slowly, and there is a great deal to do.

The area began to decline in the early 20th century when the mansions of the rich were mostly turned into casinos and nightclubs. The upper levels became notorious brothels, adorned with skimpily dressed girls who would stand on the balconies to lure in custom. Now, however, it is full of ordinary people going about their daily business or simply taking a stroll. Furthermore, some of the old buildings nearby have been turned into schools, and as they have no playgrounds, you will often see the children in their red and white uniforms having sports lessons or just playing on the Prado's raised walkway. Sometimes there are small art markets or open-air concerts; it is a place where spontaneous events happen.

Take a short detour off the Prado to the ornate **Hotel Mercure Sevilla**, which was a notorious Mafia hang-out, and featured prominently in Graham Greene's *Our Man in Havana*: secret agent Hawthorne stayed in Room 501. Beautifully restored since the mid-1990s, the Sevilla has a wonderfully Spanish ambiance, with a cool lobby and a delightful blue-tiled patio café, complete with fountain.

The national art collection

Between Agramonte (Zulueta) and Avenida de las Misiones are two of Havana's most important museums, presenting two very different aspects of Cuba. The first of them, in a modernist building dating from 1954, is the excellent *Arte Cubano* section of the **Museo Nacional Palacio de Bellas Artes ㉗** (National Museum of Fine Arts; Trocadero between Zulueta and Monserrate; Tue–Sat 10am–6pm, Sun 10am–2pm;

charge; combined ticket available for this and the *Arte Universal* section, *see pages 161–2*).

The museum reopened in 2001 after five years of extensive renovation. It contains the largest collection of works by Cuban artists in the country, and the excellent 20th-century section includes pieces by Wifredo Lam, Carlos Enríquez, René Portocarrero, and Eduard Abela, well displayed in a series of interlinked air-conditioned galleries. It is generally considered the best museum in the city.

Museum of the Revolution

Directly opposite the Fine Arts Museum is the **Monumento Granma**, which is part of the **Museo de la Revolución ㉘** (Refugio between Zulueta and Monserrate, also known as Avenida de las Misiones; tel: 7-862-4091; daily 10am–5pm; charge), housed in the former presidential palace. The 18-meter (56ft) yacht *Granma* was used by Fidel, Che, and 80 other guerrillas to cross from Mexico to Cuba in 1956. The boat is painted brilliant white with green trim and set in a huge glass case

A weekend walk down the shady center of the Prado.

BELOW: geometric sculpture at the *Arte Cubano* section of the Museo Nacional Palacio de Bellas Artes.

The patio of the Museo Nacional Palacio de Bellas Artes.

BELOW: a Mariano Rodriguez painting in the *Arte Cubano* section of the Museo de Bellas Artes.

as one of the revolution's great icons. Around the yacht, in a fenced-off and closely guarded area, are other relics of the revolution: a tractor converted into a tank by rural guerrillas; an old Pontiac with a double floor for smuggling arms and documents; and the bullet-riddled delivery van used for an attack on the Presidential Palace in 1957 in an unsuccessful attempt to assassinate Batista. March 13, the anniversary of the attack, in which 35 rebels and five palace guards were killed, is commemorated each year.

There are also airplanes and a tank that were used to repulse the CIA-backed Bay of Pigs invasion (the invading boats are decorated with a skull and crossbones), and a fragment of the U2 spy plane shot down over Cuba shortly before the Missile Crisis of 1962. The star-shaped monument to the Heroes of the New Fatherland, with an eternal flame, is just like the Kremlin's master model in Moscow. Every day at 3pm a changing of the guard ceremony is held here.

The Presidential Palace was worked in and lived in by all Cuba's presidents from its completion in 1913 until 1957, when Batista built the present Palacio in what is now the Plaza de la Revolución. The delicious white-and-gold interior was created by Tiffany's of New York.

The memorabilia laid out with quasi-religious reverence in these splendid rooms offers a vivid picture of the revolution, and the earlier struggle for independence. There are blood-stained uniforms from the failed attack on the Moncada Barracks in 1953, as well as the heavy black coat that Fidel wore during his trial, when he made his famous "History will absolve me..." speech. Information panels about the exhibits all have English translations, and quite good ones, at that. Allow several hours to see it all.

The end of the road

Not far from the Presidential Palace, at the bottom of the Avenida de las Misiones, before it meets the Malecón, the **Museo Nacional de la Música** has an extensive collection of Cuban instruments, but is currently closed for renovation.

Set proudly and unmissably on an island in the middle of a swirl of traffic and parkland is the **Monumento de Máximo Gómez** ㉙, who was one of the great campaigners for Cuban independence, although he actually came from the Dominican Republic.

On the waterfront opposite stands a small 16th-century fortress, the **Castillo de San Salvador de la Punta** ㉚. Like El Morro across the water, the fortress was designed by Italian engineer Juan Bautista Antonelli during the reign of the Spanish king Felipe II. In the 17th century, to further protect the harbor against pirate incursions, a heavy chain linked the two fortifications. On the seafront there are metal floor plans of all the fortresses around the harbor.

Fortresses across the bay

From Old Havana, a tunnel dips beneath the bay to the **Castillo de los Tres Santos Reyes Magos del Morro**, which is usually known simply as **El Morro** ㉛ (daily 8am–8pm; charge – it costs less if you simply want to walk round the ramparts). This 16th-century

fortress, with 3-meter (10ft) -thick walls constructed from blocks taken from Cuba's coastal reef, took more than 40 years to complete. It still dominates the eastern skyline, especially at night when floodlit. The views from here are superb, whether around the bastion's vertiginous ramparts, back toward the city, or out to sea, from where the main **lighthouse** can be seen 33km (18 nautical miles) away. It is absolutely stunning at sunset.

The castle was once a vital part of the city's defenses. On the lower level, closer to the harbor, is the **Batería de los Doce Apóstoles** (Battery of the 12 Apostles), with each of its 12 cannons bearing one of their names. In colonial times, these guns would be fired to announce the closing of the city gates – a rite now re-enacted in the neighboring fortress of San Carlos de la Cabaña (*see page 166*).

A great chain used to run between El Morro and the Castillo de la Punta in Old Havana. The chain closed the bay to pirate ships in the days when Sir Francis Drake sailed these seas. The pirate Henry Morgan was told by

Watching the world go by in one of the many streets that have not been renovated.

BELOW LEFT AND BELOW: model of Che Guevara and view of the interior, Museo de la Revolución.

WHERE

To get to the fortresses you can take a taxi (around CUC$5), or get on any of the buses that run through the tunnel. Alternatively you can get the HabanaBusTour from the Parque Central for CUC$5, which will allow you to hop on and hop off at stops all along the line all day; the route going to Playas del Este will drop you at La Cabaña. From El Morro to the Castillo de San Carlos it's about a 20-minute walk. Travel agencies run tours here, as well.

BELOW: El Morro fortress, built to defend the city.

former English prisoners in Havana that he would need at least 1,800 men to take the city – he did not even try. Bizarrely, there are still several pieces of modern artillery directed out from El Morro toward the Straits of Florida, in symbolic defiance against a *yanqui*-inspired invasion.

There are three **museums** at El Morro castle, focusing on navigation, the history of the castle, and on pirates. You will also find one of Havana's most atmospheric restaurants, Los Doce Apóstoles, just outside the wall *(see page 168)*.

Castillo de San Carlos

The **Fortaleza de San Carlos de la Cabaña** ❸❷ (daily 9am–10pm; charge, increased 6–10pm for *El Cañonazo*) was built from 1764–74, after the departure of British invaders. It, too, has two interesting **museums**. One of them documents the fortress in colonial days, when many independence fighters were shot here. A good number of Batista's followers met the same fate after the revolution in 1959, when Che Guevara used the fortress as

his headquarters (the focus of the second museum).

In the first year of the revolution, those found guilty of such crimes as murder and torturing prisoners under the Batista regime were executed here. Bullet holes from the firing squads pepper the walls by the front gate.

At 9pm every evening, the atmospheric ceremony of the **firing of the cannon** (called *El Cañonazo*) is conducted in period military dress, in commemoration of the obsolete practice of closing the city gates. Although nowadays they only fire blanks, the noise is authentic, and the ceremony is fun, especially as local people often outnumber tourists.

Much of the fortress is in a fairly dangerous condition – there are a lot of sheer drops from the high walls, which are neither roped off nor signposted, so take care when exploring and keep a close eye on children. You will find an excellent restaurant, La Divina Pastora, at the foot of the fortress on the waterside *(see page 168)*, as well as several upscale tourist shops selling arts, crafts, and clothes. ❑

RESTAURANTS, PALADARES, BARS, AND CAFÉS

Restaurants

Price categories are for a three-course meal for one with a beer, or *mojito*. Wine puts the price up:
$ = under $25
$$ = $25–35
$$$ = over $35

Al Medina
Casa de Los Arabes,
Calle Oficios, 12, between Obrapía and Obispo
Tel: (7) 867-1041. Open daily noon–11pm. **$$**
Tasty Arabic dishes, falafel, hummous, couscous in the courtyard of a lovely old colonial mansion attached to the Casa del Arabe. The menu is padded out by Cuban dishes.

A Prado y Neptuno
Prado corner Neptuno
Tel: (7) 860-9636. Open daily noon–midnight. **$$$**
Modern restaurant opposite the Hotel Parque Central on one corner and Hotel Telégrafo on the other. The Italian chef serves good Italian food and excellent pizza, but leave room for the delicious tiramisu.

Bar Cabaña
Calle Cuba, 12, corner of Peña Pobre (by the seafront)
Tel: (7) 860-5670. Open daily 10am–midnight. **$$**
Good *criolla* and international food served in an unpretentious setting.

Café del Oriente
Calle Oficios, 112,
Plaza de San Francisco
Tel: (7) 860-6686. Open daily noon–midnight. **$$$**
This is an extremely formal restaurant, with a resident pianist and a full international menu. The food is very good, but there's not much atmosphere. Tea, coffee, or cocktails at tables in the square may be a better bet.

Café el Mercurio
Calle Oficios, corner of Plaza de San Francisco
Tel: (7) 860-6118. Open daily 9am–midnight. **$$**
Good spot for breakfasts and for light meals throughout the day – salads, omelets, etc. Particularly recommended are the ice creams and cocktails, especially the excellent *mojitos*.

Café Taberna
Calle Mercaderes, 531, corner of Brasil (Teniente Rey)
Tel: (7) 861-1637. Open daily 11am–midnight. **$$**
Rather greasy Cuban food in cheerful, atmospheric surroundings, done out in 1950s style with a Beny Moré theme. There's a tremendous band of elderly *son* and mambo specialists to serenade you while you eat. And there's dancing later on. This was the first coffee house opened when the British took Havana in 1762, and was named after its owner Juan Batista de Taberna.

Don Giovanni
Calle Tacón, 4, between Empedrado and O'Reilly.
Tel: (7) 867-1036. Open daily 10am–midnight. **$$**
Pretty blue and white balconies and reasonable Italian food. They serve pizzas, including one with lobster, mushrooms and olives.

El Castillo de Farnés
Avenida de Bélgica (Monserrate), 361, corner of Obrapía
tel: (7) 867-1030. Restaurant open daily noon–midnight; bar daily 24 hours. **$–$$**
Pictures of Fidel and Raúl adorn the bar – this is supposed to have been one of their favorite haunts and they came here with Che at 4.45am on January 9, 1959 after Castro's victory speech on arrival in Havana. There are authentic Spanish dishes on the menu. The chickpeas (*garbanzos*) with ham are a specialty and are worth trying.

El Floridita
Calle Obispo, 557, corner Monserrate
Tel: (7) 867-1300/1301. Open daily noon–1am. **$$$**
Havana's most fabled dining spot, and Hemingway's favorite for his daiquirís (the best in town, but not cheap), is elegant but dark and overpriced. You pay for the name (and the waiters' red jackets) as well as for the food. Main courses include grilled lobster, shrimp flambéed in rum, turtle steaks, and other exotica. If you just want to check it out, you could simply opt for a daiquirí at the bar.

El Mesón de la Flota
Calle Mercaderes, 257, between Amargura and Brasil (Teniente Rey)
Tel: (7) 863-3838. Restaurant open daily 11am–11pm; bar daily 24 hours. **$–$$**
A restaurant-bar in Old Havana serving authentic and delicious tapas and full Spanish-influenced

RIGHT: entertainment at La Mina.

meals. There are good Spanish wines, beer on tap, and excellent service. Flamenco performances daily. All very refreshing.

El Patio
San Ignacio, 54, Plaza de la Catedral
Tel: (7) 867-1034. Open daily noon–midnight. $$$
Go for the fabulous location, in an old colonial palace, rather than the food. You can eat either on the ground floor, surrounded by palms and serenaded from the grand piano, or upstairs in the Parillada del Marqués. Reserve a table overlooking the plaza. International menu.

Hanoi
Calle Brasil (Teniente Rey), 507, corner of Bernaza
Tel: (7) 867-1029. Open daily noon–midnight. $
Despite the name, the food is *criolla*. Lots of pork, shrimp, and rice, cheap, set three-course meals or *combinados*. Cheap cocktails, live music, and a relaxed atmosphere.

Jardín del Eden
Hotel Raquel, Calle Amargura, corner of San Ignacio
Tel: (7) 860-8280. Open daily L & D. $$
Havana's only kosher restaurant. Delicious food (no pork or seafood, of course) in the Hotel Raquel's elegant restaurant, with a chan-

delier and attractive stained-glass screens. Surprisingly reasonable prices.

La Barca
Avenida del Puerto, corner Obispo
Tel: (7) 866-8807. Open daily noon–midnight. $$$
Opposite the old yacht club overlooking the seafront road and the water, a pleasant open-air restaurant with good Spanish dishes, seafood, and steaks. Part of the Habaguanex chain and efficiently run.

La Bodeguita del Medio
Calle Empedrado, 207, off Plaza de la Catedral
Tel: (7) 867-1374. Open daily noon–midnight. $$$
Bohemian atmosphere with creole cooking in this old Hemingway haunt, but the quality of the food and service suffers due to the constant flow of tourists. Walls downstairs are decorated with the autographs of celebrities who have eaten here over the years, but the roof terrace is a more congenial place to sit. Reservations advised.

La Divina Pastora
Fortaleza de La Cabaña
Tel: (7) 860-8341. Open noon–11pm. $$$
At the foot of the Cabaña fortress, La Divina Pastora offers a stunning view of the Havana skyline. A good place for a meal or a drink before the 9pm *cañonazo (see page*

166). Among the seafood specialties is fillet of red snapper stuffed with shrimp.

La Dominica
Calle O'Reilly, corner of Mercaderes.
Tel: (7) 860-2918. Open daily noon–midnight. $$
You can sit inside or out at this lovely courtyard restaurant. Excellent pizzas and pasta and other Italian-influenced dishes. Good band.

La Lluvia de Oro
Calle Obispo, 316, corner of Habana
Tel: (7) 862-9870. Open daily 8am–early hours. $
The name means Golden Rain. This is a good place for a snack and a drink in a very local Cuban atmosphere with live (and loud) music.

La Mina
Plaza de Armas
Tel: (7) 862-0216. Open daily noon–midnight. $$$
Cuban *criolla* cooking, or sandwiches and pasta, in a restaurant with a beautiful courtyard and a broad terrace right on the Plaza de Armas. Very popular with tourists. Strolling musicians.

La Zaragozana
Monserrate, 351, between Obrapía and Obispo
Tel: (7) 867-1040. Open daily 10am–midnight. $$
Filling *criolla* and Spanish dishes, including thick bean soups, fish, and paella, but the quality is rather inconsistent. The restaurant tends to be livelier at lunch time than in the evening.

Los Doce Apóstoles
Castillo del Morro
Tel: (7) 863-8295. Open daily noon–11pm; bar 11pm–2am. $$
Next to the El Morro Fortress and named for its battery, this restaurant serves fish and pork dishes with all the trimmings, though the setting

is arguably better than the food.

Los Nardos (Sociedad Juventud Asturiana)
Paseo de Martí (Prado), 563, between Teniente Rey and Dragones
Tel: (7) 863-2985. Open daily noon–midnight. $
This is a quirky and popular place, with a busy, buzzing atmosphere. No reservations taken, so you have to wait in a well-regulated line outside till a table is free. Decorated with soccer memorabilia with trophies from the 1930s. Good wine list. Huge portions, of pork, lamb, Uruguayan beef, chicken, fish, shrimp, and lobster with all the trimmings. The service is efficient and friendly. You don't have to queue if you go to the restaurants upstairs: El Trofeo, which serves Cuban and international food, or El Asturianito, serving Cuban and Italian food, with good pizzas.

La Torre de Marfil
Calle Mercaderes, 121, between Obispo and Obrapía
Tel: (7) 867-1038. Open daily noon–midnight. $–$$
Tasty Chinese food, better than you'll find in Chinatown, in pleasant surroundings with lanterns and Chinese decorations.

Marinero El Templete
Avenida del Puerto, 12–14 corner Narciso López
Tel: (7) 866-8807. Open daily noon–midnight. $$$
Next to La Barca and under same management but slightly more elegant, up-market ,and expensive. You can eat inside or in the open air overlooking the waterfront. The food is good and you can choose from meat, fish, or lobster.

The Roof Garden
Hotel Sevilla, Calle Trocadero, 55
Tel: (7) 860-8560. Open daily

7–10.30pm. **$$$**
The food is good but the views are the reason many people come here for dinner. Panoramic vistas of Old Havana on three sides. Wonderful, elegant, candlelit ambiance, really special when they throw open the huge windows to let in the night-time breeze off the sea.

Vuelta Abajo
Hotel Conde de Villanueva, Calle Mercaderes, 202, between Lamparilla and Amargura
Tel: (7) 862-9293. Open daily L & D. **$$$**
Named after a tobacco plantation in Pinar del Río, this cool, stone-arched restaurant specializes in old *criolla* favorites, such as *pescado trapiche* – fish with ginger, and *fonguito* – streamed, seasoned plantain.

Paladares

Doña Blanquita
Paseo de Martí (Prado), 158, first floor, between Colón and Refugio
Tel: (7) 867-4958. Open daily noon–midnight. **$**
One of Havana's best-known *paladares*. The usual Cuban dishes of pork, chicken, rice, and beans, and excellent *malanga con mojo* (a *yuca*-like vegetable with garlic sauce). It's pink, kitsch, and great fun, with plastic flowers and candles on the tables. Try for a table on the sweet little balcony overlooking the Prado.

La Julia
Calle O'Reilly, 506, between Bernaza and Villegas
Tel: (7) 862-7438. Open daily noon–11pm. **$**
One of the real old-style *paladares* where you feel

as if you are eating in someone's home – although the dining room opens out onto the street. Excellent *comida criolla* – some of the best *frijoles* (fried beans) you will find – together with good prices and good service from members of a friendly family – make this a recommended choice.

La Moneda Cubana
Calle San Ignacio, 77, between O'Reilly and Empedrado
Tel: (7) 867-3852. Open daily noon–late. **$**
This very small *paladar* has four set-price menus on offer. They are the usual criolla dishes, but they are well cooked. Fish and omelets make an appearance, too. Lots of pesos and bank notes from all over the world are glued to the walls. Despite the restaurant's name, you have to pay in CUCs, not *moneda nacional*.

Bars and Cafés

Bar El Louvre, Hotel Inglaterra
Parque Central
The terrace bar is a great place for people-watching. Among other things there are good fresh fruit juices, home-made lemonade, and what some say are the best ham and cheese sandwiches in Havana (and there's internet access in the lobby). There is always a group of musicians playing, and as often as not it's *Guantanamera*.

Bar Monserrate
Avenida de Bélgica (Monserrate), 401, corner of Obrapía
Good, reasonably priced cocktails in a bar with a laid-back, local atmosphere, next door to the far more swish and expen-

sive El Floridita.

Bosque Bologna
Calle Obispo, 424
A cheerful place on this busy street, with green-painted trellises, and live music day and night.

Café de Paris
Calle San Ignacio, 202, corner of Obispo
Live music and street-style pizza, but fried chicken and fries seem most popular.

Casa de las Infusiones
Calle Mercaderes, between Obispo and Obrapía
An attractive courtyard bar where you can get a variety of infusions (herbal teas), along with soft drinks and cocktails – but no beer. Also serves snacks and light meals.

Café el Escorial
Mercaderes, 317, corner Muralla
A European-style coffee house serving different blends of coffee and a variety of cakes, with tables outside on the corner of Plaza Vieja.

Café O'Reilly
Calle O'Reilly, 203, between Cuba and San Ignacio
An atmospheric little bar with a spiral staircase leading to a small upper room where you can sit on the tiny balcony and drink one of the best cups of coffee in Havana. Good fruit juices, too. Tapas and other snacks are available. On the adjacent corner the bar has an open-air barbecue area with a few tables.

Hotel Ambos Mundos
Calle Obispo, 153
Take the ornate elevator to the rooftop bar for a drink with a wonderful view. The ground-floor piano bar is pleasant, too, in a hushed and intimate kind of way.

> Price categories are for a three-course meal for one with a beer, or *mojito*. Wine puts the price up:
> **$** = under $25
> **$$** = $25–35
> **$$$** = over $35

RIGHT: the courtyard of Don Giovanni.

CUBA'S COLONIAL ARCHITECTURE

Colonial architecture in Havana may not be as decorative as that found in other Spanish colonies such as Peru, but it has a simple, solid elegance

Old Havana is, without doubt, the finest showcase of colonial architecture in Cuba. Its features are seen all over the island, however. Other cities particularly worth visiting for their architecture are Camagüey, Gibara, Remedios, Santiago, and, especially, Trinidad.

The strongest influence on Cuban colonial architecture came, of course, from Spain, in particular from Andalusia, where the so-called Mudéjar style – a fusion of Christian and Arabic architectural traditions that developed in medieval Spain – predominated at the time of the colonization of Cuba. Many of the early buildings in Havana were built by Mudéjar craftsmen, who came by ship from Seville and Cádiz and adapted the styles they knew to suit the conditions in the Caribbean: primarily the hot climate and the relative paucity of materials. The talent of these craftsmen lay above all in carpentry. Woods such as mahogany and cedar were abundant in Cuba at that time, and were used to construct ceilings, doors, columns, and railings, as well as furniture.

The other predominant style is Baroque, which reached Havana in the late 18th century, and was primarily used in the building and decoration of churches. This more flamboyant, sophisticated architecture proved to be a perfect medium for expressing the new-found confidence of a nation enjoying its first real economic boom – though the wealth was concentrated in the hands of a few. While undoubtedly grander than anything that had gone before, fusion with the existing Mudéjar styles kept Cuban Baroque relatively simple.

BELOW: restrained Baroque: the swirls on the facade of Havana's cathedral are typical of Cuban Baroque. Because the local limestone was hard to work with, the style was less elaborate than that found in Europe, and some believe that to be a good thing, more in keeping with the Caribbean surroundings.

LEFT: the high-timbered ceilings of the Parador de los Tres Reyes restaurant in Camagüey are typical of 19th-century colonial architecture.

How to be Cool in Cuba

The most striking features of Cuban colonial design are solutions to the problem of how to keep cool – namely, by creating the maximum amount of shade and ventilation.

● Courtyards: many houses were laid out around a courtyard, with arcades enabling residents to move from room to room in the shade.

● Doors: these were very tall and had small windows or *postigos* that could be opened to provide light and ventilation without having to disturb the residents' privacy by opening the whole door.

● Ceilings: vaulted ceilings *(alfarjes)* were not easy to build but were higher than flat ones and kept rooms cooler.

● *Mamparas*: these swing doors, with decorative glass panels and fancy woodwork, were popular in the 1800s and allowed air to circulate between rooms.

ABOVE: the louvered and stained-glass windows of the Museo de Arte Colonial offer a magnificent view of the unequal twin towers of Havana's cathedral.

LEFT: much of Old Havana has now been restored to its former glory the Cuban tourism company, Habaguanex.

ABOVE: many families use antique furniture and retain pre-Revolutionary fittings for lack of modern alternatives.

BELOW: the Palacio de Ferrer in Cienfuegos is an ornate late 19th-century mansion with sea views over the harbor from its tower.

ABOVE: an 18th-century engraving of Havana's Plaza Vieja, notable for its grand houses and fine arches.

CENTRO HABANA AND VEDADO

Centro Habana is a run-down but colorful place with crumbling tenements and crowded markets, while Vedado's broad streets are quieter, more elegant, and the centerpiece is the stark, impressive Plaza de la Revolución

Bounded by the giant avenues of the Malecón to the north, Prado to the east, and Calzada de Infanta to the west, **Centro Habana** is a bustling, overcrowded district seething with life and noise. It dates mostly from the 19th century, when Havana, having burst out from its city walls, began to spread across the swampy lands and rocky pastures to its west. The restoration program has spread to Centro, notably to the Malecón, Monte, Cayo Hueso, and parts of Chinatown. But most of this district is as it has been for decades: tumbledown, narrow streets lined with tall, crumbling mansions divided between a dozen families into *ciudadelas* (little cities).

But look beyond the crumbling facades and you will see that many of these houses are true palaces, even if their glory has faded: pizzerias lit by priceless chandeliers; a narrow passageway lined with lofty marble columns; a pink marble bathroom with gold fittings, but nevertheless waterless and sometimes shared by 30 families. The street theater of everyday Havana lights up each corner and offers visitors a different kind of experience – of life as it really is lived in the city.

Behind the Capitolio

Tucked just behind the Capitolio is the **Fábrica de Tabacos Partagás** ❶

(Partagás Cigar Factory; Industria 520 between Dragones and Barcelona; tel: 7-862-4604; Tue–Fri 9.30–11am, noon–2pm; regular 40-minute tours every 15 mins; charge, tickets must be bought in hotel lobbies; no photos; store Mon–Sat all day). The famously strong Partagás cigars have been rolled here since 1845 *(see pages 212–13)*. The factory has a cigar store attached, but prices are often higher than they are in hotel stores. Real cigar smokers should resist the temptation to buy from the *jineteros* (hustlers) gathered outside. Despite the

Main attractions
FÁBRICA DE TABACOS PARTAGÁS
MALECÓN
HOTEL NACIONAL
CALLEJÓN HAMEL
COPPELIA ICE CREAM PARK
PLAZA DE LA REVOLUCIÓN
CEMENTERIO DE COLÓN

LEFT: a golden glow on the Malecón.
RIGHT: the Partagás Cigar Factory.

Old trains on display in front of Parque de la Fraternidad.

BELOW:
colorful washing on a Malecón balcony.

stories they tell, most of their cigars are fakes and definitely not worth the high asking price. Immediately behind the factory at Amistad No. 407, the equally famous **H. Upmann** cigar factory also offers guided tours. Some of the best Montecristos are rolled here.

Flanking the southern side of the Capitolio is the **Parque de la Fraternidad**, a busy, pleasant park with the Friendship Tree at its heart. This ceiba tree was planted in the soil of 17 nations by the delegates of the 1928 Pan-American conference to cement friendship between the countries of the Americas. On the west side is this area's main bus terminal, and you will see long lines for the buses.

The Queen's Avenue

The hectic **Avenida de la Reina** effectively forms the southern boundary to Centro Habana for most tourists. Somewhat confusingly, this street is also known as Avenida Simón Bolívar, and becomes Avenida Salvador Allende as it heads out toward Vedado. Two sites are worth noting among the multitude of stores and apartment blocks

along its length. First, a magnificent Gothic church with lovely stained-glass windows, the **Iglesia del Sagrado Corazón de Jesús**; and a short way farther on, the splendid **Casa de Cultura de Centro Habana** (Avenida Salvador Allende, 720 between Soledad and Castillejo; tel: 7-878-4727), which is always alive with musicians, dancers, and other aspiring artistes, who rent magnificent, decaying practice rooms for a pittance.

Running southwest from the east end of Reina is Calle Máximo Gómez, better known as **Monte**. This area has been crumbling away for decades but is now in the process of renovation. The imposing 19th-century mansions were once the summer homes of the city's colonial aristocracy, as it was cooler here than in the rest of the city during Havana's steamy summers.

The street begins to the south of the Parque de la Fraternidad, at the bustling farmers' market of **Cuatro Caminos** – the largest market in the city, with separate sections for fruit and vegetables, meat, flowers, and prepared foods. There is a *guarapera*

selling freshly pressed sugar-cane juice for around a Cuban peso a glass. This entire area is good for peso street food, such as peanut *turrón* (nougat) candy bars, reasonably cheesy pizza, *refrescos*, and *granizados* – shaved ices flavored with syrup, for those with stronger stomachs. The area has some good *paladar* restaurants, too. There is an interesting herbalist, with strong links to Santería, opposite the market, selling medicinal herbs alongside votive jars, candles, and bead necklaces dedicated to the *orishas* or gods of the religion.

Chinatown

Easily reached by heading west along Dragones from the Partagás cigar factory is the **Barrio Chino ❷** – Havana's once huge but now tiny Chinatown, centered around calles Cuchillo and San Nicolás. The first Chinese arrived in Cuba in the mid-19th century to build the country's railroads, but the community lost much of its homogeneity after the revolution, and has to a large extent been integrated into wider Cuban society. Still, many people in the area have distinctly Asiatic features and, confusingly, almost everyone is known by the nickname "Chino."

This area used to be notorious as the center of Havana's red-light district. Times have changed, and the infamous **Shanghai Theater** – described in Graham Greene's *Our Man in Havana*, and which once specialized in live sex acts and pornographic movies – has now re-opened as a nightclub specializing in karaoke. Castro and Hemingway were both regulars of the once-renowned Restaurante Pacífico, at the end of Calle Cuchillo on San Nicolás, but these days the food is not distinctively Chinese. Hemingway's son Gregory described a 1950s visit to the Pacífico with a five-piece Chinese orchestra on the second floor, a whorehouse on the third floor and, on the fourth floor, an opium den. On Calle Cuchillo, a small, not especially Chinese market is a hive of activity and does sell a few unusual things – fresh lychees and goose eggs

for example – but watch out for pickpockets. There are also several places specializing in Chinese medicine.

The neo-Romanesque Santería church, **Nuestra Señora de la Caridad del Cobre ❸** is to be found at the edge of Chinatown on calles Manrique and Salud. This glorious frescoed and golden church – its dark interior lighted by candles and full of incense, flowers, and choral music – is undergoing lengthy restoration, so you won't yet be able to appreciate its beauty. Just inside the door is a shrine to the eight saints who are the most powerful *orishas* of the Santería faith.

The Malecón

The area of Centro Havana that most tourists visit is to the north. Emerging from the Castillo de la Punta at the end of the Prado, the 5km (3-mile) **Malecón** seafront stretch is Havana's main artery, running straight through to Vedado. Hitchhikers, runners, young couples, families, wheeler-dealers, prostitutes, elderly women walking the dog – such is the cross section of city life you will see here. Salsa bands rehearse

Lanterns above the patio of a Chinatown restaurant.

BELOW: fresh produce at a farmers' market.

WHERE

Take Avenida de Italia, also known as Galiano, down from Chinatown to the Malecón. This noisy commercial street, lined with crumbling tenements, has lots of *agropecuarios* (produce markets) and CUC stores. It is also home to the Casa de la Música. Set on the first floor of a huge apartment block, it looks unprepossessing but is known for its great music.

BELOW:
waves batter
the Malecón.

in the buildings above, while children splash in the crashing (and heavily polluted) surf, or play makeshift games of baseball, fearless of the traffic as they run out to collect their balls, and musicians sit on the sea wall and play, hoping for a few pesos from tourists who show an interest. On weekend nights the Malecón turns into one huge party, when hundreds gather to dance and drink rum.

The first ornate building you see is the **Centro de Cultura Hispano-Americano**, with its second-floor balcony supported by caryatids (classical, draped female figures). Known as the Casa de las Cariátides, it reopened after extensive renovation in May 2004, and now stages temporary art and photographic exhibitions.

Many houses along the seafront here, having suffered from decades of neglect, are now undergoing desperately needed renovation, with many individual buildings having been sponsored by different Spanish provinces. Consequently, you find severely dilapidated, overcrowded buildings standing next to smartly painted new ones.

There are plans to completely rebuild the dangerously pitted seafront walkway. The spectacle of the sea roaring up against the Malecón is a part of the Havana scene, but the "big seas" (during storms, giant breakers can reach up to 10 meters/30ft) do tremendous damage to roads, paths, and buildings. In winter, the road is often closed to traffic, and on some occasions the sea wall is severely breached, flooding Centro Havana.

For the time being, at least, you can still enjoy the dramatic spectacle from September to April – the biggest and best waves are to be seen in Vedado, by the Hotel Riviera and the statue of Calixto García, where the Malecón meets Presidentes. In contrast, when the tide is low and the sea calmer, you can see the remains of 19th-century stone baths carved from the limestone at the Old Havana end of the Malecón. The area, known as the **Elysian Fields**, was a fashionable place to see and be seen. There were once separate bathing areas for men and women, and for blacks.

The Hotel Deauville at Malecón and Avenida de Italia (Galiano) is one of Centro Habana's only tourist hotels – a pretty grim-looking building, although the interior has been refurbished. Halfway along the promenade is the **Monumento a Antonio Maceo ❹**, a huge bronze statue of the 19th-century revolutionary hero. There is a code to the city's equestrian statues of heroes: when the horse is rearing up, with both hoofs in the air, the subject died in battle; if only one hoof is raised, the man died of wounds sustained in battle; if the horse has all four hoofs firmly on the ground, the hero in question died peacefully in his bed. Maceo's horse is rearing since he died fighting the Spanish in 1896. Close by is the 18th-century watchtower, the Torreón de San Lázaro.

The large tower block behind the statue, reached by sinuous drive, was built before the Revolution as a bank, but it is now Cuba's flagship hospital, the Hospital Nacional Hermanos Ameijeiras.

A couple of blocks inland is **Callejón de Hamel ❺** – take San Lazaro behind the hospital, then turn left on Calle Hospital (*see panel below*).

Vedado

West of Centro Habana, the Malecón courses through to the green and leafy suburbs of Vedado. The district was loosely modeled on Miami: the streets are identified by numbers (running east to west) or letters (running north to south); and some Art Deco buildings vaguely recall the shabbier corners of South Beach in the 1970s, before its restoration. With palm trees lining many streets, it is a pleasant place to stroll or to stay, particularly if you want to take advantage of the nightlife on your doorstep.

The suburb is heralded by the twin towers of the **Hotel Nacional ❻**, Havana's most splendid hotel, perched on a rocky outcrop overlooking the Malecón. Modeled in the 1920s on the Breakers Hotel in Palm Beach in Florida, it has serene gardens with conveniently placed chairs and tables, good views of the sea and a long, shaded veranda with comfy wicker chairs where you can escape the hubbub of the city for a while. The café bar has walls lined with pictures of those who stayed here in its glory days – movie

Callejón de Hamel is a fascinating spot, quite unlike anywhere else in the city.

BELOW LEFT: musician in the Callejón de Hamel.

Callejón de Hamel

Anyone who takes an interest in Afro-Cuban religions and the powerful, percussion-driven music and dance that accompanies their ceremonies, should check out the Callejón de Hamel in the district of Cayo Hueso – a tiny backstreet off San Lázaro and Lucena in northwestern Centro Habana. The area has been dedicated to Palo Monte and Santería, with shrines to various *orishas* and tiny stores selling art and artifacts. The walls and houses have been plastered with enormous, boldly colored murals, pieces of sculpture, old typewriters, and bath tubs turned into seats. The project was initiated in 1990 by artist Salvador González. A nattily dressed man with the air of a showman, he is fired by his religious heritage, and there is considerable local pride in his achievement, especially considering the scarcity of available resources.

It's interesting to see at any time, but Sunday is the best day to go (noon–3pm), when an Afro-Cuban band strikes up with *batá* drums and fierce dancing for the mixed crowd of tourists and local people. The atmosphere is good, but it gets very crowded, so take care of your valuables, or better still, leave them behind in your hotel. You are welcome to take photos, but expect to make a contribution. Women sit at the gated entrance offering good-luck charms and fortune telling for an "offering," and the bands' CDs are for sale.

TIP

There is a television
station in Vedado's
hotel zone, from which
Castro traditionally
made his speeches.
When he was due to
arrive the streets were
blocked off and
residents were not
allowed out on their
balconies.

stars such as Errol Flynn, Frank Sinatra, Ava Gardner, and Clark Gable, plus more recent celebrity visitors, such as Naomi Campbell.

The Malecón rolls on past the **Monumento al Maine** , dedicated to the 260 US sailors who were killed when their ship blew up in Havana in 1898 *(see page 48)*. A plaque on the monument declares, "Victims Sacrificed by Imperialist Voracity in its Eagerness to Seize the Island of Cuba." The US eagle that once topped the two graceful columns was felled by an angry mob with a crane in 1960.

The **US Interests' Section of the Swiss Embassy** – a faceless mass of concrete and tinted glass – lies a little father west. Throngs of over-dressed Cubans, hoping to join the *"Señores Imperialistas"* with an entry visa, gather in a little park on Calzada and K as they wait to be interviewed by the US consulate.

Protests against US policies are also held here and monuments come and go in line with events. These have included tit for tat measures: an electronic billboard scrolling out illumi-

nated propaganda was blocked by 138 black flags, each with a white star, symbolising those who had died as the result of violent acts against Cuba since 1959.

A couple of blocks south, on calles 13 and L, is a building right out of Gotham City, designed by the firm of architects (Shreve, Lamb, and Harmon) who built the Empire State Building in New York. The families of many famous revolutionaries lived here. Next door, by the park, is the Hospital Camilo Cienfuegos (convertible pesos only), specializing in eye diseases. Another Vedado landmark is the blunt, curved **Edificio Focsa** : although reminiscent of Stalinist architecture, it was actually built in the capitalist 1950s, and the Russians liked it so much that they copied the design for 10 buildings in Moscow.

La Rampa

The Hotel Nacional overlooks the junction of the Malecón and Calle 23 – known as **La Rampa**. This famous commercial artery houses many of the city's airline offices, the International

The Posada Debâcle

In 1976 forme CIA agent Luís Posada Carriles was jailed in Venezuela for his part in bombing a Cuban airliner, en route from Caracas to Havana, killing all 73 people aboard, but he escaped nine years later. In 2005 he arrived in the United States, where he was charged with illegal entry. To the anger of both Cuban and Venezuelan authorities, the charges were dropped two years later, even though the US Justice Department described him as a danger to the community, and "an admitted mastermind of terrorist bombs and attacks." Both governments are pressing for his extradition, which to date the US has refused to grant. Posada is also under investigation for an alleged role in the bombing of the Copacabana Hotel in Havana in 1997, in which an Italian tourist was killed.

Press Center, a few nightclubs, an excellent jazz club, and a whole host of fairly cheap but good snack bars.

One block away, on Calzada de Infanta, is the **Museo Casa de Abel Santamaría** ❾ (Mon–Fri 10am–4pm; free), home of the joint leader (with Castro) of the 26th of July Movement in the 1950s, tortured to death after the failed Moncada attack of 1953. Castro attended many meetings here. Today, it contains Santamaría memorabilia.

To the west is the **Hotel Habana Libre** ❿, a tall building emblazoned with a bold blue-and-white ceramic mural. Inaugurated three months before the fall of the Batista dictatorship as the Havana Hilton, Fidel and his embryonic government took over an entire floor for several months in 1959. The first-floor café that was the scene of a famous poison attempt on Castro – who used to spend late nights here chatting to kitchen staff (the cyanide capsule intended for his chocolate milkshake broke in the freezer) – has disappeared in a refurbishment that replaced the atmospheric 1950s interior with a bland, modern design.

Opposite the Habana Libre is the famous **Coppelia Ice Cream Park** ⓫, built by the revolutionary government to replace the notoriously elitist Vedado ice-cream parlors (where poorer and darker-skinned clients need not even have bothered lining up). The domed building, occupying a whole block, was designed by Mario Girona in 1966, based on an idea by Celia Sánchez, friend and companion of Fidel Castro and heroine of the Sierra Maestra campaign. It was in the park that the opening scenes of the 1994 film *Fresa y Chocolate* were filmed – the title refers to the two most common flavors, sometimes the only ones available – strawberry and chocolate.

Tourists are entitled to wait for two hours or more with everyone else if they wish to buy ice creams and pay in *moneda nacional*, but it is quicker (and more expensive) to pay in CUCs at one of the stands on the fringes of the park. The ice cream is still the best in Cuba, but it is less rich and creamy and more icy than it used to be – employees say that less butter is used now because of the cost.

Savoring the very special ice cream at Coppelia Ice Cream Park.

BELOW: all are welcome at Coppelia.

Statue of Alma Mater in front of Havana's university.

BELOW: enjoying the sunset.

Around the university

Two blocks southeast of here, the **Universidad de La Habana** ⓬ is a lovely group of classical buildings in golden stone placed around a cool and leafy garden, reached by climbing an impressive flight of steps at the head of San Lázaro. Anyone can stroll around the campus, and it is a good place to meet young Cubans, who love to practice their English. In the Faculty of Mathematics lies the **Museo Antropológico Montané** (Mon–Fri 9am–noon, 1–4pm; charge), with an excellent collection of pre-Columbian artifacts including the famous wooden Taíno Tobacco Idol, dating from around the 12th century, found in Maisí, at the far eastern tip of Cuba.

Opposite the university is a stark **monument to Julio Antonio Mella**, containing the ashes of the student who founded the Cuban Communist Party and was assassinated in Mexico in 1929. On January 28 – José Martí's birthday – a tremendous torchlit march starts from the monument.

Around the corner, the **Museo Napoleónico** ⓭ (San Miguel, 1159; tel: 7-879-1460; closed for renovation) is housed in a delightful mansion with a small garden. Much of this unexpected collection of Napoleonic memorabilia was brought by Julio Lobo, a 19th-century politician, from his travels in Europe. It includes Napoleon's death mask (made by one of his doctors who later moved to Santiago de Cuba, where he performed the first cataract operation), pistols from the Battle of Borodino, and a fine library.

Where Calzada de Infanta meets Avenida Salvador Allende (also called Carlos III) you'll find the **Quinta de los Molinos** ⓮ (closed to the public), reached via a tree-shaded drive. This was the site of 18th-century snuff mills built alongside the Zanja Real watercourse to Old Havana (*see page 156*), and parts of the 16th-century aqueduct have been incorporated into the water garden and grotto. Now quiet and neglected, the gardens were popular in colonial times, when the rich owners of summer palaces nearby could inspect slaves before they went to market. They are now home to La Madriguera, a center for young artists, and a music

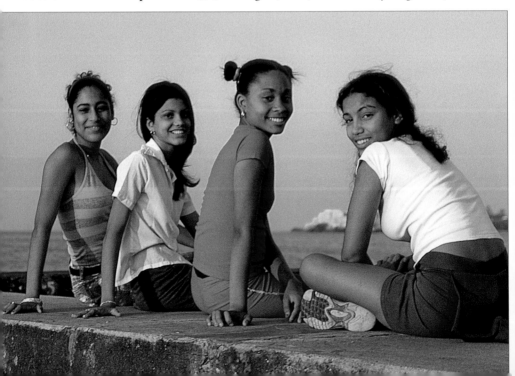

venue where musicians are often found practicing beneath the trees.

Revolution Square

South of here is the **Plaza de la Revolución** ⑮, the governmental heart of modern Havana. It is an extraordinary place – a vast, bleak square, big enough to hold the masses who came to hear Fidel's famous eight-hour May Day speeches, but normally empty of anyone except camera-toting tourists and the taxis that brought them. The exception to this is October 9, the anniversary of Che's death, when schoolchildren come here to lay flowers.

The whole region has been given over to eastern European-style monolithic architecture, where bureaucrats labor behind concrete walls. Yet the Revolution is not to blame: most of the buildings, including the Martí monument, went up during Batista's time, when the dictator expressed his taste for intimidating, uninspired design, as seen in the gray former Justice Ministry, finished in 1958, that now houses the Central Committee of the Communist Party.

At the center is the mighty **Monumento José Martí** ⑯ (tel: 7-859-2347; Mon–Sat 9am–5pm; charge), which houses an informative museum, including the original design plans for the plaza and Martí monument. Ascend the monument (extra charge) for an impressive 360-degree view of the city: Habana Vieja looks a very long way away. Behind the monument is the monolithic Palacio de la Revolución, where senior ministers, including Fidel Castro, have their offices. Visitors are not permitted to photograph the palace, or loiter behind the monument.

The Ministerio del Interior is Cuba's most sinister and secretive organization (although vast, it has just one number listed in the phone book, which no one ever answers), yet it is housed in Cuba's most photographed building. The outside wall has a giant mural of Che Guevara executed in black metal, and best viewed at night when clever lighting gives the face an eerily three-dimensional look. The plaza is also the location of the Television and Radio Information and Communications Building, the Biblioteca Nacional, and the Teatro Nacional de Cuba (tel: 7-879-3558) – a stark building containing three theaters, the lively Café Cantante, a piano bar, a discotheque in the basement, and a large sculpture garden where works by Cuban artists are displayed. On the east side of the plaza is the terminus for Astro, the long-distance bus company used by Cubans.

Avenida de los Presidentes

From the Plaza de la Revolución make your way (on foot or by taxi, depending on stamina) along the broad Avenida G, also called the **Avenida de Los Presidentes**, which crosses La Rampa, and is lined with lush, formal gardens and the former homes of the rich, most now government buildings. En route, you pass a monument to the murdered Chilean president Salvador Allende, and a gigantic marble tribute to past Cuban presidents. Once a favored hang-out for disaffected youths, it has

BELOW: the mural of Che Guevara in the square.

There is a philatelic museum – the Museo Postal José Luis Guerra Aguiar (open Mon–Fri 8am–5.30pm, charge) – to the northeast of the square, with exhibitions of stamps from all over the world.

BELOW: leaping from the rocks in front of the Malecón. **RIGHT:** a view of Casa de las Américas.

now been cleaned up. Where Avenida G meets the Malecón stands a monument to Calixto García.

A couple of blocks west, at Calle 17, between Avenidas D and E, is the **Museo de Artes Decorativas** ⓱ (tel: 7-830-8037; Tue–Sat 11am–6pm, Sun 9am–1pm; charge). It has a wonderful collection of European and oriental decorative arts, especially porcelain, which is displayed in a series of furnished rooms ranging from a rococo salon and Regency dining room to a gorgeous Art Deco bathroom. Many of the treasures in this museum belonged to María Luisa, Condesa de Revilla de Camargo, a member of the wealthy Gómez Mena family. She lived here from the 1930s until she fled after the revolution, leaving her collections of fine art hidden in the basement.

Where Avenida G crosses Línea, you find the delightful **Museo de la Danza** (Línea, corner G; tel: 7-831-2198; Tue–Sat 10am–6pm, Sun 9am–1pm; charge), where guided tours are available of the personal collection of Alicia Alonso, and other memorabilia from the Ballet Nacional de Cuba.

Next door to the Hotel Presidente is the elegant cultural center, the **Casa de Las Américas** ⓲ (Calle 3, 52, corner l; tel: 7-838-2706; www.casadelasamericus.com; Mon–Fri 8am–5pm; charge). Housed in a landmark Art Deco building, it contains archives, a fine collection of Latin American art in the Sala Latino-americana, contemporary Cuban art in the Sala Contemporánea, and hosts workshops, lectures, and other cultural events. There is also a good book and music shop. Next door, the Galería Haydée Santamaría also exhibits the work of Latin American artists, including paintings, sculptures, engravings, and photography.

At the intersection of Avenida de los Presidentes and the Malecón, beside the Calixto García monument, is the José Martí sports ground, built in 1961 and a fine example of the use of concrete in the 1960s, painted in bright colors to relieve the effect on the eye. From here, the Malecón heads west. There is an artisans' market, the Feria del Malecón, on the corner of Avenida D, and just beyond rises the Hotel Riviera, built by mob boss Meyer Lansky as a last attempt to re-create Las Vegas in the Caribbean. Lansky had a suite on the 20th floor, which can be booked by hotel guests. The interior of the Riviera is still pleasantly evocative of the 1950s, but the hotel has been both dwarfed and outclassed by the Hotel Meliá Cohiba next door, which was Cuba's first five-star hotel *(see page 342)*.

Paseo

If you turn inland again by the Riviera, parallel with Avenida de los Presidentes is Paseo, another of the major thoroughfares of Vedado, which runs from the Malecón to the Plaza de la Revolución. The main point of interest along this street is the **Casa de la Amistad** (Paseo, 406, between calles 17 and 19; tel: 7-830-3114), in a beautiful coral-pink 1920s mansion. This is the head office for the Cuban Institute for Friendship among the Peoples and also houses the Amistur travel agency, which specializes in social tourism. However, of more interest to the visitor may be the restaurant and bar and the music on offer; there is usually something of interest going on here.

A few blocks away, on Calle 8 between 15 and 17, is the **Parque John Lennon** ⑲, a nicely landscaped park occupying one block, where the centerpiece is a realistic bronze statue of John Lennon, lounging nonchalantly on a park bench and inscribed with the line "Dirás que soy un soñador, pero no soy el único" (You may say that I'm a dreamer, but I'm not the only one). The statue was unveiled by Castro himself in December 2000. It's a favorite hang-out spot for young people and there are occasional concerts.

City of the dead

You could turn right (west) on Paseo or get a taxi from Plaza de la Revolución – there are usually several there – to the **Cementerio de Colón** ⑳ (Columbus Cemetery, entrance on Calzada de Zapata; tel: 7-830-4517; 8am–5pm; charge includes a guided tour), with its arched entrance gate, one of the largest

necropolises in the world. Work began in the 1860s, when *habaneros* ran out of catacombs. A competition for its design was won by a Spaniard, Calixto de Loira y Cardosa. Although the Latin motto reads "Pale Death enters both hovels and the palaces of kings," Calixto ensured the dead could be separated by social status. He died before it was completed and became one of the first to be buried here. Wealthy *habaneros* competed to create the most impressive tombs, and the result is a morbid atmosphere that would have appealed to Edgar Allan Poe: a stone forest of Grecian temples and columns, crucified Christs, and angels of mercy. The mausoleums are an eclectic mix of Gothic and neoclassical styles, and stone dogs lie at their masters' feet.

Cubans make pilgrimages to the tomb of Amelia Goyre de la Hoz, La Milagrosa (The Miraculous One), who died in childbirth. She was buried in 1901 with her child at her feet, but when exhumed the child was supposedly found in her arms. Nobody seems clear about *why* she was exhumed, but she is an object of devotion. ❑

When Meyer Lansky owned the Hotel Riviera he was listed, for tax reasons, as the hotel's kitchen manager.

BELOW:
John Lennon's statue in the little park named after him.

RESTAURANTS, PALADARES, BARS, AND CAFÉS

Restaurants

Price categories are for a three-course meal for one with a beer, or *mojito*. Wine puts the price up:
$ = under $25
$$ = $25–35
$$$ = over $35

1830
Malecón, 1252 and 22, Vedado
Tel: (7) 838-3090.
Open daily L & D. $$$
Located just before you go under the tunnel to Miramar at the mouth of the Río Almendares in the **Torreón de la Chorrera** castle by the sea, this romantic restaurant is known for it excellent chef and cabaret shows. There is a bar, live music, and a pleasant garden.

Casona de 17
Calle 17, 60, between M and N, Vedado
Tel: (7) 838-3136. Open noon–midnight. $$–$$$
Serves reasonably priced Cuban dishes, and more international food in the elegant surroundings of an old villa, opposite the Focsa Building. Two air-conditioned indoor restaurants and an Argentine-style barbecue-grill on the patio.

El Conejito
Calle M, 206 and 17, Vedado
Tel: (7) 832-4671. Open noon–midnight. $$
The architecture and decor is a strange mix of English and Swiss styles. It specializes in rabbit *(conejo)*, with lots of different sauces and styles, but serves a wide range of international dishes.

La Roca
Calle 21, 102, between L and M, Vedado
Tel: (7) 834-4501. Open daily noon–2am. $–$$
A classic 1950s club – with an atmospheric cocktail bar – that has been well renovated. Well cooked, if rather bland, international menu, with a choice of meat, fish, and shellfish. One of the few restaurants in Cuba to offer a cigar after dinner. A word of warning: the air conditioning is fearsome.

La Torre
Focsa Building, calles 17 and M, Vedado
Tel: (7) 832-7306.
Open noon–midnight. $$$
Sitting at the top of Havana's highest building, La Torre offers a fantastic panoramic view. The menu, which is dominated by steaks and fish, has a decidedly French influence.

Polinesio
Hotel Habana Libre, Calle 23, Vedado
Tel: (7) 838-4011.
Open daily noon–midnight. $$–$$$
Attached to the Hotel Habana Libre but with access from the street, so it feels a bit less like a hotel restaurant. The food is also different, as they serve a variety of Chinese and Indonesian dishes. Once a Trader Vic's, and still using the same decor, it has been in operation for decades and is highly thought of.

Restaurante Monseigneur
Corner of O and 21, Vedado
Tel: (7) 832-9884. Open noon–1am. $$

Located opposite the Hotel Nacional, the Monseigneur (called Monseñor by Cubans) cellar restaurant is famous as a former meeting spot for 1950s Mafia bosses. The Cuban singer, the late Bola de Nieve, made it his home, too, and his piano is still there. The restaurant now has a long seafood menu and a moody ambiance.

Restaurant Tien Tan
Calle Cuchillo, 17, between Zanja and San Nicolás.
Tel: (7) 861-5478.
Open daily 11am–midnight. $$
Extensive menu of genuinely Chinese food with chefs who actually come from China. Serves good stir-fries, and duck as well as pork and chicken.

Trattoria Marakas
Hotel St John, Calle O, 206, between 23 and 25, Vedado
Tel: (7) 833-3740. Open daily L & D. $$
The Trattoria serves authentic Italian food, including pizzas cooked in a wood-fired oven. There are pasta dishes, steaks, and interesting salads on offer, as well.

Paladares

Bellomar
Virtudes, 169 A between Industria and Amistad, Centro
Tel: (7) 861-0023. Open daily noon–11pm. $–$$
This is a pleasant *paladar* run by a friendly couple; the tables are set in a passage, one behind the other in a row. The food is traditional Cuban and well cooked, with tasty fish and chicken dishes

accompanied by rice, beans, and salads.

El Gringo Viejo
Calle 21, 454, between calles E and F, Vedado
Tel: (7) 831-1946.
Open daily noon–11pm. $
"The Old Gringo" is popular for its efficient service as well as the menu, which features seafood as well as the usual offerings. The decor is of wall-to-wall movie memorabilia.

El Monguito
Calle L, between 23 and 25, Vedado
Tel: (7) 831-2165.
Open daily noon–midnight. $
Opposite the Havana Libre hotel, this small restaurant in the family living room serves traditional, tasty *criolla* food: pork, chicken, and fish with *congrís*, fried plantain and salad. Plastic tables and chairs are decorated with plastic flowers, the outdoors brought indoors.

La Guarida
Calle Concordia, 418, between Gervasio and Escobar, Centro
Tel: (7) 866-9047, www. laguarida.com.
Open daily lunch and dinner.
$$–$$$
You must book well in advance, as this *paladar* featured in the famous Cuban film *Fresa y Chocolate* – or, rather, the film featured the crumbling tenement building, and the *paladar* followed two years later. It is always full. The decor is kitsch and eclectic, the food is varied and excellent, and portions are "nouveau" without being small. The prices are high, as the restaurant trades on its movie connections, but it is well worth a visit.

La Tasquita
Jovellar 160, between Espada and San Francisco, Centro
Tel: (7) 873-4916.
Open daily noon–2am. $
Very good food at excellent prices make it well worth seeking this place out. Meat dishes such as pork, chicken, or fish come with all the trimmings: rice and beans, sweet potato, and good salads. Unusually, this is a non-smoking *paladar*.

Las Mercedes
Calle 18, 204, between 15 and 17, Vedado
Tel: (7) 830-1302. Open daily noon–midnight. $$
Smart, with good-quality tables, chairs, and tablecloths. The room is decorated with fairy lights, and Jorge Pérez and his family provide a friendly atmosphere and like to get to know their customers. Some visitors eat here every night of their stay in Havana, appreciating the home cooking.

Los Amigos
Calle M, between Calles 19 and 21, Vedado
Tel: (7) 830-0880.
Open daily noon–midnight.
$$
A *paladar* offering good food, served among kitsch Christmas decorations, wind chimes, and religious icons. There is often entertainment after dinner, and it is popular with Habaneros as well as tourists.

Los Tres Chinitos
Zanja, 355 and 357, between Manrique and San Nicolás, Centro
Tel: (7) 863-3388.
Open daily noon–1am. $
On the edge of Chinatown. A reasonable place to come and try Cuban Chinese food, although if

you change your mind they also have a pizzeria here too.

Nerei
Calle 19, 110, between calles L and M, Vedado
Tel: (7) 832-7860. Open daily noon–midnight. $
Good Cuban dishes and fast, friendly service, but note that a 10 percent service charge is added. *Lechon asado* (roast suckling pig) is a specialty, and it does taste very different from the usual slices of pork. *Malanga con mojo* (starchy tuber with garlic sauce) is another favorite. Eat in a dining room furnished with antiques, or outside on a plant-filled terrace.

Bars and Cafés

Bar-Café Centro de Prensa
Calle 23, corner of Calle O, Vedado
A pleasant place for a drink, where you can feel as if you are joining the intellectual café society. It

closes at 7pm, though.

Café Neruda
Malecón, 353–7, corner Manrique
A great, modern, open-air bar with a glass front, located in the shell of a ruined building on the seafront. Run by Habaguanex, it has flair and style while prices of drinks, meals, and snacks are moderate. It is a very popular place to stop while strolling along the Malecón and there are usually lines of young couples waiting outside on weekend nights.

Opus Bar
Calzada, corner of Calle D, Vedado
Above the Teatro Roldán, this is a tranquil, comfortable bar.

Hotel Nacional
Calle O and 21, Vedado
An excellent *mojito* or daquirí on the hotel's broad, landscaped terrace overlooking the sea is one of the delights of Havana, especially when the sun is going down.

LEFT: enjoy a *mojito* before your meal.
RIGHT: doorman at the Hotel Nacional.

AROUND HAVANA

The area around Havana contains an eclectic mix of things to see – from classy Miramar in the west to the Parque Lenin, a delightful botanical garden, a couple of Hemingway sites, and an eastern beach

Visitors to Havana generally concentrate on La Habana Vieja, Centro, and Vedado, but there are other areas not far away that are well worth visiting if you have time.

Continuing westward from Vedado, where the previous chapter left off, you will soon come to the suburb of Miramar, which is divided from Vedado by the Río Almendares. You can cross into Miramar by tunnel, close to the bay, or farther inland by the road bridge, an extension of La Rampa (Calle 23).

Miramar

Miramar ❶ is a suburb of broad, tree-lined avenues, once the home of Havana's wealthiest residents, and still pretty smart compared with much of the city, although many of the buildings have seen better days. It is also an area that seems to have no center, perhaps because it was modeled on Las Vegas, rather than on colonial Spanish cities. High-rise hotels, luxury apartments to rent to foreigners, and business centers have sprung up all over the area.

Quinta Avenida (Fifth Avenue) is a broad promenade, planted with vividly flowering trees and bushes, where most of the foreign companies who have chosen to defy the US ban and invest in Cuba have their offices. Signs are everywhere: Benetton, Castrol, Bayer,

Philips. It is also the home of the city's foreign embassies, housed in beautiful buildings, set in lush gardens.

Quinta Avenida is home to one of the city's quirkiest museums – the **Museo del Ministerio del Interior** (Av. 5 corner Calle 14; tel: 7-203-4432; Tue–Fri 9am–5pm, Sat 9am–4pm; charge), which catalogs the history of the police force as well as the CIA's numerous attempts to destabilize the Cuban state and to assassinate Castro.

A little farther along, between calles 24 and 26, there is a pretty little park,

Main attractions
MIRAMAR
MARINA HEMINGWAY
TROPICANA
PARQUE LENIN
EL RINCÓN
FINCA VIGÍA
SANTA MARÍA DEL MAR

LEFT: an old Chevrolet at Marina Hemingway.
RIGHT: a weathered facade in Miramar.

A Night at the Tropicana

Cuba's unique brand of escapism is showcased here in breathtaking glamor, a colorful spectacle where cabaret meets carnival

The roulette tables may be gone, but not a great deal else has changed in the Tropicana nightclub – which has been Havana's most famous cabaret spot ever since it first opened in 1931, and the only place of its kind that has operated more or less continuously from the days when the Mafia and their hedonist friends lavished money on nightlife in Havana, through the austere years of the revolution. Internationally famous as one of the best shows in the world, the Tropicana (Calle 72, 4504, between Avenida 43 and 45, Marianao, western Havana; tel: 7-267 0110 has all the glitz and glamor of a casino show, without the casino. It has been called the Moulin Rouge with Cuban music and rhythm.

Shows start at 10pm every evening except Monday, weather permitting, and last 1 hour and 45 minutes. Billed as an open-air paradise "*bajo las estrellas*" (under the stars), it is forced to cancel shows regularly in the rainy season. Doors open

from 8.30pm, when guests start arriving for drinks or dinner. The place is lit up like a Christmas tree: blue neon signs announce the entrance, and a huge fountain with statues of frolicking naked women is bathed in blue and red. A small band warms up the crowd at the entrance, to add to the carnival atmosphere.

The setting is breathtaking. Tables fan out like sunbeams around the semicircular stage, with enough room to seat 1,400 and stand many more; tropical trees enclose the amphitheater in a sheltering cocoon; among the foliage, large neon lights spell out the names of legends who performed here in pre-revolutionary times, such as Carmen Miranda and Nat King Cole. On a good night, the warm tropical air is seductive and the stars are visible through the treetops. This being Cuba, there may also be the odd cat running around between the audience's legs, bringing the tone back down to earth.

With the triumphant blare of a 20-piece band, the show begins. Women in silver lamé coats and top hats float across the stage on trapezes. Dancers leap past in a blur of feathers, glitter, and long legs. A bizarre pageant may be thrown in. Then, as if to mock the power shortages elsewhere, dancers appear with giant, blazing candelabras sprouting bizarrely from their heads.

It's the sort of extravaganza preserved elsewhere in the world only in casinos, although many of the costumes have echoes of carnival processions in Rio de Janeiro or Trinidad. Cubans love their vast, hectic, titillating shows, but few can afford a night at the Tropicana; lesser versions can be seen around the island – the best, also called the Tropicana, in Santiago de Cuba.

One reason the Tropicana has survived is that it brings in tourist revenue: entrance fees are 70, 80, or 90 CUCs depending on the seat and the age of the quarter-bottle of rum (with mixer and cigar – the smoke can be overpowering) included. The most expensive seats are closest to the stage; you get a better view from the mid-range ones, which are slightly raised. Transport, snacks, or dinner (the food and service are heavily criticized) can be arranged at extra cost. The Tropicana is a prime haunt for Cuba's most gorgeous *jineteras* (prostitutes) who hunt out single men, and introduce themselves as "dancing students" who just happen to be catching the show. The discotheque attached to the club goes on, very loudly, till 2am. ❑

LEFT: Tropicana's extravaganza has changed little over the decades.

shaded by enormous, ancient banyan trees. Heading from here toward the sea you will come to the **Maqueta de la Habana** (Calle 28, 113, between 1st and 3rd Avenues, tel: 7-202-7322; Tue–Sat 9.30am–5pm; charge). This vast scale model of the city took 10 years to construct, and is the largest of its kind after a model of New York. Every street, every house, every vacant lot, every tree is faithfully represented, made out of cigar boxes; different colors show from which periods the districts date.

Back on Quinta, farther west at No. 6502, between 62 and 66, the giant **Russian Embassy** towers over Miramar. This huge, ugly complex of offices and apartments once housed the various delegations of the Soviet Union. Now the independent former Soviet states have moved out and have their own embassies, leaving the greatly reduced Russian mission somewhat lost and lonely, but hard to overlook.

Close by, on the seafront, is the **Acuario Nacional** (National Aquarium, 3rd Avenue, between calles 60 and 62; tel: 7-202-5872; www.acuarionacional.cu; Tue–Sun 10am–6pm; charge),

which has an endangered-species breeding program, and treats injured animals before returning them to the wild. Unfortunately, it also stages three dolphin and sea-lion shows throughout the day (small extra charge) and is a great favorite with local families, especially on weekends, when it gets quite crowded. Note that Cuba is in the habit of capturing wild dolphins, removing them from their natural habitat and families so they can be confined and trained for human entertainment, a practice condemned by conservation groups worldwide. Opposite is a little complex of bars and restaurants.

Just inland from the Russian Embassy, on Avenida 5B, between calles 66 and 70 (the western end of Avenida 7), is the **Fundación La Naturaleza y el Hombre Antonio Nuñez Jiménez** (Mon–Fri 9am–3pm; advance booking essential; charge). This fascinating place displays the canoe in which naturalist Antonio Nuñez Jiménez and his team traveled from the source of the Amazon to the sea in 1987. There is a wealth of objects gathered from the indigenous people they met,

The stark Russian Embassy building.

BELOW:
Maqueta de la Habana.

Marina Hemingway is a center for all kinds of water sports.

including lots of erotic ceramic figures. The foundation also has an excellent photographic collection, and Oswaldo Guayasamin's portrait of Fidel Castro.

Retracing your steps eastward, another attraction is the Teatro Karl Marx (tel: 7-209-1991), on Primera Avenida (corner Calle 10), which is good for concerts and movie premieres.

Nightlife and sea life

South of Miramar, in Marianao, is the **Tropicana** nightclub *(see page 188)*, while to the west extend endless green suburbs, such as **Cubanacán** and **Siboney**, where many government offices are located, and a lot of party

functionaries live. Cubanacán is also the location of the Instituto Superior de Arte, and a large conference center.

At the farthest outskirts of Havana, in what was once a fishing village called Santa Fé, is the marine resort called **Marina Hemingway ❷**. There are hotels and villas for rent, several expensive restaurants and duty-free stores, and a popular center for sport fishing, sailing, and scuba diving *(see Activities, page 363)*. From the marina, the coastal road carries on west toward the province of Pinar del Río. It passes a few small resorts, such as **Playa Baracoa**, and **El Salado**, pleasant, sleepy places with wooden houses along

Around Havana

the seafront and small rocky beaches, before it reaches Mariel (*see page 201*).

Lenin lingers on

Directly south of Havana on the airport road (officially called Rancho Boyeros, but Avenida Independencia on most street signs) is **Parque Lenin ❸** (park daily; attractions Wed–Sun 9am–5pm; free entry, but charges for some amenities and attractions), a vast stretch of gently rolling parkland with tall trees and bamboo stands. After years of stagnation in the "Special Period," the park is slowly gaining a new lease of life. Some rides and shows, and the 19th-century miniature steam railway, have reopened and there are new cafés serving Cubans in pesos and foreigners in CUCs. Among the attractions is an artificial lake with rowboats, a monument and museum dedicated to the park's creator, Celia Sánchez; and, most famously, a giant, well-tended stone head of Lenin – one of the last such monuments in the world.

South of the park is the largest botanical garden in Latin America, the **Jardín Botánico Nacional ❹** (Wed–Sun 9am–4pm; Mon–Tue by arrangement; charge). Looking after the vast areas of pasture and woodland is quite a struggle, and some areas are sorely neglected. The beautiful Japanese Garden is well maintained, however, and there are attractive greenhouses with large collections of tropical, desert, and temperate flora (there are poinsettias the size of Christmas trees), as well as an extensive herb garden, which supplies medicinal plants to many of Havana's *yerberos* (herbalists). The entrance fee includes the services of a knowledgable guide. The garden has a herbal tearoom, a botanical bookstore, a plant store, and one of Cuba' very few vegetarian restaurants (*see page 195*).

Across the road **ExpoCuba ❺** (Wed–Sun 10am–5pm; charge) is a sprawling area of pavilions celebrating Cuba's achievements in science, health, education, and the arts.

About 8km (5 miles) down Avenida

de la Independencia from the Parque Lenin turning is the small town of **Santiago de las Vegas**, a sleepy place that wakes up just once a year for the **Procession of the Miracles**. On the eve of December 17, the day of San Lázaro – patron saint of the sick, and also worshiped by followers of Santería (*see pages 83–5*) – people come from all over Cuba to the little church of **San Lázaro** at **El Rincón ❻**, just south of town, to pray for help or forgiveness. Thousands of people – a mixture of penitents and those who come just to join in – process slowly through the town to the church, where the pilgrimage culminates with a Mass held at midnight. The scenes inside the church are often emotional, with people shouting "¡Viva Lázaro!" "¡Viva Cristo!" Spirits run so high that the security forces always turn out in force in case of trouble.

The eastern suburbs

The suburbs east of Havana offer a slice of life you won't see in the city, but if you only have a short time in Cuba you will have plenty to do in Old Havana

Insignia for the members-only Club Náutico la Habana located at Marina Hemingway.

BELOW: trying out a vintage kart on display at Marina Hemingway.

En route to Regla or Casablanca on the ferry, you may see passengers dropping paper into the sea – this means they are hoping to rid themselves of their problems in a Santería ceremony.

BELOW RIGHT: classic American car in Guanabavicoa.

and Vedado, and if you have longer you will almost certainly be visiting some of the better-known towns on the island. These small towns, although they get a mention, will not be high on most visitors' lists.

The ramshackle little town of **Casablanca** can best be reached from Old Havana by ferry *(lancha)*, which will pick you up at the foot of calles Luz and Santa Clara and take you to the other side of the harbor. Alternatively you can walk about 15 minutes from the fortress of La Cabaña. Casablanca is famous for the statue that dominates the bay, the figure of Christ, carved from Italian marble, and very similar to the more famous one in Rio de Janeiro. Sometimes known as **El Cristo de Casablanca**, it was carved by Cuban sculptor Jilma Madra, and inaugurated in December 1958, shortly before the fall of Batista. In the early years of the revolution the statue was struck by lightning and the head fell off. The government had the figure repaired – to the consternation of some communists who felt it a "waste of the people's money" to repair a reli-

gious monument. The other noticeable structure here is the domed, white national observatory, the **Observatorio Nacional** (no public access). You can continue on from Casablanca east to Matanzas via the electric Hershey train, built when the Hershey family operated the sugar refinery at Santa Cruz del Norte *(see page 195)*.

If you want to visit **Regla,** the best way to get there is also by ferry from the foot of calles Luz and Santa Clara in Old Havana, but it is not the same ferry that goes to Casablanca. Regla is ringed by heavy industry, but the old town is still quite pleasant, and its main forms of transportation are trucks and horse-drawn carts. The main reason people come here is to visit the early 19th-century **Iglesia de Nuestra Señora de Regla,** (daily 7.30am–5.30pm). This church is dedicated to the black Virgen de Regla, the patron saint of Cuba's sailors. Her counterpart in Santería is Yemayá, goddess of the sea. You will see worshipers making offerings here, many dressed in blue, or wearing blue-and-crystal beads – the colors of Yemayá. Her day

Small Town with Big Connections

If you have your own transportation, and time to spare, you might like to make a brief trip to the southwest of Havana (some 37km/22 miles along the Autopista del Mediodía), to San Antonio de los Baños, which may be the most filmed small town in the developing world. Just 8km (5 miles) away is the Escuela Internacional del Cine (International Film School), whose students, who come from 50 countries in Latin America, Asia, and Africa, often use San Antonio and its residents in their graduating projects. Gabriel García Márquez is one of the three founders and a benefactor of the school, which he has often visited to teach classes in screenwriting. Other notables who have worked with the school include Robert Redford and Francis Ford Coppola.

San Antonio is known, too, for its annual International Humor Festival (in April), and has a small Museo del Humor, which exhibits satirical cartoons. It is also the birthplace of both the composer-singer Silvio Rodríguez (in 1946), whose political lyrics have made him a national icon; and of the late Eduardo Abela (1889–1965), whose cartoon character, El Bobo (The Fool), which appeared in a daily newspaper in the 1930s, created biting social criticism. El Bobo is now the town symbol, standing at its entrance. There is a gallery named after the artist, but it exhibits the work of local artists and does not contain his works.

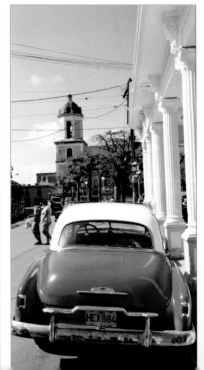

is September 8, when there is a procession in her honor. The church also has an altar to Santa Bárbara, twinned in Santería with Changó, god of war and machismo. Offerings here are in red, the color of Changó. His feast day is celebrated on December 4. The **Museo Municipal de Regla** (Calle Martí, 158 between Facciolo and La Piedra; tel: 7-797-6989; Tue–Fri 9am–6pm, Sat 9am–7pm, Sun 9am–1pm; charge) has information and displays of Yoruba culture and the links with Santería.

Afro-Cuban center

Santería is strong in **Guanabacoa ❼** as well, a town renowned in Cuba for its connections with Afro-Cuban religions. Though the outskirts are grim and faceless, the town has an agreeable **plaza** and several interesting churches (in the process of restoration).

The **Museo Histórico de Guana-bacoa** (Calle Martí, 108, between Versalles and San Antonio; tel: 7-897-9117; Tue–Sat 10am–6pm, Sun 9am–1pm; charge) is best known for its exhibitions on Afro-Cuban cults. There is also lots about local resistance to the British invasion of 1762. Less heroically, Guanabacoa was a nexus for the slave trade. Wander along **Calle Amargura** (Bitterness Street), where slaves were dragged en route to their executions. A festival celebrating Cuba's African roots is held in Guanabacoa the last week of November every year.

Guanabacoa also has an interesting Jewish cemetery, started at the beginning of the 20th century. As well as graves of victims of the Machado dictatorship there is a memorial to victims of the Holocaust.

Driving to Guanabacoa, you take a turning off the Central Highway, 5km (3 miles) east of Havana. Alternatively you could take bus Ruta 3 from Parque de la Fraternidad, or the ferry to Regla and then another bus from there to Guanabacoa. There are also guided excursions which include the town on a trip to nearby Cojímar (see below).

Heading east

The former fishing village of **Cojímar ❽**, 16km (10 miles) from Old Havana, is popular for its Hemingway connection, but now it is a concrete mess. The

A marble statue of Christ keeps watch over the harbor.

BELOW: fire-breathing dancer in Guanabacoa.

The late Gregorio Fuentes, pictured here in Cojímar, was Hemingway's fishing guide for nearly 30 years.

BELOW: Finca Vigía has been beautifully renovated in recent years.

seafront took a battering in the 2008 hurricanes and the wharf where Hemingway kept his boat, the *Pilar*, was smashed. Hemingway used the village as the setting for *The Old Man and the Sea* and celebrated his Nobel Prize here in 1954. There is a bust of the author made from boat propellers donated by local fishermen and housed in a gazebo by the cube-shaped Spanish fortress, now occupied by the military.

Just off the highway before Cojímar is the **Villa Pan Americana**, a complex of sports facilities, apartments and a hotel built for the 1991 regional games. The volunteers who took on the huge task of building the complex now live in the athletes' apartments, though some are still used by athletes competing at the nearby stadium (Estadio Panamericano).

Across an inlet to the east of Cojímar lies **Alamar**, a suburb built by volunteers, known as micro-brigades, after the revolution. Originally planned for 40,000 people, it now has closer to 100,000, mostly in a depressing array of five-story walk-up apartment blocks. Despite or because of the grim surroundings, a strong musical culture has sprung up in Alamar. Many young bands rehearse in this dingy neighborhood, which stages an annual international rap festival, held in August at the **Casa de la Cultura de Alamar**.

Southeast on the *autopista* (Via Monumental) is the suburb of **San Francisco de Paula**, 12km (8 miles) from the city center, with the Hemingway Museum at **Finca Vigía** ❾ (tel: 7-910-809; Wed–Mon 9am–4.30pm, closed when it rains; charge). Journalist Martha Gellhorn, soon to be Hemingway's third wife, was not content to live in a room at the Hotel Ambos Mundos. She found a house called Finca Vigía – a former cattle farm on the site of a Spanish fort. The couple bought it in 1940 for US$18,500, and, although Gellhorn later divorced him, Hemingway stayed on at the *finca* for most of his life. The house lies at the end of a long, leafy driveway and is surrounded by lush gardens. The views over Havana are splendid. The mansion looks much as he left it, but meticulously renovated by a joint US-Cuban project to restore the house and preserve the author's papers (http://fincafoundation.org. Among the relics are 9,000 books, Hemingway's original Royal typewriter, and innumerable bullfighting posters and animal heads – mementoes from Spain and Africa. As a precaution against theft, visitors can only look in through the open doors and windows, but you get an excellent view of the large, airy rooms and their contents. Close to the main house is a four-story tower, from which the estate gets its name – *vigía* means "lookout." The pool where Ava Gardner swam naked and Gary Cooper once lolled, tanning his famous torso, is still there.

Santa María del Rosario ❿ nearby is a lovely place with tall trees, colonial houses, and pleasant inhabitants. The main attraction is the 18th-century **Catedral de los Campos** – best visited on Sunday afternoon (Mass at 2.30pm), the only time you can be fairly sure of seeing the Baroque paintings and

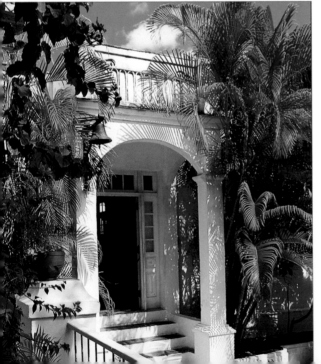

statues. Across the shady plaza is the restored **Casa del Conde de Bayona**, home of the Count of Bayona, a sugar baron notorious for executing a group of rebellious slaves. The execution site is marked on the **Loma de la Cruz** (Hill of the Cross), up a steep street from the plaza. The plain wooden cross was erected as a warning to other slaves, and two flanking crosses were added in 1959 to represent the thieves crucified with Christ.

Playas del Este

Beyond Alamar stretch a series of beach resorts known collectively as the **Playas del Este** (Eastern Beaches). This is where *habaneros* come to enjoy the sea and sand. The closest beach is **Playa Bacuranao**: on a small horseshoe-shaped inlet, it is a favorite with Cuban families and is packed in July and August.

After this is Tarará, where there is a marina and a famous hospital where victims of the Chernobyl nuclear explosion are treated. Then comes a 16km (10-mile) stretch of open sea, sand dunes, and coconut palms. The sand starts at **El Mégano** and continues to **Santa María del Mar ⓫**, which has a good beach and is the nicest section of this coast, with a number of seafront hotels. Farther on is **Guanabo**, an old seaside town with a lively beach and a number of wooden bungalows built in the 1920s and 1930s, which are very popular with Cubans. Much of this stretch of coast can be seen by taking a ride on the hop-on, hop-off HabanaBusTour.

Farther east lies **Santa Cruz del Norte**, site of Cuba's largest rum distillery (home of Havana Club). Inland is the decommissioned **Central Camilo Cienfuegos** sugar mill, founded by the the Hershey Chocolate Company during the sugar boom in 1917.

The coast road continues past attractive **Playa Jibacoa**, a good spot for family vacations and with some good walking opportunities; then along the **Litoral Norte** (North Coast) where beach resorts sit amid coastal vegetation. While much of the route along the Vía Blanca is attractive, there are also parts spoiled by heavy industry and smelly oil wells right by the sea.❑

Enjoying the Playas del Este.

RESTAURANTS

El Aljibe
Avenida 7, between calles 24 and 26, Miramar
Tel: (7) 204-1583. Open daily noon–midnight. **$**
Open-air dining; specialty is *pollo al aljibe*, chicken with rice, beans, potatoes, and salad. Unprepossessing menu but delicious recipe and very popular. First opened in 1947, it closed in 1961, but was reopened in 1993 by the state with the original owner bringing his famous dish back to life.

El Eco-Restaurant El Bambú
Jardín Botánico, Carretera El Rocío, Km 3.5, Boyeros
Tel: (7) 643-7278. Open: L daily for foreign tourists. **$**
Eat all you want for a set price from a huge array of vegetarian dishes, ranging from soups, salads, and rice dishes to puddings and fresh fruit juices. Most products grown on the premises, and cooked with solar power.

El Tocororo
Calle 18, 302, and Avenida 3ra, Miramar
Tel: (7) 204-2209, 202-4530. Open daily noon–midnight. **$$$**
Housed in an attractive Miramar villa, with a striking array of Art Nouveau lampshades. There are two dining rooms: one for *criolla* food, one for Japanese dishes, and a tapas bar (till 2am). It's expensive, but excellent. Book ahead.

La Cecilia
Avenida 5ta, between 110 and 112, Miramar
Tel: (7) 202-6700. Open daily noon–midnight. **$$$**
Surrounded by foliage, this relaxing restaurant serves everything from *ajiaco criolla*, a tasty meat and vegetable soup, to grilled sirloin steak. The fish is prepared with subtle seasonings. Live music with dancing Thur–Sun.

La Cocina de Liliam
Calle 48, 1311, between Avenidas 13 and 15, Miramar
Tel: (7) 209-6514. Open L & D, closed Sat. **$$**
Lovely setting with tables set in a pretty garden. Very good and tasty Cuban dishes, which are popular with the Cuban clientele so reservations are recommended.

La Fontana
Avenida 3ra, 305, corner Calle 46, Miramar
Tel: (7) 202-8337. Open daily noon–midnight. **$$**
The Cuban food here attracts Cubans and foreigners alike and its popularity means that reservations are advisable, particularly at night.

> Price categories are for a three-course meal for one with a beer, or *mojito*. Wine puts the price up:
> **$** = under $25
> **$$** = $25–35
> **$$$** = over $35

VIÑALES AND THE WEST

Cuba's westernmost province is one of its most beautiful, a lush and lovely landscape where tobacco, bananas and pineapples are grown, where fields are tilled by ox-drawn plows, and the white sandy beaches are never far away

Main attractions
LAS TERRAZAS
SOROA ORCHIDEARIO
VIÑALES
PARQUE NACIONAL DE LA GÜIRA
PINAR DEL RÍO
CAYO LEVISA
PUNTA MARÍA LA GORDA

Jutting out to the west of Havana, the province of Pinar del Río looks and feels quite different from the rest of Cuba. This is the country's tobacco heartland. Physically, it is dominated by a string of rounded limestone mountains called *mogotes*, around Viñales; in their shadows are lush green tobacco fields – *vegas*. Southwest of the *mogotes* lies the area known as Vuelta Abajo that produces the world's finest tobacco leaves, the dream of cigar connoisseurs from Paris to New York.

The atmosphere in Pinar is several degrees more gentle and relaxed than the rest of Cuba – a fact that the great Cuban intellectual Fernando Ortíz has argued is a legacy of the centuries-old tobacco tradition. While eastern Cuba is devoted to sugar cane – a crop whose harvesting is back-breaking work in the fierce Caribbean sun – the cultivation of tobacco is refined, intimate and even elegant. Pinar's plantations are minuscule compared to the endless cane fields of the east, and only a fraction of the numbers of workers are required. Everything is done by hand, from the picking of the leaf to the rolling of the cigars. In some *vegas*, linen nets protect the plants from the sun while harvesters remove their hats, so as not

to bruise the fragile, valuable leaves.

Pinar del Río has historically been one of the least-developed provinces of Cuba. For centuries, the central government looked first toward the east (after Havana, that is), and even vacationing *habaneros* avoided Pinar for the beaches of Varadero and attractions of Santiago. One of the revolution's aims was to bring Pinar more up to par with the rest of the country but rural life is still somewhat reminiscent of the 19th century. Bullock carts are

PRECEDING PAGES: plowing in the Viñales valley. **LEFT:** tending the crops at a Viñales tobacco plantation. **RIGHT:** revolutionary monument in Pinar del Río.

Western Cuba

N

20 miles

20 km

Gulf of Mexico

Golfo de Guanahacabibes

Archipiélago de los Colorados

CARIBBEAN SEA

Golfo de Batabanó

Archipiélago de los Canarreos

Isla de la Juventud

La Habana

Matanzas

Tarara

often the main form of transportation and regularly block traffic on highways; the use of oxen and mules for transportation is not exclusive to this region, but Pinar's reliance on them is greater than elsewhere. This is partly because oxen are used for plowing the tobacco fields; their hooves do far less damage to the soil than tractors. Thatched *casas de tabaco*, with steeply pitched roofs for drying the leaves, still dot the landscape, although some have been replaced by similar sheds roofed with sheets of corrugated iron. You will see traditional palm-thatched cottages – *bohíos*. At a time of severe building shortages, the government began constructing new *bohíos*, using traditional, abundant, natural materials. The villages are small and dreamy, each with a crumbling colonial church, palm-fringed plaza – and the inevitable bust of José Martí.

Head west, *compañero*

In its efforts to bring Pinar closer into the national fold, the Castro government pushed through an impressive six-lane *autopista* (highway) from Havana. Today it is little used; except for a few trucks and army vehicles, your rental car or tour bus is likely to be the only moving thing on it. Clustered in the shade under bridges are droves of hitchhikers going to buy food in the provinces or visit relatives – be generous with your space since many of them may have been waiting for hours. In the summer, when students are on holiday, the problem is worse, but always exercise caution. People have frequently been hit by vehicles when they step out into traffic to hitch a lift.

Following the highway, the provincial capital of Pinar del Río, 178km (110 miles) from Havana, can be reached in only three hours. Slower, but more appealing, is the old Carretera Central, a two-lane road that winds through smaller towns and is thick with cyclists. The third and most picturesque option is the rough-and-ready Carretera Norte, which follows the coast. Note that it is considerably easier to get out of Havana and join any of these three routes by first following the coastal road to **Mariel ❶**. During the summer of 1994, *balseros* (rafters) embarked on the hazardous crossing toward the US from all along this coast, in a great refugee crisis that strained political relations between the two countries. Mariel was also the scene of a great exodus in 1980, when more than 120,000 Cubans were allowed to leave, picked up in boats from Miami. This port used to be filled with Soviet ships, but now it is busy with a free-trade zone (*Zona Franca*). An horrendous cement works rains white powder on the town, which gives it its gray, ashen appearance.

Beyond Mariel, the scene grows more rural. The coast road passes glorious blue seas edged with scrubby beaches, and inland the landscape is agreeably pastoral. Many roads are unmarked, but local people will give directions. If heading inland, the road from Mariel soon joins the highway or links up with the Carretera Central at Guanajay. Although all Cuban *autopistas* are now pretty well provided with fuel and

BELOW: the verdant and fertile Viñales valley.

The area around Soroa and San Cristóbal is the only region in Cuba where grapes – introduced from Spain – are grown for wine production. The industry is still in its infancy, but some of the wines are worth trying.

BELOW: braving the waterfall at Soroa.

rest stops, drivers should remember to fill up with gas before heading to the remoter parts of the province.

The verdant sierra

Traveling through the interior, the highways enter the steep hills of the **Sierra del Rosario**. The first detour, just before the provincial boundary, is the biosphere reserve and eco-resort of **Las Terrazas** (there's a small charge, payable at checkpoints). In 1967 the government built a colony here, on 5,000 hectares (12,300 acres) of land, in an attempt to assist the rural community after indiscriminate tree-felling had all but denuded the countryside. The terraces were created to help prevent further soil erosion. Now run as a tourist complex on principles of sustainable development, the little colony flourishes, its forested terraces tumbling down to a long artificial lake that is lit at night and has a small café suspended over the water on a pier. A recent addition to the area's tourist attractions is a zip line, called a canopy tour, across the lake into the trees. The community is the base for several

artists who sell crafts and paintings from their workshops. There is also a **museum** of pre-Columbian artifacts. The Hotel La Moka here is a beautiful modern hotel built in traditional Cuban style.

At the **Eco-Center** (Centro de Investigaciones Ecológicas) you can hire guides who specialize in the forest's flora and birdlife and will lead you on forest trails. The San Juan River Trail ends at the fabulous **Baños de San Juan** where you can bathe in a deep mountain pool fed by a waterfall. You can also rent bicycles for about CUC$1 an hour.

Just across the provincial border, 8km (5 miles) from the main highway, is **Soroa ❷** – less a village than a crossroads in the dripping forest (much of the sierra has been declared a Unesco Biosphere Reserve). Do not attempt to drive the back road from Las Terrazas to Soroa, which was blocked by a landslide in 2009. Go back down to the *autopista*. Soroa is best known for its **Orchideario** (Orchid Garden; daily 8am–4pm; charge), maintained behind large gates: on its extensive, pleasant grounds are some 700 types of orchid, more than 200 of them indigenous, and most of them in flower between December and March.

Signposts by the road also direct hikers to a *mirador* (lookout) – a 20-minute walk – and a **waterfall**, as well as the **Villa Soroa-Castillo en las Nubes** complex. This is a good place for a break from the road, with a pleasant dining room (although the food is only average) and views across the sierra to the plains from a sunny, silent terrace. Soroa is now very much a part of the tourist trail but this is still a pleasant place to sit and watch the river and listen to the cicadas – an amazing rattling sound that rolls through the forest like a Mexican wave. Visitors can stay at the Villa Soroa in cabins set in a lush landscape or in one of the *casas particulares* along the road.

West of Soroa, the Carretera Central passes the provincial town of **San Cristóbal**, whose red-tiled roofs and colorful buildings are falling to pieces. As in all such outposts, motor vehicles are few and far between. Slightly to the southwest, on the railroad line, is **Los Palacios**, and a rough dirt road that heads to the remote and barely populated southern coastline. In the swampy land here is **Maspotón ❸**, where a Club de Caza (hunting club) operates small bungalows. Pigeon and wild duck are common in the winter months, and trout fishing is good year-round.

Che's redoubt

Back on the Carretera Central, the route passes the **Presa La Juventud** (Lake of Youth), and there's a detour north to the village of **San Diego de los Baños**. This pretty little town, by the side of a gorge cut by the fast-flowing Los Palacios River, was once famous for its spa. Public thermal baths were inaugurated in 1951 but they have been closed since the passage of Hurricane Ike in 2008. You can still get a massage, but treatments with volcanic mud and mineral water are currently unavailable. There is a milky radioactive pool that glows in the gloom of the bathhouse, which is said to stimulate the hypothalamus area of the brain and rejuvenate the nervous system.

The tropical forests of the **Parque Nacional La Güira ❹** can be reached

Imported from the Far East, the Red Ginger Lily (Etlingera elatior) *is now found all over the Caribbean and is one of the species cultivated at the Orchideario.*

BELOW: graceful statue in the Parque Nacional La Güira.

Polo Montañez

Born Fernando Borrego in San Cristóbal in 1955, Polo Montañez became popular both within and outside Cuba for his *guajiro* (country) music. His first and best-known album was *El Guajiro Natural* (The Authentic Countryman). Polo joined his father's band when he was 10 years old, and never stopped playing or singing, even when he had to take on a variety of manual jobs to earn a living. He rarely left Pinar del Río, and never strayed from his roots. His music was undeniably Cuban, yet it was unlike any other, for he developed his own distinctive style. There was widespread mourning when Polo died following a car accident on his way home from Havana in November 2002. The lively Cultural Center in Viñales, not far from his home town, has been renamed the Polo Montañez Center in his honor.

Guayabita del Pinar is a liqueur specific to the region.

BELOW: an ornate but crumbling building houses the Museo de Ciencias Naturales.

by road, or by crossing the suspension bridge across the river by the spa. This was part of an aristocratic estate in colonial times and still contains a mansion and sculpted garden. The surrounding forest, dotted with lakes, plays host to a rich birdlife and is home to the native Cuban deer.

The neighboring **Cueva de Los Portales** was the HQ for the Western Army under Che Guevara during the 1962 Missile Crisis, and was declared a National Monument in 1987. You can visit free of charge, although if there is a guide there he will appreciate a tip. A path leads into a tunnel, parallel with the Río Caiguanabo, and off to one side is the chamber from where Guevara led his operation. Stalagmites and stalactites are interspersed with evidence of his occupation, but this is not a museum as such. The camping complex here, with a dozen comfortable cabins set among lawns and pines joined by rope walkways, was designed by Celia Sánchez. It is a pleasant, inexpensive place to stay, although it is primarily for Cubans and foreigners can only stay there if there is space.

Provincial capital

The one exception to the prevailing laid-back atmosphere of the province is the hectic regional capital, **Pinar del Río ❺**. A settlement has existed here since the 1570s, but development really began only after 1774 – comparatively late in the Spanish colonial period. Pinar lacks the clear grid pattern that makes other Cuban towns so straightforward to explore. The streets are unusually narrow and confusing, packed with cyclists. Be warned, too, that for a relatively small place, the town contains an unusual concentration of *jineteros* (street hustlers).

The main street, José Martí, has a number of impressive, if decrepit, buildings: the **Palacio Guasch**, dating from 1909, stands out for its fairy-tale Moorish design mixed with other architectural styles. It is in a somewhat sorry state, but houses the **Museo de Ciencias Naturales Tranquilino Sandalio de Noda** (Natural History Museum; Tue–Sat 9am–6pm, Sun 9am–1pm; charge), crammed with stuffed animals and with a curious collection of concrete dinosaurs in the courtyard.

A short walk east is the **Museo Provincial de História** (Calle Martí 58; Tue–Sat 9am–5pm, Sun 9am–1pm; charge), housed in a colonial mansion and with a collection of local memorabilia ranging from 18th-century furniture to the pistols, radios, and rifles of local revolutionary heroes. Next door, the fully restored, 19th-century, neoclassical **Teatro Jacinto Milanés** is one of the prettiest theaters in the country.

More interesting for visitors are two factories in Pinar. Near Plaza de la Independencia, at the eastern end of Martí, is the tiny **Fábrica de Tabaco Francisco Donatién** (Maceo 157, corner Tarafa; tel: 48-723 424; Mon–Fri 9am–noon, 1–4pm, Sat 9am–noon; charge, no photos allowed), where a constant stream of tourists watches workers rolling a variety of cigars, and where there is also a small shop opposite, the Casa del Habano. South on Isabel Rubio is the **Fábrica de Bebidas Casa Garay** (Isabel Rubio 189, between Ceferino Fernández and Frank País; Mon–Fri 9am–noon, 1–4pm, Sat 9am–noon; guided tours; charge), which produces a liqueur called Guayabita del Pinar,

distilled from sugar cane and the small *guayabita* fruit, a tiny, wild guava that grows around Pinar. Tours take you past the vats of liqueur and end up in the gift shop, where the concoction can be tasted and, of course, bought.

The Viñales valley

The touristic core of the province lies north of Pinar in the **Sierra de los Órganos**, a region protected as the Parque Nacional de Viñales and dominated by the bizarre flat-topped mountains that protrude sheer from the fields on the valley floor. These *mogotes* are fists of hard limestone that were left behind when the softer rock around them eroded over millions of years. In the Jurassic period the *mogotes* were the pillars of vast caves that subsequently collapsed; today, covered in luxuriant foliage, they have the air of overgrown ruins.

From Pinar, a narrow road with splendid views winds 27km (17 miles) up into the sierra until it reaches **Viñales ❻**. The long rows of single-story houses and the porches on which people sit in rocking chairs, are

Tobacco crops and thatched drying barn.

BELOW: view of the *mogotes* across the fertile Viñales valley.

Nearly all the *casas particulares* in Viñales cook excellent food for their guests at very reasonable prices – and some of them mix a mean *mojito*, as well.

colorfully painted. Local residents have discovered the benefits of tourism: Viñales has more rooms to let than any small Cuban town except Trinidad; there were said to be 280 at the latest count. There are a couple of lively music venues *(see page 211)* and a general air of friendliness. Viñales has been badly hit by hurricanes in recent years and the loss of the avenue of trees down the main street in 2008 has changed the rural aspect of the town.

At the east end of the main street (Salvador Cisneros), almost opposite the Cupet gas station, is the pretty little **Jardín Botánico** (daylight hours; donation appreciated), first planted in the 1930s and maintained by the same family ever since. A wide selection of flowers and fruits is cultivated, as well as some oddities, like a tree decorated with beer cans, and another with plastic dolls' heads. They will show you around and tell you the name of everything, before offering you slices of seasonal fruits on their shady porch.

BELOW: a Viñales tobacco plantation worker.

There's a little Museo Municipal at the western end of the street (No. 115) in the house of local War of Inde-

pendence heroine, Adela Acuye (1861–1914). It gamely stays open until 10pm, but seems to receive few visitors.

A good way to get to know the area is to take the little tourist bus that runs from the main square seven times a day (first bus at 9am, CUC$5). The tour lasts just over an hour and takes in all the main sights and hotels; you can get off where you like, and continue on a later bus.

There are two hotels worth visiting even if you aren't staying there. The **Hotel Los Jazmines** has the most attractive position. The views across the valley are exceptional. The **Hotel La Ermita** is closer to Viñales (a 20-minute walk, above the town to the east). It has more distant views of the valley, but at dusk the scenery is stunning: the sun turns brilliant orange as it slides behind the mountains while a thin mist gathers in the valleys, isolating the distant strings of palm trees in a haunting tropical soup.

Agricultural heartland

It is a short drive (or a pleasant walk) from Viñales into the shaded valleys

Insider Knowledge

The Parque Nacional de Viñales has a Visitors' Center, housed in a bright yellow building just past the Hotel Los Jazmines, 3km (2 miles) from Viñales. It offers a limited amount of information on the area's agriculture and geology, as well as guided walking tours (in English if required) into the valley, stopping to visit a tobacco-drying house. It is convenient if you are staying in the Hotel Los Jazmines, but if you are in a *casa particular*, the owner will probably be able to arrange similar walks more cheaply (although you are less likely to get an English-speaking guide). In Viñales, everyone knows someone who can perform such services. If you want to go horse trekking, for example, a guide and a horse will be produced and a price quoted; and if you want to buy cigars, you'll be spoiled for choice.

between the *mogotes*, whose rich, red soil is perfect for tobacco growing. Along the isolated tracks, *guajiros* (farmers) cycle past wearing straw hats and puffing huge cigars, or trot past on horseback. In the fields, simple wooden or iron plows are pulled by placid oxen (*bueyes*) instead of tractors, and these animals are often used to pull carts as well. You will see the steep-roofed *secaderos*, sheds in which tobacco is dried, and the small homesteads where local farming families live. Most of the farmers here grow a mixture of tobacco, maize, bananas, and pineapples, all on a small scale, and most keep a pig and some chickens, as well as the working *bueyes* and horses.

The **Mural de la Prehistoria**, an enormous, garish painting that covers the flank of the Dos Hermanas Mogote, about 4km (2 miles) west of Viñales, was commissioned by Castro in the 1960s to portray the emergence of Socialist Man from the primal wilderness. One of Diego de Rivera's students, Leovigildo González, took on the commission, directing dozens of local painters. It is regularly touched up by artists who dangle precariously from the cliff top on rope swings.

A collection of caves

The *mogotes* are riddled with underground rivers and limestone caves. Heading north of Viñales, the road passes the **Cueva de San Miguel**, a small cave through which you walk to reach **El Palenque de los Cimarrones**, a bar, restaurant, and museum (noon–4pm). A couple of miles farther on, in manicured grounds amid towering rocks, is the **Cueva del Indio** ❼ (Indian Cave; daily 10am–5.30pm; regular tours last 25 minutes; charge) – so named because the indigenous Guanahatabey people used it as a cemetery and refuge during the Spanish Conquest. You climb steps to the cave then follow a contorted limestone tunnel down to an underground lake, on which you can take a boat trip (part of the guided tour).

There is a pleasant hotel (El Rancho San Vicente), with a restaurant and a bar set beside a deep natural pool, with shacks outside selling touristy goods. You can visit the spa with its sulphur-

Some 4km (2½ miles) from Viñales is a small community called Los Acuaticos, founded in 1943 by a santero, Antoñica Izquierdo. The residents venerate water, and bathe three times a day in the clean water here, which they believe keeps them healthy, and they refuse outside medical care.

LEFT AND BELOW: a boat trip on the underground lake is included in the Cueva del Indio guided tour.

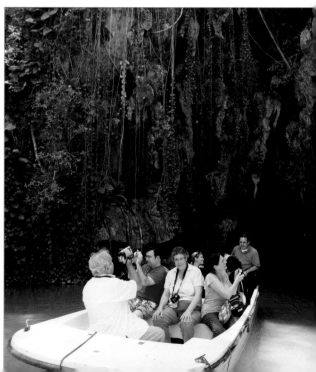

The *Guajiro*

Looking like a cowboy who's lost his steers, the *guajiro* is usually seen welded to his horse, shaded by his broad-brimmed hat

A *guajiro* is a Cuban peasant farmer – the romanticized version of the *campesino*, or rural worker. The true *guajiro* is country-born and bred, devoted to the land, fiercely independent, and firmly set in his ways. Both by tradition and preference, he lives in a *bohío*. These rustic cottages, their roofs thatched with palm leaves, can still be seen, with rocking chairs tipped up on the front porch, a horse tethered at the door, a television aerial atop the roof, chickens scratching in the yard, and a few pigs rooting outside.

The stereotypical *guajiro* is taciturn and mistrustful of outsiders, especially people from the city and farming bureaucrats – the ones who set quotas and prices for whatever they've told him to plant. In recent years, more and more *guajiros* – persuaded by the state – have joined their land with others to form larger cooperatives. But he's still a *guajiro*, guiding his ox-pulled plow through the fields, dressed like his predecessors in old boots, baggy pants, long-sleeved shirt, and broad-brimmed straw hat; breaking his dawn-to-dusk day with a midday meal then relaxing with a cigar and a shot of rum.

The first *guajiros* were the tobacco farmers of western Cuba, sons of Spaniards who revolted against the Spanish tobacco monopoly in 1717. Although plantations based on slavery soon dominated Cuban agriculture, they always co-existed with small farms owned and worked by free men. No matter what the crop or where they grew it, these farmers had little in common with the plantation owners, who operated on a totally different scale, with a large workforce of slaves. They also had little in common with freed slaves.

Though unsophisticated, the *guajiro* has unwittingly made his contribution to Cuban fashion with the *guayabera*, a white cotton shirt he always donned for a down-home *guateque*, or party. In the 1800s, Cubans rebelling against Spain adopted the *guayabera* for dress parade; in the early 20th century, Havana bohemians took a fancy to it and brought the look into their clubs. It is still the favorite dress shirt of many Cubans.

Typically, the *guajiro* enlivens the *guateque* with a dance that expresses his exuberant energy: called a *zapateo*, it is a toe-and-heel jig that keeps couples hopping around energetically between drinking shots of *aguardiente* (raw rum) and eating hunks of roast pork.

Despite lacking formal education, the *guajiro* brought poetry to the Cuban countryside in the form of the *décima*, which originated in 16th-century Spain. It consists of 10 octosyllabic rhymed lines, improvised and usually sung in counterpoint, accompanied by three main instruments – a guitar, a *tres* (similar to a mandolin), and a lute – with *claves* (wooden sticks) and a dried gourd for percussion. The songs will usually describe the *guajiro*'s life of joy and pain, trust and deception, success and failure, but they are sometimes witty polemics on a current topic.

Typical of rural Cuba is the *guajira* ballad, first sung by roving troubadours, and much later commercialized for radio. The most famous *guajira* is the one that groups of musicians play in every square and bar in Cuba where tourists congregate. It is Joseito Fernández's *La Guantanamera*, sung in praise of a girl from Guantánamo, using verse written by independence hero José Martí: "I am a sincere man from the land where the palms grow... Guantanamera, *guajira*, Guantanamera..." ❏

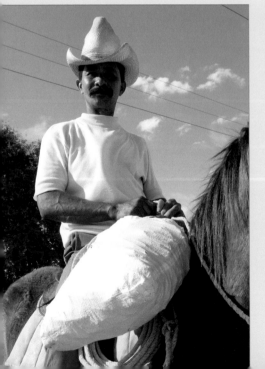

LEFT: a *guarijo* at work in Holguín.

ous water and have a mud bath, massage, physiotherapy, or acupuncture (usually closed in the low season). There's also the Cueva del Indio restaurant, open for lunch only, where you buy tickets to visit the cave.

Seventeen kilometers (10½ miles) southwest of Viñales, in the village of El Moncada, is the **Gran Caverna Santo Tomás** (daily 9am–5pm; 90-minute guided tour; charge), said to be Cuba's largest cave system. Visitors are provided with headlamps (like miners' lamps) but the lack of other artificial light makes it unsuitable for the caustrophopic.

Two cays on the gulf

A well-signposted road leads westward and then north from El Mondaca, passing mangrove swamps on the last part of the journey, to **Cayo Jutías**, a tranquil little sandy beach reached via a long causeway. (There's a gas station at Santa Lucía, just before you get to the causeway.) You pay CUC$5 to gain access. A *ranchón* (thatch-roofed restaurant and bar) is open for lunch and drinks until 6pm right by the shore.

There are thatched umbrellas for shade on the beach and a kiosk where you can rent snorkeling equipment or sunbeds. Snorkeling is best right out on the reef beyond the sea grass. Take insect repellent as flying insects can be a nuisance.

The road north of Viñales runs through spectacular countryside directly to the coast, ending up at **Puerto Esperanza** a small, soporific fishing outpost, where benches are laid out beneath palm trees by the mangrove-lined coast. Just past the Cuevo del Indio, on this road, is a more oft-traveled route: a turn-off east leads through La Palma to **Palma Rubia** ❽, from where it is a 25-minute boat trip to **Cayo Levisa** ❾: get there by 9.45am at the latest to catch the 10am sailing, or there isn't another departure until 6pm. Return ferries are at 9am and 5pm. This small island has the best beaches in Pinar del Río province, with sparkling white sands. There is a comfortable, unpretentious resort where, thanks to the fishing industry, lobster is the specialty. This is a place to chill out, though there is some good diving – the nearby reef has abundant black coral and other rarities.

TIP

The Cubanacán office is at Salvador Cisneros 63, and Havanatur at 65, one on either side of the Víazul office in Viñales, for tours, transport, and accommodation reservations.

BELOW: Cayo Levisa is great, whether you want to be lazy or active.

Attractive conch shells on the beach – don't be tempted to take them home.

BELOW: Punta María La Gorda in the far west.

The coastal route heading back to Havana via **Las Pozas** and **Bahía Honda** is often rough, potholed, and narrow, so should be approached with caution. The Sierra del Rosario, Soroa, and Las Terrazas can also be accessed from just east of Bahía Honda. This is a return to more traditional sugar-growing areas, and in winter harvest time the road can be jammed with trucks. The views of the Caribbean are pleasant, but the beaches are not the best, and much of the coastline is taken up by mangroves rather than sand. The best of them is probably **Playa Herradura**, some 8km (5 miles) off the main road, to the north of Cabañas.

The end of the road

Heading west from Pinar del Río, the route passes the town of **San Juan y Martínez** ❿. Between here and **San Luis** is the district of **Vuelta Abajo**, where it is generally regarded that the finest tobacco leaves in the world are grown. Despite its tiny size, the most famous – and therefore the most photographed – field of all is the **Hoyo de Monterrey**.

Increasing numbers of travelers venture west beyond this point. Although the roads are in reasonable condition, invasions of land crabs can cause havoc with your car tires at breeding times (March–April). The Carretera Central leaves the hills for more monotonous terrain. You pass the planned city of **Sandino** – named after the Nicaraguan revolutionary hero, and partially populated by Cubans forcibly transferred from the Escambray mountains during the 1960s for supporting the counter-revolution – and end up at the fishing outpost of **La Fé**.

You can continue west from La Fé to **La Bajada**, where the road branches south to **Punta María La Gorda** ⓫ (Fat Maria's Point), named for an obviously well-fed Venezuelan girl abandoned here after being kidnapped by pirates. The beach is lovely, but most people come for the diving. There are some sheltered offshore reefs of black coral, some good wrecks to explore, a wide range of marine life, and great visibility. The **International Diving Center** offers a range of dive packages including accommodation and food.

La Bajada marks the beginning of the **Península de Guanahacabibes Biosphere Reserve** and the site of the Guanahacabibes' last stand against the Spanish. At the information center you can arrange an entry permit and guided walks. The area has an excellent reputation for birdlife, including several rare endemic species. The roadway along the **Bahía de Corrientes** sparkles with fine, white-sand beaches, and dolphins may sometimes be seen in the blue seas of the bay. Beyond this, the Gulf of Mexico stretches into the distance. Cuba's most westerly point, **Cabo de San Antonio** ⓬, is 52km (32 miles) on a good road from La Bajada. There is a small new hotel and marina, near the Roncali lighthouse, built in 1849. Diving and fishing are offered as well as refueling and provisioning for visiting yachts. There are a few caves to explore and some pretty beaches, but otherwise the region is very isolated. ❑

RESTAURANTS AND BARS

Restaurants

Price categories are for a three-course meal for one with a beer, or *mojito*. Wine puts the price up:
$ = under $25
$$ = $25–35
$$$ = over $35

Las Terrazas
El Romero
Las Terrazas, Autopista Habana–Pinar del Río, Km 51
Tel: (48) 778-600–1. Open daily 9am–9pm. $
A vegetarian restaurant in this "eco-community" between Pinar del Río and Viñales. All ingredients are home-grown and organic – and dishes are quite innovative, too.

Pinar del Río
El Aguila de Oro
Rafael Morales corner Calle Antonio Maceo
Open 11am–11pm. $
Not far from the cigar factory, this pleasant restaurant and bar is in an old colonial building and looks like a plantation house. Exceptionally cheap because it charges in pesos Cubanos.
El Marino
Isabel Rubio corner Calle Martí
Tel: (48) 750-381.
Open noon–11pm. $
Nautical themed restaurant serving good food for pesos Cubanos. Even dishes with lobster can be had here at a fraction of the normal price. Quite smart, with a dress code of no shorts or sandals

and no smoking.
Rumayor
Carretera Viñales, Km 1½
Tel: (48) 763-051.
Open noon–10pm, closed Thur. $–$$
Restaurant and amphitheater surrounded by garden and trees. The house specialty is smoked chicken *(pollo ahumado)*. Known for its Tropicana-style cabaret show Fri–Sun, starting at 11pm, followed by a disco until about 3am.

Viñales
La Casa de Don Tomás
Calle Salvador Cisneros, 140
Open daily L & D. $$
Completely rebuilt in 2010 after the 2008 hurricane destroyed the former lovely old house in the main street, set in flowery gardens with a terrace. The food is nothing special but it is a nice place to come for a drink.
Palenque de los Cimarrones
Carretera Puerto Esperanza, Km 36, Viñales.
Tel: (48) 796-290. Open daily 11am–4pm. $$
Reached through the Cueva de San Miguel. You get an Afro-Cuban show with your lunch. Grilled chicken and game are the specialties. On Fri and Sat nights there is a cabaret followed by a disco.
Restaurant Jurásico, Mural de la Prehistoria
Carretera Pinar del Río–Viñales
Tel: (48) 796-260. Open daily noon–7pm. $$
The mural may be a bit odd but the food is great. Charcoal-grilled pork with

all the trimmings is the specialty.

Bars

Pinar del Río
Bar La Esquinita
Isabel Rubio. Open daily 8pm–late.
Live guitar music.
Creador
José Martí 113
A cultural institution for young artists and musicians and at night a place where they get together to arrange concerts for up-and-coming bands.
La Picuala
(at the back of the Teatro Milanés)
Live bands and a fashion show on Wed and Fri and Sat from 9pm.
Viñales
Casa Polo
Calle Salvador Cisneros, beside church in the plaza

Named after a renowned local singer who died in a car accident in 2002, this place is open all day, serving drinks and snacks, with taped music. Live music, often very good, starts around 10pm, followed by a disco, till about 2am.
El Viñalero
Calle Salvador Cisneros, 105
Renovated in 2009, this is a very local, friendly spot for a beer or a rum – and if there's no music you can sit on the terrace and hear the music from the Decimista opposite.
Patio del Decimista
Calle Salvador Cisneros, 102
A lively spot, where you can sit at tables inside or out with a rum or a beer. Live music every night from 9pm or 10pm.

RIGHT: La Casa de Don Tomás.

SECRETS OF THE CUBAN CIGAR

Thanks to the ideal climate and soil, plus centuries of expertise in cultivating the tobacco crop, Cuba produces the world's finest smokes

The big fat Cuban cigar holds almost as important a role in the national identity as rum and salsa. Tobacco is grown on smallholdings in parts of eastern, central, and western Cuba, but the most highly prized comes from the *vegas* (plantations) around the town of San Juan y Martínez and San Luís in the western province of Pinar del Río, in an area called the Vuelta Abajo.

It is this region's leaves – the most important of which are grown under cheesecloth to protect them from direct sunlight – that end up in Havana's cigar factories, to be made into world-famous brands such as Cohiba, Montecristo, and Romeo y Julieta. Around 100 million cigars are exported each year, and the industry is one of the island's chief hard-currency earners.

In order to stamp out the black market in counterfeit cigars, official cigar boxes now bear a holographic seal. A box of Cohibas bought on the street may look much like the real thing, with the packaging and cigar bands pilfered from a factory, but the tobacco is likely to be inferior. It's best to buy from an official shop (the best are in tobacco factories), where prices are much higher but still only a fraction of what you would pay abroad.

If you get the chance to inspect the contents of a box before you buy, check that the cigars are of a similar color (the darker the color, the stronger the flavour), and that if you squeeze them they readily spring back into shape and don't crackle.

ABOVE: it was the women who traditionally sorted tobacco leaves by placing them across their thighs, giving rise to the myth that cigars are rolled on the thighs of dusky maidens.

LEFT: the finished product – sealed boxes of genuine Montecristo cigars.

RIGHT: the harvested leaves are sewn together in pairs and hung on a pole to dry for about 50 days before being stacked for fermentation.

CUBAN CIGAR FACTORIES

Cigars for domestic consumption are made in small-scale factories across the country, while those for export are produced in Havana's large, famous factories such as Partagás and La Corona.

The highlight of a factory visit is seeing a room full of *torcedores* (cigar rollers) dexterously blending together the filler, binder, and wrapper leaves. The best rollers can produce as many as 150 cigars a day. All rollers are allowed to smoke as many cigars as they want on the job. To help pass the time and prevent boredom, a lector takes the podium to read from a newspaper or book.

Visitors are often allowed to watch other parts of the cigar-making process, such as the sorting of leaves into their various strengths, and the color grading, banding, and boxing of the final product. Before cigars can leave the factory, *catadores* (tasters) smoke random samples from selected batches to ensure their quality.

ABOVE: harvesting of tobacco is done by hand from January through March, with two or three leaves picked from each plant every five days, starting from the bottom.

BELOW: Alejandro Robaina (1919–2010) was the only grower to have a brand of cigar named in his honor after a lifetime of producing the very best leaves for wrapping cigars on his privately owned 40-acre (16-hectare) farm in Pinar del Río.

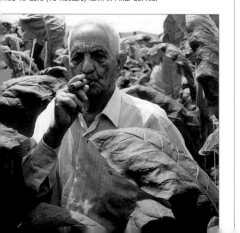

TOP: five types of leaves are used to make a cigar: "fillers," *ligero*, *seco*, and *volado*, mixed together in the middle to determine the flavor, wrapped in the "binder," *capote*, which is then enveloped in the soft, silky "wrapper," *capa*.

ABOVE LEFT: every brand of cigar has its own emblem and many of the old labels have become collectors' items.

BELOW: the pitched roofs of tobacco drying sheds were traditionally thatched, but successive hurricanes have led to other materials being used in some cases.

West Central Cuba

0   20 km

0   20 miles

N

Cayo Cruz
del Padre

Cayos
Arenas

Cayos
Falcone

Santa Cruz
del Norte

Arcos de
Canasí

Playa Jibacoa

❶ Puente
Bacunayagua

Península de
Hicacos

Punta
de Morlas

Cayos de las
Cinco Leguas

Varadero ❹

Reserva Ecológica
Varahicacos

Bahía de
Matanzas

Bahía de
Cárdenas

Bahía de Santa Clara

Caraballo

Pan de
Matanzas
381

Matanzas ❷

Camarioca

Sale

La Teja

Bainoa

Ceiba
Mocha

Aguacate

Gelpi

Cárdenas ❺

Corral

❸

Las Cuevas
de Bellamar

Guanábana

Limonar

José
Smith
Comas

Martí

Itabo

Minas
de Motembo

Alturas de Bejucal

Madruga - Coliseo

Coliseo

La Habana 251

Madruga

San Antonio
de Cabezas

Juan
Gualberto
Gómez

Carlos
Rojas

Máximo
Gómez

Carlos
Rodríguez

Motembo
Viejo

La Palma

Pipián

San José
de los Ramos

Israel
Ruiz

San
Nicolás

Unión
de Reyes

San Miguel
de los Baños

Jovellanos

Perico

Banagüises

México

La Habana

Nueva
Paz

Alacranes

Bolondrón

Pedro
Betancourt

Matanzas

Colón

Los
Arabos

CARRETERA CENTRAL

Héctor
Molina

Llanura

Cársica

Puerto
Rico Libre

Meridional

Agramonte

Palmillas

Playa del
Caimito

Tasajera

El Estante

Autopista Nacional

Pedroso

y

de

Guareiras

Rafael

Ensenada
de la Broa

Hatiguanico

Negro

Torriente

Colón

Manguito

Jagüey
Grande

Calimete

Hanabana

Punta
Sombrero

Ciénaga Occidental
de Zapata

❻ Australia

Amarillas

Santo
Tomás ❽

La Boca de Guamá

Aguada de
Pasajeros

Maneadero

Gran Parque Natural Montemar

Palpite

Laguna
del Tesoro

Real
Campiña

Rodas

Península de Zapata

Ciénaga de Zapata

Llanura de Zapata

Buenaventura

Playa
Larga

Covadonga

Yaguaramas

Abreus

Cienfue

Cayo del
Masío

Cueva de
los Peces

Cayo
Ramona

Horquitas

Antón
Recio

Cienfu

Cayería de Diego Pérez

Las Salinas ❾

Bahía de Cochinos

Ciénaga Oriental de Zapata

El Rincón

❿ Playa
Girón

Juragua

Castillo de

Cayos Blancos

Punta
Palmillas

Caleta
Buena

Colo

Golfo
de Cazones

Isla de
la Juventud

Archipiélago de los Canarreos

Punta
del
Este

Cayo
del Rosario

Cayo
Rico

Cayo
Largo

Cayos
de Dios

CARIBBEAN

ATLANTIC OCEAN

Archipiélago de Sabana

Around Cienfuegos

Rodas,
La Habana
Jaime
González
Parque José
Martí Cienfuegos
0   1km
0   1 mile

Hotel Jagua Palacio
del Valle
Cementerio
Tomás Acea
El Junco

Calle 37 (Prado)

Caunao

Cayo
Carenas
Bahía de
Cienfuegos

Cayo
Picuas

Cayos Jutías
Isabela
de Sagua

Cayos del
Pajonal

Cayo
la Vaca

Jagua
La Milpa
Hotel Pasacaballo
Pasacaballo
Castillo Nuestra Señora
de los Ángeles de Jagua

Cayo
Ocampo

La
Campana
Laguna
Guanaroca

Cuba
Libre

Rancho
Luna

Arimao

Cayo
Santa
María

Punta
Colorados
Hotel
Faro de
Luna
Hotel
Rancho Luna

hita Carahatas
ho
Quintín
Banderas

Sagua la
Grande
Playa
Uvero

Quemado
e Güines
Embalse
Alacranes
Sitiecito

Granadillo
El
Santo
Playa
Juan
Francisco

Cayo
Fragoso

a la Grande
Viana
Perucho
Figueredo

Villa

Encrucijada

Cayos de
la Virazón

Cayos de la Herradura

Rodrigo
Cifuentes

Cayo
Conuco
13

Cayos de la Herradura

Manacas
Santo
Domingo

Clara

Mata

Sagua la Chica

San Antonio
de las Vueltas

Cayo
Conuco

San
cos
Jicotea
Hatillo

Camajuaní
Remedios
Taguayabon
12
Caibarién

Bahía de Buena Vista

Esperanza
Santa Isabel
de las Lajas

Santa
Clara
11
Díaz

Embalse
Minerva

Zulueta
Buena
Vista

Alturas
Simón
Bolívar

ruces
Ranchuelo
San Juan de
los Yeras

Falcón
473
Placetas

Remates
de Ariosa

Yaguajay

Nela

351
General Carillo

del

Caunao

San Fernando
de Camarones
Potrerillo
Mataguá
Báez

Jarahueca
Meneses
Iguará

Mayajigua

Nordeste

Jatibonico del Norte

Alturas
de Santa Clara

Calabazas

435
Chambas

Embalse
Avilés
348
Jorobada
La
Moza
Barajagua

Manicaragua
489

Autopista Nacional

Zaza
Jiquima
Sancti
Spíritus
Jarahuegas

Florencia

Los Guaos
ao
Jardín
Botánico
Soledad

El Nicho
14

Cumanayagua
Fomento
Cabaiguán
La Rana

Tamarindo

Arroyo
Blanco
Marroquí

Escambray
San Francisco

Embalse
Hanabanilla

Pico San
Juan 1140
Jibacoa

Güinia de
Miranda

Santa
Lucía
Guayos
Taguasco

Ciego de Ávila

nao
La
anes
Sierrita

Sierra del Escambray
Parque Nacional
Topes de Collantes
15

Zaza
del Medio
16
Jatibonico

Majagua

illo
Inglés
Yaguanabo

Topes
de Collantes
Pico de
Potrerillo
Muñoz

931
20

Macizo de Guamuhaya

Condado

Loma de Banao
843

Sancti
Spíritus

Embalse
Zaza

Jatibonico del Sur

Río Hondo
La Boca

Valle de
los Ingenios
18
Torre de
Manaca-Iznaga

Caracusey

Banao

Limones
Palmero

Llanura de Júcaro - Morón

Playa
Ancón
19
Trinidad
Casilda

San
Pedro
Playa
Tayabacoa

Guasimal
La Sierpe

Negros

Península
de Ancón
Punta
Manatí
Bahía de
San Pedro

Heriberto
Orellanes
El Jíbaro

Mapos
Romero
Palo
Alto

Tunas de Zaza

SEA

VARADERO AND MATANZAS

Cuba's prime resort for package tourism, Varadero
is a world apart from the rest of the island,
including the area's own peaceful hinterland and
the nearby cities of Matanzas and Cárdenas

The province of **Matanzas** is the largest in Cuba, yet most visitors will never go there unless they are staying in the glitzy beach resort of Varadero. The province couldn't have a grander point of entry than the **Puente Bacunayagua ❶**. This impressive bridge, the highest in the country, spans the 112-meter (370ft)-deep gorge of the Bacunayagua River dividing the provinces of Havana and Matanzas. The Yumurí valley meanders away to the distant mountains beyond. Turkey vultures wind lazy circles above the near-silent gorge. Cicadas sing. Few vehicles pass. There is a small restaurant and café here – an obligatory pit stop for bus parties, and deservedly so: the view is impressive.

City of the slaughter

About 20km (12 miles) east is the provincial capital of **Matanzas ❷**, founded more than 300 years ago. The highway passes right by the city's supertanker port, capable of receiving 150,000-tonne oil tankers and linked by pipeline to the Cienfuegos Oil Refinery, 187km (116 miles) to the south.

Matanzas Bay was first navigated by Sebastián de Ocampo in 1509, but the city itself wasn't established until October 1693, when Severino de Balmaseda, the provisional governor of Cuba,

traveled from Havana to Matanzas with a team of surveyors to parcel out lots to new settlers from the Canary Islands. The city's name means "slaughter," and was originally thought to refer to a massacre of a local indigenous tribe, but recent study suggests it had more to do with the killing of herds of pigs kept nearby to resupply ships.

Local farmers started out growing tobacco, but by the end of the 18th century they had converted to sugar. Sugar and the slave trade made the city immensely rich, and during the 19th

Main attractions
PUENTE BACUNAYAGUA
MATANZAS
TEATRO SAUTO
CUEVAS DE BELLAMAR
VARADERO
XANADÚ
CÁRDENAS

PRECEDING PAGES: Mantanzas' Museo Farmacéutico. **LEFT:** handicraft barrow, Varadero. **RIGHT:** Puente Bacunayagua.

TIP

If you would like to try to catch a performance at the Teatro Sauto, you could call in advance (tel: 45-242-721). There is usually something on on weekends.

century the local aristocracy became major patrons of the arts. Matanzas developed a rich café society and many poets and artists made their home here. During the 1895–8 War of Independence, it was the center of a battle between Spanish general Arsenio Martínez Campos and two of Cuba's most important national heroes, Máximo Gómez and Antonio Maceo. On January 1, 1899, in **Plaza de la Vigía**, in the center of town, the Spanish Army handed over control of the town – not to the Cubans, but to General J.P. Sanger of the US Army.

The square still has a reminder of that conflict: the **Statue of the Unknown Soldier**, erected in 1919 on the spot where Matanzas was founded. Here, too, is the neoclassical **Teatro Sauto** , which has glorious ceilings and wonderful acoustics. Unusually, it also has a floor that can be raised to convert it into a ballroom. It was built in 1862–3 by Daniel Dallaglio after he won a competition. It is open for visitors (daily 8.30am–4pm; charge) and for performances of theater, opera, and dance, usually on weekends. In the past

such international stars as Sarah Bernhardt (1844–1923) and Andrés Segovia (1893–1987) have performed here to audiences of 650 people, seated in wrought-iron seats and, more recently, the renowned Spanish dancer and choreographer Antonio Gades.

Adjacent to the square is the **Museo Histórico Provincial** in the **Palacio del Junco** (Milanés between Magdalena and Ayllón; tel: 45-243-464; Tue–Fri 10am–6pm, Sat 1–7pm, Sun 9am–noon; charge), which holds hundreds of documents and artifacts relating to the history of Matanzas; slavery in the sugar plantations is given unusually detailed treatment here. The house itself was built in 1840 by a wealthy sugar plantation owner.

To the south of the theater toward the river you find the **Parque de los Bomberos** (Firemen's Park), with an elegant neoclassical fire station and a perfectly preserved vintage fire truck. On the same side of the street as the nearby **Galería de Arte Provincial** (daily 9am–5pm; charge) is **Ediciones Vigía**, which produces limited editions of marvelous handmade books:

BELOW: the Museo Farmacéutico in Matanzas has a vast and fascinating array of items.

you can tour the workshops (Mon–Fri 9am–4pm). The street crosses the Río San Juan at the rotating **Puente Calixto García**, a bridge built in 1849. A couple of blocks west of Plaza de la Vigía on Calle 282 stands the neoclassical **Catedral de San Carlos Borromeo** **C**, currently undergoing restoration.

A healthy tonic

Perhaps the most important attraction in Matanzas overlooks the main square, **Parque La Libertad**: it is the **Museo Farmacéutico** **D** (Calle 83/Milanés 4951, between Santa Teresa and Ayuntamiento, tel: 45-223-197; Mon–Fri 10am–6pm, Sun 8am–noon; charge), housed in the three-story dispensary of two 19th-century doctors, Juan Fermín Figueroa and Ernesto Triolet. Considering the shortage of common medications in present-day Cuba, this may be one of the best-stocked pharmacies in Matanzas. Among the most important pieces here are porcelain medicine flasks, hundreds of pharmacy books, and a dispensary table that won a bronze medal at the 1900 International Exposition in Paris. Displayed in an adjacent laboratory are ancient utensils, a wood-burning brick oven, and an *alambique,* or still, in which water, alcohol, and essential oils were distilled for medicinal purposes.

Don't leave town without visiting the **Ermita de Monserrate** sanctuary, currently under renovation on a hill, at the northern end of Calle 306 (Domingo Mujica), which offers a panoramic view of the city and the Yumurí valley beyond.

A slave's cavern

There are many interesting caves in the region. The most important are **Las Cuevas de Bellamar** **3** (Mon–Sat 9am–8.30pm, Sun 9am–5pm; 45-minute tours at half past the hour in the morning, and a quarter past in the afternoon; charge), 5km (3 miles) southeast of Matanzas. After a slave working an open lime pit in 1861 dis-

covered the cavern, 1,000 tonnes of rock had to be broken and extracted to clear the entrance; the work revealed one of the Caribbean's largest and most beautiful underground formations. According to a US traveler, Samuel Hazard, writing in 1897, anyone who hadn't visited the Bellamar Caves hadn't really seen Cuba. This is a slight exaggeration, but the caves are impressive. The Salón Gótico (Gothic Hall), 80 meters (265ft) long and 25 meters (80ft) wide, contains stalagmites with names such as La Mano de la Mujer (The Woman's Hand) and La Capilla de los Doce Apóstoles (The Chapel of the Twelve Apostles). The Lago de las Dalias (Lake of Dahlias), a rocky area covered with water, is famous for thousands of tiny calcite crystals covering its roof, walls, and floor. Tours run from Varadero, but if you are coming from Matanzas, and don't have a car, take a taxi, or the No. 12 bus from Parque Libertad, which runs every two hours.

The **Vía Blanca** highway powers 32km (20 miles) eastward from the caves to Cuba's most famous international beach resort, passing towering

Stained-glass mediopunto in the glorious but dilapidated Hotel Louvre.

BELOW: visiting the Cuevas de Bellamar.

The Mantanzas-
Varadero
hop-on-hop-off
double-decker tour
buses make it easy to
travel between the
area's main sights.

BELOW: playing in
the sand on
Varadero beach.

onshore oil rigs that fly the Cuban and Canadian flags, representing one of the island's joint ventures. At night, the sky is lit up by the eerie orange glow of gas flares.

Varadero

The resort of **Varadero** ➍ is flashy in a Cuban kind of way. Nowhere else on Cuban soil can you find such a high concentration of oceanfront restaurants, nightclubs, and luxury hotels. Varadero is the ideal place to vacation if you don't want to meet too many Cubans. They are allowed here, but few can afford the rates at the foreign-run hotels unless they are being treated by a relative from Miami. Take a leisurely stroll along its palm-fringed, white-sand beach, considered one of the finest in the Caribbean, and you're likely to encounter lots of Spaniards, Italians, Canadians, and Germans – but few local people. This is Varadero's biggest problem: because there are few Cubans, there is very little atmosphere. But if you are looking for a straight-forward beach vacation, relatively free of *jineteros*, in a good modern hotel

with cable TV; with air conditioning that works; a pool and a jacuzzi; a golf course left over from the 1950s; and restaurants serving pizzas and hamburgers, then this is the place for you. The seas are warm and crystal blue but, really, you could be anywhere in the Caribbean. This is one of the few places in Cuba where women can sunbathe topless. Despite the very open sexuality of Cuba, topless bathing is, perhaps surprisingly, illegal, although it is tolerated in resorts like Varadero.

Many package-deal tourists fly directly to Varadero and never leave, so almost the only Cubans they will encounter are on the hotel staff. Foreign hotel firms pay the Cuban Government, on average, the equivalent of US$400 a month for each employee. The government pockets that money and pays workers in Cuban pesos. Hotel jobs in Varadero are much sought-after, however, due to the access to tips and the better food they provide. An industrious waiter can make the *peso convertible* equivalent of US$10 a day in tips – which is just under half the average monthly salary in Cuba.

Visiting Varadero

If you are staying in Havana and want to check out Varadero there are four buses a day *(see page 338)*. Taxi drivers hang around the Víazul office trying to tempt you to go with them instead – and if there are more than two of you it is usually a viable option. You can also go on a tour bus, which most Havana hotels will arrange. If driving, the divided highway is good (it's 144km/90 miles from central Havana). You have to pay a small toll on entry to Varadero (currently CUC$2) at a toll gate that also acts as a checkpoint to ensure Cubans have an official reason to enter the resort. Any bus will drop you off at Matanzas en route, but a more interesting way to visit that town is on the Hershey electric train from Casablanca station (=$2.80). There are five trains a day, journey time from 2½ to 4 hours.

The early years

Varadero has been something of a private preserve for much of its history. Local tribes once lived here, but the earliest historical mention of it dates from 1587, when the merchant Don Pedro Camacho began mining salt, both for local use and for Spanish fleets that dropped anchor in Havana.

Throughout the 1600s and early 1700s, pirates preyed on the few inhabitants of the 18km (13-mile) **Península de Hicacos**, along which Varadero is located. In 1726, José Antonio Gómez bought the peninsula and used it to produce salt and rear livestock. Thirty-six years later, the Varadero Hacienda – consisting of 1,140 hectares (2,800 acres) of land from Paso Malo to Hicacos Point – was sold to an aristocrat called Bernardo Carrillo de Albornos, whose heirs were still in possession of the land in the mid-19th century.

Varadero's tourist history started in the 1870s, when families from nearby Cárdenas began visiting. In that decade, they built the first palm-thatched frame houses on the northern coast, while the southern coast remained the preserve of fishermen. The beach's fame grew, however, luring visitors from Havana, who in those days arrived by ox cart. The year 1915 marked the inauguration of the Hotel Varadero – the fledgling town's first resort. Three years later, the Cuban Congress passed a law authorizing annual rowing regattas at Varadero Beach, which soon became a highlight of the local social calendar.

A stately pleasure dome

Then in 1926, the chemicals magnate Alfred Irénée Du Pont (who had made his fortune manufacturing dynamite during World War I) scored a real-estate coup with the purchase of 512 hectares (1,265 acres) of prime Varadero property for as little as 4 centavos per sq meter (11 sq ft). The lavish vacation home he built, **Xanadú**, is still standing today – one of the few tourist attractions in Varadero worth visiting. Located right on the beach, the mansion was finished in 1930 at a cost of US$338,000 – an astronomical sum back then. These days, it is a boutique hotel (very popular with golfers) with an expensive restaurant.

Even if you don't eat there, you can see the first floor and visit the bar on the top floor for a sunset drink and a fine view. The mahogany ceilings and banisters are all original, as are the Italian marble floors and the 1932 organ, one of the largest privately built organs in Latin America. Don't overlook Samuel Taylor Coleridge's poem (*In Xanadu did Kubla Khan a stately pleasure-dome decree…*), reproduced in full on the wall; or the beautiful terrace with a sweeping view of the Atlantic. There is an adjacent golf course, but the small, flat area does not make for a very satisfying game.

Foreign investment

Du Pont, who continued to buy up oceanfront property through the 1930s and 1940s, was not the only land speculator in Varadero. Others invested here, often with the complicity of corrupt Cuban officials or those with Mafia

A gardener at work in Varadero.

BELOW:
Xanadú is now a boutique hotel.

connections. The **Casa de Al**, which evokes those years, is now a restaurant housed in a mansion once owned by Chicago gangster Al Capone.

In 1950, the Hotel Internacional was constructed for US$3 million. That sparked a development boom that continued right up until the 1959 revolution. Dozens of mansions arose from one end of Varadero to the other, along with golf courses, gambling casinos, and hotels with links to the so-called "Jewish godfather" Meyer Lansky and other notorious figures of organized crime.

That all came to a screeching halt in 1959. A state-approved tourist pamphlet says that two months after Batista's overthrow, the Cuban Government passed Law 270 "proclaiming the people's full right to enjoy all beaches." Even so, for many years the only kind of tourists Castro's regime welcomed were solidarity brigades from the Soviet Union and other sympathetic countries. It was only with the end of aid from the USSR that Cuba began to court large-scale tourism from capitalist countries.

Joint ventures

It was in Varadero that the first joint venture between the Cuban Government and foreign capitalists was inaugurated in 1990 – the US$26-million, 607-room Hotel Sol Palmeras. Since then the same firm, Spain's Grupo Sol Meliá, has built more hotels. As part of its ambitious development program for the area, the Ministry of Tourism has allowed development right to the end of the peninsula (which looks like a giant building site). Even the old "Campamiento Internacional," where Cuba's youthful pioneers once stayed alongside young foreigners from solidarity brigades, has been bought for development. There are investors here from across Europe, Latin America, the Caribbean, and even China – a Chinese restaurant has recently opened. Problems with cash flow and water supplies sometimes hinder progress.

A break from the sun

Apart from Xanadú, Varadero offers very few sites of historical interest. Visitors with time to spare might like to check out the **Parque de Diversiones**

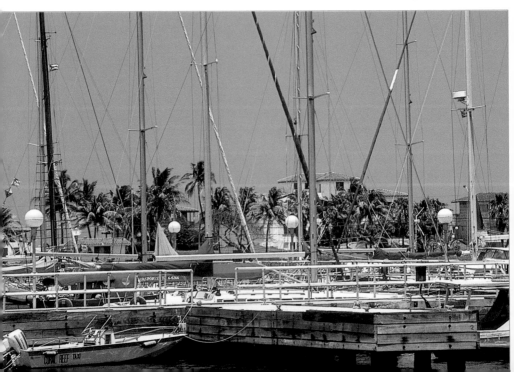

(Amusement Park) at Avenida Tercera between calles 29 and 30. There is a tiny **tobacco factory** on Avenida Primera and Calle 27, and the equally diminutive **Museo Municipal de Varadero** (Tue–Sat 10am–6pm; charge) on Avenida Playa and Calle 57, which has interesting exhibits of local flora and fauna, and some oddities, such as a two-headed shark. Varadero's municipal park, the **Parque Retiro Josone**, located between calles 54 and 59, has a pleasant flamingo lake where you can rent boats.

Halfway along the peninsula, past the main hotel stretch, the tiny, 2 sq km (0.7 sq-mile) **Reserva Ecológica Varahicacos** (daily 9am–4.30pm) gives some idea of what the peninsula was like before tourism. The Patriarca Playa trail (charge) takes you 300 meters/yds to see El Patriarca (The Patriarch) – a giant endemic cactus. At more than 500 years old, it is thought to be the longest-lived plant in Cuba, and is perhaps the only living thing in the country to have been around in the pre-Columbian age. The aboriginal paintings in the limestone **Cueva de Ambrosio** are interesting. This small cave, discovered in 1961, contains 50 well-preserved prehistoric drawings.

Cárdenas

Rent a car in Varadero and head into northern Matanzas province. The distance is minuscule but the difference in lifestyles is astonishing. Only 15km (9 miles) south of Varadero, across Cárdenas Bay, lies **Cárdenas** ❺ (pop. 104,000), a city founded in 1828. In 1850, Cuba's national flag was raised for the first time here. A plaque commemorating this can be seen on the wall of the Hotel Dominica on Avenida Céspedes. On May 11, 1898, after Spain had been defeated in the Spanish–American War, Cárdenas was shelled by US Navy ships commanded by Admiral William T. Sampson. As in many provincial Cuban towns, traffic in Cárdenas consists of horse-drawn carts rather than cars, which sit in backyards, immobilized by the lack of (or cost of) gasoline.

Cárdenas became the center of world media attention in 2000 as the home town of Elián González, the

Jellyfish warning on the Varadero shore.

BELOW: a display in the Museo de la Batalla de Ideas focuses on the picture that shocked the world.

A girl's best friend... Dogs are good company in the countryside.

BELOW: statue of Christopher Columbus in front of the cathedral in Cárdenas.

"tug of love" boy *(see box, page 90)*. The streets of this small dusty town were once filled with his image, but now he has returned to everyday life with his father, it is almost as if the huge media circus never happened, except that the town now has the **Museo de la Batalla de Ideas** (Calle 12 and Plaza Echeverría, Tue–Sat 9am–5pm, Sun 9am–1pm; charge). Housed in a well-restored 19th-century building, and inaugurated by Castro in July 2001, the six-room museum documents in lively detail the tireless campaign for the repatriation of "Eliancito," as the little boy was known. Exhibits on display include a striking modern sculpture of José Martí holding a child in his arms.

Cárdenas is also home to the eclectic **Museo Municipal de Oscar María de Rojas** (Plaza Echeverría between Avenidas 4 and 6 Este; Tue–Sat 9am–5pm, Sun 8am–noon; charge), named for a local revolutionary hero. This natural history museum has several exhibition halls devoted to Cuban coins, weapons, shells, butterflies, minerals, pre-Columbian objects, and documents from the various revolutions and wars

of independence. At the end of Calle Céspedes is a small **fortress** (**La Fuerte Roja**), now a café and a popular meeting place for local people.

On Avenida 4 Este is the **Casa Natal de José Antonio Echeverría** (Tue–Sat 9am–5pm, Sun 8am–noon; charge), the birthplace of the student killed in 1957 while leading the attack on Batista's Presidential Palace. The house itself is beautiful, and there is a monument to the student in the park outside, which is also named after him.

The city has a fine cathedral, the **Catedral de la Inmaculada Concepción** (often closed, except for Sunday Mass), on Parque Colón, with a statue of Columbus dating from 1858, said to be the first erected in Latin America. There is a mausoleum in the **Plaza de la Independencia**, containing the remains of 238 patriots who fell fighting Spanish colonialism in the late 19th century.

The quiet hinterland

The province of Matanzas has seen its glory days fade as an exporter of sugar. About 10km (6 miles) south of Cárdenas, off the road to Santa Clara, is the former sugar mill Central Azucarero José Smith Comás, decommissioned and now a museum. It is interesting to see the production process but the star of the show is an 1888 steam engine, still used to transport tourists.

Southeast of Matanzas the potholed Carretera Central offers a route toward Santa Clara, an alternative to the main *autopista*, passing by or through some pretty colonial settlements including **Jovellanos**, an old slave town with a strong Afro-Cuban tradition, which was named after an 18th-century Spanish philosopher and statesman; and on to **Colón**. This is another colonial settlement with a busy main street and sleepy squares, with some impressive, if crumbling, neoclassical architecture.

You then cross into Santa Clara province. Independent travelers may like to know that Jovellanos and Colón both have a Cupet gas station. ❏

RESTAURANTS AND BARS

Matanzas

Matanzas is distinctly lacking in eating places. The following is the only one to be recommended.

La Ruina
Calle 101, just past the Calixto García bridge
Open daily 24 hrs. **$**
Attractive location in an old sugar warehouse. Full meals or pastries or ice cream, charged in either CUCs or *moneda nacional*. There is often live music at weekends.

Varadero

Resort hotels in Varadero specialize in buffets with lots of fresh fruit, and outdoor grills, where you can get lunch without leaving the beach. The specialty restaurants in the big hotels serve decent food and are open to all.

Albacora
Calle 59 between 1a and Playa
Tel: (45) 668-050. Open daily 9am–midnight. **$$**
Excellent seafood is served on a pleasant terrace overlooking the sea (the restaurant's name means swordfish).

Casa de Al
Villa Punta Blanca, Carretera Las Américas
Tel: (45) 66-8050. Open daily noon–midnight. **$$**

Formerly Al Capone's house, now a quiet place for a drink of meal. All the dishes are themed with gangster names such as Mafia Soup or Godfather Salad. Sit indoors or outside on the terrace.

Casa de Antigüedades
Avenida 1era, corner of Calle 56, Parque Josone
Tel: (45) 667-329. Open daily noon–11pm. **$–$$**
International menu and lots of seafood in a neocolonial villa stuffed with figurines and statues.

Castel Nuovo
Avenida 1era, corner of Calle 11
Tel: (45) 667-786.
Open daily noon–11.45pm. **$$**

El Bodegón Criollo
Avenida de la Playa and Calle 40
Tel: (45) 667-784. Open daily noon–11pm. **$$**
Attempts to re-create the ambiance of Havana's Bodeguita del Medio, and serves similar cuisine. The *criolla* food is fine but don't compare the venue with the original. On the other hand, it's cheaper, and there is a sea view.

Esquina Cuba
Calle 36, corner of 1era
Tel: (45) 614-019. Open daily 10am–midnight. **$$**
A thatched *bohío* in the town center. Good *criolla* cuisine and music.

La Campaña
Avenida 1era, corner of Calle 56, Parque Josone
Tel: (45) 667-224. Open daily noon–11pm. **$**
Traditional Cuban dishes and good desserts.

La Vega
Avenida Playa between 31 and 32
Tel: (45) 611-430. Open daily noon–11pm. **$**
Pretty wooden building with seating on outdoor decking. Mostly seafood and paella.

Las Américas
Mansión Xanadu, Carretera Las Américas, Km 4.5
Tel: (45) 667-750. Open daily L & D. **$$$**
A stylish place for lunch or dinner, with good French food. Check out the cool bar on the third-floor.

Mesón del Quijote
Avenida las Américas, next to El Castillito water tower
Tel: (45) 667-796. Open daily noon–midnight. **$$**
A jolly, intimate restaurant with a Spanish theme. Well-cooked paella and grilled lobster feature. Reasonable prices, although lobster always adds to the bill.

Mi Casita
Camino del Mar, between calles 11 and 12
Tel: (45) 613-787. Open daily 6–11pm. **$$$**
Intimate, capriciously furnished and specializing in lobster and tasty Caribbean dishes.

Varadero
Resort hotels have a wide variety of bars, indoors or on the beach, with or without live music. The only independent bar worth visiting is at Mansión Xanadú (*see page 223*). Any barman will have a long list of cocktails which are fun to try.

RIGHT: the buffet at Las Américas.

THE ZAPATA PENINSULA

The best known of Cuba's wildlife havens, the Zapata peninsula is a refuge for many bird and animal species. Nearby Playa Girón earned its place in history during the Bay of Pigs invasion

The half of Matanzas province that lies to the south of the *autopista* from Havana is mainly low, marshy terrain that is primarily a destination for visitors interested in the rich Cuban wildlife to be found here, or those who want to visit the Bay of Pigs for historical reasons. It is not a place where people come to admire the towns or cities. The main town for the area is **Jagüey Grande** and the Entronque de Jagüey is the junction of the *autopista* with the access road to the peninsula. This is the heart of the world's largest citrus operation – a 40,000-hectare (103,000-acre) grove of orange and grapefruit trees owned by the Cuban Government and managed by a secretive Israeli firm.

Just south of the *autopista* is the town of **Australia ❻**, dominated by its decommissioned sugar mill *(central)*. The mill was Fidel Castro's headquarters during the battle at the Bay of Pigs, and part of it is now a municipal museum, the **Museo Memorial Comandancia de las FAR** (tel: 45-912-504, Tue–Sat 8am–noon, 1–5pm, Sun 8am–noon; charge). The next long, straight stretch of road leads to the turn-off for the Zapata peninsula, with monuments to the fallen of the Bay of Pigs all along the roadside.

Close by is the **Finca Fiesta Campesina**, a tourist venture with a little zoo, shops, coffee bars, and a small cabin-style hotel, the **Bohío de Don Pedro**, tucked round the back of the property *(see page 233)*. It is an obligatory stop on the Zapata tour, and has surprisingly appealing gardens where you can sip fresh-fruit *batidos* (milkshakes) in the bar, watch a man extract sugar-can juice (***guarapo***) for you to try, and inspect the coffee growing on the hillside. There is even an original kind of lottery where you are asked to bet on which hole a guinea pig will run into on its release.

Main attractions
CRIADERO DE COCODRILOS
LA BOCA DE GUAMÁ
LAGUNA DEL TESORO
SANTO TOMÁS
LAS SALINAS
PLAYA GIRÓN
MUSEO DE GIRÓN

LEFT: a flamingo strikes a pose.
RIGHT: rocky coastline in the Bay of Pigs.

TIP

Víazul runs a twice-daily bus service from Havana to Trinidad via Entronque de Jagüey, Playa Girón, and Cienfuegos. The bus from Varadero to Trinidad stops at Jagüey Grande but goes on to Santa Clara. It is easy to be dropped off but less easy to be picked up again, as passing buses are often full.

BELOW: speedboats make regular trips to the Laguna del Tesoro.

The Centro de Información La Finquita (tel: 45-913-224, open daily 8am–8pm), next to the café, can arrange taxi transport to Playa Larga or Playa Girón.

The Zapata peninsula

The **Península de Zapata**, 156km (97 miles) southeast of Havana, was named for its similarity in shape to a shoe (*zapato* in Spanish). An enormous swamp, it has been a refuge, first for indigenous Taíno people, later for buccaneers and charcoal makers. The entire region is now a Unesco Biosphere Reserve, the **Gran Parque Natural Montemar**.

Most of the Zapata peninsula is barely above sea level and is flooded every year during the rainy season (between June and October). About 30 percent is slightly higher, supporting a wide strip of forest some 16km (10 miles) from the southern coastline. Other elevated patches of terrain are scattered throughout the swamp, and clumps of trees grow on these patches like tiny islands. The western, triangular part of the Zapata peninsula is entirely unpopulated.

The whole area is described on maps as the Ciénaga de Zapata, divided into east and west, with the Llanura de Zapata in between (*ciénaga* means swamp, *llanura* means plain).

Many narrow, linear canals are visible from the air, connecting lagoons with the surrounding shallow seas. These were all excavated by hand by the desperately poor charcoal makers a century or more ago, to facilitate lumber transportation. There are many hidden sinkholes, so always stick to designated trails when walking. (And remember to carry plenty of bottled water with you as the swamps are very hot.) Much of the swamp area is covered by a thick mat of peat that acts like a gigantic mattress during the dry season. The underlying hard sediment of limestone frequently shows through, and, below ground, it is eroded into a network of caverns.

The Zapata's forests were once abundant in cabinet-quality hardwoods like ebony, mastic, and mahogany. Regrettably, these virgin forests have been thoroughly exploited over the centuries, and even the tallest trees today are only secondary growth. More recent logging has produced unsightly corridors through the forest. Moreover, feral pigs and the introduced white-tailed deer have devastated the plant life of the undergrowth and altered the balance of the forest species. As a result, species that you might expect to grace the forests – like orchids, ferns, bromeliads, and vines – are rarities.

Crocodile farm

Crocodiles are rare in Zapata. Two species exist – the American crocodile, and the rarer Cuban crocodile. On the road to Playa Larga, just before you reach La Boca de Guamá, is the **Criadero de Cocodrilos** (Crocodile Farm; tel: 45-913-224; daily 9am–6pm, shows 9am–4.30pm; charge) where both species can be seen.

From **La Boca de Guamá** boats carry passengers through a canal to the **Laguna del Tesoro** ❼ (Treasure Lagoon; speedboats every 30 minutes from 9am–6pm; slower ferries run about four times a day). The lake got its name because, it was said, the indigenous Taíno people of the area threw all their valuables into it rather than surrender them to the Spanish. There's a romanticized mock Taíno village at Guamá populated by life-size statues of Taínos by the sculptor, Rita Longa, as well as an interesting hotel complex. Some artifacts have been found here, but no gold.

Snail kites *(Rostrhamus sociabilis)* are abundant here. They are raptors that feed, unsurprisingly, on snails, which they extract from the shells, using their long curved beaks. One indigenous name for them was *kiewe balielie* (lord of the snails). You will also find the endemic *manjuarí* (garfish or pike) – its teeth, snout, and body are a crude parallel to those of a crocodile, and its lineage goes back some 70 million years.

A birder's paradise

Birds are the main attraction in the peninsula, with a total count of 190 species. Most of Cuba's endemic species can be found here: the bee hummingbird, Cuban parakeet, Gundlach's hawk, blue-headed quail dove, Cuban tody, Cuban trogon, two species of blackbird, two types of woodpecker, and a couple of very small owls. Some species, such as the Zapata wren and rail (close to extinction), are unique to the swamp, while others can be found in few other places – the Zapata sparrow, for instance, is only found here, in Cayo Coco, and the desert area of Baitiquirá, near Guantánamo.

Playa Larga, at the head of the Bahía de Cochinos (Bay of Pigs), is where you find the headquarters of the national park (tel: 45-987-249, email:pnacionalcz@enet.cu; daily 8am–4.30pm) and where you can organize trips with accredited guides (mandatory). You need your own transport though, or else a taxi. The hotel at Playa Larga is often booked by tour groups, but there are also a few *casas particulares*, some of which, like the hotel, are on the beach.

One of the best places for ornithologists lies north of the village of **Santo**

Crocodiles are fascinating – as long as they are at a safe distance.

The Bay of Pigs

Not far from the palm trees and tourist bungalows of Playa Girón is a defiant billboard depicting a raised rifle and the words: "Playa Girón – La Primera Derrota del Imperialismo en América Latina" (The First Imperialist Defeat in Latin America). The battle began shortly after midnight on April 17, 1961, when the 2506th assault brigade – a CIA-trained force of some 1,500 mercenaries and Cuban exiles – landed to force the overthrow of Fidel. However, El Jefe Máximo was ready for them with Soviet-built T-34 tanks and a few T-33 fighter jets, and, after two days of intense air and land battles, the 2506th surrendered. Of the invading force, 107 were killed and 1,189 were taken prisoner. Most were later released back to the US in return for a US\$53-million consignment of medicines and foodstuffs. Castro, who led the people's militia in the battle, lost 161 men and women (five of these were civilians). The Museo de Girón was built at the landing site to commemorate the events. Outside, you can inspect a couple of tanks used in the defense. Inside are two rooms full of documents, photos, and weapons and an array of artifacts, among them a 12.7mm anti-aircraft battery used against US planes, and a map showing the mercenaries' route from Puerto Cabezas, Nicaragua. Their invasion was preceded by an unsuccessful bombing raid on the Cuban Air Force, which put Castro on full alert. You can see a video compilation of footage from the era (in Spanish only).

A bottlebrush plant (Callistemon citrinus). They thrive in the Zapata peninsula.

BELOW:
scuba diving at
the Bay of Pigs.

Tomás **8**, west of Playa Larga. Many migrant birds show up here from October through April, after having flown all the way from the United States or Canada. The majority are warblers (more than 30 different species), but there are also herons, terns, and several birds of prey.

At **Las Salinas 9**, 25km (15 miles) southwest of Playa Larga, the scenery is spectacular: flamingos swoop across the milky, salt water lagoons, and crocodiles meander out across the dirt roads. The area is virtually uninhabited – there are just a dozen or so families who work in the reserve or fish for a living. Fly fishing is becoming popular but only six anglers are allowed into the reserve at any one time, and must be accompanied by a guide who will navigate through the channels and flats. You can wade or fish from the flat-bottomed skiffs for several different species.

Water birds and tropical fish

From **Playa Larga** (one of the landing sites in the notorious 1961 invasion (*see*

panel on previous page), the road skirts the edge of the Bahía de Cochinos as it runs south toward Playa Girón. Some wide canals can be found slightly inland beyond **Los Hondones** (about 10km/6 miles from Playa Larga) where water birds abound. They include coots, gallinules, ducks, whistling ducks, herons, ospreys, jacanas, migratory buntings, and peregrine falcons.

Farther along this stretch of road, look out for the many monuments to the Cuban dead of the Bay of Pigs invasion, and stop off at some of the beautiful sinkholes *(cenotes)* surrounded by forest, which are connected to the nearby sea by underwater tunnels. These flooded caverns in the limestone are full of tropical fish in all colors of the rainbow. The water is crystal clear even deep down, and surprisingly cold. You can snorkel or scuba dive in most of these *cenotes*, which is like swimming in an aquarium.

Sadly, one of the largest and loveliest, the **Cueva de los Peces** (Fish Cave; daily 9am–4pm; charge), has been spoiled by over-development. It is well signposted, and there are restaurants, a bar, and loungers on which you can sit by the lagoon and admire the scenery. You can rent snorkeling gear, and even though loud music ruins the ambiance, the swimming and the fish are still lovely. There is an abundance of lizards too, some tame enough to feed on scraps under the tables.

Playa Girón

The village of **Playa Girón** ⑩ holds an important place in Cold War history: this was the site of the United States' disastrous 1961 Bay of Pigs invasion, about which you can learn in the commemorative **Museo de Girón** (tel: 45-984-122; daily 8am–5pm; charge). The village is low and spread out, with an unattractive hotel, a collection of single-story concrete houses, and horses tethered everywhere.

At the junction there are two incongruous blocks of apartments, and here the road turns inland to Cienfuegos across a fertile plain where vegetables are grown on an industrial scale. An alternative track continues along the coast, approaching Cienfuegos from the south, but it is very rough and should only be attempted if you have a four-wheel-drive vehicle.

The western side of Playa Girón is a sanctuary for local fauna. You need authorization to go through the gate and follow the old solid-fill causeway that has slowly killed all vegetation. Flocks of rosy flamingos and spoonbills can be seen, feeding in the shallow salty lagoons, alongside other waders such as white ibises, black-necked stilts, sandpipers, and plovers.

At Playa Girón itself, you can bathe and snorkel off the beach or at several spots along the shore (designated with signs) where the seas are shallow. Farther out to sea, where the Caribbean shelf sinks vertically to hundreds of meters, scuba divers will be able to see rare black corals, spiny oysters, and ocean fish species such as amberjack and little tunny.

A little farther along the bay to the south is another excellent place to dive, the lovely cove of **Caleta Buena** (the charge includes buffet lunch; *see below*), which is also blessed with spectacular sponges and red coral. ❏

A tank at the Museo de Girón that was used to repel the US invasion.

RESTAURANTS

Price categories are for a three-course meal for one with a beer, or *mojito*. Wine puts the price up:
$ = under $25
$$ = $25–35
$$$ = over $35

Restaurants are few and far between in this region, and by far the best food can be found in *casas particulares*, where the hosts usually serve good *comida criolla* as well as fresh fish and seafood.

Bohío de Don Pedro
Finca Fiesta Campesina,
South of Entronque de Jagüey
Tel: (45) 912-825.
Open daily 7am–9.30pm. **$**
The Bohío is not the place

to head for if you are looking for a gourmet meal, but it is a reliably good pit stop on the way down to the Zapata peninsula. There is a bar, a few shops, bathroom facilities, and a pleasant garden with animals to look at while you have a drink or something to eat.

Boca de Guamá
Tel: (45) 913-224.
Open daily 9am–6pm. **$–$$**
The tourist center at the crocodile farm has shops and a restaurant, which is a regular lunch stop for tour parties, so it can be crowded if your visit coincides with one of them. The food is pretty mediocre, with the standard set meal of chicken, fish, or pork,

but you can also try crocodile meat if you are feeling adventurous. It tastes rather like a tough mixture of all three when fried.

Caleta Buena
Open daily 10am–5pm for drinks; lunch 12.30–3pm. **$**
You pay CUC$15 for a day package, which includes drinks and lunch as well as swimming in the pretty cove where the snorkeling is lovely, which makes it quite a good deal. Diving is also available for an extra (but not exorbitant) charge.

Cueva de los Peces
Open daily 9am–4pm. **$**
The "Cave of the Fish" is a restaurant and bar serving drinks, snacks, and lunch of standard *criolla* food. It is

located beside a *cenote* (sinkhole) which is full of fish and excellent for snorkeling or diving.

Punta Perdiz
Open daily 9am–4.30pm. **$**
This is a reasonable café serving drinks, snacks, and lunch (the usual food is on offer). It's the situation that is the attraction: set between Cueva de los Peces and Playa Girón, where you can go snorkeling, there is a dive center, and boat trips are available.

BIRD BONANZA

Birdwatchers will be delighted with the rich variety of birds in Cuba. Some are easy to find, but you need an expert guide if you want to discover the island's more secretive inhabitants

Cuba has a wide range of habitats: from beaches to coastal mangrove swamps, broad plains to rugged mountains, cactus semi-desert to remaining indigenous forests of cedar and ebony. Like many other large islands in the world, Cuba contains a rich collection of rare birds found nowhere else on earth, of which 21 are endemic species. A total of 357 species of birds has been recorded on the island, more than half of which use it as a winter resting spot as they migrate from North to South America.

In western Cuba an easily accessible site for birdwatching is the Sierra del Rosario. In the semi-deciduous tropical forest you can find the endemic Cuban Solitaire, as well as the Cuban Tody and the Cuban Trogon.

The Zapata peninsula is one of the best regions, particularly around Santo Tomás and the salt flats of Las Salinas, or the Laguna del Tesoro. The mixed habitat of mangrove swamp, thick scrub, forest, and saltpans attracts a wide range of birds, including most of the endemic species.

In the province of Camagüey, a good place to go is the Hacienda La Belén, in the Sierra de Najasa, a forest reserve and home to the Giant Kingbird as well as the endangered Cuban Parakeet, the Cuban Pygmy Owl and the Cuban Vireo.

Despite the proliferation of tourist facilities, Cayo Coco and the other north-coast cays near Morón are good places to see endemic sub-species, although the main attractions here are the water birds.

The east is no less rewarding, with the mountains of the Sierra Maestra, the Cuchillas del Toa, and the surrounding coast offering a variety of birds at different altitudes and habitats, including tanagers, orioles, todies, hummingbirds and woodpeckers.

LEFT: the male Red-legged Honeycreeper *(Cyanerpes cyaneus)* is a brilliant violet blue with a turquoise crown, black wings and tail, showing a flash of yellow under his wings in flight.

BELOW: the endemic Cuban Green Woodpecker *(Xiphidiopicus percussus)* is known locally as the *carpintero*, or carpenter bird.

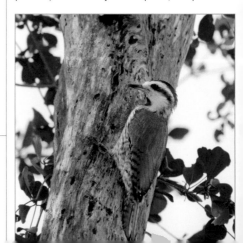

LEFT: the Cuban Tody *(Todus multicolor)* is a tiny, colorful bird which nests in short tunnels dug out of clay or tree cavities, usually found near rivers and in woodlands.

ABOVE: the Cuban Emerald Hummingbird *(Chlorostilbon ricordii)* feeds on nectar and insects and is commonly found in gardens and woodland all over Cuba.

TOURS AND GUIDES

Regulations stipulate that you must have a guide to enter a national park in Cuba, and these are of course the best places to see birds. This will be organized for you, along with your accommodations and meals, if you book a place on a birding tour with a foreign agency. Alternatively, you can do day trips with a Cuban agency such as Ecotur (www. ecoturcuba.co.cu), which has offices around the country and can take you off the beaten track to see birds in Pinar del Río, Cienfuegos, Villa Clara, or Morón. If you are traveling independently, however, you can usually arrange a specialist guide when you need one by going to the local offices of the national parks. You will have to arrange your own transport but the guide can take you to all the best places and make sure you see the species you want to see. On the Zapata peninsula, go to the headquarters of the Parque Nacional Ciénaga de Zapata in Playa Larga (tel: 45-987-249, email: pnacionalcz@enet.cu), where trips cost CUC$10 per person and some guides speak English.

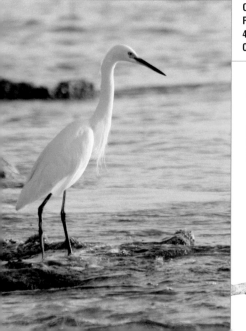

ABOVE: the swamps, mangroves, and wetlands of Cuba provide food and shelter for many migrating species as well as endemics.

FAR LEFT: the Snowy Egret *(Egretta thula)* lives in swamps, lagoons, and rivers. Some live in Cuba permanently while others migrate from North America in the winter.

LEFT: the forest-dwelling Cuban Trogon *(Priotelus temnurus)*, known as the *tocororo*, bears all the colors of the Cuban flag and is the national bird.

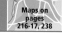

SANTA CLARA TO SANCTI SPÍRITUS

As well as hectares of sugar cane, Cuba's heartland has some lovely towns, such as buzzing Santa Clara, with its Che Guevara monument, and the little-visited gem of Remedios, plus stunning landscapes in the Escambray mountains

ast of Varadero begins a fertile green belt of land: Cuba's agricultural backbone. Formerly a monoculture with sugar cane as far as the eye can see, nowadays orchards, rice fields, vegetable farms, and enormous cattle ranches eat up the terrain and feed much of the island's population. Buses, trucks, tractors, carts, cars, bicycles, and animals all share the road, presenting a slow but picturesque parade of life in the countryside. The Ocho Vías Autopista, projected as an eight-lane highway all the way to the eastern tip of the island, is completed only as far as the other side of Sancti Spíritus. Along the way are a handful of CUC-only service stations. These offer gas, oil and air, rest rooms (of varying quality), drinks and food (proper meals in some cases), and usually one or two stores.

With a population of 800,000, **Villa Clara** province runs the gamut of rural backdrops. There are sleepy fishing villages, pretty coves, and offshore cays to the north; colonial towns and sugar-cane plantations in the center; the rolling hills of the Alturas de Santa Clara to the east; and the majestic Escambray mountains to the south.

Santa Clara's old town

Santa Clara ⓫ (pop. 210,000), the provincial capital, lies 276km (171

miles) east of Havana on the Autopista Nacional, and is well worth visiting. A university town with a large student population, it is busy and lively, day and night. There is always something going on and the music scene in particular is very active.

Santa Clara was founded in 1689 by 17 families from Remedios who (it is alleged) had been persuaded that legions of demons were afflicting their settlement (see page 38). Whatever the truth of the matter, land was parceled out and these families became the

Main attractions
SANTA CLARA
TREN BLINDADO
MONUMENTO CHE GUEVARA
REMEDIOS
EMBALSE HANABANILLA
TOPES DE COLLANTES
SANCTI SPÍRITUS

LEFT: Escambray plantation house.
RIGHT: the lovely Museo de Artes Decorativas in Santa Clara.

TIP

The views from the rooftop bar of the Hotel Santa Clara, overlooking Parque Vidal, are the best in town.

local oligarchy, building up the settlement and their fortunes by growing tobacco, sugar, cattle, and working the Malezas copper mines, as well as trading with both ends of the island. In the 19th century, prosperity increased with the arrival of the railway in 1873, and in 1895 when the island was divided into six provinces, Santa Clara became the capital city of the large province of Las Villas.

In December 1958, Che Guevara's derailment of an armored troop train on its way to Santiago de Cuba, and his seizure of the city, was the decisive victory in the struggle against Batista: this seminal moment is commemorated at sites across the town, most importantly, in Che's monument and mausoleum *(see page 240)*. It is this that brings most visitors to Santa Clara, but this pretty little city has far more to offer for those with time to spare.

Around Parque Vidal

Santa Clara's main square is the delightful, leafy **Parque Vidal** Ⓐ, with a graceful central gazebo used for concerts. A monument marks the spot where Independence hero Leoncio Vidal was killed in 1896, and benches line the promenades that cross and encircle the park – in earlier days, a fence separated the inner promenade for whites from the outer area for blacks. Colonnaded buildings from the late 19th and early 20th centuries line the square; they include the **Casa de la Trova**, and the ugly **Hotel Santa Clara Libre** Ⓑ, distinguished by a facade still riddled with shrapnel from the 1958 campaign.

On the plaza's north side is the **Museo de Artes Decorativas** Ⓒ (Parque between Lorda and Luis Estévez; tel: 42-205-368; Wed–Mon but check hours as they vary; charge), in one of the city's loveliest colonial buildings. Rooms are sumptuously furnished with colonial pieces in many different styles, but dating mainly from the 19th century.

On the nearby corner is the lovely **Teatro La Caridad** Ⓓ (tel: 42-208-548), built in the 1880s, financed by the philanthropist Marta Abreu de Estevez to bring culture to the poor people of Santa Clara. The theater,

BELOW: the armored troop train derailed by Che Guevara in 1958.

Santa Clara

0 ⸻ 500 m
0 ⸻ 500 yds

now a respected national monument, was renovated in 2009.

Marta's parents had earlier used their fabulous wealth gained from sugar and slavery to establish the city's first free clinic and primary school, in 1878. The school, a block behind the theater, was used successively as a convent, a trade school and the incipient Ministry of Education in the early 1960s, but is now the Restaurante Colonial 1878.

Santa Clara's six-block-long **boulevard**, running along Calle Independencia one street to the north of the plaza, is an enticing, brick-paved mall with iron grilles, colonial lamps, and benches at each crossing. At the western end is the **Casa de la Ciudad E**, an attractive old mansion with a motley array of exhibits, where dance classes are sometimes run; and the **Fondo de Bienes Culturales**, where local arts and crafts are sold.

Farther north, up Calle Máximo Gómez, you reach an attractive church, the **Nuestra Señora del Carmen F** (Parque El Carmen; tel: 42-205-217), built on the very hill where Santa Clara's founding families held their

first Mass. Leaving the church, go left along Calle Berenguer for a couple of blocks before turning right to the **Fábrica de Tabacos G** (Maceo between Julio Jover and Berenguer; tel: 42-202-211; Mon–Fri 9–11am, 1–3pm; buy your ticket in advance from an agency or from the shop on the opposite corner) on Calle Maceo, where there is a very good tour. Going down Maceo and turning left on Calle R. Pardo you will find the appealing **Iglesia de Nuestra Señora del Buen Viaje H** (Pedro Estevez, corner Buen Viaje; tel: 42-206-332), which is well worth visiting for its hybrid of architectural styles.

The Armored Train

Taking a short walk east along Calle Independencia from Parque Vidal and across the river brings you to the **Tren Blindado I** (Armored Train) and museum (tel: 42-202-758; Mon–Sat 8am–5pm; charge). This train, loaded with 408 government soldiers and munitions, was sent from Havana to stop the Rebel Army's advance, but was derailed at a critical moment during

Colonial style in the Parque Vidal, warmly illuminated at night.

BELOW: stunning monument to Che Guevara.

the battle for Santa Clara, when it was attacked by 23 rebels with guns and Molotov cocktails on December 29, 1958. To prevent the men and munitions getting through, Che himself ripped up the lines with a bulldozer, derailing the train, and subsequently winning the battle. Both the bulldozer and three of the train's five carriages have been preserved *in situ*.

Artists' hangout

Two blocks west of Parque Vidal, on Calle Marta Abreu, a sign above a brick facade announces **El Mejunje**. Artists, intellectuals, and bohemians of all ages meet here to sip beer and *infusiones* (herbal teas), to listen to a poetry recital or a musical group, to dance, or just to sit and chat. The cultural potion is just right for laid-back Santa Clara, and there's no place quite like it anywhere else in Cuba.

A couple of blocks farther along Calle Marta Abreu is the early 20th-century cathedral. This is the grandly named **Iglesia Parroquial Mayor de las Santas Hermanas de Santa Clara de Asís ❶**.

Going west from the church, Calle Marta Abreu joins the Carretera Central, which continues west to the *circunvalación* (beltway/ring road). Just south of the junction of the two roads is the **Plaza de la Revolución Ernesto Guevara**, the usual place for revolutionary gatherings. It is dominated by one of Cuba's finest revolutionary statues, the **Monumento Che Guevara**: a giant figure of Che, shown with his arm in a sling – he broke it when he fell from a building during the battle for Santa Clara in 1958. The bronze statue bears the legend "*Hasta La Victoria Siempre*" (Ever Onward to Victory), a refrain which appears on many a billboard around Cuba.

Beneath Che's statue is the **Mausoleo** (Tue–Sun 9am–5pm; no cameras; free), where the remains of Che and 29 of his co-revolutionaries were interred in 1997, after being recovered from Bolivia. The mausoleum, low-ceilinged and made almost entirely of stone, has the look and feel of a cave. By Che's resting place, a lamp casts a light in the shape of a five-pointed star, and an eternal flame (originally lit by Fidel)

The Town of Comandante Che

On December 28, 1958, Che Guevara's rebel troops attacked Santa Clara. Two days later, with the aid of townspeople (who braved air raids and snipers to help build barricades and mix Molotov cocktails), the rebels emerged victorious and cut Batista's communications with the east of the island, causing him to flee Cuba on New Year's Eve. Many older Santa Clara residents remember the battle well and will recount fascinating details of the events. To this day, the town remains Guevara's city: his wife, Aleida, is a native of the town; the names of institutions and numerous monuments attest to the affection in which he is held; and now he is even interred here.

When the handless mortal remains of this rebel icon were discovered after a lengthy search in Bolivia in 1997, they were brought to Cuba for burial. His flag-draped coffin lay in state in Santa Clara – the scene of his greatest triumph – for three days, and lines of those wishing to pay their final respects stretched back more than 5km (3 miles). In the town's Revolution Square, on October 8, 1997, Fidel Castro made a speech as the coffin, and those of six companions from his Bolivian campaign (including one Bolivian and a Peruvian), were laid to rest in the specially constructed mausoleum. It is now a highly revered site, visited by individual Cubans and groups of school children, as well as tourists.

burns. Few visitors fail to be moved by the aura of reverence.

There is also an interesting museum, the **Museo Histórico de la Revolución** (tel: 42-205-985; same hours as the mausoleum; free), featuring revolutionary memorabilia, some primitive broadcasting equipment used at Radio Rebelde, set up by Che at La Mesa mountain station, and some great photographs. There is also sometimes a video about Che and his role in the revolution.

Remedios

Some 48km (30 miles) to the northeast of Santa Clara (heading toward the north coast) is **Remedios** ⓬, a sleepy, engaging little colonial town and the oldest settlement in the province of Villa Clara. Founded by Vasco Porcallo de Figueroa in 1513–15 as probably the third of eight *villas*, it was moved in 1544 and in 1578 and never achieved the status of the other *villas*. A fire in 1692 meant that all the colonial buildings were built after that date. There has been very little recent urban development here, something the town has

in common with Trinidad. While it may not be as picturesque as Trinidad, Remedios scores top marks for its tranquility and lack of tourists.

Remedios did not enjoy an auspicious start, being ravaged during repeated raids by French, English, and Portuguese pirates. If that were not enough, it was subsequently occupied, according to one of the town's priests, by "infernal legions of demons," and a number of families decamped to found the settlement of Santa Clara. Commercial incentives may have also had something to do with the migration. However, many of the inhabitants ignored their cleric's warnings and stayed put.

Plaza Martí

Plaza Martí, the town's pleasantly spacious central square, has a charming bandstand and is the only town in Cuba to possess two churches on its main plaza. The most stunning edifice in Remedios is the restored **Iglesia Parroquia Mayor de San Juan Bautista de Remedios** (Mon–Fri 9am–noon, 2–5pm, or during Mass at other times,

Transport in Remedios is a leisurely affair.

BELOW: Statue of Liberty just off Plaza Martí in Remedios.

A poster advertising the parrandas *festival in Remedios.*

BELOW:
the elaborate
altar in the
Parroquial Mayor.
RIGHT:
the church tower.

or seek out the church warden at the rear; donations), bordering the east side of Plaza Martí. The old church, built in 1692 on the foundations of an earlier one, was severely damaged by a 1939 earthquake, but a millionaire penitent underwrote a 10-year renovation, discovering gold painted altars and carved beams under layers of encrusted paint and false ceilings.

The church is a religious treasure: parts of the elaborate cedar-wood altar are carved in Arab style and encrusted with 24-carat gold, seen in its full glory when the lights are turned on. The decoration continues along the edge of the mahogany ceiling – which is a breathtaking example of a Mudéjar-style vaulted ceiling (*alfarje*), and was discovered only during the restoration work in the 1940s. The ceiling is particularly rare for its floral decoration. Also overlooking the square is the attractive but run-down church of the **Virgen del Buen Viaje** (currently closed awaiting restoration), though its interior seems very plain after a visit to the Parroquial Mayor.

On the north side of Plaza Martí is the splendid **Museo de la Música Alejandro García Caturla** (Mon–Sat 9am–noon, 1–5pm, Sun 9am–1pm; charge), originally the home of Alejandro García Caturla, a lawyer who devoted his life to music and became one of Cuba's most famous avant-garde composers. Caturla broke with the conventions of his class in every way. He married a black woman and, after her death, married her sister. His worst crime, though, was his incorruptibility: in 1940, at the age of 34, he was murdered by a policeman he was about to sentence for beating up a prostitute; there are suspicions that there may have been underlying political motives. The museum exhibits Caturla's personal effects, scores, musical instruments, and recordings of some of his compositions. There are also art exhibitions, and information on other musicians and bands from the area.

A festival not to be missed

Remedios is famous for its strange and passionate street festivals, known as *parrandas*, which evolved from the percussion street bands, known as *repiques*, that advance through the streets to arouse people for the pre-dawn Mass held to honor San Juan de los Remedios on December 24. In the 19th century, this religious celebration developed into a street fair, with costumes, parades, music, and food.

The fascinating **Museo de Arte Popular las Parrandas** (Tue–Sat 9am–noon, 1–6pm, Sun 9am–1pm; charge), two blocks off the plaza at Máximo Gómez 71, displays the instruments heard during the celebrations. Neighboring districts (Carmen, identified by a sparrowhawk and a globe, and San Salvador, whose symbol is a rooster) spend the week between Christmas Eve and New Year's Eve competing for the best *carroza* (parade float). For months beforehand, artists and engineers secretly plan and build a so-called *trabajo de plaza*, a great tower of light that represents their neighborhood; it can reach up to 28 meters (90ft).

The *parrandas* start when darkness falls, with the unveiling of these incredible confections, and continue until dawn, with musicians playing traditional polkas. Paraders carry hand-made lanterns and banners, there are tableaus on dazzling floats, and fireworks as thrilling as they are menacing. Nearby Placetas and Zulueta maintain similar traditions. Enjoy the tranquility of Remedios while you can: its days as a sleepy backwater may be numbered, as it has become a picturesque and popular tourist stop on the road to Camagüey Cays.

The northern islands

Ten kilometers (6 miles) northeast of Remedios is the rather run-down fishing port of **Caibarién**, where boats dot the harbor. The wharves and warehouses along the waterfront recall the town's one-time importance as a shipping port. Caibarién has some rather mediocre beaches, on a promontory jutting out into the sea, and there is also a nautical base on the bay northeast of the port, where local people practice sailing, windsurfing, and kayaking to compete in national and international competitions.

From Caibarién, you can drive to **Cayo Conuco** ⓭. This 145-hectare

Palm trees and white sands: a Caribbean idyll.

BELOW: Cuban children enjoying the beaches on the north coast.

(363-acre) cay is a former cholera quarantine post, now a biosphere reserve, and a trail leads uphill to one of the most delightful campgrounds in Cuba. *Cabañas* (cabins) nestle in the woods, and campers can swim, fish, ride horses, cook outdoors, and enjoy nature. They share the cay with numerous species of animals, including iguanas and *jutías* (a type of rodent), as well as 172 species of plants. Remember to take insect repellent with you.

On the coast east of Caibarién, a causeway *(pedraplén)* runs out 45km (28 miles) to **Cayo Santa María** and the smaller cays closer to shore. All these cays, called the **Cayos de la Herradura**, are, or soon will be, developed for tourism. Cayo Santa María is an increasingly popular resort. There are already at least a half-dozen luxury hotels distributed among the cays, all but one of them offering all-inclusive holidays, and there are plans to construct many more.

The Escambray mountains

South of Santa Clara, the scenery of the province folds from pastoral farm-land into the Escambray mountains. At **Manicaragua**, the road splits, giving you the option to head straight on to Trinidad or west to the Embalse Hanabanilla and on to Cienfuegos.

The **Embalse Hanabanilla** ⑭ is an enormous reservoir at the top of an 8km (5-mile) climb from a turning after the village of La Moza. Perfectly located in a gorgeous location by the lakeside, with hills all around, is the Hotel Hanabanilla. You may decide simply to enjoy the views and cool off in the swimming pool, but if you wish you can also fish for large-mouth bass, hike through the woods, visit nearby waterfalls, or take a boat across the lake – a trip that is highly recommended for the glimpse it provides of mountain life.

Farmers who work small plots along the shore have their own animals, keep bees, and grow most of their food – fruit, vegetables, and coffee. Bags of beans and jars of honey and royal jelly are sometimes for sale. Coffee is a "state crop" and, legally, only the state can buy or sell the beans, but farmers often ignore the law.

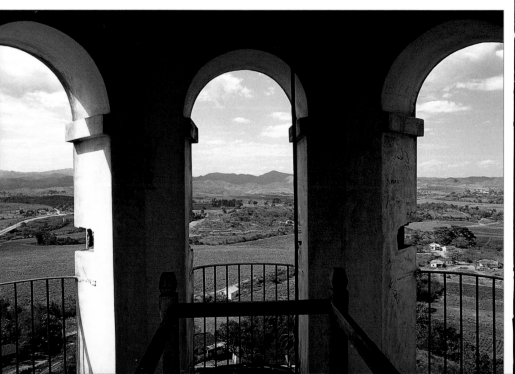

From here you could continue west on winding roads toward Cienfuegos, but our route, for the moment, goes east through the Sierra del Escambray.

Struggle in the Escambray

The majestic Sierra del Escambray is Cuba's second most famous mountain range (after the Sierra Maestra in the Oriente), with its highest peak, the Pico San Juan, topping 1,140 meters (3,700ft). Even at the height of summer, when temperatures in Trinidad or Santa Clara reach 40°C (100°F), you may still need a sweater here. Some of the heaviest rainfall in Cuba feeds the Escambray's lush jungle, where trees are laden with bromeliads and delicate waterfalls greet you at every turn; look out for the giant umbrella-like ferns, a prehistoric species. This is also an important coffee-growing region. On the lower slopes, jungle gives way to pastures and royal palms.

The Escambray provided a perfect hide-out for counter-revolutionaries in the 1960s. The number of anti-Castro guerrillas, who ranged from hardened CIA-trained fighters to local farmers adversely affected by Castro's land reforms, had reached an estimated 3,000 by 1962, when the revolutionary government instigated a campaign to defeat the *bandidos* (bandits). Counter-insurgency units combed the area, driving the bands into more and more difficult terrain until they had no option but to surrender or fight. Even so, the last groups were not killed until 1966. (There is a museum about this struggle in Trinidad; *see page 260.*)

Topes de Collantes

If, instead of turning off, you continue south from Manicaragua, the road twists and turns through spectacular scenery, with every bend offering new views of tropical vegetation, interspersed with plantation forests of eucalyptus and pine. Parrots (*cotorras*) and other bird species abound, though casual observers are more likely to hear than see them.

Eventually you come to the undulating, wooded **Parque Nacional Topes de Collantes** ⑮, 770 meters (2,528ft) above sea level. A wide variety of trees and exotic plants flourishes here: as well as pines and eucalyptus, there are cedar and mahogany among others, and orchids enjoy the damp climate.

The unattractive Kurhotel here was originally built in the 1930s as a tuberculosis sanitarium, and later developed for wider health tourism use; it still offers good hydrotherapy facilities. Tourists stay either at the Kurhotel or at the Hotel Los Helechos (both Gaviota hotels, www.gaviota-grupo.com), which offer air-conditioned rooms, saunas, mineral baths, massages, and herbal therapies.

Walks and waterfalls

For most visitors, the appeal of Topes lies in the walks, through beautiful scenery, and the exotic **waterfalls** nearby – especially **Salto Vega Grande** and the sweeping, uniquely shaped **Salto Caburní**, a 75-meter (250ft) fall. This hike involves a fairly testing 6km (4-mile) round trip; bring plenty of

TIP

Topes de Collantes offers visitors an opportunity to see the national bird, the vividly colored tocororo, otherwise known as the trogon.

BELOW:
El Nicho, one of the picturesque waterfalls near Topes de Collantes.

The burnished-yellow tower of the Iglesia Parroquial Mayor in Sancti Spíritus.

BELOW: the Yayabo Bridge.

drinking water, sunscreen and swimming gear. You have to pay to enter the National Park, and guides are compulsory. If you come here independently, arrange one through the information office at the park entrance (tel: 42-540-231). Many visitors come to Topes on a day trip from Trinidad (*see page 255*); if you are one of them, you will find the round trip by taxi costs about CUC$25–35. Cubatur or Cubanacán in Trinidad will also arrange excursions, and their Jeep or truck safaris are rewarding six-hour trips with lunch, hiking, and swimming.

From Topes the road continues dramatically downhill to Trinidad (22km/13 miles), with some stunning views of the coastline. If you are driving, be sure to stay in low gear: brake pads can wear out quickly on a hot day (*for Trinidad, see page 255*).

Sancti Spíritus

The Carretera Central and the Autopista Nacional east from Santa Clara cut through the central plains to reach the city of **Sancti Spíritus** ⓰ (pop. 87,400) – capital of the province

of the same name. Although the city in no way rivals the splendor of Trinidad, on the province's south coast, it is one of Cuba's seven original *villas* founded by the conquistador Diego Velázquez in 1514 and has a very pleasant atmosphere. The people are friendly, and there is little in the way of *jinetero* (hustler) hassle, since the town is off the main tourist routes. Avoid the ugly, industrial new town and head for the neoclassical **Parque Serafín Sánchez** and the center of the old city located to its south.

Serafín Sánchez was an independence hero who died in battle in 1896, having fought in three wars. His birthplace is now open as the **Casa Natal de Serafín Sánchez Valdivia** (Céspedes Norte 112, between Sobral and San Cristóbal; tel: 41-327-791; Tue–Sat 8am–5pm; charge), to the north of the square on Céspedes Norte.

Sancti Spíritus had an unfortunate early history: it had to be relocated from its original site after the area's native inhabitants – a plague of stinging ants – decided to fight off the invaders; and then the new city was

A Healthier City

The young Winston Churchill was a visitor to Sancti Spíritus in 1895, when working as a newspaper correspondent for the London *Daily Graphic*. Riding with the Spanish army, he became involved in a skirmish with Cuban independence fighters at Arroyo Blanco, to the east of the city. He narrowly escaped being shot, and later recalled the experience in his memoirs: "There is nothing more exhilarating than to be shot at without result." Arriving in the city, he was distinctly unimpressed, dismissing it as "a very second-rate and most unhealthy place." Perhaps he had drunk from the River Yayabo, for years the city's only source of water. There is still a tradition of drinking the river water, filtered of course, and served in a *porrón* – a small earthenware jug.

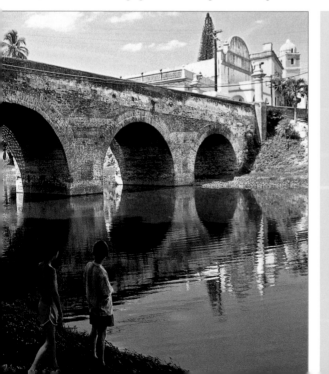

twice burned and destroyed by pirates. Therefore, none of this city's historic buildings is as old as those in Trinidad, though it does still have some delights.

Chief among them, on the **Plaza Honorato del Castillo** (also called the Plaza de Jesús), is an enchanting church, one of the oldest in Cuba, the **Iglesia Parroquial Mayor del Espíritu Santo** (Tue–Sat 9–11am, 2–5pm; free). Originally constructed of wood in 1522, it was rebuilt in stone in the 17th century after being destroyed by pirates. The tower was added in the 18th century and the cupola not until the 19th. With its rich, burnished-yellow exterior and peaceful location, this well-preserved church is one sight in the city that should not be missed.

Just to the south is the **Museo de Arte Colonial** (Calle Plácido Sur 74, between Guairo and Pancho Jiménez; tel: 41-325-455; Tue–Sat 9am–5pm, Sun 8am–noon; charge), housed in an attractive colonial mansion, and well worth visiting for its decor and furnishings alone. Built in the 18th cen-

tury by the Iznaga family, the wealthy local sugar barons, the palace is notable for having 100 doors.

The church, the nearby colonial houses of cobbled Calle El Llano, and the **Puente Yayabo**, the sturdy bridge across the Río Yayabo, built by the Spanish in 1815, have all been declared national monuments. Puente Yayabo is the only colonial arched stone bridge left in Cuba.

Lake-side peace

Cuba's largest man-made lake, the **Embalse Zaza**, just to the southeast of the city, is known for the size and number of its large-mouth bass and trout, while the surrounding woods harbor both mourning doves and white-winged doves, which attract seasonal hunters. There is a hotel here – the Hotel Zaza – which will organize excursions for visitors; and there is an international fishing competition held here in September. The reservoir area is also extremely popular with birdwatchers, as the mangrove-choked marshes of the River Zaza provide a habitat for large numbers of water birds.   ❏

Children try out the urban transportation.

RESTAURANTS

Caibarién
Saramar
Calle 14, 1502, between 15 and 17
Open daily 11am–11pm. $
A pleasant *paladar* offering the best food in the area and accepting payment in either CUCs or *moneda nacional*. Offers excellent value.

Remedios
Hotel Mascotte
Máximo Gómez, 114
Tel: (42) 395-144.
Open daily L & D. $–$$
This is really the only place to eat in Remedios. The dining room has lovely French doors opening on to the plaza. It serves standard *criolla* food and some meat

and fish dishes. Pleasant and friendly.

Santa Clara
1878 Colonial
Máximo Gómez, 8
Tel: (42) 202-428.
Open daily L & D. $–$$
Lovely old building, pleasant bar in the patio, and quite smart – men should wear long trousers at night. A variety of *criolla* dishes, nothing exciting; pork is featured highly.
La Concha
Carretera Central, corner of Danielito.
Tel: (42) 218-124.
Open daily 11am–11pm. $
Close to the Che Guevara memorial, this is the best-known restaurant in town.

Specializes in good pizzas. It can get busy with tour groups at lunch time, when there is sometimes live music.

Sancti Spíritus
Mesón de la Plaza
Máximo Gómez, 34.
Tel: (41) 328-546. Open daily 10am–10pm. $–$$
An agreeable place furnished with heavy wooden tables and chairs, popular at lunch time with tour parties, quieter in the evening. There is usually live music. The house specialty is *ropa vieja* (old clothes): strips of beef stewed with peppers and tomatoes, served with rice.
Quinta Santa Elena

Padre Quintero, between Llano and Manolico Díaz
Tel: (41) 329-167. Open daily 9am–11pm. $–$$
Pleasant restaurant in a neoclassical building by the river. You can eat on the terrace, and be serenaded with live music. Busiest at lunch time. Also specializes in *ropa vieja*, plus fish and pork. There is usually a show on Saturday night.

Price categories are for a three-course meal for one with a beer, or *mojito*. Wine puts the price up:
$ = under $25
$$ = $25–35
$$$ = over $35

CIENFUEGOS AND TRINIDAD

Two historic but very different cities and a splendid stretch of coastline, with one of Cuba's favorite beaches, offer a cultural interlude after the sugar fields and mountains of the interior

Main attractions
CIENFUEGOS
JARDÍN BOTÁNICO SOLEDAD
IGLESIA PARROQUIAL DE LA SANTÍSIMA TRINIDAD
MUSEO ROMÁNTICO, TRINIDAD
CONVENTO DE SAN FRANCISCO DE ASÍS, TRINIDAD
PLAYA ANCÓN
VALLE DE LOS INGENIOS
TORRE DE MANACA-IZNAGA

Cienfuegos province is dominated by green rolling countryside, peppered by small sleepy towns and *bohíos* – palm-thatched cottages. Palm-fringed fields run down to the Alturas de Santa Clara in the east and the distant blue Escambray mountains in the south. The 1959 revolution brought change to what was once primarily an agricultural region, and it has, around the city of Cienfuegos at least, become highly industrialized.

Cienfuegos's past

The road to Cienfuegos city from the *autopista* runs through the small town of Rodas: a pleasant but sleepy place, best known for its Ciego Montero spring, the origin of most of Cuba's fine mineral water. **Cienfuegos ❶** is known as the "Pearl of the South." It's a lovely city with most of its colonial buildings now fully restored.

Europeans first sighted the area in 1494 during Christopher Columbus's second voyage, but no settlement was established until 1819 when Louis de Clouet, a Frenchman who had emigrated to New Orleans, founded the colony of Fernandina de Jagua. It was renamed Cienfuegos the following year in honor of Cuba's Spanish governor general, who invited further settlers from Louisiana. With a little imagination you can appreciate the attempt

by its French founders to give the city a certain Parisian feel, with its parks, tree-lined boulevards, and colonnades. In 1869, a group of Cuban nationalists led by Juan Díaz de Villegas rebelled against the Spanish Government, and in October 1895, Major-General José Rodríguez organized the Cienfuegos Brigade, which later played a key role in the battle of Mal Tiempo during Cuba's second War of Independence.

Following the 1959 revolution, Cienfuegos received massive investment from the Soviet Union, which turned the region into a major industrial

---

PRECEDING PAGES: old American car, Trinidad.
LEFT: Trinidad's Plaza Mayor.
RIGHT: whiling away the day.

Marble statue in the Teatro Tomás Terry.

BELOW: a detail on the facade of the ornate Palacio del Valle.

center. At its height, the province of Cienfuegos had 12 sugar mills which could grind 39,000 tonnes of raw *caña* (sugar cane) daily, but many of them have now closed. Its port – the only deep-water terminal on Cuba's south coast, and home to a sizable fishing and shrimping fleet – handles around 30 percent of the country's sugar exports. Here you will also find the largest cement plants and oil refineries in Cuba.

The historic center

The historical center of the city is the **Pueblo Nuevo** district, which is quite a pleasant shopping center – although only for those who can use convertible pesos. However, there are more CUC stores in Cienfuegos than there are in other cities, and the residents do seem to enjoy a higher standard of living. Most of the city's best buildings are around **Parque José Martí** , the square where the first settlement was founded on April 22, 1819, under the shade of a *majagua* tree. The place where the tree stood is now marked by a bandstand. There is a series of statues

to the city's illustrious citizens, including one to José Martí, guarded by lions as well as a triumphal arch, inscribed with the date 20 Mayo, 1902 – commemorating the birth of the Cuban Republic.

The **Catedral Purísima Concepción**, dating from 1870, dominates the square and has an impressive, but shabby, interior, complete with marble floors. Nearby, on the north side, is the neoclassical **Teatro Tomás Terry** (officially known as the Teatro de Cienfuegos, Avenida 56, 2701, between Calles 27 and 29; tel: 43-551-772; daily 9am–5pm; charge), inaugurated in 1890. It was named after a rich sugar baron who arrived in Cuba as a poor Venezuelan émigré, and made a dubious fortune by buying up weak and sick slaves, nursing them back to health, and then reselling them at a profit. The ornate interior of the theater is made almost entirely of precious Cuban hardwoods with classical reliefs and nymphs providing some of the decoration. National and local performances are staged here, ranging from National Ballet productions to local comedy acts.

Nuclear City

The views from the Castillo de Jagua *(see page 254)* are impressive, but they encompass not only the delights of the coastline and the inland sea of the Bay of Cienfuegos. You also get a view of the eyesore which is the Hotel Pasacaballo and, in the distance, one of Cienfuegos's most curious and eerie sites: the concrete dome of the Soviet-designed Juragua Nuclear Power Plant, known as Ciudad Nuclear, or "Nuclear City." Construction of two 440-MW reactors began in 1983 to avoid dependence on oil imports and improve electricity supplies, but were only 60 percent complete when the USSR collapsed. Attempts were made to renegotiate the contract on commercial terms, but Cuba was unable to meet the proposed payments and construction was halted in 1992.

On the opposite side of the square, the **Museo Histórico Provincial** (tel: 43-519-722; Tue–Sat 10am–6pm, Sun 9am–1pm; charge) focuses on the city's role in the War of Independence, and is housed in a magnificent building which used to be the Casino Español, a cultural and political institution. The marble staircase is huge and grand and the rooms contain art and furniture as well as historical exhibits. On the west side of the plaza, the **Casa de Cultura Benjamín Duarte**, which occupies the former Palacio de Ferrer, the home of a rich sugar baron, is closed for renovation. It's a fine building, with a wide marble staircase and attractive wall tiles. There is a tower on the corner which was used to view shipping in the harbor, but is also great for looking out over the town.

Next door is the UNEAC cultural center (*see margin note*), with a pretty, flower-filled garden with wrought-iron furniture. There's a small movie theater here, an art gallery, and live bands perform on the weekend.

The streets around the Plaza José Martí hum with activity: particularly traffic-free **Boulevard San Fernando**, where food-stallholders, souvenir vendors, flower sellers, boot blacks, and other entrepreneurs ply their trades. Northwest of the Plaza, on a small peninsula called Cayo Loco, is the interesting **Museo Histórico Naval Nacional** (Naval Museum; tel: 43-516 -617; Tue–Sat 9am–6pm, Sun 9am–1pm; charge). There is a good deal of military history here, but there are also many exhibits to do with fishing, and some archeological and natural history items as well.

The main street, however, is the broad Calle 37, usually called the **Paseo del Prado** – a more fitting name for the longest boulevard in Cuba. It is bordered by some beautiful but unpretentious colonial buildings, mostly still private residences. South of Avenida 46, just before it hits the waterfront, the street is known as the Malecón. Always busy, and filled with traffic and gossiping crowds, it is the hub of the city's nightlife. The street is lined with statues, busts, and plaques commemorating Cienfuegos's most notable past citizens, as well as yet more impressive colonial houses.

Away from the center

One of Cienfuegos's best-known landmarks is at the very end of the Prado. At the south end of the Malecón you reach Punta Gorda, where gracious French-style mansions and plantation houses can be found. You can't miss the vast, unattractive Hotel Jagua, formerly a notorious casino hotel run by Batista's brother. However, the main attraction is the adjacent **Palacio del Valle** ❸. This kitsch mansion, done up in Moorish Revival style with a few other styles mixed in for good measure, was commissioned by businessman Acisclo del Valle. He brought in an Italian architect, and craftsmen from Morocco and France, and materials were imported from Spain, Italy, and the USA. The building was finished in 1917. After the 1959 revolution, the del Valle family fled Cuba, and for many

TIP

UNEAC stands for Unión de Escritores y Artistas de Cuba – the Writers' and Artists' Union. They have a center in each of the Cuban provinces, and they are usually worth visiting.

BELOW: climb to the top of Palacio del Valle for fabulous views.

Cienfuegos' tribute in bronze to Cuban musician, Beny Moré.

RIGHT: the tower on the Casa de Cultura in Cienfuegos.

years the palace served as a government hotel school. Then, in 1990, the Hotel Jagua, situated across from the Palacio, converted it into an expensive Italian restaurant.

Watching the sunset over Cienfuegos Bay from the third-floor balcony of the Palacio is unforgettable (they charge you 2 CUC to go onto the terrace, but this entitles you to a cocktail as well as the view). The resident pianist for many years has been the flamboyant Carmen, who wears glitter make-up and seems to know a song from every country on earth. If you decide to dine here, enjoy an after-dinner sing-along at Carmen's side and finish off the evening at the Hotel Jagua's hilarious drag-show cabaret.

Another attraction on the waterfront overlooking the bay in Punta Gorda is the Club Cienfuegos (Calle 37 between 10 and 12; tel: 43-512-891), formerly the Cienfuegos Yacht Club and still a hive of activity, with a sailing center, tennis courts, restaurants, and other social facilities. The eclectic building, with twin-domed towers linked by a balcony, is painted a brilliant white.

Around Cienfuegos

The best way to visit the **Castillo Nuestra Señora de los Angeles de Jagua ●** (daily 9am–4pm; charge, guides available) on the southern side of the beautiful Bahía de Cienfuegos is to take a ferry *(lancha)* from a terminal just south of the Parque Martí (Avenida 46, between calles 23 and 25). It departs at 8am, 1pm, and 3pm, and returns at 6.30am, 10am, and 3pm; the journey takes about 45 minutes, and costs just 1 CUC. The colonial fortress was built in 1733–45 by Joseph Tantete of France to defend the area against pirate attacks, and you enter across a drawbridge over a dry moat.

Alternatively, if you have a car or want to hire a taxi, take the road that follows the eastern side of the bay. After about 2km (1 mile) you pass the **Cementerio Tomás Acea ●**, an impressive neoclassical cemetery overlooking the bay. Guides are available here if you want a tour of the graves and monuments. You will eventually end up at the ugly, Soviet-built Hotel Pasacaballo – strangely, although it is built directly across the bay from the

Beny Moré

There is a bronze statue on the Prado at the junction with the Boulevard (Avenida 54) in Cienfuegos of Beny (or Benny) Moré, one of the best-loved Cuban musicians, who was born in nearby Santa Isabel de las Lajas in 1919. He got his first breakthrough when he won a radio competition in the early 1940s, and went on to record with the then-famous Trio Matamoros.

Beny (as he is always known) was equally at home with Afro-Cuban music as he was with mamba or the country music known as *guajira*. He is also much-loved because, when many other musical stars left Cuba after the revolution, he remained, although he was already famous in Mexico and much of Latin America, and could have had a good career outside his homeland. He is particularly honored in Cienfuegos because, at the height of his fame in the 1950s, he chose to make a recording and perform with the little-known Cienfuegos-based Orquesta Aragón and helped them reach a wider audience. A festival bearing his name is held each September.

Castillo de Jagua, all the rooms face the other way.

About 6km (4 miles) east of Pasacaballo, just where the road veers inland, is the Hotel Rancho Luna, a resort popular with Canadian tourists. Non-residents can use the Rancho Luna facilities (including the only good beach close to Cienfuegos) for around 5 CUCs. Scuba diving and snorkeling are also available here.

The road to Trinidad

En route to Trinidad, between the villages of San Antón and Los Guaos and about 23km (15 miles) east of Cienfuegos, you will come to the **Jardín Botánico Soledad** (at Pepito Tey, tel: 43-545-115; daily 8am–5pm; charge). Now a national monument, the vast garden is well worth a visit. Established in 1899, it is home to some 2,400 species, including 285 types of palm tree. It was founded by Edwin Atkins, the American owner of the Soledad sugar plantation, now called Pepito Tey.

The original aim was to produce more resistant strains of sugar cane, and from 1919 Harvard University was involved in scientific research into different types, but Atkins gradually became more interested in planting exotic species. The gardens have been in state hands since 1961 and scientists have developed sections devoted to medicinal plants, fruit trees, orchids, and palm trees.

From Cienfuegos, you can also reach Embalse Hanabanilla (*see page 244*) and Santa Clara (*see pages 237–41*) by taking the scenic road via Cumanayagua to Manicaragua, across the foothills of the **Sierra del Escambray**.

The main road between Cienfuegos and Trinidad proceeds south, across a delightful hummocky landscape, until it reaches the sea. At **La Sierrita**, 32km (20 miles) east of Cienfuegos, you can head inland into the Escambray for one of the most dramatic routes through the mountains to Topes de Collantes, which will take you close to **Pico San Juan**, the highest mountain in the Sierra del

Escambray (1,140 meters/3,740ft). The road surface is poor in places, and the inclines are steep and require concentration, but the views are magnificent. (The more usual route to Topes de Collantes runs north from Trinidad, and is one of the most popular trips from the colonial town.) Agencies in Cienfuegos offer tours to El Nicho, on the edge of Embalse Hanabanilla in Cienfuegos province, where waterfalls cascade down in falls up to 35 meters (105ft) high. It is a beautiful setting surrounded by forest and mountains, and the tour usually includes bathing in pools, hiking, cave visits, and a lunch stop.

Back on the coast road, you pass several small, empty beaches, the first of which is Playa Inglés, about 48km (30 miles) from Cienfuegos. The second is Playa Yaguanabo, 5km (3 miles) further east, where Villa Yaguanabo offers basic accommodation and meals.

Colonial sugar capital

Located in Sancti Spíritus province, 82km (50 miles) southeast of Cienfuegos, is **Trinidad** ⑱, Cuba's third-oldest settlement and one of the

Pink Ipê blossoms at Jardín Botánico.

BELOW:
a stately avenue in the Jardín Botánico Soledad.

Trinidad's cathedral, officially known as the Parroquial Mayor.

island's jewels. Its red-tiled roofs, pastel-colored buildings, cobblestoned streets, laid-back atmosphere, and historic museums make it the main place, outside Havana, that most visitors include on their itinerary.

Trinidad was founded in January 1514 by Spanish explorer Diego Velázquez, at a spot just inland from the Caribbean Sea near the mouth of the Río Arimao. From the outset, Velázquez and his men enslaved the local indigenous Taíno inhabitants but, as they soon began to die from imported diseases and overwork, the colonists started to replace them with slaves shipped in from Africa.

Throughout much of the 17th century, this area was raided by pirates, who destroyed the provincial capital of Sancti Spíritus but spared Trinidad itself. The town was also a thriving center for smugglers and the slave trade – the source of much of its wealth.

During the boom years of the sugar industry, in the late 18th century, the area around Trinidad became known as the Valle de los Ingenios (Valley of the Sugar Mills), and fabulous planta-

tion houses began to dot the countryside. When Cuba officially abolished slavery in 1886, the practice continued in more subtle forms for several years, even after the 1895–98 War of Independence. Throughout most of the 20th century, Trinidad remained economically tied to the sugar industry, though tourism is now the main source of revenue for the town.

A protected gem

In 1988, Unesco declared Trinidad and the Valle de los Ingenios a World Heritage Site, but the town had already been recognized as a National Monument back in the Batista years. There are no garish signs or political slogans in the town itself, as these are against the law.

It well deserves the praise heaped on it: painted mahogany balustrades run along the shady colonnades, massive ancient wooden doors open to reveal cool green courtyards beyond, motorized transport is light, and life in the city moves sleepily along. At night, the town is dark, lit only by low lights or the eerie glow of television

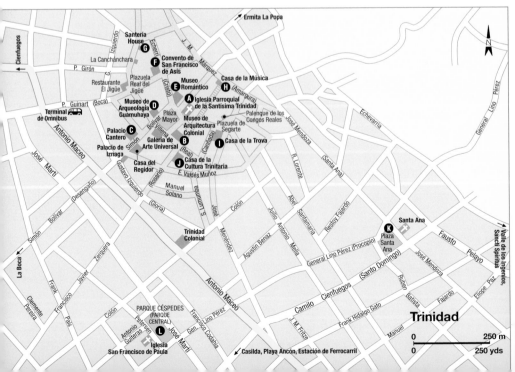

screens as the inhabitants settle down to watch an evening soap opera or movie – although the sound of music and laughter emanating from one of the bars or from the Casa de la Trova indicates that not everybody stays at home at night.

Exploring the city

Trinidad is divided into the old and the new towns. The Plaza Mayor, where the rich built their mansions, is the centre of **Old Trinidad**. Parque Céspedes is the focal point of the newer town, which is built on a grid system. The sloping streets all have a central gutter to allow rainwater to flow away easily.

The only way to explore Trinidad is on foot. Many of the streets in the old town are closed to traffic and in other parts of the town they are generally narrow and difficult to negotiate by car unless you know them well. Following a simple walking tour takes three to four hours – museum and lunch stops included – although you may enjoy the town so much that you make it last a few days. Sightseeing is best done in the morning, while it's still fairly cool and the streets are less crowded, or in the early evening, when the buildings are bathed in a delicious, pinkish light.

The heart of the city

Any tour of the town will start in the splendid yet intimate **Plaza Mayor**, one of Cuba's most photographed sights. All the museums and sites of interest are clustered around the square, with its magnificent palm trees, white wrought-iron benches, and small statues, including two bronze greyhounds. The huge, cream-colored cathedral standing at the top of the square is the **Iglesia Parroquial de la Santísima Trinidad Ⓐ** (tel: 41-993-668; daily 10.30am–1pm for visitors, Mass daily 8pm and Sun 9am for worshipers only). Begun in 1817, it is the largest church in Cuba. It is also the only church in Cuba to have hand-carved Gothic altars, and five aisles instead of three. It is known for its acoustics and it is worth catching a performance by the church choir, Piedras Vivas, singing religious music with a Cuban twist.

If you walk around the plaza in a

BELOW: view across rooftops to Convento de San Francisco de Asís.

BELOW: Trinidad has a history of producing good-quality pottery and linens although the handicraft workshops have now mostly disappeared.

clockwise direction from the church, you come to the former house of the Sánchez family, now the **Museo de Arquitectura Colonial** ⓑ (Desengaño 83; tel: 41-993-208; Sat–Thur 9am–5pm; charge), which tells the history of Trinidad's development, with maps and models showing how colonial craftsmen worked. If you are interested in architecture, ask here about two-hour walking tours of the city (they also arrange visits to the Valle de los Ingenios).

Like many buildings in Trinidad, this house, dating from 1735, was painted yellow rather than white, because white was considered too harsh on people's eyes in the strong tropical sun. When the house was restored in the 1980s, sections of yellow were left as a reminder of its original color. The museum includes an exhibition of hand-carved doors and windows, gas-lit chandeliers, and a stockade built to hold 12 slaves at a time.

On the south side of the square, the attractive balconied building contains the **Galería de Arte Universal** (Real 48; tel: 41-994-432; Fri–Wed 9am–5pm; charge) on a site where the conquis-

tador Hernán Cortés is said to have lived before departing for Mexico to conquer the Aztecs. Downstairs the gallery exhibits art. Upstairs there is a shop selling arts and crafts.

If you turn left here, down Simón Bolívar, you pass several impressive colonial mansions, before reaching the **Palacio Cantero** ⓒ, one of the city's most exquisite mansions, housing the city's **Museo Municipal de Historia** (Simón Bolívar 423; tel: 41-994-460; Sat–Thur 9am–5pm; charge), with some fine pieces of colonial furniture and interesting exhibits on the slave trade. There's a Roman-style bathhouse, and a fountain that once spouted eau de Cologne for women and gin for men. However, the finest feature is the square tower, which provides an exceptional view of the whole town.

Within a few paces of the museum are the **Casa del Regidor** (formerly the mayor's residence), and **Callejón de Pena**, a street full of private merchants' houses, and a good place to find excellent arts and crafts, particularly lace and woodwork. If you want to buy, be sure to bargain – it is expected.

Back on the west side of the square, another beautiful mansion houses the **Museo de Arqueología Guamuhaya** ❹ (Simón Bolívar 457, corner Villena; tel: 41-993-420; Sat–Thur 9am–5pm; charge). There are interesting items relating to the pre-Columbian past with developments being traced to post-Conquest times.

Elegance and romance

A strong contender for Trinidad's best museum is the bold yellow building with arches located on the same side of the square as the church: the **Museo Romántico** ❺ (Hernández 52; tel: 41-994-363; Tue–Sun 9am–5pm; charge), housed in a sumptuous mansion. The ground floor was built in 1740 and it remained single-story for 70 years until the second floor was added at the beginning of the 19th century. In 1830–60, the Romantic period, it belonged to Nicolás de la Cruz Brunet Muñoz, the Conde de Brunet, who lived in the mansion with his 12 children and a number of slaves. He made his money from sugar and cattle, owning 70 slaves at the time of his death.

In 1974, the house was turned into a museum, and its rooms were filled with period pieces collected from numerous mansions throughout the city. Here, for example, you can see a priceless 18th-century Austrian writing desk, covered with painted-enamel mythological scenes; a marble bathtub; and a wooden "throne" from 1808 used as a toilet. In the kitchen there is a limestone water filter and a set of beautiful, custom-made porcelain plates and dishes from the 1820s. The upstairs balcony has fine views over the square.

From religion to revolution

Leaving the museum, walk down Calle Echerrí (also called Cristo) to the intersection with Calle Piro Guinart. Here is the **Archivo de la Ciudad** (City Archives), recognizable by the colorful coat of arms on the facade. Directly in front is the tallest and most famous landmark in Trinidad: the **Convento de San Francisco de Asís** ❻, parts of which date from 1731. The building was enlarged and embellished in 1809 by a Spanish priest, Father

Portrait of one of the colonial aristocrats who financed their lavish lifestyles with profits from sugar plantations.

BELOW:
Trinidad street bathed in golden light.

BELOW: handmade souvenirs for sale on the Callejón de Pena.
RIGHT: cooling down on a Trinidad doorstep.

Valencia, but, after the construction of the nearby Parroquial Mayor in 1892, the convent ceased to function, and the building was turned into a barracks for the Spanish army.

Then, in 1984, in a perverse twist of history, the former convent was turned into the **Museo Nacional de Lucha Contra Bandidos** (Museum of the Struggle Against Counter-Revolutionaries; Hernández corner Piro Guinart; tel: 41-994-121; Tue–Sun 9am–5pm; charge), which concentrates on the campaign to weed out anti-Castro guerrillas in the Escambray mountains during the 1960s. Inside there is a boat in which Cuban exiles came from Florida to destroy the oil tanks at the nearby port of Casilda, and a Russian truck which was used in the search for counter-revolutionaries in the mountains.

The real beauty of this building, however, has nothing to do with politics. Climb the 119 granite and wooden stairs to the top of the bell tower. Once you've caught your breath, enjoy the view: from here, all of Trinidad is clearly visible, as are the blue waters of the Caribbean and the distant, hazy peaks of the Sierra Escambray. It is well worth the climb.

Cocktails, art, and Santería

Walking to the end of Fernando Echerrí (Cristo), you reach the area called El Fortuno. In the 18th century this area was home to several foreign pirates who were welcomed by the Trinidadians (*trinitarios* in Spanish), many of whom grew rich from smuggling and trading with these disreputable people, whom they were supposed to fear. The house located at Ciro Redondo No. 261 was said to have been built for a French pirate, Carlos Merlin, in 1754.

At the foot of Redondo, turn left into Calle Martínez Villena, heading toward **La Canchánchara**, a bar with live entertainment, and its own house cocktail, the *canchánchara*, made from rum, lime, honey, and sparkling water. The bar is quiet during the day, but comes into its own at night, and is popular with locals as well as tourists.

On the parallel Calle Vicente Suyama (also known as Calle Encarnación) is a makeshift gallery at No. 39 run by professor of art, Carlos Mata: it's typical of several private galleries that cater specifically to foreign tourists, and which have sprouted up around Trinidad since early 1994, when the government began tolerating certain limited forms of private enterprise.

One block along from La Canchánchara to your right is the spot where, in the early 16th century, the so-called "Protector of the Indians," Bartolomé de las Casas *(see page 35)*, in the presence of Diego Velázquez, conducted the first Christmas Mass in Trinidad under a stately old *jigüe* tree *(see margin note)*: this is the **Plazuela Real del Jigüe**, complete with one of Trinidad's best little restaurants.

The next stop, heading up Vicente Suyama 59, is an authentic **Santería house ⑥**, with Cuban revolutionary posters and an altar complete with a black Madonna. There's also a rock shaped like an egg, inside a pot full of seawater; the whole contraption is covered with fine lace. If you would like to go in, ask for Israel, the Santería priest, who will explain everything. He is very pleasant and knowledgable and gives an interesting little tour (a donation is appreciated).

East of Plaza Mayor

To the right of the Iglesia Parroquial Mayor, an ancient flight of cobbled steps marks the end of Calle Rosario. At No. 3 is a house built in 1732 for Fernández de Lara, Trinidad's chief inquisitor, who was responsible for upholding Christianity. Halfway up the steps is an open-air bar, La Escalinata, great for a sunset cocktail, where you can relax with a *mojito* and listen to live bands.

At the top of the steps you will find the **Casa de la Música ⑪**, a really lively spot that has live music, salsa concerts, and impromptu dancing until the early hours. The Casa also has displays of old instruments, and you can buy a range of Cuban music on CDs and tapes. There is a second entrance on Calle J.M. Márquez.

At the foot of the steps to your left along Fernando Echerrí is the Palenque de los Congos Reales, a bar open day and night where you can often catch

Many of Cuba's finest trova, son, and boleros musicians perform at Trinidad's celebrated music club, Casa de la Trova.

BELOW: Santería doll dressed in white lace at Templo de Yemaya.

Elderly local people in Trinidad have seen a lot of changes over the years.

BELOW: Playa Ancón is the main tourist resort on the peninsula.

an Afro-Cuban dance show or live music while enjoying a drink in the shady courtyard.

Slightly farther east is a triangular-shaped plaza – the **Plazuela de Sagarte**, where some of the oldest houses in Trinidad are to be found. One of these is now the **Casa de la Trova** ❶ (daily 9am–1am; free during the day, charge at night), built in 1717 and decorated with murals. It is popular with tourists and local people who come to enjoy the live music by day and night, and there is always a warm and friendly atmosphere.

One block down the hill and to your right, you come to **Calle Francisco Javier Zerquera (Rosario)** again. On the corner at No. 406 is a light-blue house that once belonged to one of Trinidad's sugar barons. Today it is the **Casa de la Cultura Trinitaria** ❶ (tel: 41-994-308; daily 7am–11pm) where there is an art gallery and classrooms, dances are held, and concerts and plays are performed. Back up the hill, notice the 18th-century walls made from rocks, bricks, bones, and bottles of all sizes and shapes, and held together

with clay, straw, and plaster. The yellow house at No. 79 is the **Casa de los Curas**, the residence for centuries of the parochial church's priests.

Trinidad's other sights

There are two other areas worth visiting outside the heart of the Old Town. A 10-minute walk from the Plaza Mayor, the **Plaza Santa Ana** ❶ has a beautiful ruined church of the same name. Also on the plaza is the former Royal Prison (Carcel Real), and there is also a restaurant, a gallery displaying local art, and a store. You may also notice a rare statue of Bartolomé de Las Casas, the Dominican friar who fought for indigenous rights in the 16th century.

To the southeast, the **Parque Central** (which is also known as **Parque Céspedes**) ❶ has no stunning architecture but is a busy spot, with a church, a cinema, and the telephone office, while in the center there are pergolas of shady vines and trailing plants. In November, the square is the focus for a week of cultural events and music.

Peninsula de Ancón

Some 12km (8 miles) south of Trinidad lies a spectacular stretch of beach, accessible either by way of **Casilda** or the more scenic route via the small fishing village of **La Boca**, where Trinidad's river disgorges its waters into the sea. The beach here is popular with local people, who can't usually be found at the main tourist resort of Playa Ancón, farther out along the peninsula. Unlike those in the tourist resorts, the beach here is not cleaned daily, but it is quite acceptable, and the area is lively, with *casas particulares* and places to eat.

Playa Ancón ❶ is an excellent long sandy stretch with warm, clear blue waters. Behind the beach, however, there are lakes and swamps, so take precautions against mosquitoes and the sandflies which appear in the evening. Bathers tend to gather on the sections in front of the Hotel Ancón and the nearby Hotel Costa Sur, where they can be within easy reach of bars and restaurants. You can use the hotel's loungers for a small fee (currently CUC$2), while straw sunshades are available if you can't find a spot under the seagrape trees.

If you don't have a car, the beach can be reached by an irregular bus service, which is not to be relied on, or by taxi (*taxistas* tout for business on the corner of Antonio Maceo and Simón Bolívar). Find other people to fill the car and make it a more economical journey. There is a public car park next to the Hotel Ancón, where taxis and coco-taxis wait to take people back to Trinidad. It is also a great cycle ride, with the road following the twinkling waters of the Caribbean.

The bicycle ride is best done fairly early in the morning or in the late afternoon to avoid the sun at its most powerful. Your hotel, or the owner of your *casa particular*, will probably be able to set you up with a bicycle for around CUC$3 a day. The quality of the bikes varies and they rarely have gears. For a tip (CUC$1) someone will watch your bicycle for you while you are on the beach.

There is a marina at Ancón, opposite Hotel Ancón (tel: 41-996-205), from where you can make excursions by boat or arrange scuba diving. Most excursions are booked through the local tour operators, but set off from here. Catamarans go to either Cayo Blanco or Cayo Macho, two offshore cays, which make a nice day trip with snorkeling, lunch, and an open bar.

Valle de los Ingenios

As you leave Trinidad on Route 12, heading northeast toward Sancti Spíritus, or to join up with the Carretera Central going east, the road passes through the spectacular **Valle de los Ingenios** ⓴ (Valley of the Sugar Mills). Like Trinidad, this lush valley is a Unesco World Heritage Site. When it was Cuba's most important sugar-producing region, there were 43 working sugar mills in the valley. However, there was a serious downturn in the valley's economy in the mid-19th century, and then it collapsed completely in 1880 when world sugar prices slumped.

In the rest of Cuba, the more efficient *central* sugar mill was becoming

The old steam train that takes tourists from Trinidad to Manaca-Iznaga.

BELOW: the lush and lovely Valle de los Ingenios.

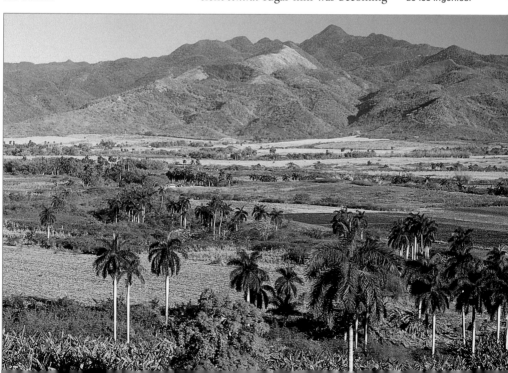

Map on pages 216–17

TIP

According to the census of 1795 there were 2,676 slaves in Trinidad. That year, the area's 82 sugar mills produced 680 tonnes of sugar, 1,000 barrels of *aguardiente*, and 700 urns of molasses.

BELOW: pressing sugar cane to make *guarapo*.
RIGHT: the Torre de Manaca-Iznaga.

the norm, and the valley's *ingenios* simply could not compete. Many of the magnificent plantation houses and mansions dating from those days are now in ruins, but some still stand, most notably the exceptionally beautiful farm belonging to the Iznaga family, which has been restored.

The quaint little **Tren Turístico**, an old steam train, goes from Trinidad station, south of the town, to Manaca-Iznaga (daily in high season, 9.30am–2pm; CUC$10).

Torre de Manaca-Iznaga

You cannot miss the farm, as it is splendidly indicated by the **Torre de Manaca-Iznaga**, 15km (10 miles) by road from Trinidad (daily 9am–4 or 5pm; charge), which rears proudly out of the green cane fields. Legend has it that the tower was built after a bet between two brothers, in which one had to build a tower higher than the depth the other could dig a well. In fact, the tower was designed originally as a watchtower to keep an eye on the slaves working in the fields, and has a bell that summoned them to work.

Birds of prey circle on the thermals, and a refreshing wind cools you as you climb up above the valley floor.

Down below, local women sell beautiful handmade lace and *guayaberas*, the traditional white cotton men's shirts. The immaculate hacienda (daily 9am–5pm) is an excellent place for a drink of *guarapo*, the freshly pressed sugar-cane juice that is milled by Cuba's only original *trapiche* (sugar press) remaining *in situ*. There are also demonstrations of sugar-cane pressing, in which you can participate, and enjoy the fruits of your labor afterward with a dash of rum. Trips to the *torre* can be arranged through tour operators in Trinidad.

If you are bound for Santa Clara, you should take the road running north from the Manaca-Iznaga tower to Güinia de Miranda. This is a little-used and potholed but beautiful route. Alternatively, the road to Sancti Spíritus curves and dips across a lovely landscape, passing the heights of the Alturas de Banao, and this is the main route for buses heading to the east, en route to Santiago de Cuba. ❑

RESTAURANTS AND BARS

Restaurants

Price categories are for a three-course meal for one with a beer, or *mojito*. Wine puts the price up:
$ = under $25
$$ = $25–35
$$$ = over $35

Cienfuegos

1869
Calle 31, corner of 54
Tel: (43) 551-020
Open daily 7am–9.45pm. **$$**
An elegant restaurant in the Hotel La Unión. Cuban and international cuisine. Not the greatest food in the world, but not bad, and a very pleasant place to sit.

Aché
Avenida 38 between 41 and 43
Tel: (43) 526-173
Open Mon–Fri noon–10pm. **$$**
The only legal *paladar* in Cienfuegos and a long-established, professional business, having opened in 1996. Generous cocktails and you can accompany your meal with wine. The menu is limited to the legal chicken, pork, or fish, but it is all good with friendly service.

Club Cienfuegos
Calle 37, between 10 and 12
Tel: (43) 512-891.
Open daily 10am–1am.
$$–$$$
There are two restaurants in this elegant colonial building: one is Italian and the other serves pretty much the usual *comida criolla* meat and fish dishes, but with a great view over the bay.

There is also a cocktail bar and a swimming pool.

El Polinesio
Avenida 29
Tel: (43) 515-723.
Open noon–10pm. **$$**
Cuban and international food. Great for people-watching; sit at one of the tables outside. The shop attached sells rum, cigars, music, and handicrafts.

Palacio del Valle
Calle 37, Punta Gorda
Tel: (43) 551-226. Open daily L & D. **$$–$$$**
Seafood, including lobster and shrimp, is the specialty in this extravagant, early 20th-century Spanish-Moorish palace.

La Verja
Avenida 54, 3306
Tel: (43) 516-311. Open daily 11am–3pm, 6pm–midnight. **$$**
The best place to eat in the town center, for its shabby elegance and stained-glass *mámparas* more than the food.

Trinidad

El Jigüe
Calle Rubén Martínez Villena, 69, corner of Piro Guinart
Tel: (41) 996-476. Open daily noon–10.45pm. **$$**
Located in the tiny, picturesque Plaza El Jigüe, this restaurant is airy with a pleasant atmosphere, live music and good *comida criolla* at reasonable prices.

El Mesón del Regidor
Calle Simón Bolívar, 424
Tel: (41) 996-572. Open daily 9am–10pm. **$$**
The setting and decor are rather better than the

food. The usual fare, including grilled steaks and fish.

Estela
Simón Bolívar 557
Tel: (41) 994-329. Open Mon–Fri from 7pm. **$$**
A *paladar* and the most popular place to eat in town, so get there early. Tables in the garden, enclosed by a high wall. Food is fresh and tasty with lots of choice and plentiful portions. Friendly hosts, good service.

Guaicanamar
Grand Hotel Iberostar Trinidad, José Martí
Tel: (41) 996-070. Open daily 7–10am, 12.30–3pm, 7–10pm. **$$$**
The only restaurant in Trinidad which could be classed as gourmet, offering items unavailable elsewhere such as

cheeses, jamón Serrano, and salmon, with a high standard of service.

Sol y Son
Calle Simón Bolívar, 283
No phone. Open daily 7–11pm. **$**
One of Trinidad's two *paladares*, this place serves good-value *criolla* food in a colonial house with a jumble of antiques and its own patio. Vegetarian options available. There is often live music, too.

Trinidad Colonial
Calle Maceo, 402 and Colón
Tel: (41) 996-473. Open daily noon–10pm. **$$**
The international and Cuban food does not quite live up to the charm of this lovely colonial mansion, but it is perfectly acceptable. Wine and canapés with live music Fri at 10pm.

EASTERN LOWLANDS

This region's economic mainstay is agriculture although tourism is growing steadily. While the area is not full of obvious attractions, it is well worth visiting the colonial city of Camagüey, and there are fine beaches along the north coast

The Carretera Central highway continues east from Sancti Spíritus through **Ciego de 85 Ávila province**. With its fertile soils and abundant water, this is Cuba's fruit bowl, producing citrus, bananas, and pineapples, in the most productive plantations on the island. To the north are the Jardines del Rey, of which Cayo Coco, Cayo Guillermo, and Cayo Paredón Grande now make up the third most important tourist development in the country. To the south are the Jardines de la Reina, popular for diving and fishing, while other watery attractions include the two largest natural lakes in Cuba, Laguna de la Leche and Laguna La Redonda, much loved by fishermen, hunters, and birdwatchers.

Pineapple town

The provincial capital, also called **Ciego de Ávila ❶**, gets its name from a 16th-century rancher named Jácome de Ávila, who cleared the original dense forest here to make a clearing, or *ciego*. He set aside part of his estate as a resting place for travelers on the east–west route, and this quickly became a settlement. Often called the "Pineapple Town" by other Cubans, its nickname is well deserved. Here, a single variety of pineapple, the sweet and juicy *Española Roja*, is grown in vast quantities that still fall short of demand.

The town, also known as the "city of portals," after the large number of neoclassical columns and pillars adorning the houses, is built on a strict grid system around **Parque Martí**, with the usual bust of the hero. There are few buildings of note apart from the **Museo de Artes Decorativas** (tel: 33-201-661; Mon–Fri 9am–5pm, Sat 2–9pm, Sun 8am–noon; charge) and the neoclassical **Teatro Principal** (just south of the square, Agüero and Honorato del Castillo; tel: 33-222-086), built in the 1920s by a rich socialite, Angela

Main attractions
CIEGO DE ÁVILA
LOS JARDINES DE LA REINA
MORÓN
CAYO COCO
CAMAGÜEY
CAYO SABINAL
HACIENDA LA BELÉN

LEFT: patio of a Camagüey restaurant.
RIGHT: setting sail from Cayo Coco beach.

Cycling is a popular mode of transportation in Morón.

Hernández Vida de Jiménez, who battled to create a cultural mecca in her home town. The theater has wonderful acoustics and is still used.

During the first War of Independence in the 1860s, the Spanish colonial government built a 67km (42-mile) defensive string of 43 forts – called **La Trocha** – across the island from Júcaro to Morón, so as to cut the rebellious east off from the rest of the island. At the junction of calles Marcial Gómez and Joaquín de Agüero is the spot where the city was founded, and a 19th-century Mapa Mural shows the first 25 blocks of the town, including the Spanish command headquarters and some of the forts along the military line.

Island pearls

South of Ciego de Ávila, **Júcaro ❷** is a pleasant, if scrappy, fishing village on the coast, and the point of embarkation for the pristine and enchanting island chain of **Los Jardines de la Reina** (The Queen's Gardens). Visits, which must be organized well in advance, are expensive week-long diving or fishing

packages, with accommodations on a floating hotel, the *Tortuga*, moored near Cayo Anclitas, or on live-aboard boats. For more information, contact Avalon (www.avalonfishingcenter.com, www.divingincuba.com) or Roxtons (www.roxtons.com), the only operators who currently have authority to run fishing and diving expeditions here. The 200km (125-mile) archipelago has been designated a marine national park.

Rooster city

Morón ❸, a real country town where people get around on foot, on bicycles, or in horse-drawn carts, lies to the north of the province and is visited mostly by people wanting easy access to the northern cays but with cheaper accommodations. Nicknamed Ciudad del Gallo (Rooster City), the town's symbol is a crowing rooster, representing the people's triumph over arrogant officialdom. In the 1950s, local citizenry raised money to have the rooster sculpted in bronze as a public monument. Dictator Fulgencio Batista got in on the act and decided to unveil the statue in what would be known as

Batista Park. Outraged residents saved their rooster from humiliation by boycotting the inauguration, but the bird was subsequently kidnapped and destroyed by misguided guerrillas.

In the calmer 1980s, Morón's rooster was born anew and placed in the **Parque del Gallo** (Rooster Park), at the entrance to Hotel Morón. The monument was sculpted by Rita Longa and is a replica of the rooster at Morón de la Frontera in Spain. In the adjacent tower an amplified recording of jubilant crowing is electronically set to activate twice a day at 6am and 6pm.

The 1924 eclectic, neo-colonial, two-story railway station is a national monument. You can ride on a steam train through sugar-cane fields to the Patria o Muerte sugar museum at the Central Patria. The **Museo de Arqueología e Historia Caonabo** (Calle Martí 374; Mon–Tue 8am–4pm, Wed–Sat 8am–9pm; charge) was built originally as a bank in 1919, but after a spell as the offices of the telephone company it became the municipal museum, showcasing archeology and local history.

North of Morón are popular places for fishing, hunting, and boating: **Laguna La Redonda**, where catfish abound, and **Laguna de la Leche**, milky-white from sodium carbonate deposits that attract flamingos. This is Cuba's largest natural reservoir; its size and central location made it strategically important during the 1895 War of Independence: Cuban *mambí* fighters crossed it on numerous occasions to deliver munitions from Camagüey to Villa Clara, thus evading La Trocha. An Aquatic Carnival is held here in July (sometimes in August or September).

The northern islands

Cayo Coco ❹ covers an area of 595 sq km (230 sq miles) with 22km (13 miles) of white sand and crystal-clear water. There are nine beaches of varying sizes on the northern coast. Several of them are now dominated by large, all-inclusive resorts only meters from the shore. A 27km (17-mile) causeway that shoots straight through a mirror of water links the cay to the mainland.

Cayo Coco is named after the white ibis, known locally as a *coco*, one of the island's more striking inhabitants,

A rooster is the mascot for the town of Morón.

BELOW: bananas are one of the many crops grown in this fertile region.

Eastern Lowlands

BELOW: Camagüey's Gran Hotel and the city beyond.

along with the rosy flamingo. The area is a protected zone, as much of the wildlife, including 156 bird species, is endangered. Many Cuban ecologists are concerned about the long-term effects of development, especially the way the causeway has obstructed the free flow of currents. The expansion of hotels is also having an impact on wildlife – hotels routinely spray against mosquitoes, for example.

The causeway continues west to **Cayo Guillermo** – also rapidly developing for "sea and sand" tourism and as a base for scuba diving and fishing – and east to **Cayo Romano** and **Cayo Paredón Grande**, far less developed, with empty white sand beaches.

Camagüey's capital

The province of Camagüey, the largest in Cuba, has its fair share of sugar-cane fields, rice paddies, and citrus groves, but far more important are its cattle pastures, supporting both dairy and beef cattle. *Vaqueros* (cowboys), wearing broad-brimmed hats and dangling machetes, can be seen herding stock from astride their horses, lassos fly-

ing. Rodeos are a popular entertainment. **Camagüey** , the capital of the province, is Cuba's third-largest city (pop. 325,000). It was one of Diego Velázquez's seven original settlements, founded as the Villa of Santa María del Puerto Príncipe in 1514. It was twice moved, then razed by Henry Morgan's crew in 1668. It was rebuilt soon after, with a street plan that seems designed to help ambush future invaders.

Camagüey is a place of beauty, culture, and tradition. The old town is a delight: narrow, twisting streets wind from the river, lined by rows of small, rainbow-colored, stuccoed houses, with lush courtyards set back from the street that can be glimpsed through ancient wooden doors. But don't come expecting to find another Trinidad: Camagüey is quite different.

The local hero

The city's most famous son, Ignacio Agramonte (1841–73), was the fighting general of Camagüey's rebel forces during the first War of Independence (he died in action in 1873). The **Museo Casa Natal de Ignacio Agramonte**

Honoring Famous Sons

Camagüey has spawned a number of eminent men, several of whom have achieved international fame. Ignacio Agramonte *(see above)* is the great warrior who battled for five years against the colonial Spanish but never lived to see independence (the inhabitants of Camagüey are called *agromonteros* in his honor). **Casa Natal de Nicolás Guillén** (Hermanos Agüero 58 between Príncipe and Cisneros, tel: 32-293-706) is the birthplace of a more recently famous Camagüeyan, Nicolás Guillén Batista. The house is now an art and cultural studies school, with a library, rather than a museum. You are free to wander around but there is not a great deal to see. The world-renowned writer *(see page 115,* was born here in 1902, but only lived here until 1904. There is a small bronze portrait of the poet at the front of the house, and photos and poems on the walls inside. Carlos J. Finlay's birthplace at Cristo 5 between Lugareño and Callejón del Templador (tel: 32-296-745) is also open to the public. He was born in 1833 to a family of mixed French and Scottish origins and later pursued his scientific studies in Paris and Philadelphia. His discovery in 1881 that the Aedes mosquito was the vector for yellow fever affected the world's health. By controlling the mosquito population, the spread of both yellow fever and malaria were checked, a factor of particular importance in the construction of the Panama Canal. Finlay became the chief health officer in Cuba at the beginning of the 20th century and died in Havana in 1915.

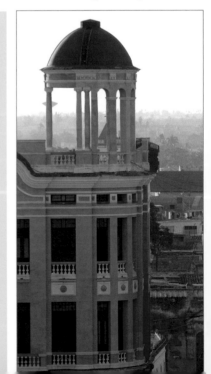

(Avenida Agramonte, 459, Plaza de los Trabajadores; tel: 32-297-116; Tue–Sat 9am–7pm, Sun 8.30–11.30am; charge) is a museum in the hero's birthplace – a lovely 18th-century mansion, sumptuously furnished with period pieces. The *tinajones* are a prominent feature – round, wide-mouthed earthenware jugs, modeled on the big-bellied jars that came from Spain filled with wines and oils. Cuban versions were created by local potters to solve a pressing problem: Camagüey had almost no water sources, and rainfall, while abundant, was seasonal. You still see *tinajones* in the shady courtyard of many Camagüeyan households, and water sellers still ply the streets. Ranging in size from large to enormous, some of the *tinajones* still in use were made more than a century ago.

More city sights

North of here sits the splendid **Teatro Principal B**, which draws the biggest audiences when the Ballet de Camagüey or the local symphony orchestra perform. Calle Padre Valencia brings you back to the attractive 18th-century church, **Nuestra Señora de La Merced C** (opening hours vary), across from Agramonte's birthplace on the **Plaza de los Trabajadores**. Considered one of the most splendid churches

Bronze head of poet, Nicolás Guillén.

BELOW: statue of local hero, Ignacio Agramonte.
BELOW RIGHT: freewheeling in Camagüey.

in the country when it was first built in 1747 and now a National Monument, La Merced has benefitted from (ongoing) restoration: the 20th-century decorated ceiling is particularly striking. The ghoulish may go down the steps beside the altar to see the catacombs.

Avenida Agramonte leads you to another important church, also dating from the 1700s: **Nuestra Señora de la Soledad** ❶. Its red-brick exterior looks unpromising, but inside you are greeted by glorious decoration on the arches and pillars, topped by a splendid vaulted ceiling. Before continuing south to the heart of the city, you can make a diversion north along Avenida República (which becomes Avenida de los Mártires beyond the train station) to the **Museo Provincial Ignacio Agramonte** ❶ (Avenida de los Mártires 2; tel: 32-282-425; Tue–Thur and Sat 10am–6pm, Fri noon–8pm, Sun 10am–2pm; charge), with an eclectic collection ranging from stuffed animals to archeological finds. It is best known, though, for its fine-art collection. A cavalry barracks in the mid-19th century, the building was converted into a hotel in the first half of the 20th century but became a museum in 1955.

Continuing on the route south, you reach **Parque Ignacio Agramonte** ❶, the nearest thing Camagüey has to a main square. The dramatic mounted figure of Agramonte is the centerpiece. On the south side, the 19th-century **Catedral** ❶ is worth a peek. Its wooden ceiling is its best feature. If you ask, you may be allowed to climb spiral steps to the bell tower for a wonderful view (donation appreciated).

Another recently restored church is **Nuestra Señora del Carmen** ❶, which lies several blocks west of the square along Calle Martí, on the beautifully restored **Plaza del Carmen**. The old hospital alongside the church is now the offices of the Historiador de la Ciudad, where all the restoration works are planned. The plaza is dotted with *tinajones* as well as sculptures by Martha Jiménez Pérez of gossiping women, a courting couple, and a man reading a newspaper. The real-life models can often be seen alongside their statues. There are restaurants here

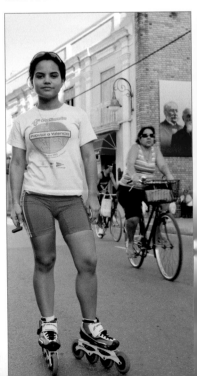

where you can sit and have a drink, or take a break on one of the benches and watch the world go by. While in this area, walk a few blocks south to the **Iglesia de Santo Cristo del Buen Viaje** . The interest here lies mainly in the adjacent **cemetery**, one of the finest in the country, much frequented by local people who like to stroll around, as well as visiting family graves. Running eastward, back toward the center, Calle Cristo has road-side flower-sellers, and a couple of local bars.

Rivaling the Plaza del Carmen for the honor of being the loveliest place in Camagüey is the restored, 18th-century **Plaza San Juan de Dios** ❶, south of Parque Agramonte. Now a national monument, the square is peaceful and surrounded by brightly colored houses with elegant wooden *rejas* (grilles), and tall doors and windows. The plaza is dominated by the **Iglesia San Juan de Dios**, a small, intimate church with a fine mahogany ceiling and altar. Adjacent, the old hospital, the first ever built in town, was where the body of Agramonte was brought before his interment in the cemetery.

It is believed that he may have been tended by Fray José Olallo Valdés (1820–89), who worked tirelessly to help those suffering from the cholera epidemic in 1835, and the wounded of the Wars of Independence. He was the last remaining brother of the San Juan de Dios order in Cuba, following religious persecution by the Spanish authorities, and was beatified in 2008 in the first-ever such ceremony in Cuba. Now the hospital is the local heritage office, Centro Provincial de Patrimonio Cultural. Two of the finest buildings on the plaza are restaurants, La Campana de Toledo and the Parador de los Tres Reyes, popular with day-trippers.

Down by the river side

The **Agromercado** ❶ (farmers' market), on the banks of the river, is a great place to appreciate the *agramonteros'* renowned love of good food. In addition to stands selling fresh produce are simple kitchens serving piping-hot meals. It's a lively spot, shaded by palms and tropical foliage, and with vendors noisily hawking their produce. And there's far more produce to hawk

TIP

The ubiquitous *tinajón* has inspired a local legend, which says that if a girl gives a man a drink of water from one, he will fall in love with her and never be able to leave.

BELOW: the Plaza San Juan de Dios is a national monument.

Preparing for a diving expedition on Cayo Sabinal.

than you find in most Cuban markets: piles of glossy mangos, tomatoes, and peppers, strings of garlic, and heaps of *mamey* make it resemble a Mediterranean marketplace. On the eastern bank of the Hatibonico River, Parque Casino Campestre was used in colonial times for cattle shows, fairs, dances, and other social activities.

Backtracking up Calle San Pablo and turning right on Calle Martí you come to the Plaza de la Juventud, to give it the official name, but local people know it as **Parque Martí** ❶. This quiet square is dominated by the Sagrado Corazón de Jesús, an imposing neo-Gothic church built in 1920 that is currently undergoing extensive renovation work.

Exploring the province

The city of Camagüey is a cultural oasis in an otherwise arid province, where cows seem to outnumber people. Second in size is **Nuevitas** ❼, the Atlantic seaport on the Bahía de Nuevitas. Despite its run-down appearance, Nuevitas is an important trading center for the rural heartland,

close to the causeway to the beautiful **Cayo Sabinal** ❽, a cay to the northwest with more than 30km (20 miles) of empty beaches. At Playa Los Pinos, there are basic accommodations and a restaurant. The cay is a nature reserve protecting flocks of flamingos and many endangered birds.

Boat trips are organized from nearby **Playa Santa Lucía** ❾, to the east, to Cayo Sabinal, but the most common route is by road from Camagüey – a journey of 105km (65 miles) through cattle country. At Santa Lucía, the 20km (12 miles) of dazzling white sands are still relatively quiet. There are half a dozen hotels of varying quality strung out along the main road, but not a great deal else. If you don't have your own transport you can get a bus from Camagüey to Playa Santa Lucía at 5am or 2pm for a few pesos Cubanos.

The area is well known for the quality of the diving. Scuba devotees recommend the area for the sheer variety of marine life at underwater sites with 33 known shipwrecks just off the coast. The Shark's Friends International Diving Center offers a variety of boat dives including shark feeding at a site in the channel between Cayo Sabinal and Playa Los Cocos, which is exciting to watch.

La Boca, a tiny fishing village on **Playa Los Cocos**, 8km (5 miles) west of the main resort, is one of the loveliest spots in Cuba, with a glorious crescent of sand that knocks spots off the strip at Santa Lucía, and a couple of seafood restaurants. Behind is a lagoon where flamingos gather.

A whistle-stop destination

Traveling eastward from Camagüey along the Carretera Central, the only town before you cross into Las Tunas province is **Guáimaro** ❿, whose main claim to fame is that it was the site of the assembly which drew up Cuba's first constitution in 1869.

South of Guáimaro, near the town of **Najasa**, the Sierra Guaicanama-Najasa is the site of the little-visited reserve of **Hacienda La Belén**. The birdlife is especially rich, with many species of parrot; you can also go horseback riding or hiking, and there is a small hotel with swimming pool. Contact Ecotur, www.ecoturcuba.co.cu, for details.

There is not a lot to detain you in Las Tunas province and most people drive straight through without stopping. The provincial capital, also called **Las Tunas ⑪**, was burned down in both wars of independence, and has no colonial landmarks. The main square, Parque Vincent García, is not unpleasant but is spoiled by traffic.

Located close by on Calle Lucas Ortiz is the **Museo Memorial Mártires de Barbados** (tel: 31-347-213; Mon–Sat 10am–5pm; charge). It is set in a two-story wooden house, the former home of fencing champion Carlos Leyva González, who was killed with 72 others when a Cuban plane was sabotaged by terrorists in 1976 (see page 178). En route from Caracas to Havana, the plane made a stopover in Barbados, when the bomber got off, leaving a bomb on board. The museum contains documents, photos, and sports implements belonging to all the victims, but especially to Carlos and to Leonardo McKenzie Grant, who was also born in the town.

The region's most famous son is El Cucalambé, the pseudonym of poet Juan Cristóbal Nápoles Fajardo, whose 19th-century *décimas* (10-line rhyming topical songs) are honored at the annual Cucalambeana Fair, when poets and singers from all over Cuba come for a festival.

The town has a traditional dish, a *caldosa* (stew) of meat and vegetables, which is served in tasty form at Quique Marina, a family-style restaurant on the Carretera Central on the western outskirts. Look for terracotta ceramics dotted about the town – Las Tunas is famous for them.

There is nothing much south of Las Tunas except mangroves and rice farms. On the north coast, near the town of Jesús Menéndez, are two fabulous beaches, **Playa Uvero ⑫** and **Playa La Herradura ⑬**. Both are completely unspoiled. On **Playa Covarrubias**, there is a single all-inclusive hotel. There is nowhere else to stay. ❑

The Spanish name for the prickly pear cactus is tuna, *and it is after this plant that the province is named.*

RESTAURANTS

Camagüey

Campana de Toledo
Plaza San Juan de Dios, 18
Tel: (32) 286-812. Open daily L & D. **$$**
Spanish-style dishes in a colonial mansion with an attractive patio; tables overlook the square or the courtyard. Busy at lunch with tour parties. Next door, Parador de los Tres Reyes (same phone) offers similar fare for a similar clientele.

El Ovejito
Plaza del Carmen
Tel: (32) 292-498
Open daily noon–9.45pm. **$$**
In a colonial house with indoor and outside tables; mostly lamb dishes. Nice spot for a drink, although the *mojitos* are overpriced.

Paladar El Cardenal
Calle Martí, 309, between Hospital and San Antonio
Open daily 11am–11pm. **$–$$**
Hearty portions of good *comida criolla* with a pleasant atmosphere make this *paladar* a popular choice.

Papito Rizo (La Terraza)
Santa Rosa 8, 1 block from Calle República
Tel: (32) 298-705. Open daily 11am–11pm or later. **$**
The best *paladar* in town, serving good Cuban food (CUCs or *moneda nacional*). Eat in the open air under a roof or in a private dining room. Friendly staff.

Ciego de Avila

Fonda La Estrella
Honorato del Castillo
Tel: (33) 266-186. Open daily noon–midnight. **$**
The best restaurant in town, decorated like an old Spanish inn, with local artifacts on the walls. Cuban food including *ropa vieja*.

Solaris
Honorato del Castillo
Tel: (33) 222-156. Open Tue–Sun noon–3pm, 6–10pm. **$**
On top floor of a 12-story building with a panoramic view. Cocktails and *comida criolla* while a pianist plays requests.

Morón

La Atarraya
Laguna de la Leche
Tel: 33-505-351. Open Tue–Sun noon–5pm. **$$**
Built over the lake with a lovely view. La Atarraya serves mostly seafood and fish dishes (*moneda nacional* or CUCs).

Las Fuentes
Martí 189 between Libertad and Agramonte
Tel: 33-505-758. Open Tue–Sun noon–3pm, 7–10pm. **$–$$**
Serves a good two-course meal of chicken or pork. You pay extra for lobster or shrimp. Nice garden with a fountain.

> Price categories are for a three-course meal for one with a beer, or *mojito*. Wine puts the price up:
> **$** = under $25
> **$$** = $25–35
> **$$$** = over $35

DREAM DIVING

Whether you're a first-time scuba diver or a pro, Cuba offers some of the most exciting diving in the Caribbean along myriad reefs and cays still relatively untouched by mass tourism

Cuba's dive sites extend all round the island and no matter where you're staying there's bound to be a dive operator within fairly easy reach. They offer a variety of reefs, walls, tunnels, and wrecks, from old Spanish galleons to modern fishing vessels deliberately sunk as dive sites. Marine wildlife is varied and plentiful and much of it is protected, including turtles and the illusive manatee.

María la Gorda, in the far west, has some of the best diving, in a sheltered bay where it is calm even when the rest of the island has bad weather. Spectacular sponges and colorful coral offer shelter to grunts, grouper, barracuda, and even whale sharks. Visibility here and off the west coast of Isla de la Juventud can usually be relied on to be good. Hotel Colony, on the Isla, is the most famous dive resort in Cuba, with 56 dive sites within reach of a dive boat. Some 40 varieties of coral can be found here, home to myriad fish of many colors, and you swim through tunnels, trenches, and pristine underwater gardens. Further east in the Jardines de la Reina there is even a live-aboard boat hotel for divers and fishermen.

Along the north coast the cays and reefs of the archipelago Jardines del Rey attract moray eels, angel fish, snappers, jacks, lobster, and rays. Marinas offering scuba diving can be found at Varadero, Cayo Las Brujas, Cayo Coco, Playa Santa Lucía, and Guardalavaca. Sometimes they suffer from rough seas if there is a weather front coming down from the eastern seaboard of the US, but generally the water is warm and inviting.

ABOVE: the reef around Cuba abounds with colorful hard and soft corals often seen to best advantage on a night dive.

BELOW: scuba divers can explore the tunnels at El Encanto, off María la Gorda where conditions are exceptional and sea life abundant.

LEFT: the Goldentail Moray Eel *(Gymnothorax miliaris)* can be found popping its head out of holes along the reef or among wrecks, its golden tail rarely visible.

SHARKS AND WRECKS

Playa Santa Lucía, north of Camagüey, has some excellent dive sites, with 33 shipwrecks discovered so far. However, it is more famous for its sharks than its wrecks. Staff at the local dive shop, now called Shark's Friends, started to feed a few sharks in the early 1980s but word got round underwater and now some 20 massive bull sharks measuring up to 3 meters (10ft) turn up at feeding time. They congregate and are fed in a channel between Playa Los Cocos and Cayo El Sabinal, close to the wreck of a Spanish merchant ship at a depth of 25–30 meters (80–95ft). The current has to be right and there is only a 45-minute slot, but it is thrilling to watch the dive masters hand-feed them, and the sharks swim up to the dive group, strategically placed a few meters away. No armor is worn but staff have spear guns at the ready, just in case. Watch your air consumption – you may run out if it is too exciting.

VE: the Longspine Squirrelfish *(Holocentrus rufus)* are ~monly found around Cuba feeding among the coral gardens or ~ng under overhangs.

ABOVE: the whale shark is one of several types of shark found in Cuban waters; November is the best month to see them off the Isla de la Juventud.

BELOW: the Yellow Tube Sponge *(Aplysina fistularis)* is a filter-feeder, consuming plankton and detritus, in turn being eaten by reef fish as well as the hawksbill sea turtle.

LEFT: the Brain coral *(Diploria Strigosa)* is a colony of tiny polyps which secrete the coral skeleton and can live to be 900 years old and grows very slowly, eventually reaching approximately 2 meters (6ft).

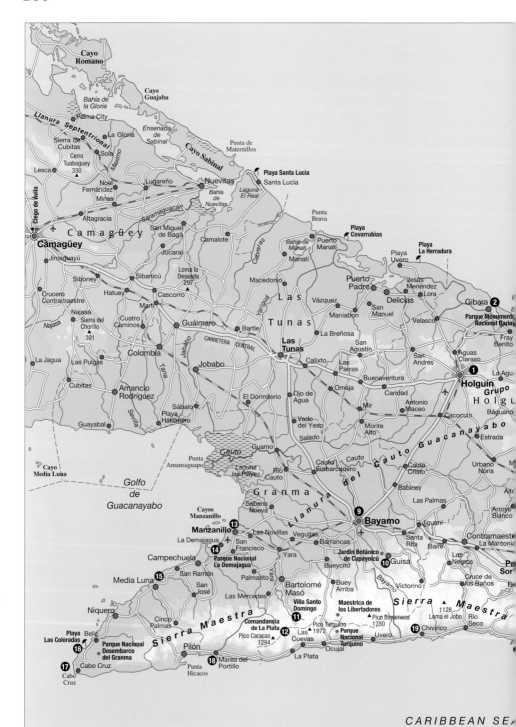

Cayo
Romano

Cayo
Guajaba

Bahía de
la Gloria   Palma City

Ensenada
de
Sabinal

Punta de
Maternillos

Llanura Septentrional   La Gloria

Sierra de
Cubitas
Cerro   Sola
Tuabaguey
330
Lesca   Lugareño   Nuevitas

Playa Santa Lucía
Santa Lucía

Noel
Fernández
Miñas   Bahía
de
Nuevitas

Laguna
El Real

Altagracia

Saramaguacán   San Miguel
de Bagá   Camalote

Punta
Brava

Puerto
Manati   Playa
Covarrubias

Playa
La Herradura

Camagüey   Júcaro

Bahía de
Manatí

Manatí   Playa
Uvero

Jimaguayú   Puerto
Padre   Jesús
Menéndez
Lora

Siboney   Sibanicú   Loma la
Deseada
297   Macedonio   Vázquez   Delicias   Gibara

Crucero
Contramaestre   Hatuey   Cascorro   Las   Maniabón   San
Manuel   Velasco   Parque Monumento
Nacional Bariay

Najasa   Martí   Tunas   La Breñosa   San
Agustín   Fray
Benito

Sierra del
Chorillo   Cuatro
Caminos   Guáimaro   Bartle   Las
Tunas   San
Andrés   Aguas
Claraso

La Jagua   Las Pulgas   Colombia   Jobabo   Calixto   Las
Parras   Buenaventura   Holguín   La Agu

Cubitas   Amancio
Rodríguez   Ojo de
Agua   Omája   Caridad   Antonio
Maceo   Grupo
Holgu

Guayabal   Sábalo
Playa
Habanero   El Dormitorio   Vado
del Yeso   Mir   Monte
Alto   Cacocum   Báguano

Cauto   Salado   Estrada

Cayo
Media Luna   Punta
Amansaguapo   Guamo   Cauto   Cauto   Urbano
Noris

Golfo
de
Guacanayabo   Laguna
las Playas   Cauto
Embarcadero   Cauto
Cristo   Alt

Río
Cauto   Babiney

Granma   Sabana
Nueva   Las Palmas   Arroyo
Blanco

Cayos
Manzanillo   Las Novillas   Veguitas   Bayamo   Jiguaní   Contramaestr
La Mantonia

Manzanillo   Barrancas   Santa
Rita   Baire

La Demajagua   San
Francisco   Yara   Jardín Botánico
de Cupaynicú   Guisa   Los
Negros   Pa
Sor

Campechuela   Parque Nacional
La Demajagua   Palmarito   Bueycito   Cruce de
los Baños   Be

Media Luna   San Ramón   San
José   Las Mercedes   Bartolomé
Masó   Buey
Arriba   Victorino   Sierra   Maestra

Niquero   Cinco
Palmas   Villa Santo
Domingo   Maestrica de
los Libertadores   1128
Loma el Jobo   Río
Seco

Playa
Las Coloradas   Belic   Parque Nacional
Desembarco
del Granma   Comandancia
de La Plata   Pico Turquino   Parque
Nacional
Turquino   Chivirico

Cabo Cruz   Pilón   Pico Caracas
1294   Las
Cuevas   Uvero

Cabo
Cruz   Punta
Hicacos   Marea del
Portillo   La Plata   Ocujal

CARIBBEAN SE

Around Santiago de Cuba

0   10 km
0   10 miles

Mayarí
Arriba

Embalse
Protesta de
Baraguá

Julio Antonio Mella

Cauto

Palmarito
de Cauto

San tiago de

La Prueba

Loma
Blanca

La Comunal

▲ 751

Mayari

Bayamo

Autopista

Nacional

Palma
Soriano

San
Luis

Dos
Caminos

Alto
Songo

Guantánamo

Los
Reynaldos

Costa
Rica

Cuba

La Maya

Guantanamo

581

Bellaire

El Cristo

Carretera Central

El Cobre

23

Santiago
de Cuba

El Caney

20

Aéropuerto
Antonio
Maceo

Parque
Nacional
Gran Piedra

Cordillera de la Gran Piedra

El Aguacate

Niceto
Pérez

Gran Piedra
1214

Granjita
Siboney

24

★ Jardín Ave de
Paraíso

Playa Mar Verde

26

El Oasis

25

Antonio
Maceo

21

22

Siboney

27

Museo Nacional
de Terrestre
★

Laguna
Sigúa Baconao

Baconao

Castillo
del Morro

Valle de la
Prehistoria

Parque
Baconao

Playa
Daiquirí

CARIBBEAN SEA

ATLANTIC

OCEAN

era

laya
uardalavaca

3

Guayacanes

vaca

•Chorro
de Maíta

Los
Angeles

Punta de Mulas

5

Banes

ortaderas

Bahía de Banes

Antilla

La Chiva

Cayo
Saetía

Playa
Corinthia

Bahía de
Nipe

6

Guatemala

Felton

7

errera

Guaro

Nicaro

Cayo Moa Grande

34

Moa

Punta Guarico

Mayarí

Levisa

Cayo
Mambí

Cebolla

Pico del Cristal
1231

El Sitio

Pico del Toldo
1175

Cañete

oma de
Mensura
995

Sierra del Cristal

Sagua de
Tánamo

Cuchillas de Moa

tipanicie de Nipe

Mayari

Santa
Catalina

Alturas

Playa Maguana

8

Mayarí
Arriba

Cuchillas de Toa

Toa

de Toa

El Yunque
de Baracoa

33

Baracoa

32

Boca de
Yumurí

San tiago
de Cuba

Bayate

Palenque

Guantánamo

Bernardo

Baracoa

Punta del Fraile

to

La Comuna

Boquerón

Jamal

Sabana

31

Maisí

La Prueba

Loma
Blanca

Los
Reynaldos

Costa
Rica

El Salvador

Museo Zoológico de Piedra
★

Honduras

Pico el Gato
1176

Sabanilla

Punta de Maisí

Alto
Songo

Jaibo

Jamaica

La Faroja

Yumurí

La Maquina

Dos
aminos

El Cristo

La Maya

El Aguacate

Niceto
Pérez

28

Guantánamo

Manuel Tames

Puñales
de Caujerí

Sierra del Purial

Jauco
Jauco

Yateras

▲747

Cajobabo

Santiago
de Cuba

Parque
Nacional
Gran Piedra

Maqueicito

Sierra del Maguey

CENTRAL

Yacabo Abajo

Imías

30

Punta
Caleta

Playa de
Cajobabo

Gran
Piedra
1214

CARRETERA

San Antonio
del Sur

Siboney

Sigúa

789
▲

Guantánamo

Caimanera

Mirador de los
Malones

Yateritas

Parque
Baconao

Baconao

29

US
NAVAL BASE

Punta
Barlovento

Eastern Cuba

N

0   20 km
0   20 miles

HOLGUÍN AND GRANMA

From the island's top archeological site
to the ragged mountains of the Sierra Maestra,
including the Pico Turquino, Cuba's highest peak,
this region has much to offer, yet attracts
surprisingly few tourists

Main attractions
HOLGUÍN: MUSEO PROVINCIAL
GIBARA
GUARDALAVACA
CHORRO DE MAITA
BAYAMO
PICO TURQUINO
MANZANILLO
PARQUE NACIONAL DESEMBARCO
DE GRANMA

Often called the "Granary of Cuba" because of its agricultural wealth, the province of Holguín has some 1.3 million people living within its borders, making it second in population only to Havana province. Its capital city, also called **Holguín ❶**, is the fourth-largest city in Cuba, with a population of 300,000. Along with its agricultural importance, it is a relatively active industrial center, having grown rapidly in recent decades, and has two universities, two large hospitals, and a brewery.

Familiarly known as the "city of the parks," Holguín is built on the traditional grid system. Five parks lie within the parallel lines of the two main streets, running roughly southeast to northwest: Maceo and Manduley (also called Libertad). The three middle plazas are linked by a recently created pedestrian boulevard along Manduley where you can find cultural venues, restaurants, and cafés, most of which charge in *moneda nacional*.

Parque Calixto García is an expansive square built around the monument to the city's most famous independence fighter, General Calixto García Iñiguez. His birthplace, a block away, is now a museum (Calle Miró 147; tel: 24-425-610; Tue–Sat 9am–4.30pm, Sun 10am–6pm; charge). Families and friends come in the cool of the evening for a stroll or to sit on benches and watch the children playing while music wafts out from the bars and clubs. Fronting the square are a striking Art Deco theatre, the local Casa de la Trova, an ARTex bar, ice-cream parlors, the modern provincial library, bookstores, and art galleries. For nightlife, in addition to the Casa de la Trova, there is also the Casa de la Música, a disco on the third floor of the Pico Cristal building, and the Beny Moré center on the corner of Luz Caballero and Maceo.

PRECEDING PAGES: coastal view from El Morro fortress. **LEFT:** Playa Esmeralda.
RIGHT: *bici-taxis* wait for customers.

You may find a rodeo taking place in Holguín, where you see this sign.

BELOW: humpbacked hills dot the landscape around Gibara.

Holguín's attractions

Most noteworthy is the building known as **La Periquera** (Parrot Cage) – so named ever since Spanish soldiers, in their blue, yellow, and green uniforms, took refuge behind the barred windows during a *mambí* attack in 1868. The building houses the **Museo Provincial de Historia** (Mon–Fri 9am–5pm, Sat 9am–1pm; charge), whose prized possession is the *Hacha de Holguín* (Holguín Axe), a pre-Columbian figure carved in polished rock; found in 1860, it has become the symbol of the province. There are also displays on slavery, and all kinds of historical memorabilia.

A half-block south of the square, on Calle Maceo 129, is the **Museo de Ciencias Naturales Carlos de la Torre** (Sun–Thur 9am–5pm, Sat 1–5pm; charge), with a fine collection of polymitas, the brightly banded snails indigenous to eastern Cuba. There are also lots of stuffed animals, including a pair of ivory-billed woodpeckers, now almost certainly extinct.

Around the corner, **Parque Peralta**, also known as the Parque de los Flores because people sell flowers here for the cemetery, is the site of the **Catedral de San Isidoro** (1720). Its rough brick arcades harbor birds and figures carved by a local artist; other treasures include the original baptismal font.

The Plaza de la Maqueta is a recently restored square one block from Maceo between Mártires and Máximo Gómez, and is well worth a visit. The old market in the center has now become the Lírico theater, and there are shops selling music, instruments, painting materials, cigars, and handicrafts, along with some art galleries. A boutique hotel will shortly join them. Artwork is everywhere, from statues to carved lamp posts.

Three blocks north of Parque Calixto García, leafy **Plaza Carlos Manuel de Céspedes** is the most picturesque square in Holguín, with a ruined church, the Iglesia San José, in the middle. The main post office is here and a couple of banks.

La Loma de la Cruz (The Hill of the Cross), to the north, is Holguín's most visible landmark and a place of pilgrimage. It's not far to walk, but when you get there you must tackle the 468 steps leading up to the top. On May 3, 1790, a group led by a Franciscan priest erected a cross on the hill (unfortunately blown down by Hurricane Georges in 1998); later the Spanish built a look-out tower for strategic reasons. The construction of the stone steps was begun in 1929, but not finished until May 3, 1950. The *Romerías de la Cruz de Mayo* are celebrated every May 3 with a procession up the hill.

Gibara, a colonial gem

The farther north you go, the better Holguín province gets. **Gibara ❷**, on the coast, 36km (22 miles) north of the capital, exudes maritime charm and colonial grace. On the road from Holguín you pass through some fabulous scenery with strange, humpbacked hills. An old iron bridge over the **Río Cacoyoquín** leads into the town along a seaside drive with a **statue of Christopher Columbus** and a small ruined garrison at the end.

With terracotta roofs, flowering patios, a weather-beaten church, cobblestoned streets, and fishing boats, Gibara is endlessly photogenic, although the town is still recovering from the battering it received from Hurricane Ike in 2008. The **Teatro Colonial** (1889) is a little masterpiece, but the pièce de résistance is the **Museo de Artes Decorativas** (Independencia 19, betweenLuz Caballero and J Peralta; Tue–Sun 9am–noon, 1–5pm, Thur–Sun also 8–10pm; charge), on the second floor of a magnificent 19th-century mansion. Besides gorgeous *mediopuntos* (Cuba's characteristic, fan-shaped stained-glass windows) and *mamparas* (decorative saloon-style doors), there is a fine collection of furniture and many Art Nouveau pieces. You can climb up to the roof terrace for a view of the town. Also worth visiting is the **Museo de Historia Natural Joaquín Fernández de la Vara** (Maceo, 12 between Martí and Luz; tel: 24-844-222), where there is an excellent collection of butterflies and moths.

In April every year Gibara hosts the Festival Internacional del Cine Pobre, a celebration of movies made for less than US$300,000. The festival was founded in 2003 by the Cuban filmmaker Humberto Solás (1941–2008) who championed films made despite the lack of a financial backer or official approval. He had a prolific output himself, even being nominated for an Oscar, and some of his films were shot in Gibara.

A controversial monument

There used to be a long-standing debate between Gibara and Baracoa about the exact place where the Europeans first landed in Cuba. Nowadays historians agree that the first landfall was made in **Bariay Bay**, east of Gibara. The peninsula has been declared a national monument, **Parque Monumento Nacional Bariay** (daily 9am–5pm; charge). A **monument**, designed to symbolize the meeting of European and American aboriginal civilizations, was erected in 1992 to commemorate the 500th anniversary of Columbus's setting foot in America. It sits on the tip

Dancers in Holguín's Casa de la Trova.

BELOW: Tune in to local radio.

Gold idol in the Museo Indocubano.

BELOW: Playa Esmeralda.

of Cayo Bariay, within sight of what is almost certainly the flat-topped mountain he mentioned in his logbook. By road, it is 7km (4 miles) north of Fray Benito, but boat trips are also arranged from Guardalavaca.

Guardalavaca

Farther east lies northeastern Cuba's main resort area, where the sea is a diaphanous blue and the beaches creamy white, fringed by tropical foliage. Guardalavaca can be reached by bus from Holguín: make a reservation at the Transtur Buró in the Pico Cristal cafetería on Parque Calixto García, for CUC$5 one way, and catch the Transtur bus outside La Begonia café. They frequently offer mid-week or weekend deals with accommodations.

The oldest part of the resort is Playa **Guardalavaca ❸** which has a village atmosphere with a cluster of hotels, restaurants and water sports facilities along a pleasant beach, as well as workers' apartments and a commercial center. West of here you reach the powdery white-sand beach at **Playa Esmeralda**. This horseshoe-shaped bay

has been taken over by the all-inclusive hotels of the Sol Meliá chain.

At the **Bahía de Naranjo** there is a marina and an aquarium (daily 9am–9pm; charge), with the usual overpriced dolphin show labeled "educational." On the eastern shore of the bay there is a marked nature trail, Sendero Ecológico Las Guanas, with a cave and a lookout.

Playa Yuraguanal and Playa Pesquero to the west are dominated by enormous all-inclusive resorts of up to 1,000 rooms each. They are isolated and there is nothing to do in the immediate vicinity of the hotels, but excursions to Gibara, Holguín, and other towns are within easy reach and the myriad bays are beautiful.

Chorro de Maita and Banes

Just south of Guardalavaca, the hilly road passes **Museo Aborígen Chorro de Maita ❹** (tel: 24-430-201; Tue–Sun 9am–5pm, Mon 9am–1pm; charge), the largest pre-Columbian burial ground known to exist in the Antilles. Archeologists' excavations have revealed 108 skeletons of the indigenous Taíno

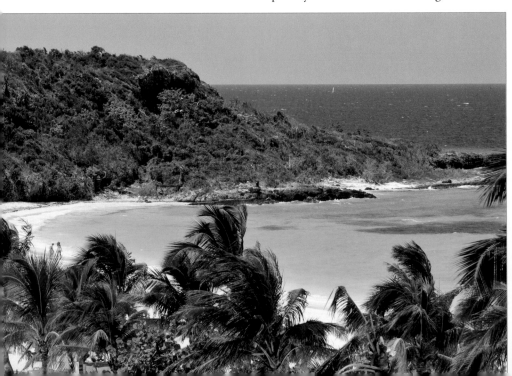

people who inhabited the area from *circa* AD 1000 to the end of the 16th century. A section of the graveyard has been excavated to show how the skeletons were buried. Two of the children wear European jewelry, and the presence of a Spaniard indicates that there must have been cross-cultural relationships in the early years.

Over the road is a reconstructed Taíno village, the **Aldea Taíno** (tel: 24-430-422; daily 9am–5pm; charge) – the most authentic of the country's reconstructed indigenous settlements.

Some of the finds from Chorro de Maíta are on display in the tiny but interesting **Museo Indocubano Bani** (Gen Marrero 305, corner José Martí; tel: 24-802-487; Tue–Sat 9am–5pm, Sun 8am–noon, 2–5pm, Fri–Sun also 7–9pm; charge) in nearby **Banes ⑤**. The utensils and jewelry are made of delicately carved and shaped shells, rocks, bones, ceramic, wood, and metal. The minuscule gold idol of a woman wearing a headdress and offering a bowl is, arguably, a joint Amerindian-Spanish effort, and is one of the few gold pieces to have been found.

Castro's birthplace

South of Banes, a former United Fruit Company town, the road runs around **Bahía de Nipe**. There is a turn-off to **Cueto**, and from there a road goes to **Birán**, Castro's birthplace. It has been reconstructed since the revolution; thatched *bohíos* have gone, replaced by rows of identical concrete houses. The old Castro residence still stands in this tiny community. A long avenue of royal palms sweeps up to the front of the elegant pink and yellow wooden house with lacy balconies, which is open to the public as the **Sitio Histórico de Birán** (tel: 24-286-102; Tue–Sat 9am–noon, 2–4pm, Sun 9am–noon; charge; phone ahead – if it rains it is closed). There are lots of family photographs on display, as well as domestic items and an ancient Ford (which belonged to Castro's father).

A slave town and the central highlands

Back toward Bahía de Nipe, **Mayarí** is an industrial town with little to interest travelers, but **Guatemala ⑥**, an old slave town right by the bay, is a gem. There are plenty of gingerbread cottages, built out of palm timber and driftwood, each delightfully individual, each a work of art: some have carved wooden gargoyles, others elaborately worked gables; the gardens are lush and colorful. A former exclusive "whites only" country club is now a bar, selling shots of rough *aguardiente* spirit for around a peso.

At the mouth of the Bahía de Nipe is the 42 sq km (16 sq-mile) island of **Cayo Saetía ⑦**, once the exclusive resort of top Communist Party officials; Raúl Castro used to be a regular visitor. The island is home to deer and wild boar, and a variety of imported animals: ostriches, zebra, antelope. Although this is a protected reserve, hunting is still allowed under strictly regulated conditions. It's a delightful spot, with lush vegetation running down to the pristine white sands and

Indigenous skeleton from Chorro de Maíta.

BELOW: riding through Gibara by buggy and horse.

DIGITAL
Granma
INTERNACIONAL

The digital version of Cuba's only newspaper, Granma, is published online daily in five languages. For the English version, go to www.granma. cu/ingles.

just one hotel, the Villa Cayo Saetía (*see Accommodations, page 352*).

The impressive **Sierra del Cristal** mountain range, reaching 1,231 meters (4,000ft) at Pico del Cristal, rolls through Holguín and Guantánamo provinces. The best place to get close to nature is the pleasant hotel at **Pinares de Mayarí**, established in 1988 to study the mountain ecology of the region (*see page 352*).

Cuba's great hero of the first *mambí* independence struggle, Carlos Manuel de Céspedes, established his revolutionary government at **Mayarí Arriba** ❽ in 1868. The area is covered with coffee plantations established by French planters who fled here in the early 19th century after the slave rebellions in Haiti. From here, a twisting road descends to Cuba's second city, **Santiago de Cuba** (*see pages 297–307*).

Visiting Granma province

Granma province was carved out of the old *Oriente* or Eastern Territory historically controlled by Santiago de Cuba. The peculiar name comes from the cabin cruiser Fidel, Raúl, Che, and

their comrades used to sneak into the country from Mexico in 1956 before they took up arms in the mountains. The stunning scenery of the Sierra Maestra is one of the area's main attractions, but so too are the numerous sites linked with the 1950s guerrilla campaign, and with the 19th-century struggle for independence.

Bayamo

Bayamo ❾ (pop. 150,000), the second of Cuba's seven original *villas*, was founded in 1513 by Diego Velázquez. It was located far enough inland to be safe from pirate attacks, and set on the navigable Río Bayamo. This flowed into the **Río Cauto**, the longest river in Cuba and the major transportation route for the eastern end of the island when coastal trade was faster than overland trails. It wasn't until 1902 that eastern and western Cuba were linked by rail through the center of the island, and the Carretera Central roughly paralleling it was only finished in 1932.

Bayamo is famous for its role in the Cuban independence struggle and was the first city taken by the rebels. In

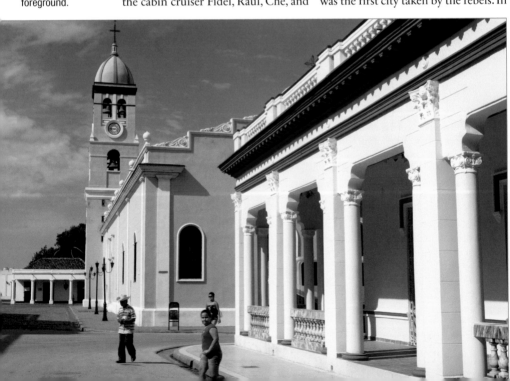

BELOW: Iglesia de San Salvador, with boutique hotel in foreground.

the main square, **Parque Céspedes**, is the **Ayuntamiento** (town hall) where Carlos Manuel de Céspedes, the rebel president, signed the document abolishing slavery in the liberated zones. Across the plaza is the **Casa Natal de Carlos Manuel de Céspedes** (Maceo 57 between Donato Mármol and José Joaquín Palma; tel: 23-423-864; Tue–Sat 9am–5pm, Sun 9am–noon; charge), where he was born in 1819. Built of marble, it emerged unscathed from the independence wars and was for years the local post office.

The museum recounts Céspedes's life, from his days as a law student to the rebel presidency, with documents, photos, period furnishings, and family memorabilia. Next door, at Maceo 55, is the **Museo Municipal** (tel: 23-424-125; Tue–Sat 8am–2pm, Sun 9am–1pm), which has rooms exhibiting natural history, architectural history, and the War of Independence.

Plaza del Himno Nacional

A block from the central square, the **Iglesia de Santísimo Salvador** was the church where *bayamese* patriot Perucho Figueredo first performed a stirring march for the independence fighters that later became Cuba's national anthem. The square outside the church is now called the Plaza del Himno. The church was burned down when Spanish troops re-took Bayamo, and residents decided to torch their own city and flee to the hills. They did, however, save the wooden altar to the Virgen de Dolores, and the stone font at which Céspedes and Figueredo were baptized, which can be seen in the rebuilt church.

A descendant of the Father of the Homeland, Onorio Céspedes, is Bayamo's historian and director of **La Casa de la Nacionalidad Cubana** (House of Cuban Nationality, Plaza del Himno 36 between Antonio Maceo and Padre Batista; tel: 23-424-833).

Boulevard

Running south from Parque Céspedes is the main shopping street, General García, most of which has now been converted into a pleasant pedestrian boulevard, sometimes called Paseo Bayamez. Quirky lamps and benches along its length give

The mansion in which the Casa de la Nacionalidad Cubana is situated was acquired by the state in 1990 and intended originally as a maternity home, before being opened the following year as a research institute.

BELOW LEFT: a bust of Carlos Manuel Céspedes, who declared rebellion against the Spanish.

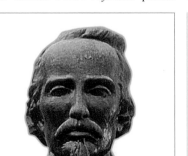

Céspedes and Cuban Rebellion

On the morning of October 10, 1868, Bayamo-born Carlos Manuel de Céspedes rang the great bell at his sugar plantation, La Demajagua, south of Manzanillo. With that stroke he emancipated his slaves and, in the resonant *Grito de Yara* (Cry of Yara), he declared open rebellion against Cuba's colonial rulers, thus beginning the first War of Independence against Spain. As with the US Civil War a few years earlier, emancipation was not the main reason for the war, but it was always an important subsidiary, and became an increasingly necessary weapon. Other landowners were soon to begin freeing their slaves and arming them for battle.

Céspedes's bold action was the climax of 15 years of conspiracy during which he and his friends used Masons' lodges and chess tournaments in Bayamo and Manzanillo as a cover for anti-colonialist plots. He led the rebel forces as president of the Republic in Arms until October 1873, when factional infighting forced him from power. By now almost blind, he accepted his removal with great dignity, and retired to San Lorenzo in the Sierra Maestra to teach letters and chess. He had just finished a chess game one afternoon in March 1874 when Spanish troops raided the town and ordered him to surrender. He refused and was shot down.

Stitching by hand at the old carriage workshop in Bayamo.

BELOW: mechanized sugar cane-cutting in the Sierra Maestra.

it artistic interest. Here you can find shops, banks, the telephone and internet office, post office, pharmacies, cafés, restaurants, and a few small museums, including a waxworks, an aquarium, an archeological museum, and a *maqueta* or scale model of the town.

Parks, plazas, and entertainment

Turn west off the boulevard along Calle Masó and head downhill to the river and a large park. Here a busy market sells meat, seasonal fruit and vegetables. Open-air concerts are sometimes held here, too, and there is an amusement park and a pleasant swimming spot in the river.

The **Plaza de la Patria** is a huge open space with historical monuments and statues, created in 1982 by the architect Miguel Delarrá. To its north is the railway, to the west is Avenida Amado Estévez, and to the east are the buildings of Reparto Jesús Menéndez. Political rallies, sporting events, concerts, and Carnival (at the beginning of August) are held here. At the base of the administrative building you can

see the largest *vitral* in the Americas. There are several open-air cafés and La Taberna, selling local and national beers in *pesos cubanos*.

What was formerly known as Plaza Luis Ramírez López, on Calle Línea between Milanés and William Soler, has been redeveloped as a recreational center called **El Guajiro Natural**. A restaurant, bar, café, and literary center are open daily from 10am until midnight, while from Thursday to Sunday there is an open-air cabaret with live music, and a show with dancers from 8pm until about 3am.

Guisa

Guisa ⑩ is a pretty village in the foothills of the Sierra Maestra, 14km (8 miles) southeast of Bayamo off the road to Santiago. On a hill overlooking the little town is the Mirador de Guisa, with a restaurant and bar, very popular at weekends as an out-of-town excursion because of the lovely views up into the mountains with a reservoir sparkling in the distance. Calixto García used this hill to take up his position before a battle in 1897 in the

War of Independence, and it was used again during the revolution some 60 years later.

Just before you get to Guisa, turn right off the road to the **Jardín Botánico de Cupaynicú** (charge, guides available). Of the 13 botanical gardens in Cuba, this is the third largest, after Havana and Cienfuegos, but it contains some of the oldest trees, at more than 300 years old. Just over half of the 104 hectares (257 acres) have been left as a protected reserve containing native forest, with the rest divided into fascinating and beautiful collections of medicinal plants and edible plants and another of palms. A guided tour is well worthwhile and birdwatchers will find it a rewarding visit. There is no public transport to speak of, so you will need to hire a taxi or rent a car or bicycle.

Into the Sierra Maestra

To experience fully the rugged beauty of the southeastern mountains, the best base is the **Villa Santo Domingo** ⓫, south of the road linking Bayamo and Manzanillo on the coast. The mountain road veers off at **Yara**, passing through the small town of **Bartolomé Masó** and steeply up into the heart of the sierra.

During the guerrilla war, Santo Domingo was a rebel camp with a mess hall and workshops. Today, these have been adapted for feeding and entertaining campers. Cabins are partially hidden in the forest by the Yara River. The **Turquino Parque Nacional** offices are at Santo Domingo; come here to arrange a guide (mandatory) for any of the hikes up the mountains. Tours set off at 9am and you should be there some time in advance. Take water and snacks and sunblock, of course. From here a 3km (2-mile) road goes up the steepest (40-degree gradient) incline in Cuba, finishing at Alto de Naranjo (950 meters/3,116ft), a parking lot for the vehicles ferrying walkers. The trail to the right goes to the Comandancia de la Plata, while the trail to the left heads up Pico Turquino.

Castro's old rebel headquarters in the mountains are at **La Comandancia de La Plata** ⓬. The trail is 3km (2 miles) up and down hill; parts of it are steep and if it has been raining it can be slippery and muddy. Halfway there you come to the house of the Medina family, who were the first in the area to help the revolutionaries. Their little family farm looks much the same today, with pigs and chickens roaming around and coffee beans drying on the ground.

At the command station there is a small museum, Castro's bedroom and kitchen, the old hospital and Radio Rebelde hut, all small wooden buildings spread out over the hillside. Quiet, beautiful, and very atmospheric, you get a good idea of how tough life must have been. Birdwatching is good here and you can see the national bird, the Cuban trogon. After being banned for 50 years, photography is now allowed, for a charge.

Hikes up Cuba's highest mountain, **Pico Turquino** (1,972 meters/6,470ft), are exciting and beautiful *(see panel below)*. Between outcroppings of

Celia Sánchez, whose family home is now a museum.

Peak Fitness

To hike up to the Comandancia de la Plata from Villa Santo Domingo costs CUC$20 and to Pico Turquino costs CUC$53 for a two-day hike, both with mandatory guide. Add transport up to Alto de Naranjo car park and back, CUC$5, and CUC$5 to take photos. The overnight stop for Pico Turquino is at Camping Joaquín and, as numbers are limited, this should be organized well in advance. It can be done in one day if your guide is willing. There is also access from the Caribbean side of the Sierra Maestra at Las Cuevas (between Ocujal and La Plata on the coast road). Day trips are offered by Sol y Son, in Santiago, for CUC$90, which involve a Jeep pick-up at 5am, a two-hour drive to Las Cuevas, a four-hour hike up, a lunch stop and a four-hour hike down, getting back to Santiago around 7pm. It is tough, so take plenty of water and sunscreen.

It is possible to go up Pico Turquino from Santo Domingo and down the other side to Las Cuevas (or vice versa, 2–3 days), or hike to Pico Turquino one day and Comandancia de la Plata the next, spending the night on the mountain. Go to the national park HQ in Santo Domingo (no phone) soon after 7.30am to ensure there will be a guide available. Even so you may have to come back another day as numbers are limited, routes may be closed, or the weather may be against you. There is no national park office on the Las Cuevas side and no guides wait there.

An elegant shopping arcade in Manzanillo, with pronounced Moorish influences.

BELOW: detail of an ornate bandstand in Manzanillo.

mineral and sedimentary rocks, deep-green conifers stand alongside precious cedar, mahogany, and trumpetwood trees. The slopes are dotted with delicate wild orchids and graceful ferns. Although it can be cold and windy, the temperature rarely drops to freezing and there is never any snow. You can't see anything from the summit of Turquino, but the views from just before you reach it are magnificent.

Manzanillo

On the Gulf of Guacanayabo, 48km (30 miles) west of Bayamo, the fine harbour at **Manzanillo** ⑬ made it the main fishing center and principal shipping terminal for the sugar brought in by truck or rail from the little mill towns farther south. However, during the difficult times of the Special Period, the port was closed and 3,000 men lost their jobs. Imports of food and building materials have restarted, but large cargo ships can no longer come in, as the harbor has silted up. Fishing is still an important activity, though.

Like Bayamo, Manzanillo is steeped in rebellion, early on as a smuggling port, then during the Wars of Independence. Cuba's first communist cell was organized in Manzanillo in the 1920s, and the only communist mayor, Paquito Rosales, was democratically elected there in the 1940s. In the same decade, Jesús Menéndez, the incorruptible leader of the sugar workers' union, was assassinated on Manzanillo train station platform.

During the 1950s, Celia Sánchez organized an underground campaign here in support of the 26th of July Movement. The **Celia Sánchez Memorial**, with its colorful tiled murals of sunflowers and doves, is seven blocks southwest of the main square along Calle Martí, which is partly pedestrianized as a boulevard.

On the large **Parque Céspedes**, several colonial buildings show a marked Arab influence – particularly the delightful, brightly colored *glorieta* or bandstand in the center of the square. You still see people playing the *órgano oriental*, a type of hand-operated organ brought from France in the 19th century. The Museo Histórico Municipal is on the park (José Martí 226; charge), with colonial history in one section and displays on the 20th-century political struggle in the other. Walk past the little colonial church, Iglesia de la Purísima Concepción, and up Maceo toward the sea. At Villuendas, one block away, you come to the theater, reopened after a closure of 30 years, and opposite it the small Hotel Venus, also restored, to be used by visiting artistes.

On the seafront drive, Avenida 1 de Mayo, you find the little Parque Masó, El Golfo seafood restaurant, and for night-time entertainment, the cabaret Costa Azul (tel: 23-573-158; show 9pm–1am). From here the Malecón stretches west along the coast, past a statue to singer Beny Moré, a few fish restaurants and road-side stands, and out to the Proyecto Recreativo, a large open public space where there are nightclubs, cabaret and open-air nightlife. A bit further on, on a hill overlooking the city, is the multicolored, concrete Hotel Guacanayabo, busy and noisy during the Cuban holiday season but unaccustomed to foreign tourism.

Liberty bell

Parque Nacional La Demajagua ⓮ (Mon–Sat 8am–5pm, Sun 8am–1pm; charge), on the coast just 10km (6 miles) south of Manzanillo, is where Céspedes rang the bell to call for independence and the abolition of slavery in 1868 *(see box, page 289)*. The plantation is now a park, with the great bell firmly anchored in a stone wall by some old machinery, and a tiny museum. It is a pleasant place to stop on the way along the coast, with pretty views over the sea and cays offshore.

Past La Demajagua, the road follows the coast 50km (30 miles) through cane fields to **Media Luna** ⓯, the little town where Celia Sánchez was born in 1920. Her father was the local doctor and a follower of José Martí. The family home, a green and white traditional wooden house, is now a museum, the **Casa Natal de Celia Sánchez Man-** duley (Avenida Principal 111; Tue–Sat 9am–5pm, Sun 9am–1pm; charge). Celia Sánchez became a prominent underground organizer and was the first of the underground movement to make contact with Fidel after the landing of the *Granma*. Eventually, she joined the rebel forces and was a part of the revolutionary leadership up to her death in 1980.

Parque Nacional Desembarco de Granma

The road continues another 23km (14 miles) along the coast to **Niquero**, a busy town full of horses and carts and *bici-taxis*, with a functioning sugar mill and a pleasant hotel with a sea view, as well as some interesting French-style plantation houses.

At **Playa Las Coloradas** ⓰, 17km (10 miles) south of Niquero, there is a pleasant beach and a Campismo Popular site with basic cabins. A bit further on is the entrance to the **Parque Nacional Desembarco del Granma**. A visitor center has been built with a replica of the yacht *Granma*, close to the *bohío* of Angel Pérez Rosabal, the

TIP

The Campismo Popular at Playa Las Coloradas is chiefly for Cuban holiday-makers, but foreigners are welcome and there are facilities for camper vans. Reservations through Campismo Popular in Bayamo, or through Cubamar (www.cubamarviajes.cu) in Havana.

BELOW: the coastline, going toward Santiago.

A Holguín Province farmer in his field.

first person to help the 82 guerrillas when they landed on December 2, 1956. From the visitor center, where you have to get a guide, you follow a concrete boardwalk to the landing site, crossing the mangrove and sawgrass swamps that Fidel, Raúl, Che, and their band waded through, heavily laden with guns and ammunition while wearing heavy fatigues *(see page 58)*. The rebels were quickly surrounded by Batista's troops, and were nearly annihilated at the tiny village of Alegría de Pío. At one time the revolutionary force was reduced to only 12 men. An annual reconstruction of the event is staged each December by hundreds of young people, making the journey from Mexico before heading off into the Sierra Maestra.

A few kilometers further on, on the left side of the gravel road is the **Sendero Ecológico El Guafe** (charge includes guide), a 2km (1-mile) circular trail through the dry tropical forest. There is lots of wildlife in the forest and birdwatching is very rewarding. The tallest cactus in Cuba, called *El Viejo Testigo* (The Old Witness), was bat-tered by the 2008 hurricanes but still stands. The guide will also show you evidence of Amerindian habitation, burial sites, and ceremonial areas. The Ciboney once lived in the caves along this coast. Their diet consisted of fish, small animals, and native plants; they collected shells and stones to make tools and weapons, and crushed rocks into colored powder for painting. Clearly visible on the walls of several caverns are black and red (sometimes blue and brown) drawings.

At the end of the road, still within the national park, is **Cabo Cruz** ⓱, marked by a 19th-century lighthouse and fishing village, marking what is effectively Cuba's most southerly point. There is a restaurant, but if it isn't open when you arrive, a road-side stand by the sea wall sells freshly fried fillets of *minuto pescado* served in a bun, for a few *pesos cubanos*. The marine terrace along this part of the coast is replete with caverns: fissures in the rocky surface expose drops of up to 70 meters (240ft) with vertical walls that open into enormous underwater chambers. Fascinating coralline formations and one of Cuba's largest collections of the coveted queen conch hug the rocky shore. The dry surface of the terrace reveals sturdy cacti poking through the rocks. Lizards scuttle underfoot, while cormorants, egrets, and gulls wheel overhead.

The dramatic south coast

Between Media Luna and Niquero a road turning takes you along the Río Sevilla through sugar-cane plains and the foothills of the Sierra Maestra before coming to the beautifully sited harbor town of **Pilón**. Along the way, just before you get to Ojo de Agua, look out for signs and plaques marking the places where three groups of Castro's men crossed the road in underground water conduits on their journey from *Granma* to the Sierra Maestra, aiming to meet up at Cinco Palmas.

From Pilón the road hugs the coast, sandwiched between mountains and the Caribbean, all the way to Santiago de Cuba, with some of Cuba's most dramatic scenery along the way. There are occasional rock falls, and stones get washed up from the beach, so drive carefully, and always keep an eye out

for cows, goats, and other animals. Take plenty of fuel, water, and food for the journey. **Marea del Portillo** ⓲, once a small fishing village, has been developed as a medium-sized resort, very popular with Canadians in winter. Diving is possible off the reef, with shipwrecks and coral caves to explore, and guests can take trips into the local mountain villages.

La Plata (not to be confused with the Comandancia de La Plata inland) is the site of the rebels' first attack on Batista's army on May 28, 1957. A museum (Mon–Sat 8am–6pm, Sun 8am–noon; charge) in the village focuses on this battle and other aspects of the guerrilla campaign. Nearby, **Las Cuevas** has a pleasant beach, and is the trailhead for the climb up to Pico Turquino from the coast *(see page 291)*. The road continues through Ocujal and Uvero to the fishing village of **Chivirico** ⓳, famous for its bat-filled caves, **Las Cuevas de los Murciélagos**, and its **international scuba center**, based at the Hotel Brisas Sierra Mar Los Galeones, before eventually reaching Santiago. ❑

Cuban rock iguanas inhabit the southern coastal region.

RESTAURANTS

Bayamo

El Polinesio
Parada between Pío Rosado and Cisneros
Tel: (23) 423-860.
Open daily L & D. $–$$
A *paladar* with live music on the terrace at night. Cuban and international food of better quality than at state restaurants, however, you have to pay in CUCs.

El Ranchón
Balneario la Vega, on the river bank
Open daily noon–9pm. $
Lovely location, country-style restaurant, and good *comida criolla*, particularly roast pork. Food is priced in *pesos Cubanos*, drinks in CUCs or pesos.

Guardalavaca

El Ancla
Playa Guardalavaca
Tel: (24) 430-381.
Open daily 9am–10.30pm. $$
Perched on a rocky promontory above the sea, a lovely location to dine on seafood and a pleasant change from all the hotel buffets.

Holguín

Isla Cristal
Pico Cristal building, 3rd floor, Parque Calixto García
Tel: (24) 425-855.
Open noon–3pm, 5–10pm. $
Nice view over the plaza, international and Cuban dishes, reasonable food, lots of chicken.

La Ternura
José A Cardet 293 between

Angel Guerra and Cables
Tel: (24) 421-223.
Open daily from 6pm. $
A good *paladar*, upstairs. Typical food of pork and chicken with *congrís* enlivened by pork steak stuffed with ham and cheese. Prices in *moneda nacional*, but you can pay in CUCs.

Taberna de Pancho
Avenida Jorge Dimitrov
Tel: (24) 481-868. Open daily 12.15–4pm, 6.15–10pm. $
Right by Hotel Pernik and close to Plaza de la Revolución. Rustic wooden tables and chairs, wooden barrels, traditional music, a quiet, pleasant place for a burger and a beer or a full meal.

Salón 1720
Frexes 190, corner Miró
Tel: (24) 468-150.
Open daily L & D. $–$$
An elegant restaurant in a colonial building. The quality of the food doesn't match up, but it is OK and the service is attentive. Standard chicken and pork dishes, also lamb, beef, and lobster. There is a pleasant bar in the same building, and live entertainment.

> Price categories are for a three-course meal for one with a beer, or *mojito*. Wine puts the price up:
>
> **$** = under $25
> **$$** = $25–35
> **$$$** = over $35

SANTIAGO DE CUBA

Cuba's second city has a heroic revolutionary past,
beautiful squares, and a vibrant musical tradition
that includes the country's most vigorous carnival

N estled alongside a sweeping bay at the foothills of the Sierra Maestra mountains, surrounded by slopes covered with sugar cane, coffee, fruit, and vegetables, **Santiago de Cuba** ⑳ is Cuba's most exotic and ethnically diverse city. Multicultural, it is where many Haitians, both of white French ancestry, and of black African descent, settled after fleeing the slave uprisings in their country at the end of the 18th century, bringing with them the cachet of their Afro-French culture to blend with that of Afro-Hispanic Cuba. Isolated and remote, it is Cuba's second-largest city with a population of 475,000.

The city has its share of structural decay, yet it's not nearly as run-down and dilapidated as Havana. Some areas are traffic-free, but generally the streets are congested and full of fumes in the heat. There is some beautiful colonial architecture – you'll see plenty of graceful hanging balconies, gingerbread latticework, and wrought-iron gates throughout the city, but Santiago suffered greatly from the privations of the "Special Period." There is a lot of poverty here and visitors have to put up with harassment from hustlers and beggars. For the same reason, there is more need for care against crime, especially when walking through town alone at night. On the other hand, most

of Santiago's residents are extraordinarily friendly and helpful.

Santiago is renowned for producing much of Cuba's most important music, and this rich musical tradition, mingled with the remnants of French customs, gives the city a sensual, somewhat sleazy, New Orleans-like atmosphere. Wandering around can be confusing at times because some of the city's streets have two or three names, but Santiago is still ideal for walking if you can manage the hills of the old city and deserves several days' exploration.

Main attractions
ANTIGUO CUARTEL MONCADA
PLAZA DOLORES
MUSEO BACARDÍ
PARQUE CÉSPEDES
CATEDRAL DE N.S. DE ASUNCIÓN
CASA DE VELÁZQUEZ
CEMENTERIO SANTA IFIGENIA
CASA DE LA TROVA

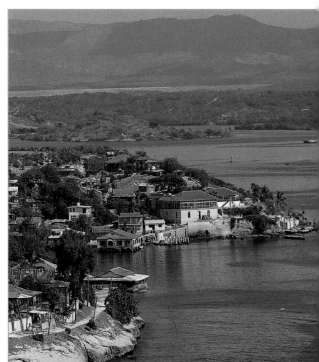

LEFT: Plaza de la Revolución, Santiago.
RIGHT: view over the bay.

Bastion of nationalism

Founded by the Spaniards in 1514, Santiago was Cuba's capital from 1524 until 1549. Because of its deep, natural harbor and Caribbean coastline, it also served as the center of the island's prosperous slave trade in the 1700s and 1800s. In 1898, Spain's surrender to the United States took place in Santiago, but then the city gradually slipped into second-class status after the government based itself in Havana.

Today, Santiago is the island's only official "Hero City," revered for being a bastion of Cuban nationalism and the cradle of the revolution. It was here, on July 26, 1953, that the revolution began with the failed assault by Castro and his rebels on the Moncada Garrison, then the second-largest military post in Cuba. It was also here that Castro accepted the surrender of Batista's army in 1959. The town's motto is "Rebelde Ayer, Hospitalaria Hoy, Heroico Siempre" (Rebellious Yesterday, Hospitable Today, Heroic for Ever).

Touring the town

The first thing you see when you enter Santiago is the stark **Plaza de la Revolución**, dominated by a vast, equestrian statue: the **Monumento Maceo**. Beneath the monument is a museum containing holograms of revolutionary items connected with the great fighter, one of the major figures in Cuba's 19th-century struggle for independence. The plaza stands at the junction with the Avenida de los Libertadores, a broad street lined with flowering trees and busts of the Moncada rebels.

Some distance down Avenida de los Libertadores you come to the Parque Histórico Abel Santamaría. On the other side of the road is the **Antiguo Cuartel Moncada ⒶⒶ**, now half a primary school, half a museum, the **Museo Histórico 26 de Julio** (Moncada Barracks; entrance on Avenida Moncada; tel: 22-620-157; Tue–Sat 9am–8pm, Sun 9am–1pm; charge), dedicated to the Moncada assault and the 1959 revolution. Batista had the

bullet holes filled in, but these have now been reconstructed for effect. Inside are revolutionary memorabilia: guns, grenades, documents, photographs, Castro's khaki uniforms, and Che Guevara's muddy boots. The museum is visually strong, and there are multilingual guides. Surprisingly, the museum is hardly signposted; you enter by taking a turning left off Avenida de los Libertadores.

Opposite, in a park of the same name, is the impressive **Monumento Abel Santamaría ⒷⒷ**, a tribute to Fidel's second-in-command in the 1953 attack on Moncada. It was Santamaría's job to create diversionary fire at the nearby hospital – a task he performed too well, in fact: unaware that the main assault had failed, he and his men continued firing until the hospital was surrounded. Despite pretending to be patients, the unfortunate rebels were caught and tortured, and most were executed.

Batista's men gouged out Santamaría's eyes and presented them to his sister, Haydée, a fellow revolutionary, to make her talk, but she realized that

The July 26 assault on the Moncada Garrison initiated the revolution.

BELOW: statue of Antonio Maceo in the Plaza de la Revolución.

TIP

Santiago seems to have more than its fair share of wonderful old cars, many of which are now used as taxis. You can find big old Buicks, Packards, Chevys, Chryslers, Studebakers, Hudsons, Edsels, and Fords. Treat them with respect, you may find you are getting into a 1940s Oldsmobile. If the driver holds the door open for you, he is probably not just being gallant, but making sure you don't slam it so it falls off.

BELOW:
the Moncada Barracks is now home to a museum and a school.

he could not have revealed the movement's plans and kept silent herself. Eye hospitals in Cuba now bear Abel Santamaría's name, as does a national medal given to young people who show extraordinary achievement in their studies or work. The park itself is a shady, well-used spot, where plants struggle to survive, boys play baseball, and groups of elderly people take exercise classes.

Ferreiro and Vista Alegre

Walking south from here, you reach Avenida Victoriano Garzón. If you go left up the avenue you come to the junction with Avenida de las Américas, locally known as Ferreiro after the family that owned most of the land here before the revolution. This is one of the city's most modern and most wealthy areas, with the landmark red, white, and blue **Hotel Santiago**. Nearby is a buzzing farmers' market, and, next to the **Hotel de las Américas**, a small, rather neglected park, the **Bosque de los Héroes ©**, which has monuments dedicated to Che Guevara and his comrades who fell

in Bolivia. It was the first monument to Che in Latin America. Just east of here, flanking Avenida Manduley, is the attractive **Vista Alegre** district. There are several museums and cultural centers for those interested in Afro-Cuban culture and religion, including the Centro Cultural Africano Fernando Ortiz (Avenida Manduley, 106), the Casa del Caribe (Calle 13 corner Calle 8), and the Museo de la Religión (Calle 13, 206, corner Calle 10).

Toward the colonial center

To reach the old heart of town, however, turn right and look out for **Hotel Rex**, on the left just before you reach **Plaza de Marte ©**. Now a basic peso hotel, the Rex is only notable as the place where Fidel Castro and his fellow guerrillas ate their last meal before the Moncada Barracks attack in July 1953. From Plaza de Marte, a noisy square where taxis gather, and goat-pulled carts take children for rides at weekends, head down the busy, commercial Calle Aguilera to **Plaza de Dolores ©**, a pleasant open space with lots of benches under the trees, as well as the tables of numerous restaurants. It is known as *Bulevar*, and is more a widening of Calle Aguilera than a formal square. The Cafetería la Isabelica here is a local institution, open 24 hours, but watch out for *jineteros*. Also on the plaza is the Complejo Don Antonio, which is a complex of places to eat, including Chinese, Cuban, international, and Italian food. In a former church, the Sala Dolores is known for its recitals of choral and orchestral music.

Santiago's museums

Continuing down Calle Aguilera, you come to the **Museo Provincial Emilio Bacardí** ➏ (entrance on Pío Rosado; tel: 22-628-402; Mon noon–8pm, Tue–Sat 10am–8pm, Sun 10am–6pm; charge, guided tour in English), Santiago's most interesting museum. It was founded in 1899 by Emilio Bacardí Moreau, a Cuban writer and the first mayor of Santiago, although he is more famous for his Caney Rum distillery, which was moved to Puerto Rico after the revolution to produce the re-named and globally popular Bacardi Rum.

The museum contains some first-rate Cuban art (including works by the talented José Joaquín Tejada Revilla), some colonial European paintings and memorabilia from Cuba's wars of independence, historic documents, flags, maps, and weapons. There is also an archeology section with indigenous artifacts, an Egyptian mummy, bought by Emilio Bacardí, a keen collector, on a visit to Egypt in 1912, several skeletons from Paracas in Peru, and a shrunken head.

From here it is a short walk to one of old Santiago's most important and most vibrant streets, **Calle Heredia**, which has a couple of museums worth a quick visit. The most interesting is the small **Museo del Carnaval** (Heredia, corner Carnicería; tel: 22-626-955, Tue–Sat 9am–6pm, Sun 9am–noon; charge), where there are some great costumes and *cabezudos* (big-headed carnival figures) and faded photographs depicting carnival's history. In the courtyard you can watch Afro-Cuban music and dance sessions daily (except Saturday) at 4pm – but be prepared to be pulled into the action.

Santiago is a city full of music, enjoyed by people of all ages.

BELOW: Santiago's rooftops against a mountain backdrop.

Nearly opposite, the **Casa Natal de José María Heredia** (Tue–Sun 9am–6pm; charge) is the birthplace of José María Heredia, one of the first Cuban poets to champion national independence. It's a peaceful, attractive house with original furnishings, and there are occasional poetry workshops held in the courtyard.

The central square

In the very center of the city is **Parque Céspedes** , a colonial square with a bust of Carlos Manuel de Céspedes in the middle, where you will find young and old, rich and poor, gathering to exchange news or simply watch the world go by. It is also a place where you are likely to get a lot of requests for money or soap from the persistent *jineteros* (hustlers) of both sexes who congregate here.

Dominating the park is the **Catedral de Nuestra Señora de la Asunción** (daily 8am–noon; free), a vast basilica rebuilt four times since the first one was completed in 1524, because of earthquakes or pirate attacks. The current building dates from 1818, with fur-

ther restoration and decoration added in the 20th century. There is a good, painted wooden altar, and hand-carved choir stalls, and, it is said, the remains of conquistador Diego Velázquez, though these have never been located. It also contains a small museum (Mon–Fri 9.30am–5.40pm; charge), entered to the left of the cathedral.

Directly opposite the cathedral is a splendid neo-colonial white building with blue shutters. This is the **Ayuntamiento** (town hall), from the balcony of which Castro announced the triumph of the revolution on January 2, 1959.

Also on the square is the elegant **Hotel Casa Granda** . The interior, restored in the mid-1990s, has an air of faded grandeur. A drink on the roof terrace at sunset is delightful. The hotel was once a high-society spot where the Cuban elite gathered on the rooftop terrace to sip rum, dance, and smoke cigars. Anyone who was anyone could be seen here, and famous patrons included many famous movie stars, singers, and sports champions, including Babe Ruth, the baseball player.

However, during the 1950s it was a sinister place that teemed with US spies and Cuban rebels. One of the hotel's former guests was the author Graham Greene, who came here to interview Castro (the interview never took place) and used the setting for a scene in his book *Our Man in Havana*, when his protagonist, Wormold, stayed here.

Cuba's oldest house

In the northwest corner of Parque Céspedes, distinguished by its black-slatted balconies, is the **Casa de Velázquez** Ⓚ which houses the **Museo de Ambiente Histórico Cubano** (tel: 22-652-652; Sat–Thur 9am–5pm, Fri 2–5pm; charge, multilingual guided tour, camera fee). A solid-stone structure with Moorish-style screened balconies, glorious cedar ceilings *(alfarjes)*, floor-to-ceiling shutters, and two lovely courtyards, the house was built between 1516 and 1530 and is said to be the oldest home in Cuba. In the 16th century, Governor Diego Velázquez used the first floor as his office and the upper floor as his residence. Among its collection are European tapestries, crystal, paintings,

ceramics, and antiques. *Peñas* (musical performances) are sometimes held here, and you may hear musicians practicing in the courtyards.

Just behind the square, to the southwest, is the **Balcón de Velázquez** Ⓛ (CUC$1 to take photos), an open paved area on the site of the first Spanish fort in the city, which has very good views of the harbor.

Away from Parque Céspedes

Bartolomé Masó (also called San Basilio) is a cobblestoned street lined with antique gas lamps, running parallel to Heredia. Look out for the **Restaurante Santiago 1900**, in a grand colonial home that once belonged to Emilio Bacardí. With a series of balconies set around a courtyard with a central fountain, and furnished with 19th-century antiques and crystal chandeliers, it retains some of its original elegance. It's a better spot for a drink than a meal, however *(see page 307)*. The **Museo del Ron** (San Basilio 358, corner Carnicería; tel: 22-623-737; Mon–Fri 9am–5pm; charge) explains

Antique bust at the Museo de Ambiente Histórico Cubano.

BELOW LEFT: Santiago street scene.

Music on Calle Heredia

Calle Heredia is a good venue for the arts and you may well witness here some of the finest musicians in Cuba. The local office of the Unión de Escritores y Artistas de Cuba (UNEAC; Cuban Writers' and Artists' Union) stages poetry readings, arts shows, lectures, and literary discussions. Another venue is the unprepossessing ARTex shop, which sells various crafts and souvenirs, and hosts good bands in the relaxed atmosphere of the pretty courtyard at the back.

The most famous venue is the renowned **Casa de la Trova**. Musicians consider it an honor to be asked to play here – treading as they do in the footsteps of a string of Cuban greats – and so it attracts some very accomplished artists. All week long, local musicians perform acts that range from somber Spanish guitar classics to vibrant Afro-Cuban drumming, from solo acts to 12-piece bands, trained professionals to talented amateurs. Upstairs there is a dance floor and lounge used at night, known as the Salón de Grandes Personas. Tables and chairs are set on the wooden balcony running the length of the room above the street. Daytime concerts are held downstairs for a minimal charge. Tour agencies offer evening packages that include transport, drinks, and a CD, but it is cheaper to come independently. Note that you are not allowed to record the music.

Cuban Health Care

One of the major successes of the revolution was the development of an exemplary health service, now being exported around the world

The flood of middle-class, educated professionals leaving Cuba after the revolution took with it over half the 6,000 doctors previously working on the island. Health care was already fragmented and failing the poor so it became one of the key areas for attention, along with the literacy campaign. Private health care was abolished and a state-run, national system was introduced. Huge efforts were made to eradicate infectious diseases, improve maternity care and reduce mortality rates, while large numbers of young people were recruited to train as doctors and other health professionals.

The next stage, in the 1970s, developed the idea of community health care. Polyclinics were built around the country to provide specialist services not previously available outside big cities. Then, in the 1980s, the Family Doctor program was introduced to provide care on a micro level; each doctor in charge of 120 families, a ratio rarely seen in the developed world and only beaten by Israel.

The success of initial policies enabled the government to embark on preventative care, led by a massive immunization and screening program; 95 percent of the population has been vaccinated against 12 diseases, some of which have been eradicated. Everyone has been tested for HIV and most people are tested annually. Ante-natal screening has prevented any babies being born HIV-positive since 1998. Other indicators also highlight the enormous success in improving the health of the nation: UN statistics show infant mortality has fallen from 70 deaths per 1,000 live births in 1955–60 to only 5 deaths in 2005–10 (UK down from 24 to 5, US from 26 to 6), while life expectancy has risen in the same period from 61 to 77 years for men and from 64 to 81 years for women. This has been achieved with one of the lowest rates of spending per person on health care in the world.

A by-product of the investment in training has, however, left Cuba with a surplus of doctors. Some of them have left the profession to work in the tourist industry, where they can earn more money as waiters or guides. Others work abroad and have become a valuable tool in the state's foreign policy initiatives. In the 1990s 600 Cuban doctors were seconded to the South African health service for three years to make up a shortfall when their own doctors emigrated. Groups of doctors work in polyclinics throughout the Caribbean, while teams of Cubans operate in Caracas shanty towns in return for a cheap supply of oil. Many of these take the opportunity to defect to the USA, but the majority return home when their time is up.

Whenever there is a natural disaster or emergency, Cuban doctors and paramedics from the Henry Reeve Medical Brigade are usually first on the scene – they set up field hospitals in Haiti after the 2010 earthquake long before the US emergency services arrived, with 30 doctors deployed to join the team of 344 already in the country before the disaster. The brigade was set up after Hurricane Katrina hit New Orleans in 2005, but the offer of help was rejected by President Bush. Since then, they have been deployed after earthquakes in Pakistan and China, the tsunami in Indonesia, and major flooding in Guatemala and Bolivia.

Thousands of foreign students from developing countries have also benefitted from training in Cuba, returning to their native lands after years of subsidized education as fully-fledged doctors fluent in Spanish and skilled in salsa.   ❑

LEFT: better health care has improved life expectancy.

the history of rum in Santiago and has an atmospheric little bar for a post-tour rum tasting. The street leads down to Avenida Jesús Menéndez and Parque Alameda, flanking the harbor.

Off to the left, before you reach the harbor, is one of the prettiest streets in the city, **Padre Pico**, which climbs up steps to the top of a steep hill southwest of Parque Céspedes, in the **Tivolí district**. The streets here are lined with houses that were once home to prosperous French refugees fleeing the slave rebellion in Haiti.

At the corner of Padre Pico and Diego Palacios (Santa Rita) is the **Museo de la Lucha Clandestina** (Museum of the Underground Struggle; tel: 22-624-689; Tue–Sun 9am–5pm; free), a lovely mustard-yellow colonial mansion with fine views of the city, reached via a slope fringed with bougainvillea. It is dedicated to the heroes of the 26th of July Movement and highlights the help that local people gave to the revolutionaries. In 1956 guerrillas fire-bombed the Batista police headquarters here, but it has since been beautifully restored.

Farther south, on Calle Jesús Rabí, is the Casa de las Tradiciones, in a large colonial house with a central courtyard, a great place to come at night for authentic *trova*, and a lot more local than the Casa de la Trova.

The broad, dusty promenade by the seafront is not particularly scenic, but you may want to venture down here to visit the cigar factory, the **Fábrica de Tabaco César Escalante** (Mon–Fri 9–11am, 1–5pm; charge).

Santa Ifigenia

Some distance northwest (taxi recommended) is the **Cementerio Santa Ifigenia** (Avenida Crombet, Reparto Juan G. Gómez; tel: 22-632-723, daily 8am–5.30pm; charge includes a guide). Once segregated by race and social class, the cemetery has both massive mausoleums and unpretentious graves. Carlos Manuel de Céspedes, Emilio Bacardí, and Cuba's first president, Tomás Estrada Palma, are among the famous figures buried here.

The tomb to receive most visitors, though, is that of the patriot José Martí, whose marble vault has the figures of

Laundry drying in the breeze on a Santiago rooftop.

BELOW LEFT: Santiago musician. **RIGHT:** an impressive gas guzzler.

The Bacardí family tomb in Santa Ifigenia Cemetery.

BELOW AND RIGHT: changing of the guard at the impressive José Martí mausoleum, Cementerio Santa Ifigenia.

six women carved around the outside bearing the symbols of Cuba's provinces. Buried within the mausoleum is earth from each of the Latin American countries inspired by Martí to assist in the independence struggle; the countries' names are inscribed on wall plaques. The national flag is draped over Martí's sarcophagus, which is so positioned as to catch the sun throughout the day. Accompanied by martial music, a uniformed armed guard is changed every half hour. The remains of 38 of the Moncada rebels are also buried here, in a special wall just inside the cemetery entrance.

Back to the center

You could ask your cab driver to return to the center via the **Casa Natal de Antonio Maceo** (Los Maceo 207 between Corona and M Delgado; tel: 22-623-750; Mon–Sat 9am–5pm; free), a modest house where the great man, nicknamed the Bronze Titan, was born. It exhibits photos, personal possessions, and Maceo's battle flag.

From here, you can walk along Calle General Banderas where there is a museum dedicated to two of Santiago's revolutionary heroes, the **Museo Hermanos País** (General Banderas 226, corner Los Maceo; tel: 22-652-710; Mon–Sat 9am–5pm; charge). Frank País was a poet, teacher, and army rebel who led the 26th of July Movement in Oriente. His younger brother, Josué, was also active in the movement. Both were gunned down in the street in separate incidents in 1957, and their boyhood home is a national shrine.

On your way back to the center stop at the memorial to Vilma Espín (1930–2007) (Sánchez Hechavarría, also known as San Jerónimo, between Calvario and Carnicería), opened in April 2010 on the 80th anniversary of her birth, in the house that was the headquarters of the 26th of July Movement. Each exhibition room charts a different period of her life, from her childhood in Santiago, her time as a student, as part of the clandestine movement, as a revolutionary fighting in the Sierra Maestra, as a mother and wife to Raúl Castro, and then her important work with the Federation of Cuban Women (FMC). ❑

RESTAURANTS AND BARS

Restaurants

Price categories are for a three-course meal for one with a beer, or *mojito*. Wine puts the price up:
$ = under $25
$$ = $25–35
$$$ = over $35

Santiago has long been a great place for bars and nightspots, but not so good for restaurants. However, things are now changing with the opening on Avenida Victoriano Garzón of several new restaurants, cafeterias, and food stalls, all of which charge in *moneda nacional*.

Café Catedral
San Pedro, corner San Basilio
Open daily 9am–5pm. **$**
Beneath the cathedral, this is a good, cheap place to pick up a sandwich with great coffee.

Casa Granda
Hotel Casa Granda, Parque Céspedes
Tel: (22) 686-600
Open daily L & D. **$$**
An elegant venue in Santiago's most atmospheric hotel. Eat in the dining room, on the broad terrace, or in the rooftop bar/restaurant. International food and pleasant, if not very rapid, service.

El Barracón
Avenida Victoriano Garzón between Martí and Primera
Tel: (22) 661-877.
Open daily 11am–11pm.
$–$$$
Decorated with a slavery theme; life-size images of slaves at the door to welcome you; the walls are stone, the crockery earthenware, the furniture rustic and wooden. The food is good *comida criolla* but the service is slow.

El Baturro
Aguilera, corner San Félix
Open daily noon–11pm. **$**
A popular place serving cheap Cuban food.

España
Avenida Victoriano Garzón, corner Cañedo
Open Mon noon–5pm, Tue noon–4pm, 6pm–midnight, Sat–Sun until 2am. **$**
One of the new restaurants operating in *moneda nacional*. The outside is blue with tiles reminiscent of public baths, but inside is quite smart with waiters in neat uniforms; men should wear jackets. In the cellar, decorated with barrels, there is a choice of wine.

La Reyna
Avenida Victoriano Garzón between calles 5 and 6, Ferreiro
Tel: (22) 626-731. Open daily noon–4pm, 6pm–midnight, Sat–Sun until 2am. **$**
A popular peso place serving fish and seafood, wine available. Air-conditioned dining room with only six tables, walls decorated with photos of underwater scenes.

Santiago 1900
Calle Masó (San Basilio), 354, between Pío Rosado and Hartmann
Tel: (22) 623-507. Open daily L & D. **$**
In a beautiful mansion that was the Bacardí family home. There's a great courtyard with a fountain, an upstairs patio, and a dim though elegant dining room. There is often live music, too. Unfortunately the food isn't very good and they tend to run out of things, especially if they have been catering for a group.

Zunzún
Avenida Manduley, 159, corner of Calle 7, Vista Alegre
Tel: (22) 641-528. Open Mon–Sat L & D, Sun L only. **$$$**
Marble floors, crystal chandeliers, and attentive waiters. Such elegance is rare in Santiago, and so is the menu. Both meat and fish are prepared with panache, and the lobster is excellent.

Bars

Santiago bars and clubs are pretty much interchangeable, so some of these venues are also mentioned in the Nightlife section (*see page 359*).

Bello Bar
Hotel Meliá Santiago, Avenida de las Américas
A quiet bar on the hotel's 15th floor, with wonderful panoramic views.

Café de Ajedréz
Plaza Céspedes
A good local bar (small and easy to miss). Great coffee all day; music at night.

Patio de ARTex
Calle Heredia, 304
Rum, beer, coffee, and snacks in the patio behind the ARTex shop; two daily sessions of live music.

Casa de la Trova
Calle Heredia, 208
There's music here, afternoon and evening, and drinks are not expensive.

RIGHT: enjoying a drink at the Patio de ARTex.

AROUND SANTIAGO

Several interesting trips can be made from Santiago de Cuba, including one to the spectacular Morro Fortress, to El Cobre, the island's most holy Catholic shrine, an historic coffee plantation, and some great beaches

Within easy striking distance of Santiago are several sights that shouldn't be missed. A rental car provides the most convenient way of exploring these, but if you don't want the risk of getting lost they are also accessible either with tour agencies or by hiring a taxi for an individual trip or for the day – make sure you strike a deal and agree an itinerary before you set off.

Most sights are located east of Santiago. West of the city you'll find a scattering of pleasant beaches, such as **Playa Mar Verde** ㉑, not to mention the stunning drive along the coast into Granma province.

A Spanish fortress

To the south of the city, perched above Santiago Bay, is the Spanish fortress of **Castillo del Morro** ㉒, now a World Heritage Site, housing the Museo de la Piratería (tel: 22-691-569; daily 8am–8pm; charge). A taxi from Parque Céspedes will cost CUC$25 for the round trip, with waiting time. Construction on this stunning fortress began in 1638, to a design by a specialist Italian architect, Juan Bautista Antonelli, son of the man who built El Morro in Havana.

It was destroyed in 1662 by English forces commanded by Sir Christopher Myngs, an expedition in which the pirate Henry Morgan took part, and

rebuilt between 1690 and 1710. It has an elaborate labyrinth of drawbridges, moats, passageways, staircases, and barracks, all executed with marvelously precise angles and a geometric beauty – many people think it is more impressive than Havana's fort. Its dark, dank inner cells, complete with built-in iron shackles, once housed African slaves in transit, and a small chapel still contains a wooden cross carved by a 16th-century Spanish artist. Look out for the contraption that was used to haul mighty stone balls up from the store

Main attractions
BASÍLICA DEL COBRE
CASTILLO DEL MORRO
CAYO GRANMA
LA GRAN PIEDRA
CAFETAL MUSEO LA ISABELICA
GRANJITA SIBONEY
VALLE DE LA PREHISTORIA

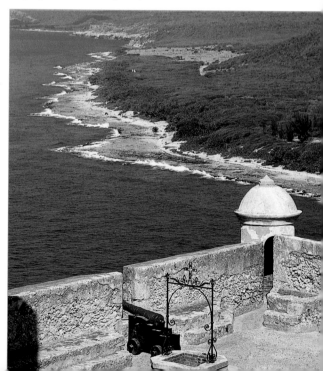

LEFT: the Basílica del Cobre.
RIGHT: a detail of Castillo del Morro.

You can get a ferry to Cayo Granma from the Ciudamar pier.

BELOW: flower seller on the road up to El Cobre.

to the cannon above. The views across the bay and along the coast are splendid. You can have an excellent lunch here *(see page 313)* or just buy snacks or drinks (and souvenirs, of course) from the stands outside.

The ferry boat to **Cayo Granma** – a small island community just inside the mouth of the Bay of Santiago – departs from the Ciudadmar pier 1.6km (1 mile) along the coast from the small beach at the foot of El Morro (you will see it signposted as you drive up to the fort on the Carretera del Morro). Ferries (CUC$2) depart roughly every hour throughout the day and follow a roundabout route linking the island with several little communities on the bay shores. Ferries also depart from Punta Gorda on the bay, about a CUC$6 taxi ride from the center. The island was formerly called Cayo Smith, for the wealthy English slave trader who once owned it, but the name was changed after the revolution.

Cayo Granma today has about 750 residents, some of whom still fish and build boats for a living, although most commute by ferry to factory and office jobs in Santiago. Since there are no cars or hotels on the island, it has a tranquil, old-time atmosphere. It has a beautiful beach, a small park where local people gather for games of dominoes, a school, a few stores, and a good seafood restaurant *(see page 313)*. Many residents offer rooms, and the island makes a pleasant, relaxing place to spend a night.

Virgin or goddess?

Of all the monuments in the Santiago region, the most famous is the shrine to the Virgen de la Caridad del Cobre, 19km (12 miles) northwest of the city. The **Basílica del Cobre** ㉓ (daily 7am–6pm; free) is named for the first open copper mine in the Americas, which supplied the ore for Havana's artillery works, the largest in the New World, around 1600.

Although the mine was producing copper until a few years ago, the place has long been identified with an object that some people believe is far more precious, which three young men found floating in the Bay of Nipe off Cuba's northern coast, in 1608. This is

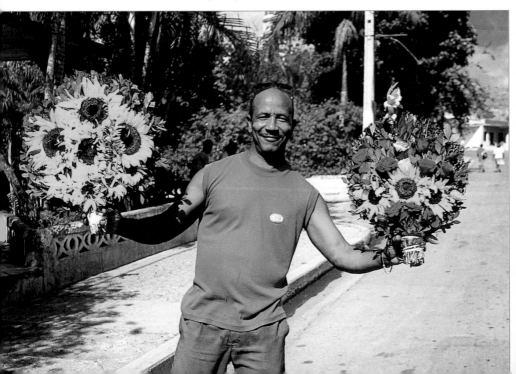

a 30cm (1ft) -tall wooden statue of a mestizo (mixed-race) Virgin carrying the infant Christ on her left arm, and holding a gold cross in her right hand. At her feet was the inscription, *Yo soy la Virgen de la Caridad* (I am the Virgin of Charity). Legend has it that she had been floating for almost 100 years, since an indigenous chieftain – who had been presented with the statue by the conquistador Alonso de Ojeda in 1510 – had set her adrift to protect her from the evil intentions of other less Christian native *caciques* (chiefs).

Through the years, the Virgin has been invoked to protect freedom, perform miracles, offer consolation, and heal the bitterness of battle. In 1916, at the petition of veterans of the War of Independence, the Pope declared her the patron saint of Cuba. The Virgin's sanctuary was inaugurated on her saint's day, September 8, in 1927, and thousands of worshipers flock to the church every September 8, for the Virgin is also worshiped as Ochún, the magnetic and sensual Santería goddess of love and rivers. Pope John Paul II visited the basilica during a trip to Cuba in 1998, and there is a bust of him outside the main door.

On the hilly drive from Santiago you will pass flower sellers offering yellow blooms that people buy as gifts for the Virgin/Ochún. The cream-colored church, surrounded by bougainvillea, looks stunning against the wooded slopes behind. Inside, above the altar is an air-conditioned niche that holds the diminutive figure of the Virgin, dressed in a gold-encrusted satin gown and crown.

The Virgin is displayed to worshipers during Mass, then the figure is rotated so that it can be seen only by climbing stairs above the Shrine of Miracles, where grateful believers leave braces, crutches, flags, armbands, coins, medals, locks of hair, and other *ex-voto* offerings. There is even a piece of the Berlin Wall, and the athletics shirt of the famous Cuban 800-meter Olympic gold medalist, Ana Quirot.

It is said that the mother of Fidel and Raúl Castro laid an offering here for the safety of her boys when they went off to fight in the Sierra Maestra. Well, that worked.

El Cobre attracts hordes of persistent touts and beggars. Be careful if you are carrying valuables, and be firm in refusing to buy statues of the Virgin (unless, of course, you really want one).

From the basilica you can see the **Monumento al Cimarron**, a sculpture commemorating a revolt by African slaves forced to work in the copper mines. A steep hike to the statue will be rewarded with stunning views. In one of the abandoned mines a lake has formed; the high but fluctuating mineral content means that the water – which has proved effective for some skin conditions – can be green one day and blue the next.

Gran Piedra

The highway east of Santiago, which follows the Caribbean coastline, is a marvelous road that slips between the sea and a rocky cactus desert with the blue-green mountains beyond. An

Ernest Hemingway donated his Nobel Prize to the Virgen de la Caridad, but unfortunately it was stolen from the Shrine of Miracles. It was soon recovered but is now safely stored away.

BELOW: the Virgen de la Caridad is an object of veneration.

Jardín Ave de Paraíso is named for the flamboyant Bird of Paradise flower (Strelitzia reginae).

BELOW: a sheltered bay in Santiago province.

80,000-hectare (200,000-acre) area, the **Parque Baconao**, has been recognized as a biosphere reserve by Unesco.

Thirteen kilometers (8 miles) into the mountains is a well-marked turn-off to **Gran Piedra** ㉔, taking you from dry and dusty desert into cloud-capped mountains shrouded in rainforest, up a long access road (under-powered or overloaded cars may struggle to make it). Each twist and turn in the road reveals a new vista across the mountains. At 1,214 meters (4,300ft) above sea level, you come to the Gran Piedra (Great Rock), with fabulous views across the mountains and out to sea, where even the lights of Jamaica can be seen on a clear night. It's ideal for climbing. Most people come for the day, but you can stay at the Villa Gran Piedra, an "eco-lodge" with comfortable rustic cabins along the mountain ridge, and unbeatable views. There is a CUC$1 charge to climb the steps to the Gran Piedra.

Close to Gran Piedra, the **Jardín Ave de Paraíso** (Bird of Paradise Garden; daily 8am–5pm; charge) should not be missed. First laid out in 1860 in the grounds of a coffee plantation, it was subsequently used to provide flowers for hotels, celebrations, and formal presentations. The gardens are beautifully landscaped, covering 45 hectares (111 acres) and the flowers are breathtaking, especially the brilliant *ave de paraíso* for which the garden is named.

Coffee and rebellion

In a lovely spot 2km (1 mile) or so along a dirt road east of La Gran Piedra, the **Cafetal Museo La Isabelica** (daily 9am–5pm; charge) is one of the area's few relics of the plantation era. This 19th-century estate, now a Unesco World Heritage Site, gives an insight into what life on a coffee plantation was like. The house originally belonged to a family of French descent, refugees from Haiti's slave rebellion (1789–1804). It is said that the plantation was named for the owner's mistress, an enslaved woman whom he later married.

Back on the main highway is **Granjita Siboney** ㉕ (Tue–Sun 9am–5pm; charge), the farmhouse where Fidel Castro and other rebels planned the

Antique Autos

Before the revolution American cars were freely imported into Cuba, and some of the most flashy were brought in by Hollywood film stars and Mafia hoods. Since the US trade embargo in 1961 there have been no new imports and the American cars you see on the roads now date from the 1940s and 1950s, and are held together with a lot of ingenuity and tender care. In the late 1980s, the government began selling some of the old cars to foreign investors, offering Cuban owners new Ladas instead, but many fine examples of old Buicks, Chevys, Studebakers, and others ended up in the Museo Nacional de Transporte Terrestre *(see opposite page)*, and in the Depósito de los Automóviles in Havana *(see page 154)*. Many of them are also used as taxis to ferry tourists around.

1953 attack on the Moncada Barracks in Santiago *(see page 299)*. It has been converted into a museum, displaying the usual collection of bloodstained clothing and the check from the Santiago restaurant where the *compañeros* had their last supper before the failed assault. The weapons were hidden in a well in the garden. The road along the coast is peppered with monuments to those who died at Moncada.

Back to the coast

About 2km (1 mile) away, the village of **Siboney** ㉖ has a pleasant, although not outstanding, beach, as yet undeveloped for foreign tourism but much used by local families. **El Oasis** a little farther on is an artists' colony with a store. Just after El Oasis, another excellent small beach, **Playa Bucanero**, is a well-developed tourist resort. The Club Bucanero Hotel caters mostly to German and Canadian package tourists.

One unmissable site for anyone interested in Cuban kitsch is the **Valle de la Prehistoria** ㉗ (daily 8am–5pm; charge), some 24km (16 miles) east of Santiago. This dinosaur theme park was created in 1983, with a collection of life-sized models. There is also a good little museum, the **Museo de Ciencias Naturales**, packed with interesting facts on local flora and fauna.

The **Museo Nacional de Transporte Terrestre** (daily 8am–5pm; charge), up a left-hand turn a little farther east, is also worth visiting for its collection of vintage cars – including the Cadillac that belonged to renowned Cuban singer, Beny Moré – and the display of more than 2,000 miniature cars.

At **Playa Daiquirí** on the coast south of here the daiquirí was invented, as an anti-malarial tonic for miners, even if it was "perfected" in Havana's El Floridita bar. Unfortunately, Playa Daiquirí is reserved for the military.

The best place to aim for is **Playa Cazonal**, with an all-inclusive hotel, though the shallow water makes for limited swimming. Just beyond lies **Laguna Baconao**, a lagoon surrounded by hills. There's a restaurant, a couple of boats, and a small crocodile enclosure.

The paved road ends by the lake. Beyond lies a restricted military zone – do not go any farther. ❏

The Villa Daiquirí has another historical connection, too: it was on Daiquirí Beach that Teddy Roosevelt and his Rough Riders came ashore during the Spanish–American War of 1898.

RESTAURANTS

Casa de Pedro El Cojo
Sigua
Tel: (22) 356-210.
Open daily, all day. **$**
Just outside Sigua, directly south of La Gran Piedra, this is a pleasant thatch-roofed restaurant *(ranchón)* that serves fish (mostly) with the usual accompaniments. Compay Segundo entertained friends here in his latter years, and there is an Eliades Ochoa song of the same name on a *Best of Buena Vista* album.

El Cayo
Cayo Granma,
Bahía de Santiago
Tel: (22) 690-109.
Open daily noon–7pm. **$**
This pretty little blue-and-white building by the water

houses Cayo Granma's only restaurant. You can eat good *criolla* food here – mainly fish – in pleasant surroundings. Booking for lunch is advisable.

La Jaiba Azul
Baconao
Open Tue–Sun 9am–6pm. **$–$$**
Near the black sand beach and convenient for lunch on a day trip out of the city. It specializes in seafood, including lobster. Prices are in *pesos Cubanos*, making it very good value.

El Morro
Carretera del Morro, Km 9
Tel: (22) 691-576.
Open daily noon–4pm. **$$**
This place serves what is probably the best *criolla* cooking in the Santiago

area, with a varied menu that includes spicy shrimps and lobster. It's right next to Castillo del Morro with cracking views of the coastline. Booking is advisable.

Hotel Villa Gran Piedra
Gran Piedra
Tel: (22) 686-147 and 651-205. Open daily D only. **$**
The restaurant in this "eco-lodge" is open to non-residents as well as guests, and serves traditional Cuban food.

Los Robalos
Baconao
Open Tue–Sun 9am–6pm. **$–$$**
Over the bridge from La Jaiba Azul, giving you a second option. This restaurant specializes in crab dishes.

La Rueda

Calle Montenegro s/n, Siboney
Tel: (22) 039-325, 399-325.
Open daily 9am–9pm. **$**
The food is pleasant and the service friendly, but the main reason this little place is well known is as the birthplace of Buena Vista musician, Compay Segundo. It also goes by the name of Museo/Sitio de Compay Segundo and is decorated with his personal possessions.

Price categories are for a three-course meal for one with a beer, or *mojito*. Wine puts the price up:
$ = under $25
$$ = $25–35
$$$ = over $35

BARACOA AND THE FAR EAST

The US military base of Guantánamo is synonymous with the "war against terror," but it is the lush mountain landscape, the pristine beaches, and the laid-back town of Baracoa that draw visitors to the east

The main reason most visitors venture east of Santiago de Cuba is to visit Baracoa, the most popular destination in the region, which has been opened up to tourism. If you want to go straight from Santiago to Baracoa, there is a daily Víazul bus. The 4½-hour journey down the road called La Farola is delightful; views are splendid and bends are tortuous, so it's preferable to have somebody else doing the driving.

However, there are a few other places of interest in the surrounding area for those who have rented a car and want to explore at leisure.

Guantánamo

To get to **Guantánamo** ㉘ you take the Autopista Nacional from Santiago, then, after about 15km (9 miles), go east on the Carretera Central. The road then becomes motorway again about 20km (12 miles) before Guantánamo.

There's no immediately obvious reason to make the trek from Santiago to Guantánamo, but it is a pleasant, well-kept provincial town. It was founded in 1819 and lies between the Jaibo, Bano, and Guaso rivers just north of where they flow into the Bay of Guantánamo. During the 19th century the town received a large influx of immigrants from Haiti and Jamaica, many of them French, fleeing the slave

revolt. As a result, some of the architecture has a French Caribbean feel, with pretty wooden balconies and wrought ironwork, although there is a predominance of the neoclassical style of the late 19th- and early 20th-century Spanish Cuba. There is also a rather unfortunate late 20th-century 12-story apartment tower.

City life revolves around **Plaza Martí**, a pleasant leafy square shaded by laburnum trees (glorious in March), and with an attractive golden-colored church, the 19th-century **Iglesia**

Main attractions
GUANTÁNAMO US BASE
LA FAROLA
BARACOA
RÍO YUMURÍ
EL YUNQUE
PLAYA MAGUANA

LEFT: lazy day on the Río Yumurí.
BELOW: Guantánamo street mural.

TIP

There is a small
museum near the Plaza
de la Revolución, north
of Guantánamo city
center, which contains
the space capsule in
which the first Cuban
went up into space.

Parroquial Santa Catalina de Ricci. It's worth at spending least an hour exploring the streets around the main square. There are some attractive old houses on the parallel calles Pedro Agustín Pérez and Calixto García, north of Parque Martí, while Los Maceo, one block east, is buzzing with shoppers. Seek out the unusual **market**, a neoclassical structure occupying an entire block.

Musical heritage

The town's French heritage has had a lasting impact on its musical traditions and rhythms. Go to the **Tumba Francesa** (Serafín Sánchez 715, between Jesús del Sol and Narciso López; Tue 9.30am–1pm, Thur 9.30am–noon, Sat 9.30am–2pm) to see the colorful folk dance and music which originated in Haiti. It was created in the 1890s by freed slaves to preserve the traditions that had grown up on the coffee plantations in the area. The dancers re-create the movements of their ancestors to the beat of the Premier drums and the Catá (a wooden percussion instrument), both of which came from the Dahomeyan region of Africa. There is

a shop selling Haitian-style handicrafts and other souvenirs.

Everyone visiting Cuba will hear the haunting *Guajira Guantanamera* song, based on the words of a poem by José Martí. The *guajiro* is not only a peasant farmer *(see page 208)*, but also a rural style of *son*. This developed in the mountains around Guantánamo and became known as *son changüí*. It has a very complex rhythm and much improvisation on the bongos, but it has been kept alive in the **Casa de la Trova** (Pedro Agustín Pérez corner Crombet; Tue–Sun 9am–noon, 2–6pm, 7pm–midnight) and in the **Casa del Changüí** (Serafín Sánchez 710 between Jesús del Sol and Narciso López; tel: 21-324-178; Tue–Fri 7am–11pm, Sat–Sun 10am–2am). Here you can find the *changüí* bands playing their bongos and marimbulas (African thumb bass).

Caimanera and the base

The only reason most people come here is for a view of the controversial US naval base, one of the last vestiges of the Cold War, and the place now

BELOW:
driving over
La Farola, en
route to Baracoa.

best known as the site of the infamous Camp Delta, where men suspected of terrorist involvement have been detained in conditions that have aroused widespread disquiet.

Guantánamo itself offers no views of the base, which actually extends to the south of the city. If you want a glimpse of it, there are two options open to you. The first and most difficult option is to pass through two Cuban military checkpoints, to **Caimanera**. The necessary papers can be obtained from the Ministry of the Interior (MININT) office on Calle José Martí in Guantánamo, but independent travelers will find it difficult and very time-consuming to get hold of a pass. Visitors staying at the Hotel Caimanera on a pre-booked itinerary through a tour agent get a pass included in their booking. The hotel is the closest you will get and has a three-story observation tower overlooking the **US Naval Base ㉙**. Look up: on all sides of town are the omnipresent tunnels where residents are to go in case of an emergency.

Los Malones

For the average visitor, the best view they will get of the US base is through binoculars from the **Mirador de los Malones**, off the Baracoa road about 24km (15 miles) east of Guantánamo. You can arrange a visit by booking a tour at one of Santiago's central travel agencies, ideally a couple of days in advance, or at a *buró de turismo* in the hotel in Guantánamo. The area is controlled by the military and tours are sold by Gaviota, the military's tour agency. A guide will accompany you into the Cuban military zone that surrounds the base and then along a bumpy dirt track to the lookout point. You will be shown a model of the base, and given a few vital statistics before climbing the stairs, where a telescope allows you to pick out vehicles and people moving around, and spot the US and Cuban flags flying by the perimeter fences.

Up into the mountains

You could make a detour into the mountains northeast of Guantánamo, toward Palenque, where the village of **Boquerón** is home to the **Museo Zoológico de Piedra** (Stone Zoo, Carretera a Yateras, Km 18; Mon–Sat 9am–6pm; charge), the handiwork of Ángel Iñigo, a coffee farmer who has carved over 100 animals out of the limestone. Some large sculptures are carved *in situ* from outcrops or large boulders, others from smaller rocks, and all stand amid a beautiful garden. Almost all were carved from pictures in books: Ángel has never seen most of the animals he has so faithfully sculpted. The zoo is now run, and the more recent figures carved, by Ángel's eldest son, Angelito. From here, access is prohibited, and you must retrace your steps to Guantánamo and the Baracoa road.

Along the coast

The road east out of Guantánamo passes pleasant little farming communities and beaches at **Yacabo Abajo** and **Imías**. At **Playa de Cajobabo ㉚**, next along the coast, José Martí and

Playa de Cajobabo.

BELOW: a creature in the Stone Zoo, Boquerón.

US Guantánamo

This little piece of the island of Cuba is in fact US-occupied territory with one of the worst human rights records in the world

The naval base sits in the southeast corner of Cuba, an enclave of US military might, occupying 116 sq km (45 sq miles) of Cuban territory. For decades, it has been one of Uncle Sam's most-favored ports, known to sailors as Gitmo. Founded in 1898 after 600 US Marines landed here to fight in the Spanish–American War, the base was formally established in 1901 by the Platt Amendment. Until 1959 it was a good-time assignment where sailors overindulged in cheap rum and accommodating women. Saloons and brothels dotted the streets of nearby Guantánamo city.

Following Castro's takeover, brothels and bars were closed, commerce between Americans and Cubans forbidden, and security on the base tightened considerably. Many Cubans still worked there, but had to get a bus then walk through the gate after vehicular traffic was prohibited.

Since 1960, Castro has not cashed any of the annual US$4,085 rent checks issued by the US Treasury, as to do so would acknowledge the legitimacy of the base. Guantánamo, according to Castro, is "a dagger plunged into the heart of Cuban soil," but it remains in US hands until the two countries agree to end the arrangement, or the US decides to abandon the base. The Platt Amendment was repealed in 1934 and theoretically the US lease on Guantánamo expires in 2033.

Surrounded by barbed wire, Gitmo is an isolated installation guarded by 500 Marines. About 8,000 people live here, including civilians and military families. It contains housing, a school, health spa, a movie theater, a shopping center, and a McDonald's. Children watch Saturday-morning cartoons picked up by satellite from US television networks, and military planes fly in with supplies. Servicemen and women stationed on the base conduct defense exercises, maintain warships, and monitor Cuban airspace. Rifles slung over their shoulders, they patrol the perimeter, which is mined with explosives. Though neither the US nor Cuba will confirm the figure, it is estimated that about 100 Cubans a year enter the base illegally by swimming through the shark-infested waters or jumping the fence. Dozens of these have died in the attempt. In the early 1990s, the camp held Haitian refugees who fled their country after a coup, and in 1994 it became a temporary refugee center for thousands of Cuban rafters who had been picked up at sea by the US Coast Guard.

As Cuba poses little military threat to the US, the base had little strategic value except as a thorn in Castro's side, until 2002, when it became the site of the now-notorious Camp Delta, the subject of international controversy, which holds people suspected of belonging to al-Qaeda or the Taliban. There were in fact three camps, one of which has been closed. There was controversy over the insistence of the Bush administration that detainees, despite being held as "enemy combatants," should be denied the protection of the Geneva Convention. Terrible stories emerged concerning torture and human rights abuses of the prisoners, who were held indefinitely without trial. The election of President Barack Obama in 2008 brought hopes of change. In January 2009 he suspended the proceedings of the Guantánamo military commission for 120 days and promised that the facility would be shut down within a year. Many prisoners were released or transferred, but 193 remained in January 2010, waiting for a correctional center in Illinois to be made ready as their new prison. ❏

LEFT: detainee attending a "life skills" class.

Máximo Gómez came ashore to begin the fight against the Spanish in 1895. However, it is not a particularly interesting beach destination. From here, the road divides, turning north to Baracoa, and east to **Punta de Maisí**.

Few people take the road to Maisí. It is in poor repair, and requires a good four-wheel-drive vehicle and a skilled driver, not to mention a strong nerve, as it bends higher and higher up the stone mountain terraces. It passes through dry, scrubby desert land with dramatic mountain scenery rising to the north. The vast limestone terraces are full of caves with stalactites and stalagmites. Below the coffee-growing town of La Máquina, the village of **Maisí** ❸❶ sits on a wide coastal plain of dry shrubby vegetation and cacti. There is a lighthouse on Cuba's most easterly point, only 80km (50 miles) from Haiti, but this is a military zone and you will be denied access.

Instead, take the route heading north (inland) from Cajobabo to Baracoa – along the hair-raising but well-maintained road over the mountains. Known as **La Farola** (The Beacon), it twists through some fearsomely acute bends. The crash barriers are disconcertingly broken in places and warning notices appear regularly – "Caution: 72 Accidents on this Bend So Far." The risk is compensated for by the wonderful scenery: magnificent mountain vistas, wild jungle, coconut groves, and coffee and cocoa plantations. You will be approached by vendors of wonderful fruit and snacks, such as *cuchuruchos*, grated, flavored coconut neatly encased in palm leaves, but if they offer you anything made of polymita snail shells, say no, as they are endangered and protected by international law.

Cuba's first town

Some believe Columbus landed first at **Baracoa** ❸❷ in October 1492, but there is little evidence for this. The explorer was looking for the Orient, but no matter: he found the *oriente* (east) of Cuba. "A thousand tongues would not suffice to describe the things of novelty and beauty I saw," he recalled. The town nestles beneath El Yunque, a flat, anvil-shaped mountain that was described by Columbus in his log.

Baracoa Bay.

BELOW: view over Baracoa after a tropical storm.

"This is the last church in Cuba to be renovated," said an elderly lady, mopping the church floor after rain flooded through holes in the roof. "We are farthest from Havana, so it takes a long time for money to get here."

Baracoa certainly was Cuba's first town, founded by Diego Velázquez in 1512, and was also the first capital of Cuba and the starting point for the Spanish conquest of the rest of the island. Three years later, Santiago, and then Havana, took over the role of capital. Baracoa remained isolated up until La Farola was built in 1962; prior to that, access was possible only by sea.

The streets, impossibly picturesque in the late afternoon light, are absolute heaven for photographers, with their neat lines of one-story, pastel-colored houses with red-tiled roofs and lush vegetation. This laid-back air is a result primarily of Baracoa's isolation, with Havana 1,070km (670 miles) away. While Baracoa is still well off the main tourist trail, the town's combination of friendly people, attractive scenery, and distinctive cuisine make it a great place to spend some time. There are several small hotels and dozens of *casas particulares*, but no large resorts.

The best place to get an overview of the town, the bay, and the unnervingly short runway of Baracoa's tiny airport on the far side is from the gardens of

the Hotel El Castillo *(see page 355)*, up a long flight of steps or a steepish slope on a clifftop. The building was originally a castle, built in 1770 to keep out the British; it later became a prison, and more recently a hotel.

Baracoa life

Life in Baracoa revolves around leafy **Parque Independencia**, also known as Parque Central, where legend has it that the indigenous chief Hatuey was burned alive by Spanish conquistadors *(see page 35)*: the supposed spot where he died is marked by a bust, directly opposite the entrance to the **Catedral de Nuestra Señora de la Asunción** (Tue–Sat 8am–noon, 2–4pm, Sat 7–9pm, Sun 8am–noon; free), although his death is more likely to have occurred in Yara, near Manzanillo. The church was built in 1805, replacing the original, destroyed by pirates in 1652. It is sadly in need of renovation, but Mass is still held here. What is believed to be Columbus's Cruz de la Parra *(see box opposite)* is kept inside. There are several peso food stalls and cafés around the parque, particularly at lunch time.

BELOW: cutting sugar cane is hard work.

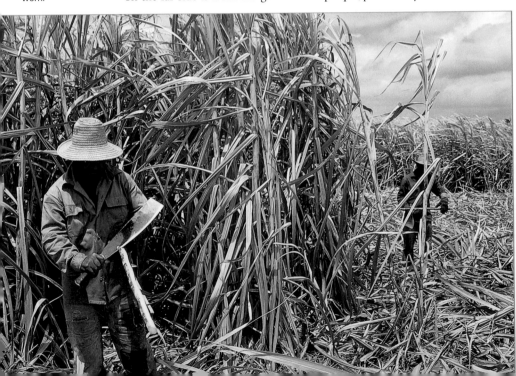

The town's two main streets, Maceo and Martí, are where everything happens. Check out the small but lively **Casa de la Trova** (Antonio Maceo 149; Tue–Sun from 9pm), which really gets going at about 10pm, and is a popular gathering place. Dancers are always welcome if you want to join in. In neighboring **Plaza Martí**, each Saturday is "La Fiesta" – a lively affair with loud street music and plenty of rum, roast pork, and snacks for sale. Farther along Maceo (No. 124) is the **Casa de la Cultura**, where there are exhibitions of modern art by local artists, and regular live music, including a nightly show of Afro-Cuban music using traditional instruments and costumes.

The Malecón

Baracoa was particularly badly hit by the hurricanes of 2008, but work is now being done to cheer up the **Malecón**, Baracoa's seafront boulevard. Gaviota has opened a few cafeterías, all called Costa Norte, and has renovated the iconic La Rusa hotel (you can't miss it, it's bright yellow). La Rusa was a Russian woman who abandoned the Soviet

Union in the 1950s, came to Cuba, and ended up supporting the rebels. Fidel and Che both stayed here, and guests fight over the rooms where they are said to have slept.

At the eastern end of the Malecón is the small but well-preserved **Fuerte Matachín** (1802), which houses a small **Museo Municipal** (tel: 21-642-122, daily 8am–noon, 2–6pm; charge). Outside the fort is a chunky statue of Columbus and a large wooden cross. The museum contains a mixture of displays on the indigenous Taíno, local history, and a few Baracoan characters.

At the western end of the Malecón, close to the bus station, is **La Punta** fortress, now a restaurant, with a statue of a defiant-looking Hatuey outside. From here there is a great view of the bay, on the far side of which is a good hotel, the Porto Santo, and a small airport (two flights a week to Havana).

Baracoa's past

If you climb a flight of steps on the inland side of Antonio Maceo toward a neighborhood called Reparto Paraíso, you pass the outdoor El

Bass saxophonist rehearsing in Baracoa.

BELOW LEFT: a monument to Columbus on the Malecón.

A Cross Debate

In Baracoa almost every resident can, and will, tell you the story of the Cruz de la Parra (Cross of the Vine), fashioned from hardwood, which Columbus reputedly brought from Spain and planted here. It vanished and was later found amid the backyard blackberry bushes of a colonizer's house in 1510. This historic cross survived pirates, fires, vandals, and other hazards, although relic-hunters have chipped away at the edges and it is now about half the size it used to be. Standing 1 meter (3ft) tall, it is now kept safe in the cathedral, with its edges encased in metal.

That, at least, is the story. But did Columbus really bring the cross? The church maintains that he did. So does Alejandro Hartmann, director of the local history museum, the Museo Municipal (in the Fuerte Matachín) in Baracoa. But a host of scholars disagree. Everybody has a conflicting notion – and everyone can back it up with data. In 1989, carbon-dating tests appeared to indicate that Baracoa's wooden cross was planted in Cuban soil in the late 15th century, which supports one strand of the Columbus theory, making it chronologically possible, but it is made from the native seagrape tree *(Cocoloba diversifolia)*, which could not have been brought from Spain. So the mystery deepens, but the cross is still revered.

Close to the mouth of Río Yumurí is the Tunel de los Alemanes (German Tunnel). This impressive natural rock formation, through which the road runs, is so-called because, in pre-revolutionary times, a German family lived close by, and charged drivers of motor- and horse-drawn vehicles for passing through.

BELOW: coconut is used in the preparation of many Baracoan dishes.

Ranchón disco, then walk along pretty, rural tracks lined with little houses in lush gardens, with children playing, goats roaming, and chickens pecking in the dust.

The **Museo Arqueológico** (Mon–Fri 8am–5pm, Sat 8am–noon; charge) is tucked away up a narrow path, in the Cueva del Paraíso. It contains objects found in and around Baracoa, including a skeleton of a Taíno chief called Guamá, who fought the Spanish for 10 years. The story is that he was murdered by a single blow to the head, dealt by the man, possibly his brother, whose wife he had stolen. There is also a replica of the Taíno tobacco idol, found nearby in 1903, and said to be the most important in the Americas. The original is in Havana's museum of anthropology *(see page 180)*. The cave is part of the Majayara terrace, and there are stalagmites and stalactites and petroglyphs. Yara and Majana are the two other terraces in this geological area, in between which there are many caves, full of petroglyphs, once used by the Taínos. The museum runs archeological tours of the area.

Excursions from Baracoa

Legend says that those who sleep in Baracoa's **Bahía de Miel** (Bay of Honey) will never want to leave. Disappointingly, the city beach, at the eastern end of town, is gritty and gray, and the sea rather muddy. Going east from Baracoa through the small settlement of Jamal, there are some beautiful (and gentle) walks through countryside where the crops are a mixture of bananas, coffee, cocoa, and avocados, where pigs snuffle in the undergrowth and chickens roam. At Río Yumurí, 30km (20 miles) east of Baracoa, a boatman is usually available to take visitors on a short trip. The green river is delightful, flowing between high cliffs, and you may see and hear Cuba's national bird, the trogon (also known as the *tocororo*).

Baracoa's horizon is dominated by **El Yunque 33** (The Anvil), looming at 560 meters/1,800ft, to the west of the town. Archeologists have found shells and skeletons left by the Taíno people who, during the conquest, took advantage of the mountain's cliffs and natural look-out points, as did anti-Spanish rebels during the 19th century.

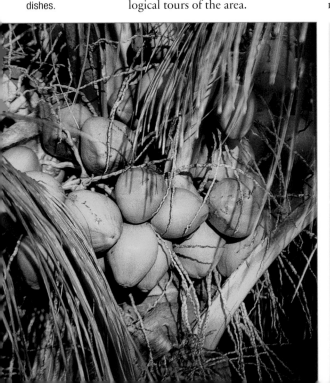

A Regional Cuisine

Baracoan food typically uses spices, coconut, and chocolate. Food is cooked in coconut oil and *lechita* (coconut milk), giving the whole town a heavenly smell when cooking starts. Local dishes include *bacón* (a plantain tortilla filled with spicy pork), and *tetí* – small red fish caught in the river estuaries between August and December; they have a gelatinous protective wrapping, which dissolves upon reaching fresh water, and are tasty raw or in omelets. Tamales are mashed plantains wrapped in a banana leaf, instead of the maize used elsewhere. Rice is colored yellow with annato seeds, while "Indian bananas" are boiled in their pink skins and dressed with garlic and lime juice. The Casa del Chocolate at Antonio Maceo, 121, famously serves hot chocolate with salt as well as sugar.

The slopes are cloaked in virgin rainforest, part of which is protected by the rarely visited **Cuchillas de Toa** mountain reserve. This is one of the wildest regions in Cuba, with excellent potential for hiking and some wonderful flora, such as wild orchids. You can climb El Yunque in a couple of hours; bring plenty of water and good footwear, as the path can get muddy and slippery. A guide is compulsory. The path runs from Campismo El Yunque, near the base of the mountain, but you can also rent horses and hire guides for the trip at Finca Duaba, just outside Baracoa, along the Moa road.

The Finca, which, like all the tourist facilities here, is part of the Gaviota chain, has a restaurant that serves Cuban food, and organizes demonstrations showing how local crops, such as cocoa and bananas, are cultivated. At **Playa Duaba**, near the mouth of the Duaba River you can swim in either fresh or saltwater.

The best beach, and one of the finest in Cuba, is **Playa Maguana**, 22km (14 miles) from town, where there's a good hotel (*see page 355*). A coral reef ensures

that the 3km (2 miles) of sugar-white sand is lapped only by gentle waters.

Tour operators, Cubatur (Maceo 149; tel: 21-645-306), Ecotur (Coronel Cardoza 24; tel: 21-643-665), and Havanatur (Martí 202; tel: 21-645-358) in Baracoa can organize excursions of the area led by knowledgable local guides, who can incorporate interesting additions, such as visits to cocoa farms. Here, you can learn how the cocoa pods are harvested and transformed into a variety of delicious products including chocolate, which you can taste and buy.

The road northwest from Baracoa takes you into Holguín province, along a dramatic route that skirts the mountains and the sea. It is rough going in the early stages, with many potholes, so allow three hours for the drive to **Moa ③**. Unless you are a metallurgist, you won't want to spend much time in Moa. This is mining country, with possibly the world's largest reserves of nickel and cobalt. Nickel production is an important industry, but one that results in belching chimneys and polluted seas and rivers washing up against blackened hills. ❏

Chocolate bars fresh from Baracoa.

RESTAURANTS AND BARS

Baracoa
El Castillo
Calle Calixto García
Tel: (21) 645-165.
Open daily L & D. $$
The hotel restaurant has a varied menu including spicy soups and fish cooked in coconut-milk sauce. Good three-course set menu.
Finca Duaba
Carretera Mabujabo, Km 2.
Tel: (21) 645-206. $$
A farm close to town; the restaurant serves good barbecued meats.
La Colonial
Calle Martí, 123
Tel: (21) 645-391. Open daily D only. $
A delightful *paladar*. Two small dining rooms and interior patio lively with

caged birds. Menu varies, depending on availability.
La Punta
Malecón s/n
Tel: (21) 645-224.
A pleasant open-air restaurant with a good reputation within the walls of one of the three forts.
Porto Santo
Carretera del Aeropuerto
Tel: (21) 645-105. Open daily L & D. $$
Hotel restaurant; international menu and barbecue, just outside Baracoa.
Villa Maguana
Playa Maguana, Carretera a Moa, Km 22.5. Tel: (21) 641-204. Open daily 7am–9.45pm.
A pleasant beach bar and *parrillada* for snacks, meals, and drinks.

Guantánamo
La Cubanita
Calle Martí, 864. No phone.
Open daily L & D. $
A great little *paladar* serving well-cooked *comida criolla*, charged in *moneda nacional* and very cheap.
Vegetariano
Pedro A Pérez
Open daily noon–2.30pm, 5–11pm. $
One of the very few vegetarian restaurants in Cuba.
Taberna Las Ruinas
Calixto García
Open daily 10am–1am.
The shell of a ruined building is the backdrop for this restaurant. It offers an extensive menu for lunch and dinner, and the bar is open late with live music.

Bars
Baracoa
Casa de la Cultura
Maceo, 124
Music most nights.
Casa de la Trova
Maceo, 149
Lively at night with traditional *son*.
El Patio de ARTex
Maceo, 120
Pleasant courtyard bar; live music and other events.

Price categories are for a three-course meal for one with a beer, or *mojito*. Wine puts the price up:
$ = under $25
$$ = $25–35
$$$ = over $35

SOUTHERN ISLANDS

Most important are the Isle of Youth, with good diving, caves with indigenous paintings, and the prison where Fidel Castro was once incarcerated, and Cayo Largo, with its sugar-white beaches

ocated off the main island's south coast, each of the islands of the Archipiélago de los Canarreos has its own distinct personality. Isla de la Juventud (Isle of Youth) is quiet and rural, with a colorful history as a pirate refuge, home for US settlers, and prison camp for revolutionaries; Cayo Largo has a string of hotels and little else; other cays, like Cayo Rosario, are just virgin specks of sand wallowing in the blue Caribbean.

The real Treasure Island

Isla de la Juventud, the largest by far of Cuba's subsidiary islands with an area of 3,020 sq km (1,180 sq miles) and a population of around 87,000, can be reached either by plane from Havana or by the ferry that departs from the port of Surgidero de Batabanó. The latter is a time-consuming option, and one that is usually only undertaken by travelers with time to spare *(see margin tip on page 328)*. Accommodations for visitors are in Nueva Gerona, the capital, and the Hotel Colony on the southwest coast, a dive resort with a marina.

Over the centuries, the island has seen immigrants from Spain, England, Scotland, China, Japan, Jamaica, the Caymans, and the USA, and it has had a similarly varied history in terms of the names it has been given.

Indigenous peoples called it Camarcó or Siguanea, but Christopher Columbus renamed it La Evangelista when he landed here in 1494, on his second voyage to the New World. By the 17th century it was known as Isla del Tesoro (Treasure Island) because of the pirate treasure allegedly buried here (thus inspiring the name, at least, of Robert Louis Stevenson's classic adventure tale, published in 1883). By this time, the Spaniards, who finally got around to colonizing the island in the 1840s, had renamed it Colonia

Main attractions
ISLA DE LA JUVENTUD
NUEVA GERONA
MUSEO DE LA LUCHA CLANDESTINA
PRESIDIO MODELO
PUNTA DEL ESTE
CAYO LARGO
CAYO ROSARIO

PRECEDING PAGES: idyllic island beach.
LEFT: repairing fishing nets. **RIGHT:** Nueva Gerona harbor.

BELOW: playing dominoes on a street in La Fé, the capital of Isla de Juventud.

Reina Amalia. Later names include: the Isla de los Deportados, when it became a dumping ground for criminals and rebels deported from the mainland; La Siberia de Cuba, in recognition of the isolated prison where Castro and others spent several years in the 1950s; Isla de las Cotorras (Isle of Parrots), as the habitat of the brightly colored birds that are still the trademark of the island's bottled water; and, until 1971, Isla de Pinos (Isle of Pines). Finally, it acquired its present name in the 1970s, a symbol of the influx of young people to the island.

An island education

In 1971, Cuba began taking students from countries in the Developing World and educating them for free on the island, thus hoping to spread solidarity for the Cuban Revolution across the under-developed world. At its height, the program included 60 boarding schools with 150,000 students. However, the flow of foreign students dwindled, due to economic difficulties in Cuba, and political changes in their own countries. The

last foreign students completed their studies in 1996, although the schools still remain.

Town with a *yanqui* touch

The point of arrival on the island is invariably **Nueva Gerona ❶**, which looks a little like a small village in the USA's West at the turn of the 20th century: the older houses are wooden, with spacious, columned verandas, shuttered windows, and carved doors with brass knockers. The similarity is no accident, since many of the town's first pioneers came from the United States in the early 1900s, lured by unscrupulous US land dealers.

It was these midwesterners who planted the island's first citrus groves, which now cover some 25,000 hectares (62,000 acres). Along the river-side road is a wooden bungalow built by a Swedish-American family whose last surviving member lived there for 60 years before finally returning to the US. Her parents, like hundreds of other Americans, believed the island would soon become another state in the Union by vote of the US Congress.

Isla de la Juventud

They built houses and planted orchards in places they named McKinley, Columbia, Westport, and San Francisco Heights. They spoke English, worshiped a Protestant God, and when they died they were buried in the **Cementerio Americano**, which is maintained today as a historical site. The starkly simple headstones – most of them dating from between 1905 and 1925 – contrast sharply with the more flamboyant mausoleums, statues, and vaults that decorate the **Cementerio Católico** in town.

Cayman and Jamaican islanders added their Caribbean English to that of the Americans in those early years, while a size able group of Japanese settled as farmers. This mix, together with Spanish merchants, Chinese storekeepers, and Cuban landowners, provided a lively diversity in island life.

Getting around the town

Today, downtown Nueva Gerona consists of an eight-block grid, so everything is within easy walking distance. This area has stores and eateries (mostly just snack places). There are also a couple of nightspots: La Movida, Calle 34 between 18 and 20, is a popular open-air disco that attracts a young student crowd; and the Disco next to Villa Gaviota hotel, where techno music attracts the younger set after midnight.

Calle 39, the main street of downtown Gerona, also known as Calle Martí, has been radically refurbished with pretty pink tiles and fresh coats of paint on every building. The street runs along one side of **Parque Central** (also called Parque Guerrillero Heróico on some newer maps). The square is located between calles 37 and 39, running north to south, and between calles 28 and 30 running east to west. Elderly residents sit and watch the world go by during the day but it gets livelier at night.

In the square stands the island's oldest church, **Nuestra Señora de los Dolores**, a typical Latin American colonial-style church, which was built in 1929 to replace an older one that blew away in a hurricane. One of the oldest buildings here, dating from 1853, is the former Casa de Gobierno, now the **Museo Municipal** (Calle 30; tel: 46-323-791; Mon–Fri 9am–10pm, Sun 9am–1pm; charge), which houses exhibits of local interest.

At Calle 39, between calles 24 and 26, is Ecotur, the main agency that runs tours of the island (tel: 46-327-101). The staff are very helpful, and all tours to the southern (military) zone *must* be booked through them. A tour guide is compulsory, to get past the military checkpoint. You will need to rent a car to get there, in most cases. Tours are best booked well in advance, as is car rental, as there are only a couple of four-wheel-drive jeeps available (try Havanautos, on the corner of Calle Martí and Calle 32; tel: 46-324-432, or one of the hotels).

The **Academia de Ciencias y Planetario** (Calle 41, corner 46; Tue–Thur 8am–7pm, Fri 2–10pm, Sat 1–5pm, Sun 9am–1pm; charge) covers natural history and archeology, and is worth visiting for the replica of the Punta del

Working in the cane factory in Nueva Gerona.

BELOW: Nuestra Señora de los Dolores in Nueva Gerona.

Este cave paintings if you don't have the time to see the real thing.

On the corner of calles 24 and 45 is the local **Museo de la Lucha Clandestina** (Tue–Sat 9am–5pm, Sun 8am–noon; charge), devoted mainly to the underground campaign in the run-up to the revolution. *El Pinero*, the ferry boat that carried Fidel Castro and his fellow revolutionaries back to the mainland after their release from prison, is now just a rotted hull on the river bank between calles 26 and 28. You may be surprised to see a nearby statue of a cow: it is dedicated to **Ubre Blanca** (White Udder), a local cow who broke world milk-production records.

A prison island

If you travel a few kilometers east of town in Reparto Chacón, on the road to Playa Bibijagua, you can't miss the **Presidio Modelo ❷** (Model Prison). It was built between 1926 and 1932 using the plans from a prison in Joliet, Illinois, to house Cuba's hardest cases – most famously Fidel Castro and other revolutionaries after the failed attack on the Moncada Barracks in 1953.

As political prisoners, Castro and his *compañeros* fared a good deal better than the common inmates. They were housed in the hospital wing, where they studied and imposed their own group discipline without much interference from the prison officials.

The prison was closed in 1967. An impressive **museum** (tel: 46-325-112; Tue–Sat 9am–4.30pm, Sun 9am–1pm; charge), which includes Fidel Castro's (rather comfortable) old cell, recounts the prison's grim past.

Cuba's 19th-century revolutionary hero, José Martí, also spent time imprisoned on the island in 1870, when he was awaiting deportation to Spain for expressing anti-colonial ideas. For a few months between his grueling prison labors and his exile, Martí stayed at the **Finca El Abra** (Tue–Sat 9am–4.30pm, Sun 9am–1pm; charge), a country estate where the Sardá family nurtured him back to relative health. The farm is located 3km (2 miles) west of town just off the road to the Hotel Colony, near marble quarries – the source of material for the floors, facades, and carved objects seen all over the island.

A spa town

La Fé ❸, southeast of the island capital, used to be the market town for the surrounding farmlands, and is far more attractive than Nueva Gerona, with green parks and tree-lined streets. There is a radio station, public library, post office, and telephone company, while ruins just off the square are what is left of an old hotel. In the early 20th century, La Fé was a well-known spa resort: the medicinal springs are located nearby, close to the deteriorating hotel and baths.

Not far from the town center is **La Cotorra** spring, in a perfect little park enclosed by an iron fence with a ceramic parrot (*cotorra*) at the gate. This is the spring that supplies the island's bottled water. Inevitably there are some brilliantly colored parrots, who screech at visitors from their cage perches.

Pirates' Coast

From La Fé and Nueva Gerona, roads lead west to the **Hotel Colony ❹** on **Ensenada de la Siguanea** (Siguanea Sound), completed at the end of 1958, just in time for the rebels to take it over. The bay here is picturesque but too shallow for good swimming – the pool is the best place for that.

Across the bay, though, is **Cabo Francés**, with the spectacular scuba sites of the **Costa de los Piratas**. At more than 50 marked sites, divers can see coral of every shape, size, and color, giant sponges, tropical fish, and crustaceans, underwater caves, tunnels, and rock formations. The site is of particular interest as it contains the sunken remains of a great sea battle between the pirate ships of Thomas Baskerville and the Spanish fleet in the 16th century. And near Punta Francés are three Spanish galleons lying together.

The scuba center at the Hotel El Colony (*see page 355*) provides full-day diving trips, moving from site to site, with lunch aboard. There is an international marina here, too, as well as plenty of opportunities for deep-sea fishing trips.

The south coast of the island, from **Punta Pedernales** in the west to **Punta del Este** in the east, is breathtaking. However, the entire area inland of Cocodrilo and nearby **Caleta**

Playing for guests at the Hotel Colony.

BELOW: bicycles are the usual form of transportation.

Ancient Ciboney
pictographs.

Grande is a military zone and off limits unless you pre-arrange a visit with Ecotur in Nueva Gerona.

This beautiful area is practically uninhabited except for the little town of **Cocodrilo** ❺, settled by English-speaking Cayman islanders at the beginning of the 20th century. Their descendants speak a lilting Caribbean English, though this is beginning to die out as younger generations slowly adopt Spanish. There are numerous magnificent white sand beaches, as yet untouched by tourism and development, but accessible on day trips.

The coast is backed by thick forests of pine and hardwoods. The region is separated from the north by the mosquito-ridden **Ciénaga de Lanier** (Lanier Swamp) and this geographical isolation once made the area a plunderer's paradise, especially for lumbermen who felled trees and shipped logs to all the ports of Cuba and the Caribbean. Reforestation has fortunately been a priority since the early 1960s.

An hour's drive southwest of Nueva Gerona is a **crocodile farm** (daily 9am–5pm; charge) which breeds native crocodiles for release into the wild. The caretakers will give you a tour of the hatchery and breeding pens. Crocodiles are released when they are four or five years old. The Isle of Youth and the Zapata peninsula are the only places in the world where the endangered Cuban crocodile can be found.

Indigenous cave paintings

Punta del Este ❻, in the southeast corner of the island 60km (37 miles) from Nueva Gerona, is beautiful. Except for the ferocious mosquitoes, it is altogether magnificent. It is so far mercifully free of intrusive tourist development, and likely to remain so as long as the restrictions on entering the zone are in place.

Just inland from a sparkling, pristine beach is a series of mysterious **caves** where the indigenous Ciboney inhabitants painted pictographs 3,000 years ago. The caves are one of the most important archeological finds in the Caribbean, first discovered by a shipwrecked French sailor in 1910 and then explored by the Cuban anthropologist Fernando Ortíz in 1922.

The main cave is considered the Ciboneys' Sistine Chapel. It is a single spacious chamber with a fairly low ceiling containing seven natural vaults and more than 235 drawings of circles, arrows, triangles, and serpentine lines. The whole is a great red and black mural which is believed to represent a lunar calendar, including human figures and animals in the world the Ciboney knew and imagined.

Cayo Largo

East of the Isle of Youth, myriad tiny cays lie scattered in a wide arc. Most are uninhabited and inaccessible from the mainland. All have delicious beaches of white powdery sand and magnificent diving amongst the coral and the shipwrecks: the Nueva España treasure fleet that went down in 1563 on the reefs somewhere between Cayo Rosario and Cayo Largo provides just a fraction of the more than 200 known

BELOW:
a crocodile farm
resident.

wrecks in this area. So far, all but one of these dream islands are undeveloped and only accessible by boat. Plans are afoot to develop Cayo Rico, just west of Cayo Largo, but nothing has happened there yet.

The only cay currently geared to tourism is **Cayo Largo**, which has 27km (17 miles) of white beaches, but is no more than 3km (2 miles) wide at any point. The cay is accessible by plane from Havana or Varadero, and day trips are organized by tour agencies in Havana *(see page 369)*.

In 1985, before Cuba plunged into schemes to attract international tourism, the slogan for this pristine island was "Thus it all began." Then came the building boom, the package tours, and the airport disco reception with watery rum cocktails. Even the boat trip to swim and have lunch at lovely **Playa Sirena** has been over-commercialized. An indication of its international tourist status is that Cayo Largo now accepts euros.

Still, Cayo Largo remains popular with travelers looking for sun, sea, and sand, and not much else – anyone interested in Cuba or Cuban people would be better off going elsewhere.

Getting away from it all

There is, however, an escape: from Cayo Largo, you can take day trips to nearby islets that have no tourist installations at all. But you cannot travel between Cayo Largo and Isla de la Juventud by boat or plane, so you won't be able to "island hop" and visit both places on the same trip.

Other accessible places include **Cayo Iguana**, inhabited by hordes of these friendly reptiles (which can also be seen on the main island). **Cayo Rosario**, west of Cayo Largo and almost as large, is a crescent-shaped beach, backed by high sand dunes. It is enclosed by a sandbar that forms a natural lagoon of clear blue water over fine pearly sand, with minuscule pink shells piled in the ridges of the sea bed. The calm water is lovely for swimming. The cay also has a freshwater river. For the time being at least, the only inhabitants are the large iguanas and other, more elusive, wild animals and birds that exist in this sensitive environment. Long may it last. ❑

A family of starfish in shallow waters on the the Cayo Largo shoreline.

BELOW LEFT: ready to sail.

Coral Reef

From the top of the headland above Punta del Este, a long coral reef is visible about 3.5km (2 miles) offshore. Blue waves crash against the coralline wall in a spray of foam that rolls onto the inner lagoon. The calm, nearly transparent water affords a marvelous view of the sea bed – a clean, sandy plain rippling in undulating zigzag crests that look like tiny dunes. At some points, a fine seagrass carpets the sea floor, revealing queen conch shells, with their shiny pink mouths; large king helmuts shaded from dark brown to a lustrous cream; and conical top shells. Starfish adorn the sandy bottom, on which white coral appears in a thicket of gorgonians, with delicate hands and multiple fingers swaying in the water. Snorkelers can explore as far as this, and the experience is wonderful, but full diving gear (and some experience) is needed if you want to swim through the coralline wall into the extraordinary reef garden beyond. It is formed of the most varied green, white, yellow, violet, and pink corals imaginable, all surrounded by an almost transparent liquid mass.

These corals can be found only where the sea is less than 100 meters (330ft) deep and where the temperature never drops below 19°C (68°F), so this is a perfect environment for them. At a deeper level, squirrelfish, hogfish, barracudas, and sharks may also be spotted.

✱ INSIGHT GUIDES   **TRAVEL TIPS**

CUBA

ACCOMMODATIONS

ACTIVITIES

A – Z

LANGUAGE

TRANSPORTATION

GETTING THERE AND GETTING AROUND

By Air

The availability of flights to Cuba and the airlines in service are subject to change and vary according to season, so always check. There are international airports at Havana, Varadero, Holguín, Santiago de Cuba, Ciego de Avila, Cayo Coco, Cayo Largo, Santa Clara, Las Tunas, Manzanillo and Camagüey. *Cubana de Aviación*, the national airline, flies scheduled and charter routes between Cuba and other cities in the Americas and Europe, serving primarily Havana, but also Holguín, Santa Clara, Camagüey, and Santiago de Cuba. Most flights are positively no-frills, but Cubana flights provide the cheapest, quickest, and easiest route into Cuba.

From Europe

Cubana (www.cubana.cu or www.cubajet. com) flies from: London (Gatwick), Paris, Moscow, Madrid, and Rome. Flights from London (twice weekly) usually make a stop in Holguín.
Air France (www.airfrance.com) has scheduled flights to Havana from Paris; there are good connections from other European cities.
Iberia (www.iberia.com) operates scheduled flights from Madrid with connections from London and other European cities.
Virgin (www.virgin-atlantic.com) operates direct flights twice a week from Gatwick to Havana. These are more expensive than those with a stop in Europe. Flight time from London on a direct flight is about 9 hours.
There are various **charter flights**

from Gatwick, Luton, Stansted, Manchester, and other regional airports in the UK to Havana, Varadero, and Holguín. Dutch charter airline **Martinair** (www.martinair.com) flies from Amsterdam to Havana, Varadero, and Holguín, usually booked through package-tour operators.

From Latin America and the Caribbean

Cubana flies to and from: Buenos Aires, São Paulo, Santiago de Chile, Santo Domingo, Mexico City, Cancún, Guatemala City, Caracas, San José, Bogotá, and Lima.
Many Latin American and Caribbean airlines also serve Cuba, with scheduled and charter flights available. **Mexicana** (www.mexicana. com) flies between Mexico City and Havana, and there are also frequent flights from Cancún and Mérida in Yucatán. There are regular connections between Havana and various Central American cities with local airlines (www.grupotaca.com); and **Air Jamaica** (www.airjamaica.com) flies to Havana.

From Canada

Cuba is accessible by air from Montreal and Toronto. **Cubana** runs scheduled flights from Montreal and Toronto, while **Air Canada** (www. aircanada.ca) flies from Toronto to Havana, Varadero, Santa Clara, Holguín, Cayo Coco, and Ciego de Avila. Direct flight time from Montreal to Havana is 4 hours; 3 hours 45 minutes from Toronto. There are also charter flights from Ottawa.

From the US

Travel restrictions remain in force and US citizens are not allowed to fly to

Cuba. However, since 2009, Cuban Americans have been allowed to visit relatives in Cuba regularly and there are direct flights from Los Angeles and Miami to Havana or Cienfuegos (Cuba Travel Services, www.ctcharters. com). Those with their visas (such as accredited journalists, academics, or businessmen) can buy air tickets from **Marazul Tours**, Tower Plaza Mall, 4100 Park Avenue, Weehawken, NJ 07087, tel: 800-223-5334 or visit: www.marazultours. com. There is often a long waiting list on these flights, and US currency restrictions apply.
Americans keen to visit Cuba sometimes travel via Canada, Cancún, Jamaica, or Nassau, although the latter is not recommended as there is a US customs office there which monitors flights arriving from Cuba.
Cuban officials do not stamp travelers' passports; they simply stamp their tourist cards. Visitors from the US are welcome as long as they steer clear of "subversive" activities.

Tourist Cards

Remember to keep your stamped tourist card in a safe place as you will need to surrender it when you leave the country. Visitors may also be required to produce their tourist card, along with their passport, when changing traveler's checks, booking into a *casa particular* or a hotel, if traveling independently.
Photocopies of passports are not acceptable – it has to be the real thing.

Airline Offices

In Havana, international and domestic airline offices, and some tour operators, are mostly located on La Rampa, a stretch of Calle 23 between Calle M and the Malecón, in Vedado.

On Departure

If you do not have a transfer to Havana airport as part of your deal, you should take a taxi. Buses do not go close enough to the airport. Allow at least 45 minutes for the trip from Old Havana to the airport. Be at the airport at least 2 hours before an international flight; security and customs checks can be lengthy.

Airport departure tax for international flights is CUC$25, which *must* be paid after you have checked in, in cash, in *pesos convertibles*. You can exchange foreign currency into CUCs at the airport, but this can be time-consuming and best not left until the last minute.

By Sea

There are over 20 marinas and nautical centers for people traveling on chartered (or private) yachts. There is no ferry service. A few cruise lines stop in Cuba, ships dock in Havana, in Cienfuegos, or in Santiago de Cuba. The US forbids any vessel from calling at a US port if it has previously stopped in Cuba.

GETTING AROUND

Cuba is a long, thin island, about the length of England, and distances between towns can be greater than expected. All transport radiates from the Havana hub. There are road and rail links between Havana and Pinar del Río in the west and Havana and Santiago de Cuba in the east, while many towns are also connected with Havana by air. Both Havana and Santiago de Cuba are ports. Their old, historic centers are by the water, with newer suburbs sprawling in an arc around them, making departure by road from the centre to the airport or *autopista* time-consuming.

From Havana Airport

José Martí International Airport, tel: (07) 649-5666 for international flight information; (07) 266-4133 for domestic flights. Most international flights operate from Terminal 3, where there is a 24-hour tourist information desk (tel: 07-642-6101, but phones

are rarely answered), numerous car-rental desks, bars, restaurants, and an exchange desk. Some charter flights use Terminal 2.

Tourist taxis are always available: the fare is around CUC$25. (The airport is about 18km/11 miles from central Havana.) Drivers from Cubataxi gather at the terminal and hustle for your custom. It is illegal for **unlicensed cabs** to drive tourists to or from the airport, and the police keep an eagle eye out for offenders.

By Air

Flying is the most convenient way to travel for anyone with limited time and a desire to see various corners of the island. Most services originate from Havana. The national airline, **Cubana** (www.cubana.cu), has regular scheduled flights to 13 Cuban cities from the capital. New destinations are being added all the time, so check with your tour operator or with the airline. The addresses of Cubana offices are:
Havana: Calle 23, 64, corner of Infanta, Vedado, tel: (07) 838-1039, 834-4446, and at the airport, Terminal 3, tel: (07) 649-0410.
Baracoa: Calle Martí, 181, tel: (0121) 645-374.
Bayamo: Calle Marti, 58, between Parada and Rojas, tel: (0123) 423-916.
Camagüey: Calle República, 400, corner of Correa, tel: (0132) 291-338, 292-156.
Ciego de Avila: Calle Chicho Valdes (Carretera Central), 83, between Maceo and Honorato Castillo, tel: (0133) 201-117.
Holguín: Edificio Pico de Cristal, Calle Libertad, corner of Martí, 2nd Floor, Policentro, tel: (0124) 468-148 and at the airport, tel: (0124) 468-114.

BELOW: one of the shiny vintage cars.

Public Transportation

Fuel shortages have prompted drastic cuts in inter-urban and inter-provincial public bus services. Many Cuban cities rely on horse-drawn carts that use the same urban routes buses once used to follow. You will also see open-backed trucks, sometimes with a tarpaulin "roof," carrying passengers in many towns.

In Havana, thousands of Chinese-made bicycles have been introduced, but there are many more non-cyclists who wait two hours or more for a bus every day. In some places, it is mandatory for Cuban state-owned cars and trucks to pick up hitchhikers; but the farther you go into the countryside the fewer vehicles you see. Tourists are not obliged to pick up hitchhikers but it is rather churlish not to. What is more, local people often make good company and can be very helpful in giving directions on Cuba's poorly signposted roads.

Santiago de Cuba: Calle Enramada (Saco) 673, corner of San Pedro (Gen Lacret), tel: (0122) 651-570/8.
Varadero: Avenida 1era, corner of Calle 55, tel: (0145) 611-823.

Aerocaribbean and **Aerogaviota** operate charter flights to Cayo Largo, Cayo Coco, Cayo Santa María, and other popular destinations.

Aerocaribbean: Calle 23, 64, corner of Calle P, Vedado, Havana, tel: (07) 879-7524, 870-4965.

Aerogaviota: at the airport, tel: (07) 203-0686, 203-0668.

For most visitors, especially those who do not speak Spanish, it is better

Puncture Repairs

The nearest petrol station may be able to help if you have a flat tire. Otherwise, ask around for the local *ponchera*. Since self-employment was legalized, many Cubans have set up puncture-repair workshops. Most of these deal mainly with bicycle tires, but many can handle car inner tubes.

to purchase tickets for domestic flights from a hotel reception desk or a recognised travel agency *(see page 369)*. They do not charge commission for making the airline booking.

By Bus

City buses, known as **guaguas**, are crowded and uncomfortable, but they are cheap and traveling on them does help immerse you in local life (take care of your valuables). They are motorized in Havana and Santiago de Cuba, but in many cities they are horse-drawn and foreigners are not encouraged to use them. A hop-on, hop-off bus service for tourists is in operation in Havana, called the HabanaBusTour, cuc$5 per day, with two routes, one from the Plaza de Armas to Vedado and the other out to Playas del Este via the Castillo del Morro. A similar service runs from Varadero to Matanzas.

Long-distance buses are a good, and relatively inexpensive, way of getting around the island.

Víazul is a recommended cuc-only bus service offering fast, comfortable, air-conditioned vehicles, with toilets, and plenty of luggage capacity, that operate between the major centers. From Havana to Santiago there are four buses a day, but the best one is the **express**, the overnight service that leaves Havana at 6.15pm, as it takes just over 12 hours, and stops only once, in Camagüey. The other services take just under 16 hours (although that is still usually faster than the train).The cost is the same whether you take the express or not: currently cuc$51 single. There are four Víazul buses a day from Havana to Varadero (3 hours), one a day to Viñales (3 ½ hours), and two a day to Trinidad (just under 6 hours), as well as many other destinations, including a direct service from Varadero to Trinidad, and from Santiago to Baracoa. Be sure to wear something warm as the air conditioning is fierce.

The Víazul station is by the city zoo on Avenida 26 and Zoológico,

Nuevo Vedado, tel: (07) 881-1413, www.viazul.cu.

Provincial offices are at:
Varadero: Calle 36 and Autopista Varadero, tel: (045) 614-886.
Viñales: Salvador Cisneros, 63, tel: (08) 793-195.
Trinidad: entrance on Gustavo Izquierdo on the corner with Piro Guinart; tel: (041) 994-448.
Santiago: Avenida Libertadores, 457, tel: (0122) 628-484.
Camagüey: Carretera Central s/n, corner Perú, tel: (032) 270-396.

At busy times of year, and on popular routes, reserve your ticket in advance, at bus terminals, at the desk at Havana airport, through a **Cubatur** office (in most towns) or, in Havana, through the **Infotur** office at Calle Obispo 524. Online reservations are 8 percent more expensive.

You pay a deposit and receive a voucher, which you exchange for a ticket at the bus station. You still have to turn up about 45 minutes in advance, but it's safer than lining up for a ticket without a reservation.

There are also long-distance bus services run by **Astro** (Terminal de Omnibus Nacional, Avenida de la Independencia and 19 de Mayo, near the Plaza de la Revolución, tel: 07-870-3397), but these are reserved for Cubans only.

Tour Buses

Hotels can book reasonably priced excursions to a wide range of destinations on modern, comfortable, air-conditioned buses. Tourist agencies will also book tours; contact: Cubanacán, Cubatur, and Havanatur *(see Tour Agencies, page 369)*.

By Train

The Cuban railroad was the first in Latin America, but it may be the last in efficiency and comfort today. Trains are crowded and services have been reduced – almost all are now locals that stop at every station. All are achingly slow and prone to breakdown. Little or no food or water is to be had, so take provisions with you, and a flashlight and toilet paper.

Seats on Cuban trains are always booked well in advance with long waiting lists, but there are always seats reserved for those paying in cucs. For peace of mind, you should book your ticket a day in advance, and arrive at least an hour before departure to check in, and before 7pm if taking a night train: unassigned seats will be re-allocated to those on the waiting list if you have

not confirmed that you are traveling.

In Havana buy your tickets in advance at LADIS (Ferrocuba) office on Arsenal and Aponte, open daily 8am–8pm, tel: (07) 860-3161. You must pay in cash, in cucs, and bring your passport. Trains leave from the Estación Central de Ferrocarril, on Egido (Avenida de Bélgica) corner Arsenal, tel: (07) 861-1920.

At many provincial Ferrocuba offices (in the stations) staff are not accustomed to dealing with foreigners and take the same unhelpful (or downright rude) attitude they inflict on fellow Cubans. They are also unlikely to speak English. Persist if you are told that there are no seats: it is unlikely that this is the case.

From Havana the train to Santiago de Cuba leaves every other day, theoretically at 3.15pm, cuc$30, taking at least 15 hours, usually many more. In summer an extra train, the *especial*, is also laid on.

Fly/Drive

There are several fly/drive options from airports in Havana, Varadero, Camagüey, Holguín, and Santiago. It is convenient because negotiations have been done in advance and your car is waiting when you arrive.

Driving

Renting a car gives the greatest degree of independence, and allows you to reach corners of the island that otherwise would be hard to get to. Highways and secondary roads are fairly well maintained, except for the potholes. Otherwise, driving is safe and Cubans are helpful with directions – though often vague when it comes to distances. There are very few road signs; a good map is essential; or be prepared to pick up hitchhikers who can direct you. Do not drive after dark; Cubans often drive with headlights on full beam and animals may wander onto the road. Away from cities, traffic congestion isn't a problem: you may travel miles without seeing another vehicle – even stretches of the *autopista* can be empty. In towns, traffic usually moves at the speed of bicycles and horses.

Car Rental

Current rental charges range between cuc$45 and cuc$100 per day, depending on the vehicle, plus a deposit of cuc$200–300. The fee and deposit must be paid in advance (cash, non-US credit card, or traveler's checks). Unlimited milage is included but insurance and fuel are extra. The tank should be full when you start (check that it is – it's a common scam for staff to underfill it) and you must return the car empty – there are no refunds.

There are two grades of insurance: Grade A at around cuc$12 a day covers theft only, Grade B at cuc$15 a day covers all risks except loss of radio and spare tire. Additional drivers are charged at a flat fee of cuc$12–15 each, or cuc$3–5 per day.

Check the car carefully for damage and scratches. Draw attention to anything you find, and insist any damages are noted on the paperwork. Car-rental agents have all kinds of ruses for not returning the full deposit. Be sure to take out the maximum insurance cover possible; it is well worth the extra cost, in case of even minor scrapes or mishaps.

If you are involved in an accident or have something stolen from the car, report this to the police and be sure to get the right paperwork (denuncia) or you will not be able to claim insurance in Cuba or at home. The business at the police station will be time-consuming and may take many hours.

Cars can be rented through the desks of the major hotels in the cities and beach resorts. The main rental companies are Rex (www.rexcarrental.com), Cubacar (www.transtur.cu), Vía Rent-a-Car (www.gaviota-grupo.com), Transtur (www.transtur.cu), and Havanautos (www.havanautos.cu). They are all state-owned and there is little competition. They also rent cars with drivers. Other websites to try include www.havanacarhire.com and www.carrentalcuba.com.

Gas (Petrol)

Buying gas used to be a nightmare. It still is for most ordinary Cubans who have no access to cucs. Tourists and anyone else with convertible currency, however, can now make use of the **Cupet** gas stations, which you will find in all the main towns and, increasingly, in smaller provincial towns all over the island. Cupet stations normally offer minimal mechanical backup, as well as snack bars. Most are open 24 hours.

Private Cars & Taxis

You may prefer to let someone else do the driving. One way Cubans are making cucs now is by driving visitors around (though the many crackdowns have hit unlicensed drivers hard). Some charge a flat rate for a half or

whole day of sightseeing or for a particular excursion, for example from Havana to Varadero or Havana to Viñales and back. The price should be less than the cost of an organized tour with a state agency if two or more of you are traveling together. Always agree a price before you set off.

It is possible to organize a car and driver for a week – as long as you pay for all their food and lodging.

It will not always be apparent, but some private taxis are licensed and some are not – depending on whether the driver pays the hefty license fee-cum-tax imposed by the government. As you walk around the streets of Havana and other towns and cities you will constantly be asked if you want a taxi – most of these will be private operators, legal or illegal.

It is supposedly illegal for private taxis – legal or illegal – to ferry passengers to any airport or to Varadero, the Playas del Este, or any other tourist resort. A Cuban caught doing this will be heavily fined and may lose his license – even his car, if it's not a first offense. Hence, some "street" taxis will now refuse to take you to these destinations.

Note that if you find a private driver willing to take the risk, and are stopped by the police, you too could end up spending several hours at a police station while the paperwork is done – though it will be the Cuban who suffers in the end.

There is only one state taxi company: Cubataxi, tel: (07) 855-5555 in Havana, although the cars vary as there used to be several different companies and their logos still exist. You can call them or pick them up from designated ranks (usually outside hotels, and major

museums). They are usually cheap, friendly, reliable, and metered (starting at cuc$1, then up to cuc$1 per kilometer, depending on the car). **GranCar** tel: (07) 881-0992, operates a taxi service in the shiny old vintage cars that all visitors appear to love, at cuc$25–30 per hour.

Coco-taxis

These are the little round, yellow, two-seater motorbike taxis that are fine (and fun) for short distances. They charge a minimum of cuc$3, and cuc$5–10 per hour.

Bici-taxis

These little rickshaw-type vehicles, drawn by bicycles, can be fun and are inexpensive – but agree a fare before you start, usually cuc$1–2 in town centers. They are not really supposed to take tourists, but they do, especially outside Havana.

Horse Carriages

In provincial towns horse-drawn wagons (called coches) provide an inexpensive bus service, and are widely used by local people. In tourist areas, such as Havana or Varadero, more luxurious carriages are available for sightseeing tours.

Cycling

Cycling is the way many Cubans get around, and you will have no trouble finding someone to mend a flat tire (see box page 338). There are cycle lanes on many roads outside towns. Bring a strong lock, and be careful where you park, or you may find yourself going home without your bicycle. Don't cycle in the middle of the day when the sun is at its height, nor after dark as roads are poorly lit and you may hit a cow.

BELOW: one of the best-known rental agencies.

A CCOMMODATIONS

HOTELS AND CASAS PARTICULARES

Looking for a Hotel

Many of Cuba's tourist lodgings have been, or are in the process of being, upgraded – and so are their prices. Foreign tour operators and hotel chains pay about half the listed price for groups of 15 or more, giving them space for the attractive packages of which the vast majority of tourists take advantage. Price categories given here reflect the rack rate an independent traveler will pay for a room. Low-season prices can be considerably lower than those provided here.

Tourist hotels are run by a variety of enterprises, and it is possible to ascertain the standard of the hotel from the name of the enterprise that manages it. For example, hotels run by **Islazul** tend to be two-star or three-star, while those run by **Gran Caribe** or **Cubanacán** are often four-star. In Old Havana there are many delightful boutique hotels in renovated mansions run by Habaguanex. They

Cuban Addresses

A few points on understanding addresses. An address written as Calle Martí 65, esq. Céspedes means it is at 65 Martí Street on the corner of (or intersection with) Céspedes Street. Similarly, Calle Martí 65, entre 9 y 11 means it is at 65 Martí Street between streets 9 and 11. You will also see Avenida 1ra or Avenida 5ta, which mean 1st Avenue or 5th Avenue. Piso 1º or Primer Piso means first floor. We use the anglicized form in our listings, but you will encounter the Spanish form in written material.

come in a variety of sizes, ages, and prices, but all one high standard with helpful, efficient staff and can be booked online at www.habaguanexhotels.com, where you often find good deals. In the resorts, there are joint-venture hotels run by foreign companies, such as **Sol Meliá** (from Spain), whose rooms may be booked from the UK, tel: 0808-234 1953. Most rooms have private bathrooms, but even three-star hotels may occasionally lack hot water. You can expect air conditioning, but in a two-star place you may just get a fan (ventilador).

Campsites

Campsites operated by **Campismo Popular** are in every province. Campers sleep in huts (cabañas) not tents. Group showers and latrines prevail. Most sites are designed for Cuban tourists, and open only in July and August but a few are used for international tourism and open all year round. They have better amenities, such as flush toilets and hot water. International sites include **Campismo Los Cocos**, near Havana, and **Villa Santo Domingo** in the Sierra Maestra, in Granma province.

Reservations can be made with **Cubatur** on arrival (see page 370) or, better, booked from abroad through a specialist tour operator.

Private Rooms
(Casas Particulares)

Renting rooms in private houses has been legal since 1996, but they must be registered with the authorities and are subject to strict regulations. There are illegal, unregistered casas particulares, but these can be unsafe.

Commissions and Scams

The owners of casas particulares can book rooms for you in other towns, passing you along a network of contacts. This is a reliable service but you will pay an extra cuc$5 per night more than you would pay if you booked independently. Any taxi driver or tout taking you to a casa will receive a cuc$5 commission, too. If you have made a reservation by phone your host will probably meet you at the bus terminal. Don't be taken in by touts trying to divert you to other houses in order to get a commission.

● Casas particulares should display a blue sign, shaped rather like an anchor, on or above the front door.
● It is illegal for a Cuban to rent an entire apartment – but people do.
● It is illegal to rent more than two rooms – but people do.
● It is illegal to let unless you register with the government and pay hefty taxes – but people do.
● Cuban hosts must fill out a form with visitors' details, and present it to the police. You can now put a legally registered casa on your tourist card as your official place of residence.

There are thousands of casas particulares in Havana and hundreds in provincial towns, especially Santiago, Trinidad, Viñales, and Baracoa. Try the internet: some have their own websites. One useful site is www.casaparticularcuba.org. The best way to find a casa is by recommendation from a fellow traveler.

ACCOMMODATIONS LISTINGS

OLD HAVANA

Beltran de Santa Cruz
Calle San Ignacio, 411, between Muralla and Sol
Tel: (7) 860-8330
www.habaguanexhotels.com
A lovely 18th-century former mansion, with beamed ceilings, stained glass, and blue-painted balconies. Eleven air-conditioned rooms overlook the courtyard and service is friendly and helpful. Only breakfast is available but there are lots of restaurants in the area. **$–$$**

Hostal Conde de Villanueva
Calle Mercaderes, 202, between Lamparilla and Amargura
Tel: (7) 862-9293
www.habaguanexhotels.com
In the heart of Old Havana this is a specialist cigar-smokers' hotel (there's a giant model cigar in the lobby and rooms are named after tobacco plantations but there are three non-smokers' rooms as well). Small and atmospheric, with a beautiful colonial patio. It has its own cigar bar and Cuban restaurant. **$$$**

Hostal del Tejadillo
Calle Tejadillo, 12, corner of San Ignacio
Tel: (7) 863-7283
www.habaguanexhotels.com
Thirty-two rooms are set around two plant-filled courtyards. There's an air-conditioned restaurant and bar, plus babysitting, and laundry facilities. Rooms, with lofty ceilings, all have minibars, safes, telephones, cable TV, and fans (there's no air conditioning), while some have kitchenettes. **$–$$**

Hotel el Comendador
Calle Obrapía, corner of Baratillo
Tel: (7) 867-1037
www.habaguanexhotels.com
Small, attractively restored 18th-century house in the heart of Old Havana with harbor views, reopened end

of 2010 after further renovation works. Quiet, with attractive air-conditioned rooms (with hairdryers) and a tapas bar on the ground floor. **$$**

Hotel Florida
Calle Obispo, 252, corner of Calle Cuba
Tel: (7) 862-4127
www.habaguanexhotels.com
Bang in the heart of Old Havana, this 19th-century building surrounds a lovely courtyard with marble floors and pillars. There is an elegant restaurant and a piano bar. Rooms have high ceilings, air conditioning, minibar, 24-hour room service, safe, and satellite TV. **$$$**

Hostal Los Frailes
Calle Teniente Rey, 8, between Oficios and Mercaderes
Tel: (7) 862-9383
www.habaguanexhotels.com
A small, attractive colonial building recently converted to an hotel in the center of Old Havana, with the gimmick of having its bellboys dress up in monks' habits. It has 22 comfortable rooms overlooking the courtyard with air conditioning and private bathrooms but no windows. Four suites with balconies look out on to the street and do have windows. **$$–$$$**

Hotel Inglaterra
Parque Central (Prado, 416), between San Rafael and San Miguel
Tel: (7) 860-8595/96/97
www.hotelinglaterra-cuba.com
Built in 1875, this historic hotel has entertained a long list of celebrities and is a national monument. A cool, gold and white lobby, a lovely 24-hour café-bar, with live music from the grand piano or a (rather deafening) mariachi band. The restaurant next door is beautiful, gently lit by chandeliers and stained

glass, but the food doesn't live up to the decor. The small rooftop bar holds a salsa cabaret every night except Tuesday. The interior rooms tend to be rather stuffy but quiet, while those with balconies looking out over the Parque Central or the Gran Teatro, next door, are light but noisy. **$$**

Mercure Sevilla
Trocadero, 55, corner of Prado
Tel: (7) 860-8560
www.accorhotels.com
The renovated Sevilla opened in 1908 and was hugely popular with the American Mafia in the 1930s. Now operated by the French hotel chain, it has a wonderfully Spanish ambiance, with a cool, tiled lobby and delightful blue-tiled patio café complete with fountain. The ninth-floor restaurant, in what used to be the ballroom, has huge windows thrown open to catch the breeze and spectacular night-time views – and the food is now very good. **$$**

NH Parque Central
Calle Neptuno, between Zulueta and Prado (Paseo de Martí)
Tel: (7) 860-6627
www.hotelnhparquecentral.com
A business hotel of international standard with efficient air conditioning, excellent bathrooms, good service, and a business centre. There is even Wi-fi in the lobby. It has a rooftop pool, a jacuzzi with sterling views, a gym, and numerous bars, cafés, and restaurants. The food is good in the extremely formal ground-floor restaurant. **$$$**

Hotel Plaza
Agramonte, 267, Parque Central
Tel: (7) 860-8583
www.hotelplazacuba.com
Favored by European tour groups, the Plaza has a grand columned lobby, while the café-bar on the ground

floor has a fountain, and is full of parrots and palms. Three rather mediocre and over-priced restaurants, but breakfast on the roof terrace is undeniably pleasant. Rooms are on the poky side, but all have delicate stained-glass windows and tasteful prints. **$–$$**

Hotel Raquel
Calle Amargura 103, corner of San Ignacio
Tel: (7) 860-8280
www.habaguanexhotels.com
In a beautifully restored Art Nouveau building, with a gorgeous lobby full of marble, stunning stained glass, and Jewish decorative symbols, and a delightful roof terrace with views over Old Havana, the Raquel is a real treat. There's a little gym and sauna, too, and the only kosher restaurant in Havana. Fourteen of the 21 rooms have views, while all the mini-suites have balconies. **$$**

Hotel Santa Isabel
Calle Baratillo, 9, between Obispo and Narciso López, Plaza de Armas
Tel: (7) 860-8201
www.hotelsantaisabel.com
A beautiful, renovated colonial palace, in the heart of Old Havana. A vision in turquoise and stone with a lovely courtyard. Five-star, popular with package tours.

ACCOMMODATIONS

ACTIVITIES

A – Z

LANGUAGE

The best rooms are on the third floor with balconies overlooking the Plaza, while the café is also good for people-watching. Excellent restaurant. One of the nicest hotels in the city. **$$$–$$$**

Hotel Saratoga
Prado, 603, corner of Dragones
Tel: (7) 868-1000
www.habaguanexhotels.com
A renovated neoclassical building opposite the Capitolio; all modern facilities and Wi-fi in communal areas. Rooms and service are of a high standard. There's a rooftop pool and terrace with a great view over the Capitolio and along the Malecón to Vedado and a good tapas restaurant. **$$$**

Telégrafo
Prado, 408, corner Neptuno
Tel: (7) 861-1010
www.habaguanexhotels.com
This hotel first opened in 1860, but moved to this location in 1888 with only one floor. It closed for rebuilding and expansion in the 1990s and reopened in its present, modernized form in 2001. Very smart and efficient, the decor mingles the old with the new, with a state-of-the-art restaurant set amid the bare brick arches of the original building. **$$$**

Hostal Valencia
Calle Oficios, 53, corner of Obrapía
Tel: (7) 867-1037
www.habanaguanexhotels.com
Just 10 rooms around a glorious vine-draped courtyard in a beautifully restored colonial mansion. Rather noisy in the morning, but the rooms are delightful, with original colonial features. Staff are very friendly. Usually booked well in advance. **$–$$**

Casas Particulares

Most *casas particulares* in Havana charge about CUC$25–35 per room per night. Breakfast is usually extra (typically CUC$3–5 per person) and is usually large and very good – fresh fruit, fruit juice, coffee, and eggs any way you want them.

Casa Humberto
Compostela, 661, between Luz and Sol
Tel: (7) 860-3264
Two large air-conditioned rooms with private bathrooms, and breakfast served on a shady plant-filled terrace outside your door. One tiny double room on the roof, where there's a huge terrace, with hammocks, for all guests' use. Run by a pleasant young couple, Humberto and Miladys.

Casa Maritza
Luz, 115, between San Ignacio and Inquisidor
Tel: (7) 862-3303
One double room in a beautiful colonial house near the harbor, with an internal patio. Private bathroom.

Eugenio Barral
San Ignacio, 656, between Jesús María and Merced
Tel: (7) 862-9877
Quiet, clean and friendly, with antique-furnished rooms overlooking an interior courtyard. Excellent breakfasts served in an ornate dining room.

Evora Rodríguez
Prado, 20, between San Lázaro and Cárcel
Tel: (7) 861-7932
E-mail: evorahabana@yahoo.com
Stunning apartment on ninth floor with views over the fortresses at the mouth of the harbor and up the Paseo del Prado. Huge rooms of hotel standard with spacious bathrooms; the living area is crammed with plants and there are large windows and balconies making it light and airy. English spoken.

Federico Llanes
Cárcel, 156, between San Lázaro and Prado, 3rd floor
Tel: (7) 861-7817
E-mail: fllanes@gmail.com
Good sized rooms with tiled

floors and air conditioning, new bathroom fittings, lots of hot water, and nice touches you don't always find, such as a wall safe, CD player, phone, and desk as well as lots of hanging space for clothes. English spoken.

Fefita y Luís
Prado, 20, 5th floor, apt B, between San Lázaro and Cárcel
Tel: (7) 867-6433
Two rooms. It's centrally located, and the owners, the food, the views of Old Havana, and the comfortable beds are all wonderful.

Juan y Margarita
Obispo, 522, between Bernaz and Villegas
Tel: (7) 867-9592
A light, two-bedroomed apartment with bathroom. No kitchen but the living/dining room has a fridge and television. Extremely central.

Rafaela y Pepe – Los Balcones
San Ignacio, 454, between Sol and Santa Clara
Tel: (7) 867-5551
Two comfortable air-conditioned rooms, with balconies, share a bathroom in this friendly house full of antiques, plants, and bric-a-brac. The owners are the parents of Eugenio Barral *(see above)*.

CENTRO HABANA AND VEDADO

Hotel Deauville
Calle Galiano and Malecón, Central Havana
Tel: (7) 866-8812
www.hotetur.com
Long used by tour groups, the Deauville has been refurbished although it still looks a bit grim from the outside. Rooms are comfortable but TVs, lamps, showers, etc. tend not to work. There is, however, a pleasant rooftop pool and breakfast is good. Not the nicest part of Havana, but within walking distance of Old Havana, and right on the Malecón. **$$**

Hotel Habana Libre
Calle L, between 23 and 25, Vedado
Tel: (7) 834-6100
www.solmelia.com
A time capsule of 1950s design for decades, the Habana Libre is – after a US$20-million refurbishment – just another high-rise modern hotel. It is, however, far more pleasant and comfortable than before. Rooms are spacious and comfortable. The higher you go, the more expensive because of the views. The hotel has a pool, several decent bars (including the

rooftop Bar Turquino) and restaurants, a bank, and a range of shops. **$$$**

Hotel Habana Riviera
Paseo and Malecón, Vedado
Tel: (7) 836-4051
www.habanarivierahotel.cu
Built by Mafia boss Meyer Lansky in 1957, it is rather overshadowed by the Meliá Cohiba next door. However, it has an excellent swimming pool, complete with original diving platform, and rooms with sea views. The lobby retains a 1950s appearance and atmosphere, and there's the lively Copa Room cabaret. Good value. **$$**

Hotel Meliá Cohiba
Paseo and Primera, Vedado
Tel: (7) 833-3636
www.solmelia.com
Cuba's first five-star hotel, opened in 1995, on the seafront. It's not pretty, in architectural terms, but it is luxurious, the service is excellent, and most of its 460 rooms have sea views.

Above: Hotel Nacional, Havana.

Filled to bursting with restaurants, cafés, bars, nightclubs, and shops, as well as a gym, a business center and, of course, a swimming pool. Some rooms are equipped for visitors with disabilities. **$$$**

Hotel Nacional
Calle 0 and 21, Vedado
Tel: (7) 836-3564–67
www.hotelnacionaldecuba.com
Once Havana's top hotel, and still pretty classy. The rich and famous of the city's golden age in the 1940s and 1950s used to stay here – you can see their pictures in the corridors and the Bar of Fame. The neoclassical building is undeniably elegant. There are beautiful tropical

gardens, tennis courts, and two pools – can be used by non-guests (CUC$15, but you get CUC$15-worth of food and drink included). There are lovely views along the Malecón, and the Cabaret Parisien is the next best thing to the Tropicana, and cheaper too. **$$$**

Hotel Presidente
Calzada, 110, and Avenida de los Presidentes, Vedado
Tel: (7) 838-1801
www.hotelesc.com
Built in the 1920s and one of the first high-rise buildings, the hotel has an impressive marble-floored lobby, filled with antiques. About half the 158 rooms have sea views; some rooms are rather small. The pool is beloved by *jineteras*

(hustlers) and the music tends to be loud. **$$**

Hotel St John's
Calle 0, 206 between 23 and 25, Vedado
Tel: (7) 833-3740
www.gran-caribe.com
Budget hotel with intermittent hot water and noisy air con, but it is well-located for Vedado nightlife, a stone's throw from the Malecón. Some of the rooms have sea views, the higher the better. There's a small rooftop pool and nightclub with cabaret act. **$$**

Hotel Victoria
Calle 19, 101, corner of M, Vedado
Tel: (7) 833-3510,
www.hotelvictoriacuba.com
A quiet, unassuming, classically elegant hotel in a good position, but with only

31 rooms, the Victoria is usually booked up. The restaurant is average, favoring seafood. There is a small pool, a business center, and a bar that serves excellent coffee. **$$-$**

Casas Particulares

Armando Gutiérrez
Calle 21, 62, Apt 7, between M and N
Vedado
Tel: (7) 832-1876
email: abelcodina@yahoo.es
A comfortable and spacious air-conditioned room in an apartment on the fourth floor (there is an elevator) with private bath, a terrace with great views, and friendly owners who speak English and French.

Melba and Alberto
Galiano 115, Apt 81, between Animas and Trocadero, Centro
Tel: (7) 863-5178
mobile 0526-48262
Email: barracuda1752@yahoo.es
The entrance off the street is not obvious and rather unwelcoming but once you go up in the elevator to the eighth floor you are in a comfortable home with great views over Havana from the balconies. There are two rooms, one has its own balcony. You can use the kitchenette, which is useful for snacks, but Melba serves tasty, filling meals.

AROUND HAVANA

Miramar

Hotel Comodoro
Calle 84 and 3ra, Playa
Tel: (7) 204-5551
www.hotelescubanacan.com
A resort complex that caters for all-inclusive vacations as well as business travelers. There are rooms and bungalows, all airy and pleasant. Excellent swimming pool, and small private beach. Transfers three times a day to Old Havana. **$$**

Hotel Meliá Habana
Avenida 3ra, between 76 and 80, Miramar

Tel: (7) 204-8500
www.solmelia.com
This is a large modern hotel of international standard (409 rooms, including a number of suites) offering smooth service and all-round excellence. Rooms with ocean views, five restaurants, three swimming pools, private beach, and a business center (Wi-fi throughout the hotel). **$$$**

Chateau Miramar
Calle 1era, between calles 60 and 70, Miramar
Tel: (7) 204-1953
www.hotelescubanacan.com

Small by Miramar standards – 50 rooms and suites on the seafront, designed for the business traveler with internet access, and close to all the embassies and the commercial heart of the city. **$$**

Playas del Este

There are numerous concrete block hotels here, of which the following are only a selection; all of them are adequate, but none is outstanding.

Hotel Atlántico
Avenida de las Terrazas, corner of

Calle 11, Santa María del Mar

PRICE CATEGORIES

Price categories indicate the cost of a double room in high season:
$ = under $80
$$ = $80–150
$$$ = $150–250

Tel: (7) 797-1085–7
www.hotelesc.com
Bright and airy hotel on the beach with 92 air-conditioned rooms. There are two pools and excellent sporting facilities. The all-inclusive meals are plentiful but can soon get boring. **$$$**

Hotel Miramar
Avenida 7B, 47614, between 476 and 478, Guanabo
Tel: (7) 796-2507–9
Twenty-four modest but pleasant rooms, some interconnect for family use, the nicest are on the third floor, with balconies that face the sea. **$**

Villa Los Pinos
Avenida de Las Terrazas, 21, between 4 and 5, Playa El Mégano, Santa María del Mar
Tel: (7) 797-1361
www.gran-caribe.com
Another good choice, offering privacy in two-, three-and four-bedroom villas built in pre-revolutionary times. Most have their own pools, and there are tennis courts on-site. **$$–$$$**

Casas Particulares

Iriana Suárez and Rosa Machado
Avenida 1ra, 50017, between 500 and 504, Guanabo
Tel: (7) 796-3959
Delightful seafront setting with a lawn running down to a seawall, and sun loungers on a balcony affording a wonderful view. Light and bright, the room has independent access, and a living area with a kitchenette. Minimum stay of seven nights in January–February. There are other *casas particulares* in tis area, several also on the waterfront or a short walk away. Prices rise the closer you get to the sea.

VIÑALES AND THE WEST

Cabo San Antonio

Villa Cabo de San Antonio Playa Las Tumbas
Tel: (48) 778-131 ext 204
www.gaviota-grupo.com
Simple lodging in a small new hotel on an isolated beach 4km/2.5 miles from a marina, where you can arrange fishing or scuba diving. Extremely quiet and peaceful although mosquitoes can be a problem at times. Car and bicycle hire. **$–$$**

Cayo Levisa

Hotel Cayo Levisa
Tel: (48) 756-501
www.hotelescubanacan.com
A resort and diving center, and the only facility on the cay, with rustic, but air-conditioned, cabins with porches, gathered beside the beach. Water sports are available, and there is a bar, a good "international" and seafood restaurant; massage facilities. **$$**

Las Terrazas

Hotel Moka
Complejo Turístico Las Terrazas, Autopista Habana–Pinar del Río, Km 51 (take this turn, then it's 8km/5 miles farther on)
Tel: (48) 578-600
www.hotelmoka-lasterrazas.com
A beautiful hotel in Spanish-Cuban style in this purpose-built eco-complex. Forest trees pierce its split levels and patios. There are light, airy rooms in the main hotel, little cabins by the lake, and a few simple rooms in wooden huts in Baños de San Juan 3km (2 miles) from the main hotel. Swim in the waterfall-fed pool, hire a bicycle, swing down a zip line across the lake into the trees, or spend time in the nearby artists' colony. **$**

María La Gorda

María La Gorda
Tel: (48) 778-131
www.gaviota-grupo.com
A wonderful, small-scale resort popular with divers, in the far-western region of Cuba. It's a peaceful and isolated place, set amid semi-deciduous woodland. Some rooms are in cabins directly on the beach, the newer ones are behind in the trees, but guests using these sometimes suffer from mosquitoes. Diving and meals can be included in packages; there is nothing else available here so you have to eat either in the restaurant, at the buffet, or have sandwiches in the bar. **$–$$**

Pinar del Río City

Islazul Vueltabajo
Calle José Martí, 103, corner Rafael Morales
Tel: (48) 759-381
www.islazul.cu
A town-center hotel with 39 pleasant, air-conditioned rooms in a pastel-pink colonial mansion. Ask for a room away from the street, which is noisy. The food is nothing special and overpriced and there may be some hassling in the bar with people trying to sell cigars. Services include car rental, currency exchange, a tourism bureau, and excursions. **$**

Hotel Pinar del Río
Calle Martí Final and Autopista, at the eastern entrance to the town
Tel: (48) 755-070
www.islazul.cu
Renovated in 2009, this hotel is of the concrete block variety offering a range of services such as car hire, drug store, and conference facilities. A convenient stopover but not a relaxing getaway. The pool is popular with local people and can be noisy on weekends. **$**

Soroa

Villa Soroa
Carretera de Soroa, Km 8, northwest of Candelaria
Tel: (48) 523-534
www.hotelescubanacan.com
Forty-nine pleasant cabins and 10 villas (*casitas*) with good facilities in stunning landscaped gardens, plus a large pool. The houses are well equipped with everything from kitchens to VCRs or DVD players. There are five bars and three restaurants, one poor, one

mediocre – the hilltop Castillo de Las Nubes – and one good (serving *paladar*-style food). Hiking round the local sights is organized. If you want to visit and swim but don't want to stay, it's only an hour's drive from Havana, and makes a pleasant daytime excursion (there are lockers for storing clothes). **$**

Viñales

Hotel La Ermita
Carretera la Ermita, Viñales, Km 2
Tel: (48) 796-250
www.hotelescubanacan.com
Just above the town of Viñales, nicely situated at the edge of the valley. La Ermita is a modern hotel of Spanish colonial design with 62 rooms ranged around a good-sized swimming pool. Balcony rooms are the nicest, but there are great views from almost all rooms, especially lovely at dawn and sunset. Decent restaurant, and a good barbecue restaurant by the pool. Tennis court. Non-guests can use the pool for a small charge, and it can get noisy. **$**

Hotel Los Jazmines

Carretera Viñales, Km 25
Tel: (48) 796-210
www.hotelescubanacan.com
Los Jazmines is a handsome, colonial-style hotel in a magnificent setting at the top of a hill above the town, with the Viñales valley unfolding beneath. There are vine-draped gardens, a large, deep swimming pool, periodic pool-side cabaret, a children's playground, and recreation hall. There are 62 rooms in the main building and 16 cabin-style rooms in an annex – most with balconies, and offering gorgeous views. Horseback riding and other excursions are available. **$**

Casas Particulares

Soroa

Hospedaje Estudio de Arte
Km 8.5 on the road past Villa Soroa
Soroa

Email: infosoroa@hvs.co.cu
This *casa particular* is attached to an art studio and paintings are all around the house. The room is spacious and the food is excellent, typical *comida criolla*.

Viñales

There are more than 280 *casas particulares* in this little town. Most of them offer excellent food. If you get one on the south side of the main street, Calle Salvador Cisneros (left side, coming from Pinar del Río), you get great views of the *mogotes*.
Casa El Cafetal
Calle Adela Azcuy Norte Final, s/n
Tel: 01522-39175
A pretty house set in lush gardens producing fruit and coffee. Señora Marta Martínez is an agreeable hostess.
Villa Ernesto
Calle Salvador Cisneros 20 Este, on

the road to the cemetery
Tel: (48) 793-261
Email: customerservice1@gmx.us
Don Ernesto worked at Hotel Los Jazmines for 30 years as a barman and he makes a great *mojito*. He rents two rooms, each with two beds, air conditioning, and a fan.
Eloy Hernández Rodríguez
Calle Salvador Cisneros, 198
Tel: (48) 695-209
Quiet, pleasant house, one

of the first as you enter the town, and surrounded by coconut palms.
Villa Los Reyes
Calle Rafael Trejo, 134
Tel: (48) 695-225
www.villalosreyes.net
The hosts, Esthelita and Yoan, speak English and offer two double rooms in a lively house, with air con, fridge stocked with beer and water, and meals if required. English spoken.

VARADERO AND MATANZAS

Matanzas

Canimao Hotel
Carretera Matanzas–Varadero, Km 4.5, Reparto Canimar
Tel: (45) 261-014
www.islazul.cu
Located on a picturesque bend of the Canímar River on the road to Varadero, with rooms gathered around a swimming pool (which can be used by non-guests). Spacious lobby, with bar, comfy chairs and birds in cages. Comfortable rooms, two restaurants, a pool-side bar, and evening entertainment ranging from salsa lessons to Mr Canimao contests. The local Tropicana cabaret is next door, so convenient for evenings out. **$**

Varadero

Hotel Acuazul
Avenida 1ra and Calle 13
Tel: (45) 667-132
www.hotelacuazul.com

Located a couple of blocks from the beach. All-inclusive or bed and breakfast available. Basic, but friendly. It has a small pool, bar, and disco and you can use the facilities of the Villa Sotavento and Aparthotel Islazul Varazul. **$**
Arenas Doradas
Autopista Varadero, Km 12
Tel: (45) 668-150
www.gran-caribe.cu
Two-story chalets, providing 316 rooms, set in tropical gardens by the beach, east of the Sol Palmeras.
Hotel Barlovento
Avenida 1ra, between calles 9 and 12
Tel: (45) 667-140
www.hotelesc.com
Located on the seaside promenade in downtown Varadero, the Barlovento has 272 attractive all-inclusive rooms in two three-story buildings and six houses. There are two pools for adults and one for children, with lots of

entertainment. Convenient for downtown restaurants, cafés, and shops. **$$**
Los Delfines
Avenida de la Playa with Calle 39
Tel: (45) 667-720
www.islazul.cu
Small Islazul hotel, right on the beach in downtown Varadero. Friendly and pleasant but often fully booked by an Italian tour operator. The upside is that the restaurant serves good pasta. **$$-$**
Hotel Dos Mares
Corner of Calle 53 and Avenida 1ra
Tel: (45) 612-702
www.islazul.cu
A pleasant, older building in Spanish Mudéjar-style, in downtown Varadero, one block from the beach. The Dos Mares has just 34 rooms of varying sizes, with two suites for families with children. It has a seafood restaurant and a solarium, and breakfast is included in the price. **$**

Mansión Xanadú
Avenida Las Américas, Km 8.5
Tel: (45) 668-482,
www.varaderogolfclub.com
The swish mansion built for industrialist Irenée Du Pont in 1930, who made the peninsula effectively his own private resort when he bought up most of it in 1926. The property was nationalized after the revolution, but retains most

PRICE CATEGORIES

Price categories indicate the cost of a double room in high season:
$ = under $80
$$ = $80–150
$$$ = $150–250

TRANSPORTATION

ACCOMMODATIONS

ACTIVITIES

A – Z

LANGUAGE

of its original fittings. Great for golf fans, as you get free green fees on the course it overlooks; and you have use of the swimming pool at the neighboring Meliá Las Américas. There's an excellent bar upstairs, with a fine view of the peninsula. Restaurant serves international cuisine (about CUC$30–50 a head including wine). Only six rooms, so book at least a month in advance. **$$$+**
Meliá Las Américas
Autopista del Sur
Tel: (45) 667-600
www.solmeliacuba.com
Next to the Du Pont mansion (Mansión Xanadú), the golf course, and the Plaza América shopping mall. Has a fabulous lobby with artworks, palms, and colored glass; a pleasant sun deck and a good stretch of beach. Rooms, suites, and bungalows of varying standards. No children under 18. **$$$+**
Meliá Varadero
Ctra de Las Morlas
Tel: (45) 667-013
www.solmeliacuba.com
Next to the shopping mall and convention center, this is another hotel in the Spanish-run Meliá chain, with a spectacular seven-story spiraling atrium with parrots and trailing vines, and even glass elevators. There are 483 rooms and

seven suites, all with balconies, most with sea views. **$$$**
Mercure Cuatro Palmas
Avenida 1era, between 60 and 64
Tel: (45) 667-040
www.mercure.com
The complex consists of a hotel on the beach side of Avenida Primera, and villas across the road. The villas provide less expensive accommodations. Both are designed with Spanish-type arcades and galleries beside the Centro Comercial Caiman, and convenient for shopping and restaurants. Helpful staff and a good atmosphere. **$$**
Paradisus Varadero Resort and Spa
Punta Francés
Tel: (45) 668-700
www.solmeliacuba.com
The most luxurious, ultra all-inclusive, five-star resort on the peninsula, with a spacious layout. It's relatively secluded, as it's surrounded by the Reserva Ecológica. There are 510 suites in bungalows, with sea or garden views. All the facilities you would expect, with a huge pool, diving, children's club, and lots of entertainment. **$$$+**
Hotel Pullman
Avenida 1ra, between 49 and 50
Tel: (45) 612-702
www.islazul.cu
An attractive Islazul hotel, resembling a frosted white

castle, with a pretty interior patio, and near the sea. It has a friendly atmosphere – more Cuban than most hotels in Varadero. It's small and gets booked up, so book in advance. Breakfast included **$$-$**
Sol Palmeras
Autopista del Sur, Km 8
Tel: (45) 667-009
www.solmeliacuba.com
This was Varadero's first joint venture with Spanish investors, dating from 1990, and part of the Las Américas complex. It has a slightly dated feel and there is a busy, family atmosphere. There's a touch of the jungle, complete with tropical birds, in the lobby, and a thatched bar on an island in the swimming pool. Rooms, suites and bungalows are laid out in a horseshoe shape. **$$-$$$**
Superclub Breezes Varadero
Avenida Las Américas, Km 3
Tel: (45) 667-030
www.superclubscuba.com
A rather pretentious, all-inclusive resort, with 100 rooms and 170 suites. Beautiful gardens, and facilities include a gym, water sports, and a complete scuba program. No children under 16. **$$$+**
Villa Tortuga
Calle 7, between Avenida Kawama and Playa

Tel: (45) 614-747
www.gran-caribe.com
A pleasant complex of scattered villas, with 292 all-inclusive rooms, close to the beach. Tennis court, night-time entertainment, and cars for rent. Friendly staff and good food. Good value for money. **$**

Casas Particulares

Matanzas

Hostal Alma
Calle 83, 29008, between 290 and 292
Tel: (45) 242-449
hostalalma@gmail.com
Two rooms (one double, one triple), both with private bathrooms, fridge, and drinks in an attractive colonial house with beautiful stained glass, a large terrace, and a good view from the roof. Friendly host. Breakfast and evening meal are available.
Hostal Azul
Calle 83, 29012, between 290 and 292
Tel: 5273-7903 (mob)
Email:hostalazul.cu@gmail.com
Beautiful mansion dating from the 1870s, which still retains its original tiles and other architectural features. Two large rooms with big private bathrooms available. English and Italian spoken; very experienced and hospitable owners.

ZAPATA PENINSULA

Boca de Guamá

Villa Guamá
Laguna de Tesoro, reached by boat from La Boca de Guamá
Tel: (45) 915-551
www.hotelescubanacan.com
Mosquitoes are a big problem here and the disco is very noisy, but slap on the insect repellent, cover your arms and legs, and when the last tourist leaves at dusk this becomes a place of peace and loveliness. It is a replica of a pre-Columbian village, with thatched-roof bohíos built on wooden

bridges over a lake to lodge guests. Cabins have modern amenities, and there are restaurants and a pool. You can watch flocks of wild parrots descend to feed on the nectar of the bottlebrush trees. The Villa Guamá was Fidel Castro's idea (in the early 1960s) and he used to be a regular visitor. Staff say that he always used to sleep in cabin No. 33, so there's usually competition for that room. The establishment has been well renovated and offers good value. **$**

Jagüey Grande

Bohío de Don Pedro
Autopista Nacional Km 142
Tel: (45) 912825
www.hotelescubanacan.com
One km (¹⁄₂ a mile) south of the Jagüey Grande highway junction, on the road to Australia and Playa Larga. A small, rustic complex with 10 large log cabins with palm-thatched roofs, own bathrooms, TV, fan, and fridge, and there's a small family-run restaurant. (Just down the road, the state-run Finca Fiesta Campesina

serves good *criolla* food.) Mosquitoes can be a problem in summer, so bring repellent and cover your arms and legs at night. **$**

Playa Larga

Villa Playa Larga

Tel: (45) 987-294
www.hotelescubanacan.com
Renovated in 2009, there are one- or two-bedroomed cabins with sitting rooms, by a small beach on the eastern edge of the village. It is popular with local people during the summer and tour groups at any time of year, particularly birdwatchers and fly fishermen, as it is well placed for exploring the Zapata Peninsula. **$**

Playa Girón

Villa Playa Girón
Tel: (45) 984-110
www.hotelescubanacan.com

A beach resort with 282 rooms in rather ugly concrete cabins, and a couple of equally unprepossessing blocks, about half of which were renovated in 2009. There are two pools, scuba diving and snorkeling facilities and equipment for hire, plus two bars and four restaurants, offering the usual fare. Bicycles and mopeds can be rented, and guides can be arranged for visits to the local area. All in all, it is quite a pleasant place to stay if you're not too concerned about the architecture. **$**

Casas Particulares

Playa Larga

Roberto Mesa Pujol
Caletón
Tel: (45) 987-307
Email:casamesa@gmail.com
The garden of this house runs down to the beach where there are palm trees and a volleyball net. There are two rooms for rent, both with air conditioning, private bathrooms, and car parking space. There are several other beach-front houses in Caletón also offering a superb location and they all charge around CUC$53 for two people for dinner, bed, and breakfast.

Playa Girón

Casa Luis
Carretera a Cienfuegos, on the corner of Carretera a Playa Larga
Tel: (45) 984-258
This house on the main road can be identified immediately by the lions sitting on top of columns at the entrance. Luis García Padrón has two rooms for rent and provides secure parking for cars. Friendly and helpful hosts offer excellent food, and English is spoken.

SANTA CLARA TO SANCTI SPÍRITUS

Cayo Santa María

Barceló Cayo Santa María Beach Resort
Cayo Santa María
Tel: (42) 350-400
www.barcelo.com
A family resort, huge but still only part of a four-hotel city to be built on the cay, so be prepared for views of building works. Plenty of sports facilities, pools, children's activities, water sports, a theater, and disco, but the buffet restaurant can get boring. **$$$**
Meliá Cayo Santa María
Cayo Santa María
Tel: (42) 350-200
www.solmeliacuba.com
This five-star, adults-only, all-inclusive resort has 360 rooms in bungalows set in 12 hectares (30 acres) of grounds by a gorgeous white beach, but not many have a sea view. A choice of restaurants, buffet, and à la carte, and all the usual Meliá resort facilities and services with lots of water sports. **$$$**
Meliá Las Dunas
Tel: (42) 350-100
www.solmeliacuba.com
A five-star, massive, all-inclusive resort, with 925 rooms in two-story buildings in manicured grounds so extensive that golf buggies are required to get around.

You can eat in a different restaurant every night of the week and there are lots of activities and sports. **$$$**
Occidental Royal Hideaway Ensenachos
Cayo Ensenachos
Tel: (42) 350-300
www.occidentalhoteles.com
An up-market and elegant resort spread over two lovely beaches in three sections: the Royal Hideaway, Royal Spa, and Royal Suites, with golf buggies to help you get around. Rooms are spacious with balconies and concierge service. Teenagers are welcome but no children under 12. Buffet food can get boring and the quality is intermittent but the à la carte restaurants are good. **$$$**
Sol Cayo Santa María
Cayo Santa María
Tel: (42) 351-500
www.solmeliacuba.com
A family resort, there are 298 rooms here in two-story buildings set in pretty tropical gardens, some with ocean views. There is a choice of restaurants and bars, three pools, kids' club and tennis courts, beside the pristine white beach where there are plenty of water sports on offer. **$$–$$$**
Villa Las Brujas

Cayo Las Brujas
Tel: (42) 350-199
www.gaviota-grupo.com
A world apart from the mega-resorts in the area, this small hotel was the first on the cays and has only 24 cabins, reached by an elevated boardwalk above the rocks overlooking the beach. A place to come for peace and quiet, unpretentious and excellent value above a beautiful sweep of white sand. The restaurant has indoor or outdoor seating and offers a buffet breakfast, snacks, and à la carte meals. **$$**

Corallilo

Hotel and Spa Elguea
Circuito Norte, Corallilo
Tel: (42) 686-298
www.islazul.cu
This Islazul-run spa hotel has air-conditioned rooms with bath, TV, and phone. The waters, and the mud, are reputed to be a rich source of minerals, and good for all kinds of ailments. Medical consultations and treatments available. There's a pool, massage facilities and beauty treatments, tennis courts, and motorbike rental, in case you want to get to the beach. **$**

Embalse Hanabanilla

Hanabanilla Hotel
Southwest of Manicaragua
Tel: (42) 202-399
www.islazul.cu
An unappealing concrete Soviet creation, but with a breathtaking setting on Lake Hanabanilla, at the end of a 8km (5-mile) hill, in the Escambray mountains south of Santa Clara. The lake is stocked with large-mouth bass and the hotel has its own dock and boats. There are 125 comfortable, air-conditioned rooms, a disco, well-stocked games room, 24-hour bar, and a lovely big pool. The restaurant specializes in lake-caught fish and will

PRICE CATEGORIES

Price categories indicate the cost of a double room in high season:
$ = under $80
$$ = $80–150
$$$ = $150–250

gladly cook and serve your catch. It's a good base for hiking, boating, and horseback riding, and there are waterfalls and caves to explore. **$**

Remedios

Hotel E Mascotte
Máximo Gómez, 114 (Parque Martí)
Tel: (42) 395-144
www.hotelescubanacan.com
A wonderful 18th-century mansion beautifully renovated in 2009 and part of the Encanto chain. Some rooms have French windows opening onto balconies with wrought-iron railings. The food is good and there's bags of nostalgia. The only hotel in Remedios. **$–$$**

Santa Clara

Hotel Santa Clara Libre
Parque Vidal, 6
Tel: (42) 207-548
www.islazul.cu
Basic accommodations: the 159 rooms in the dilapidated 10-story hotel have showers and radios, but don't all have air conditioning. It's not an attractive building, but conveniently sited on the main square, although it's not always easy to park nearby. A better standard of accommodation can be found at *casas particulares* in town. There are good views from the top-floor restaurant (which serves a decent breakfast), and the rooftop bar. The hotel was home to Che Guevara and many of his men after the battle of Santa Clara; its facade is still pock-marked by shells fired during the 1958 battle. **$**

Villa Cubanacan Los Caneyes

Circunvalación and Eucalyptos
Tel: (42) 218-140
www.hotelescubanacan.com
On the main *autopista* 1.6km (1 mile) west of the Che Guevara monument, this motel was designed to resemble an Amerindian settlement. The conical thatched-roof huts contain 95 comfortable, spacious rooms, with hot water, TV, refrigerators, and air conditioning. The garden setting is delightful. The pool provides the focus, with a bar, disco, and a restaurant overlooking it. Those who wish to hunt can make use of the Los Caneyes hunting lodge, and bass fishing in Alacranes dam, Cuba's second-largest reservoir. Frequently used by tour groups for overnight stays. Day passes are available for those staying elsewhere. There are taxis into town, and car rental can be organized. Excellent value. **$**

Villa La Granjita
Carretera Maleza Km 2.5
Tel: (42) 218-190
www.hotelescubanacan.com
This villa hotel lies in the northeastern outskirts of Santa Clara with palm and fruit trees in the gardens. Rooms in thatched cabins have balconies or terraces, with bars, a pool, and a children's playground. Day passes are available. **$**

Sancti Spíritus

Hotel E Del Rijo
Calle Honorato del Castillo, 12, corner Máximo Gómez
Tel: (41) 328-588
www.hotelescubanacan.com
A 16-room hotel in a well-restored mansion, built in 1827, that belonged to a renowned local doctor, for whom it is named. Renovation works included stained-glass windows with shutters and wrought-iron fretwork. Comfortable rooms, meals in a pretty courtyard with plants and a fountain, and a central location make it an ideal choice. **$**

Hotel E Plaza
Parque Serafín Sánchez
Tel: (41) 327-102
www.hotelescubanacan.com
Lovely colonial architecture with a distinctive blue facade and a central garden courtyard. There are 25 large and airy rooms with high ceilings, air conditioning, and satellite TV. Some have balconies overlooking the plaza. There's also a restaurant and a 24-hour snack bar. **$**

Hotel Zaza
Embalse Zaza (southeast of Sancti Spíritus)
Tel: (41) 328-512
Overlooking the reservoir (*embalse*), this hotel is a bit run-down, concrete-built, and outwardly unattractive, but the staff are extremely friendly and helpful and there's a pool, nightclub, and games room. Fishing and boating trips can be arranged here. Sometimes busy with tour groups. **$**

Casas Particulares

Remedios

Hostal Villa Colonial
Calle Antonio Maceo, 43 between General Carrillo and Fé del Valle
Tel: (42) 396-274
An attractive colonial house decorated with beautiful tiles and furnished with antiques, run by Frank and Arelys, who are most hospitable. There is a small patio where you can enjoy a *mojito*, two rooms for guests ,and a dining room.

La Casona Cueto
Alejandro del Río, 72, between Enrique Malaré and Máximo Gómez
Tel: (42) 395-350
A gem of an 18th-century house with lots of original features, and stuffed with antiques in the huge living room. There is a lovely interior patio with fountain. Owner Jenny Cueto offers two large rooms with modern bathrooms, plus car parking, roof terrace, and pets, including dogs, doves, and turtles.

Sancti Spíritus

Hostal Las Américas
Carretera Central, 157 Sur, between Cuba and Cuartel
Tel: (41) 322-984
Email: hostallasamericas@yahoo.es
Modern house in a large and productive garden. Two big rooms with stocked fridge, TV, DVD, MP3 player, hair dryer, and safe deposit box. Meals, snacks, and cocktails available with any special requirements accommodated. English and Italian spoken.

Hostal Puente Yayabo
Calle Jesús Menéndez, 109, between Padre Quintero and Río Yayabo
Tel: (cell/mob) 01524-08545
Email: puente.yayabo@yahoo.es
Spectacular location on the river bank beside the historic bridge over the Yayabo, this renovated 1840 house is a delight, both for the views and the hospitality of the owners, Elena and Víctor. There is a roof terrace where you can eat or enjoy a *mojito*; fishing rods available, and there's a garage.

Santa Clara

Casa Mercy
Calle San Cristóbal, 4, between Cuba and Colón
Tel: (42) 216-941, (cell/mob) 5283-6076
Email: isel@uclv.edu.cu
Excellent modernized house in city center run by friendly, experienced hosts, Omelio, Mercedes and family, who manage several languages between them. The two guest rooms and bathrooms are separate from the family quarters, upstairs and overlooking the street. Roof terrace, laundry, good cooking, any diet catered for, good cocktails, and rum tasting too.

Hostal Florida Center
Calle Candelaria, 56, between Colón and Maceo
Tel: (42) 208-161
Traditional 19th-century colonial house around an interior patio garden crammed with plants, orchids galore, as well as dogs, cats, and birds. Winner in 2008 of the architectural conservation award. The guest rooms open on to the patio and have lots of antique fixtures and fittings for decoration, while mattresses are up to modern standards. Host Angel Rodríguez is known for his cooking and speaks some English, French and Italian.

CIENFUEGOS AND TRINIDAD

Cienfuegos

Hotel E Casa Verde
Calle 37, between calles 0 and 2
Punta Gorda
Tel: (43) 551003
www.gran-caribe.cu

The newest of the boutique hotels in the Encanto chain, this pretty green house at the far end of the peninsula dates from the early 20th century and has been totally renovated with eight well-equipped rooms. Breakfast and snacks are offered, other meals taken at Hotel Jagua opposite. **$**

Hotel E Palacio Azul
Calle 37, 1202, between calles 12 and 14, Punta Gorda
Tel: (43) 555-828/9
www.hotelescubanacan.com

Only seven rooms, in a beautiful, pale-blue neoclassical mansion built in the 1920s, converted into a hotel in 2003. Three rooms have balconies, with great views, and all have air conditioning, TV, and a minibar. There's also a small dining room for breakfast and snacks. You get a great view over the harbor from the little turret on the roof. **$**

Hotel Jagua
Calle 37, 1, between calles 0 and 2, Punta Gorda
Tel: (43) 551-003
www.gran-caribe.cu

Located 3km (2 miles) south of the heart of the city, this was once a notorious casino hotel run by Batista's brother. Externally, it's monolithic and ugly, but the 145 large rooms have air conditioning, TV, and good bathrooms. There's a large pool, but no beach, and a CUC$5 cabaret show every night except Wed. **$$**

Hotel La Unión
Calle 31, corner of 54
Tel: (43) 551-020
www.hotelescubanacan.com

By far the most attractive option in town, this huge mansion has interior patios, a pretty pool, and comfortable rooms and suites with antique furnishings. Sauna, jacuzzi, internet, car rental, bars, and 1869 restaurant. **$$**

Rancho Luna Hotel
Carretera Rancho Luna, Km 18
Tel: (43) 548-012
www.hotelescubanacan.com

Set on its own small beach 18km (11 miles) southeast of Cienfuegos, Rancho Luna has motel-type cabins with 222 rooms. There is a large pool and sun deck, and it looks out on to a small beach with shallow water. There is a choice of restaurants, a cafeteria and bar, medical post, car rental, and shop. Good scuba diving in the area. Usually booked by Canadian package-tour groups. **$**

Guajimico

Villa Guajimico
Carretera a Trinidad, Km 45, Cumanayagua
Tel: (43) 540-947
www.cubamarviajes.cu

On the coast between Cienfuegos and Trinidad, specializing in scuba diving. Fifty-one small but attractive cabins, with air conditioning, in an attractive location overlooking the mouth of Río La Jutía. Fourteen dive sites, 10–15 minutes from shore. Scuba diving twice a day. Dive gear available for rent, also bicycles, kayaks, Hobie Cats, and cars. **$**

Playa Ancón

Brisas Trinidad del Mar
Península Ancón
Tel: (41) 996-500
www.hotelescubanacan.com

The most colorful of the Playa Ancón establishments, this all-inclusive hotel has 240 rooms in two- and three-story blocks around a pool – and its own bell tower. Popular with package-tour groups, it offers dance classes and beach volleyball. Ideal for families, with a children's program. Good water sports,

including scuba lessons. Tennis and gym. **$$**

Hotel Club Amigo Ancón
Carretera María Aguilar
Tel: (41) 996-120
www.hotelescubanacan.com

The three-star Ancón has undergone extensive renovation, having been badly hit by Hurricane Denis in 2005. It remains, a rather unattractive five-story block, albeit with a great location, right on the beach. Rooms are air-conditioned with bath and radio. There are several bars, a swimming pool, and bicycles for hire. **$$**

Hotel Club Amigo Costa Sur
Península Ancón
Tel: (41) 996-174
www.hotelescubanacan.com

Smaller, cheaper, and less appealing than the Ancón (above), in a similar, rather unattractive building. There is a swimming pool and rifle range. The air-conditioned rooms and cabins have bathtubs and radios. **$–$$**

Trinidad

Iberostar Grand Hotel Trinidad
Calle José Martí, 262, y Lino Pérez (Parque Céspedes)
Tel: (41) 996-070
www.iberostar.com

A hotel in a gorgeous renovated colonial building with a green-and-white facade. Just 36 standard rooms and four suites. Elegant and comfortable but no pool or external patio. No children under 15 years old. **$$–$$$**

Hotel Las Cuevas
Finca Santa Ana
Tel: (41) 996-133
www.hotelescubanacan.com

In a lovely spot overlooking the town. The hotel has 110 rooms in individual, simple but clean cabins, with private bath, phone, and radio. There is a swimming pool and bar, two restaurants, and a disco/nightclub with live entertainment most nights in a nearby cave – hence

the hotel's name. **$$**

Casas Particulares

Cienfuegos

Amileidis y Waldo
Calle 39, 5818, corner Avenida 60
Tel: (43) 518-991
Email: bellaperlamarina@yahoo.es

A period piece, built in the 1950s; furniture and fittings date from that time. Hosts are welcoming and knowledgable about the region; family atmosphere; English and Italian spoken. Terrace, lovely garden, extensive views, good food, two rooms available with private bathrooms.

Mirtha Hostal
Calle 37, 1205, between 12 and 14, Punta Gorda
Tel: (43) 526-286

Large house next door to Hotel E Palacio Azul, set back off the road; parking in front garden and Cienfuegos Bay to the rear. One room on the ground floor, the other upstairs with a terrace and sea view. Sun terrace upstairs. Owner Mirtha Bango Trujillo provides good food, laundry service, and help exploring the area.

Trinidad

There are numerous *casas particulares* in Trinidad, some excellent, some less so, but most perfectly acceptable. If arriving by bus, you will find people

PRICE CATEGORIES

Price categories indicate the cost of a double room in high season:
$ = under $80
$$ = $80–150
$$$ = $150–250

ABOVE: inside the Casa Colonial Muñoz in Trinidad.

outside the terminal offering rooms. It is better to make advance reservations.

Araceli Reboso Miranda
Lino Pérez, 207, between País and Calzada
Tel: (41) 993-598
One large, air-conditioned room with private bathroom and a roof terrace. English spoken, good meals.

Casa Colonial Muñoz
Calle José Martí, 401, between Fidel Claro and Santiago Escobar

Tel: (41) 993-673
www.casa.trinidadphoto.com
A lovely, breezy colonial house in the center of Trinidad. Huge shuttered windows in the living room; tiled floors and family heirlooms. Two large guest rooms with en suite bathrooms, fridge, air conditioning, safe box; there is parking, a patio, and roof terrace. Julio (a photographer) and Rosa

speak English and keep dogs and a horse. Photography workshops available. Book in advance.

Casa Font
Gustavo Izquierdo, 105, between Simón Bolívar y Piro Guinart
Tel: (41) 99-3683
One of Trinidad's most stylish *casas*, with crystal chandeliers and stained-glass *mamparas* (swing doors). Two rooms with air conditioning and private

baths. Reserve in advance.

Dr Rogelio Inchauspi Bastida
Calle Simón Bolívar, 312, between Maceo and Martí
Tel: (41) 994-107
Two rooms and bathrooms with fan and balcony. Friendly service and excellent food. Book in advance.

Hospedaje Yolanda
Piro Guinart, 227, between Izquierdo and Maceo
Tel: (41) 996-381
Email: yoliaye@gmail.com
Two nice rooms with air conditioning and private baths in huge, busy house. The room on the top floor has views of the coast. Opposite the bus station.

Hostal Sandra y Víctor
Maceo, 613, between Piro Guinart and Pablo Pichs
Tel: (41) 996-444
Email: hostalsandra@yahoo.com
Two rooms with private bathrooms and air conditioning, dining room, balcony, and terrace. Pleasant, well-maintained house and Sandra and Víctor offer good, filling meals with lots of variety.

EASTERN LOWLANDS

Camagüey

Hotel Colón
Avenida República, 472, between San José and San Martín
Tel: (32) 283-346
www.islazul.cu
A small, elegant, if slightly jaded, 1920s hotel in downtown Camagüey, with a lovely columned lobby, old wood-topped bar, and a stained-glass window picturing Christopher Columbus landing in Cuba. Rooms are simple and can be noisy, but have TV and air conditioning, and there's a decent breakfast served. $

Gran Hotel
Calle Maceo, 67, between Agramonte and Gómez
Tel: (32) 292-094
www.islazul.cu
The best of the hotels in town, established in 1939 in an 18th-century mansion,

right in the heart of Camagüey. Rooms surround a central patio with a fountain. The elegant restaurant on the fifth floor offers the best views in town (apart from the cathedral bell tower). There is also a 24-hour café on the ground floor. $

Hotel Plaza
Van Horne, 1, between República and Avellaneda
Tel: (32) 282-413
www.islazul.cu
Opposite the train station, with original Victorian features, a short walk from the center of town. Breakfast included in the price, poor restaurant. Friendly staff. $

Cayo Coco

NH Krystal Laguna Villas & Resort

Avenida de los Hoteles
Tel: (33) 301-470
www.nh-hotels.com
Massive all-inclusive resort complex on a lagoon, a few minutes' walk from the beach. Rooms are in blocks or in villas on stilts over the lagoon. Lots of sporting facilities, restaurants, and bars, $$$

Blue Bay Cayo Coco
Tel: (33) 302-350
www.bluebayresorts.com
There are 328 rooms and suites in uninspiring buildings, most of which face the gardens, pool, or lagoon, but 60 of them look out on to a truly lovely beach, Playa La Jaula. There is a nice wooden beach bar and thatched beach umbrellas for shade. The pool has a swim-up bar and there is an enclosed pool and play room for small

children. $$$

Tryp Cayo Coco
Tel: (33) 301-300
www.solmeliacuba.com
Modelled as a simulated colonial township, this 508-room complex is just 100 meters/yds in from a glorious white-sand beach. At the center is the airy town hall, with a colonnaded portico, tiled floors, and a central patio where reception is located. Accommodations are in terracotta tile-roofed buildings of two or three stories, and named for the flower planted in front of

TRANSPORTATION

each one, such as *azucenas* (madonna lilies), *mariposas* (butterfly jasmine), *claveles* (pinks), and so on. Gourmet, à la carte, buffet, barbecue, and other specialties are served in eight pleasantly designed restaurants. There are facilities for all the usual water sports. Trips offered by catamaran to outlying islands. Also on Cayo Coco are the Hotel Meliá Cayo Coco and the Sol Cayo Coco in the same Spanish chain, with good facilities and lots of entertainment. **$$$**

Cayo Guillermo

Iberostar Daiquirí
Tel: (33) 301-650
www.iberostar.com
Large and luxurious 4-star all-inclusive resort with rooms in blocks around the pool. Family friendly with children's club and other activities. Pleasant strip of beach with thatched umbrellas and palm trees for shade. **$$$**

Meliá Cayo Guillermo
Tel: (33) 301-680
www.solmeliacuba.com
All-inclusive hotel; 301 rooms in a low-rise, 5-star hotel on the beach, decorated in blue with a nautical theme. Thatched umbrellas give shade on the beach and a long pier stretches out into the sea. Good for honeymooners or families. **$$$**

Sol Cayo Guillermo
Tel: (33) 301-760
www.solmeliacuba.com
An all-inclusive hotel with rooms and bungalows, the nicest of which are close to the beach. Good for families; there are lots of activities and entertainment. **$$$**

Villa Cojímar
Tel: (33) 301-712
www.gran-caribe.com
An attractive, colourful 212-room Gran Caribe hotel at the eastern end of the island consisting of bungalows set among lawns and gardens. This is a good budget option but don't expect the facilities of the foreign-run resorts.

There's a lovely beach and excellent diving. **$$**

Ciego de Ávila

Hotel Ciego de Ávila
Carretera de Ceballo, Km 2.5
Tel: (33) 228-013
www.islazul.cu
The usual Soviet-designed 5-story monolith, with 143 air-conditioned rooms and a pool. Located 3km (2 miles) north of the center. Popular with tour groups. **$**

Hotel Santiago-Habana
Calle Honorato Castillo, between Joaquín Agüero and Chicho Valdés
Tel: (33) 225-703
www.islazul.cu
Renovated in 2009, this hotel is in the center of town. It comprises 76 air-conditioned rooms with private bathrooms; those at the front have balconies. **$**

Morón

Hotel Morón
Avenida de Tarafa
Tel: (33) 502-230
www.islazul.cu
Morón is a small town convenient for the cays, so it is worth choosing accommodations here if you don't want to pay for a beach resort hotel. This is a concrete hotel on the outskirts of town. The 144 rooms (not all currently in operation) have all the usual facilities, with air conditioning and private bathrooms. Suites have their own balconies. The hotel has a restaurant, bars, pool, and tourism bureau. **$**

Najasa

Hacienda La Belén
Five km (3 miles) from Najasa, 54km (34 miles) southeast of Camagüey
Tel: (32) 864-349
www.ecoturcuba.co.cu
One of the nicest rural hotels in Cuba, operated by Ecotur, with only 10 rooms and a pool. Breakfast is included and other meals are available as well as horseback riding, hiking, and birdwatching. Book in

advance. **$**

Santa Lucía

Club Amigo Mayanabo
Tel: (32) 336-184
www.hotelescubanacan.com
All-inclusive three-star hotel set 100 meters/yds from the beach, with 213 rooms and 12 suites in two blocks between pool and beach. Lots of water sports including diving, snorkeling, kayaking, and windsurfing, as well as facilities for basketball, volleyball, tennis, and dance classes. **$$**

Gran Club Santa Lucía
Tel: (32) 365-145
www.hotelescubanacan.com
All-inclusive villa complex with 108 rooms on a broad stretch of the beach and 144 garden rooms. Lots of activities for all ages, including a disco, games room, bicycle rental. **$$**

Casas Particulares

Camagüey City

Casa Miriam
Calle Joaquín de Agüero, 525, between 25 de Julio and Perucho Figueredo, Reparto La Vigía
Tel: (32) 282-120
Email:miriamhouse@yahoo.com
Well-maintained accommodation in a modern house north of the center, with two guest rooms, each with excellent bathroom, good beds, and plenty of storage space. Large roof terrace with pot plants, dogs, and cats. Miriam speaks English, is full of information, and cooks wholesome three-course meals.

Estela Mugarra Carmona
Calle Cisneros, 1161, Apt 2, between Cristo and San Isidro
Tel: (32) 295-053
Very central, right by the main plaza. Built in 1958, this apartment on the second floor still retains all its period features including solid wooden wardrobes and folding screens. Pleasant balcony on which to sit with a coffee (complimentary) and watch the world go by.

Los Vitrales
Calle Avellaneda, 3, between Gómez and Martí
Tel: (32) 295-866
Email: requejobarreto@gmail.com
Two large rooms in a colonial house with a friendly, English-speaking host. New bathrooms, new beds, and lots of original features including a colonial-era kitchen (there is a more modern one too) where they serve good traditional meals. There's a pleasant patio with lots of flowering plants.

Morón

Casa Xiomara
Calle 8, 2C, between Sordo and Calle C
Tel: (33) 504-236
Email: ysary@moron.cav.sld.cu
Morón is convenient for the cays, and accommodations here are cheaper than those on the beach. This very friendly and helpful family offers just one independent room with its own little kitchen and bathroom, set in the back garden, and surrounded by flowers. English is spoken and the food is good.

Maité Valor Morales
Calle Luz Caballero, 40-b, between Libertad and Agramonte
Tel: (33) 504-181
Email: yio@moron.cav.sld.cu
This is an up-market and professional household, with English and Italian spoken and lots of advice and information offered. There are two rooms available: one is very spacious and has two big beds and a kitchenette in it. The other is smaller and the bathroom is next door. The garage has been converted into a dining room where tour parties can be served and huge dinners are offered, but that still leaves plenty of parking space.

PRICE CATEGORIES

Price categories indicate the cost of a double room in high season:
$ = under $80
$$ = $80–150
$$$ = $150–250

ACCOMMODATIONS · ACTIVITIES · A–Z · LANGUAGE

HOLGUÍN AND GRANMA

Bayamo

Hotel Royalton
Calle Maceo, 53, between General
García and José Palma
Tel: (23) 422-246
www.islazul.cu
A small hotel in traditional
style on the main square.
Totally renovated and
reopened in 2010, rooms
are simple but smart, all
have air conditioning and
private baths. Restaurant
and bar and breakfast is
included in the room rate. $

Villa Santo Domingo
Carretera La Plata, Km 16, Santo
Domingo
Tel: (23) 565-657
www.islazul.cu
A small hotel in the
mountains, a base for trips
into the Sierra Maestra.
20 rooms in rustic cabins;
basic but a lovely location in
the forest by the river. $

Cayo Saetía

Villa Cayo Saetía
Tel: (24) 516-900
www.gaviota-grupo.com
A secluded 12-room
bungalow hotel on a pristine
beach, one of many on the
cay. There's a great variety
of flora and introduced
exotic fauna in the area.
Snorkeling, jeep safaris, and
horseback riding. $$

Chivirico

Brisas Sierra Mar Los
Galeones
Playa Sevilla, 65km (40 miles) west
of Santiago de Cuba, 12km
(8 miles) east of Chivirico
Tel: (22) 329-110 and 326-160
www.hotelescubanacan.cu
Inaugurated in 1994 by
Fidel Castro, this four-star
Andalusian-style resort is an
amalgamation of two all-
inclusive resorts; Sierra Mar
is on a lovely sandy beach
at the foot of the Sierra
Maestra mountains, while
Los Galeones is up 300
steps. A variety of
restaurants serving average
food; fitness center,
shopping mall, freshwater
pool, art gallery, games

room, disco, and cabaret.
Lots of water sports and
tennis and volleyball. $$

Guardalavaca/
Playa Esmeralda/
Playa Pesquero

Blau Costa Verde Beach
Resort
Tel: (24) 433-510
www.blau-hotels.com
One of many new all-
inclusive hotels in this area;
blocks of rooms built around
a pool complex a short walk
from a pretty arc of sand
where there are thatched
umbrellas for shade. $$$

Brisas Guardalavaca
Tel: (24) 430-218
www.hotelescubanacan.com
All-inclusive, 230 rooms in
the hotel and 200 in villas.
The hotel part is popular
with honeymooners, the
villas with families. The
hotel section is more lively;
ask for rooms away from the
disco. Facilities include
water sports center, pool,
disco, tennis courts, bikes
for rent, and several
restaurants and bars. $$$+

Club Amigo Atlántico
Guardalavaca
Tel: (24) 430-180
www.hotelescubanacan.com
This amalgamation of older
accommodation consists of
a moderately priced hotel on
the beach, a 1970s hotel
set around a pool, and a
clutch of newer villas a short
walk from the beach. $$

Paradisus Río de Oro
Resort & Spa
Tel: (24) 430-090
www.solmeliacuba.com
One of Cuba's most
luxurious resorts and the
best hotel in the area. All-
inclusive, five star, tasteful,
and expensive. There's a
spa for pampering and good
restaurants, including a
Japanese one. $$$+

Playa Costa Verde
Tel: (24) 433-520
www.gaviota-grupo.com
A large, new, all-inclusive
resort with low blocks of
spacious rooms in extensive
grounds. Cigar lounge and
piano bar, and lots of play

areas and pool for small
children. $$$

Playa Pesquero
Tel: (24) 433-530
www.gaviota-grupo.com
A vast, new, all-inclusive
resort with 1,000 rooms in
blocks surrounding the pool
area. Every facility you could
want, but characterless. $$$

Occidental Grand Playa
Turquesa
Playa Yuraguanal
Tel: (24) 430-540
www.occidental-hoteles.com
Pleasant and attractive all-
inclusive resort set back
from the beach with rooms
in several blocks. Lots of
sports, activities, and
entertainment, including a
multi-level pool complex
with waterfalls.

Sol Río de Luna y Mares
Playa Esmeralda
Tel: (24) 430-060
www.solmeliacuba.com
A 445-room hotel in
gardens in the Marine Park
Bahía de Navajo, with
excellent water sports
facilities, and several good
restaurants. The beach is a
lovely horseshoe shape and
the water is great for
snorkeling. $$$

Holguín City

Mirador de Mayabe
Loma de Mayabe
Tel: (24) 422-160
www.islazul.cu
An attractive villa in an
isolated but attractive spot
10km (6 miles) southeast of
Holguín. Accommodations
in cabins among trees. A
splendid view of the valley
from the terrace pool; rustic
restaurant and a famous
beer-drinking donkey. $

Hotel Pernik
Plaza de la Revolución and J
Dimitrov, Reparto Pedro Díaz Cuello
Tel: (24) 481-011, 481-081
www.islazul.cu
With 200 rooms, a
reasonable restaurant, large
pool, and huge lobby, this is
the biggest hotel in Holguín,
used mainly by overnighting
tour parties. There is a car-
rental desk. $

Manzanillo

Guacanayabo
Avenida Camilo Cienfuegos,
southwest of the town center
Tel: (23) 574-012
www.islazul.cu
Another Soviet-inspired
nightmare, with 112 rooms,
not all currently in use, but it
has a pool and a spectacular
hilltop view of the port. Used
mainly by Cuban families and
can be noisy. $

Marea del Portillo

Club Amigo Marea del
Portillo/Farallón del
Caribe
Tel: (23) 597-103, 597-080–4
www.hotelescubanacan.com
Two all-inclusive hotels,
with golf buggy shuttle
between the two and
shared facilities. The Marea
del Portillo section is on the
beach, but rather run-down;
the rooms and food at
Farallón del Caribe are
better. Lots of excursions:
boat trips, horseback
riding, and hiking; good
scuba diving. Cars and
mopeds to rent; plenty of
evening entertainment.
Some food items and wine
often run out, so bring any
supplies you particularly
need. $$

Mayarí

Villa Pinares de Mayarí
32km (20 miles) south of Mayarí
Tel: (24) 503-308
www.gaviota-grupo.com
At 600 meters (2,000ft)
above sea level, between
Holguín and Moa, this
peaceful complex comprises
28 log cabins in a woodland
setting. A pleasant bar-
restaurant, pool, gym,
tennis courts, and mountain
bike rental; will book

excursions to the Mensura National Park, which is excellent for hiking and birding. Mostly used by tour groups and often closed if no party is expected. **$**

Casas Particulares

Bayamo

Arturo y Esmeralda
Calle Zenea, 56 between Wiliam Soler and Capote
Tel: (23) 424-051
www.casa-bayamo.com
Modernized house with new bathrooms, air conditioning, roof terrace, laundry service, plenty of good, wholesome food. Friendly and helpful family.

Olga Celeiro Rizo
Calle Parada, 16, between Martí and Mármol, above Cubana office
Tel: (23) 423-859
Apartment with balcony off living room.
Two bedrooms with private bathroom. Friendly hosts

who can help arrange excursions.

Gibara

Hostal Vitral
Calle Independencia, 36, between García and Peralta
Tel: (24) 844-469
Superb, clean colonial house in the town center close to Malecón, known for its stained glass. Many original features and pretty patios full of flowers and a roof terrace with hammocks. Both rooms come with private bathrooms and there is a garage. Considered to be one of the best *casas particulares* in Cuba. Reserve in advance.

Holguín

Don Santiago
Calle Narciso López, 258, Apt 3, 2nd floor, between Coliseo and Segunda
Tel: (24) 426-146

Email: visionatres@yahoo.es
One room in cosy apartment in walking distance of center, good bed, reading lights. Santiago and Consuelo are friendly and knowledgable; can make alternative reservations if the room is occupied.

Isabel Sera Galves
Calle Narciso López, 142, between Aguilera and Frexes
Tel: (24) 422-529
A large colonial house in town center; two rooms with shared bathroom. A garden with fruit trees and flowers, cats and a dog.

Villa Liba
Calle Maceo, 46, corner 18

Tel: (24) 423-823
Air-conditioned rooms with private baths; reading lights, plenty of storage space; in walking distance of center.

Manzanillo

Adrián y Tonia
Mártires de Viet-Nam, 49, between Caridad and San Silvestre
Tel: (23) 573-028
A welcoming place on Celia Sánchez memorial staircase. Hosts are helpful and the room is well -appointed and comfortable. A great roof terrace for views of the bay.

SANTIAGO DE CUBA

Balcón del Caribe
Carretera del Morro, Km 7
Tel: (22) 691-011
www.islazul.cu
A nice spot by the sea next to the Morro Castle. The hotel, with 72 rooms and 24 *cabañas*, is largely unmodernized but has a pleasant atmosphere, and there's a little cabaret. It is handy for the airport, but it's also under the flight path. **$**

Hotel Casa Granda
Heredia, 201, between San Pedro and San Félix, Parque Céspedes
Tel: (22) 686-600 and 653-021
www.gran-caribe.com
Overlooking the main square, this landmark hotel built in 1914 is Santiago's nicest. The interior is splendidly grand, but some rooms are in need of renovation. There is a broad terrace bar overlooking the square. The fifth-floor bar offers fine views over downtown Santiago, and is great at sunset. **$$**

Gran Hotel Escuela
Enramada, 312, between San Félix and San Pedro
Tel: (22) 653-020/653-028
www.granhotelstgo.cu
Clean, central, and cozy. The 27 rooms are plain but quite large. The *escuela* in the name means that it is a hotel school where tourism students train – as they are usually enthusiastic, the service, and the food, are usually very good. **$**

Las Américas
Avenida de las Américas and General Cebreco
Tel: (22) 642-011, 687-225–6
www.islazul.cu
Opposite high-rise Santiago de Cuba, Las Américas has 70 rooms. Its restaurant is quite good and there is usually a pleasant, buzzing atmosphere; the cabaret is very popular and so is the pool. **$**

Hotel E San Basilio
Calle Masó, 403, between Calvario and Carnicería
Tel: (22) 651-702

www.hotelescubanacan.com
Santiago's only "boutique" hotel, this pretty, pastel-green place is very close to Parque Céspedes. It takes its name from the old name of the street (and one that many people still use). There are just eight rooms with air conditioning and TV. There is a restaurant on site. **$$**

Hotel Meliá Santiago de Cuba
Avenida de las Américas, between Avenida 4 and Calle M
Tel: (22) 687-070
www.solmeliacuba.com
Spectacular red, white, and blue modern building with glass-fronted escalators, its 15 stories can be seen all over town. With 270 spacious rooms, 34 suites, and a conference room, it's popular with business guests. Four restaurants, three pools, and a lavish cabaret/nightclub. Good view from rooftop bar. **$$**

Hotel Versalles

Alturas de Versalles, Carretera del Morro, Km 1
Tel: (22) 691-016
www.hotelescubanacan.com
Just outside the city, a pink and white stuccoed gingerbread house of a hotel in lush gardens. There are 61 rooms and one suite, all with garden views from their balconies. There's air conditioning, satellite TV, two restaurants, two cafés,

(Side tabs: TRANSPORTATION, ACCOMMODATIONS, ACTIVITIES, A – Z, LANGUAGE)

two bars, a large pool and a separate children's pool, a nightclub, and sporting facilities. Rather inconvenient for the town, so car rental is recommended. **$**

Hotel San Juan
Carretera de Siboney, Km 4.5
Reparto Vista Alegre
Tel: (22) 687-200
www.islazul.cu
On the outskirts of town, 3.5km (2 miles) from Parque Céspedes, this motel is set in lush gardens on historic San Juan Hill – the scene of the final battle in the War of Independence. Pleasant rooms, good restaurant, large swimming pool, and a shallow pool for children. **$–$$**

Casas Particulares

Amparo Hernández Liranza
Calle Santa Rita, 161, between Corona and Padre Pico
Tel: (22) 656-351
Email: amparohl@yahoo.es
One very comfortable room for rent. It's spacious

and well equipped with air conditioning, a good bathroom, fridge, and patio. The room is on the roof and has a great view from the terrace, a sunbathing area and a table and chairs under shade. Good food, English and French spoken.

Antonia Alonso Baldoneso
Calle Morua Delgado, 360, between General Portuondo and Lauro Fuentes
Tel: (22) 622-221
A neat house built in 1949 with all its period features retained. Lots of space, a comfortable room, and a convenient location close to center. English spoken by the welcoming hostess.

Casa Colonial Maruchi
Calle San Félix, 357 between San Germán and Trinidad
Tel: (22) 620-767
Email: maruchib@yahoo.es
Splendid colonial house with central patio garden full of plants and statues and lots of character. Two large rooms with bathrooms, high ceilings, tiled floors, quiet, central, convenient, English

spoken.
Casa Dulce
Calle Bartolomé Masó (San Basilio), 552, corner Clarín
Tel: (22) 625-479
Email: gdcastillo20@yahoo.es
One lovely room in an apartment on corner block; huge windows let in light and air. There's a great view over the city and the harbour from the roof terrace, where there is a table for meals and sun loungers for relaxing. Central, convenient, friendly and helpful hostess, English spoken, good food served.

Los Cactus
Avenida 10, 410, between calles 15 and 17, Reparto Vista Alegre
Tel: (22) 642-611
Rubén Rodes Estrada lives in a pretty yellow and white wooden house with large cacti growing outside, but he rents out a room in his converted garage, with independent access and a roof terrace. The black bathroom takes a bit of getting used to, but the fittings are all new. Parking, good food, and a quiet

residential location.
Jorge Juan Manchón Cusine
Avenida 6, 204, between calles 7 and 9, Reparto Vista Alegre
Tel: (22) 674-827
A well-preserved 1930s suburban house with high ceilings and tiled floors to counter Santiago's heat. Two bedrooms available, one of which has a massive bathroom, the other a smaller addition in the corner of the room. French and a bit of English are spoken.

José Luis Manzano
Avenida 6, 202, corner of Calle 7, Reparto Vista Alegre
Tel: (22) 644-272
Email: josemanzano_22@yahoo.com
Next door to the Manchón Cusine household *(above)*, this house on a corner plot dates from 1925. It's pleasantly cool, being shaded by trees, and has high ceilings and tiled floors, as well as inviting rocking chairs on the front porch. Parking available. The son of the house speaks English.

AROUND SANTIAGO DE CUBA

Gran Piedra

Hotel Islazul Gran Piedra
Carretera de la Gran Piedra, Km 14½
Tel: (22) 686-147
An "eco-lodge" with comfortable rustic cabins and bungalows set along the edge of the mountain ridge (*gran piedra* means large rock). The views are absolutely wonderful when the weather is fine. There is also a café, a restaurant, and a souvenir shop on the road beneath the rock. **$–$$**

Guantánamo

Hotel Guantánamo
Calle 13 Norte, between Ahogados and 1 Oeste
Tel: (21) 381-015
www.islazul.cu
The standard concrete

provincial monstrosity, overlooking Plaza Marina Grajales, a 15-minute walk from the town center. There are 124 rooms with good facilities and they are at least comfortable and inexpensive, if not beautiful. There is a 24-hour café, two restaurants, a nightclub, disco, and a pool. Staff are helpful in arranging excursions. **$**

Sierra Maestra

Hotel El Saltón
Carretera a Filé, Contramaestre
Tel: (22) 566-326
www.hotelescubanacan.com
Northwest of El Cobre, deep in the Sierra Maestra, this place is very rural and extremely beautiful. There are 22 rooms in wooden cabins set by a mountain lake fed by waterfalls.

The waterfall which gives the hotel its name is 34 meters/yds high, and you can stand under it for an invigorating shower, or bathe in its pool. The hotel was originally an anti-stress center, and it still offers sauna and massage facilities. You can take Jeep trips to S altón from Santiago. **$**

Casas Particulares

Lisette Foster Lara
General Pedro A Pérez, 661, between Jesús del Sol and Prado, Guantánamo
Tel: (21) 325-970
There are several casas *particulares* in Guantánamo, and they are much nicer places to stay than the faceless Soviet-style hotel. This is one of them: Lisette's house is

central, spacious, and comfortable, and the rooms have air conditioning. There is a pleasant roof terrace where you can eat outdoors if you want to, and there are a number of restaurants, bars, and music venues in walking distance.

PRICE CATEGORIES

Price categories indicate the cost of a double room in high season:
$ = under $80
$$ = $80–150
$$$ = $150–250

THE FAR EAST

Baracoa

Hotel El Castillo
Calixto García, s/n, Loma el Paraíso
Tel: (21) 645-106
www.grupo-gaviota.com
High on a cliff overlooking the town, this was one of Baracoa's three castles, built in 1770 to keep the British out. It later became a prison. It is hard to resist staying here: it has just 34 air-conditioned rooms, a gorgeous pool with a barbecue bar, lovely gardens, and a good restaurant. It also offers the best views of the town and El Yunque mountain. Reached by a steep flight of steps or a curving drive. Inexpensive, and great value. $

Hostal La Habanera
Maceo, 68, corner of Frank País
Tel: (21) 645-273
www.grupo-gaviota.com
This 10-room hotel with an ocher-facade in the center of town has been well renovated. It is spruce, there's cable TV and air conditioning in the rooms, and the beds are comfy. Can be noisy at night as the Casa de Cultura next door has loud music – but it's very atmospheric. $

Hotel La Rusa
Máximo Gómez, 161
Tel: (21) 643-011
www.grupo-gaviota.com
An aristocratic Russian, who fled the revolution in her own country and lived to see another on her adopted island, founded this simple 12-room hostelry near the waterfront. The low-rise yellow-painted La Rusa is in an enviable location and has attracted many famous guests. $

Villa Maguana
Carretera a Moa, Km 22.5
Tel: (21) 641-204
www.grupo-gaviota.com
A beautiful location on a spectacular white-sand beach with nothing else around it, 20km (12 miles) north of Baracoa. One of the very few small and intimate beach hotels in Cuba. There is a restaurant and a beach bar. Recently updated, it has 16 3-star rooms in four blocks and tranquility in abundance. $$

Hotel Porto Santo
Carretera del Aeropuerto
Tel: (21) 645-106
www.grupo-gaviota.com
Three km (2 miles) from town, and close to the airport. Beautiful location on a terraced hill with lush foliage, birds, and steps leading down to a small private beach across the harbor from Baracoa. Eighty rooms and three suites, and a small but pleasant pool; there's night-time entertainment. Car and moped rental available. $

Casas Particulares

Andrés Cruzata Rigores
Calle Wilder Galano Reyes, 23 Alto between Abel Díaz Delgado and Ramón López Peña
Tel: (21) 642-697, 5246-5755 (mob)
Email: cacaolog@enet.cu
Air-conditioned room in upstairs apartment, TV, good bathroom, terrace with seating, and a lovely view over the town and the sea. Helpful family who can organize things for you and offer services such as laundry. Their son speaks English and Italian.

Casa Colonial Lucy
Calle Céspedes, 29, between Rubert López and Maceo
Tel. (21) 643-548
A pretty colonial house with a lovely view over the town and the sea from the roof terrace. Two good air-conditioned rooms with lofty ceilings and fridge. Lucy is most helpful in arranging excursions and provides good food.

Daniel Salomón Paján
Calle Céspedes, 28, between Rubert López and Maceo
Tel. (21) 641-443, 5291-7403 (mob)
Email: fifi@toa.gtm.sld.cu
Daniel works at the museum and is extremely knowledgable about the area. He and his family are very helpful and friendly and speak some English. They rent one room with air conditioning and a large bathroom.

SOUTHERN ISLANDS

Cayo Largo

All the hotels are all-inclusive and flank the beach on the south side of the island. Gran Caribe (www.gran-caribe.cu) has five hotels and the Sol Meliá (www.solmeliacuba.com) has two. The price of packages bought in Havana or abroad varies widely, so shop around.

Hotel Playa Blanca
Tel: (45) 248-080
www.gran-caribe.cu
Probably the best resort and very popular. Rooms in three-story main hotel or in two-story blocks along the white sand beach. All well-appointed, spacious, and comfortable; service is friendly and efficient. Lots of activities, sport, and entertainment, and food is very good by Cuban standards. Jeep or scooter rental available. $$–$$$

Sol Pelícano
Playa Lindamar
Tel: (45) 248-333
www.solmeliacuba.com
Good, three-star family hotel. Buffet restaurant, beach bar, snack and pizza bars. Saltwater pool with children's section. $$–$$$

Isla de la Juventud

Hotel El Colony
Carretera de Siguanea, Km 46
Tel: (46) 398-181
www.gran-caribe.cu
On Southwest coast, 42km (26 miles) from Nueva Gerona, 77 air-conditioned rooms, some in cabins with good facilities. Miles from anywhere and surrounded by swamp and mangrove, people come for some of the best diving in Cuba and the beach is pleasant (bring insect repellent). Marinas Puerto Sol offers packages covering the hotel, the scuba center, and the marina, which provides deep-sea fishing trips. $$

Hotel Rancho El Tesoro
Carretera La Fé, Km 3, on the way to the airport, less than 3km (2 miles) south of Nueva Gerona
Tel: (46) 323-035
www.gran-caribe.cu
Refurbished in colonial style; 54 air-conditioned rooms set around a courtyard with a fountain and vines hanging from wooden beams. There is a pool and restaurant. $

Villa Isla de la Juventud
Autopista Gerona–La Fé, Km 1.5
Tel: (46) 323-290
www.gran-caribe.cu
Twenty rooms in modern bungalows, a decent pool and views. Salsa band plays afternoons and evenings. $

Casas Particulares

Isla de la Juventud

Elda Cepero Herrera
Calle 43, 2004, Nueva Gerona
Tel: (46) 322-774
Separate apartment behind the house with a living room and kitchen.

Odalis Peña Fernández
Calle 10, 3710, between 37 and 39, Nueva Gerona
Tel: (46) 321-166
Friendly, with good home cooking, Odalis can suggest unusual excursions or find transport.

TRANSPORTATION · ACCOMMODATIONS · ACTIVITIES · A–Z · LANGUAGE

ACTIVITIES

FESTIVALS, THE ARTS, NIGHTLIFE, SHOPPING, AND SPECTATOR SPORTS

THE ARTS

Museums

Many of the colonial mansions and public buildings clustered around the historic centers of Cuba's older cities are now museums. Whatever their theme, they are often worth seeing for the beauty of the buildings themselves.

The main museums in tourist centers charge an admission fee of cucs$1–3, but the cost is higher in some of Havana's top attractions, such as both branches of the Museo

Art in Havana

Havana has the lion's share of art treasures – in particular at the Arte Cubano section of the **Museo Nacional Palacio de Bellas Artes** (see page 163) which has the most representative collection of 20th-century Cuban art. The **Casa de las Américas** at Avenida 3era, 52, and Calle G, Vedado, www.casa. cult.cu, has an interesting collection of Cuban and Latin-American art, and the **Galería Habana**, Linea, 460, between calles E and F, Vedado, www.galerihabana. com, has lively and well-displayed contemporary Cuban works. **Galería UNEAC**, Calle 17 corner of Calle H, Vedado, www.uneac.org.cu, has exhibits by contemporary Cuban artists (in official favor). **Calle Obispo** in Old Havana is home to a number of galleries/sale rooms for contemporary art. Others are dotted all around the old town.

Nacional Palacio de Bellas Artes (a combined ticket is available), and the Museo de la Revolución.

Exhibits are generally labeled in Spanish, though sometimes shortened notes are given in English. The most popular museums usually have at least one guide who speaks English and sometimes French.

Opening hours are notoriously erratic, and buildings can be closed for renovation. Many museums close on Monday or Tuesday, and some open only for the afternoon on Sunday – current opening times of the major museums are given in the main text.

Music

Cubans are crazy about music. It blares from every window and accompanies every activity. Rumba, *son*, and its derivative salsa, *trova* ballads, and *nueva trova* political songs, jazz, country, and classical can be heard and seen on TV, along with modern, US-influenced rap, hip-hop and reggaeton. There is always some group performing live, whether in hotels or in local nightspots.

Son, **bolero**, and **salsa** are everywhere and live bands playing and singing traditional music can be found in the Casa de la Trova and/or the Casa de la Cultura in any town.

Most of the bars and *tabernas* of Old Havana and tourist centers such as Trinidad feature live bands (see Nightlife, pages 357–60).

Jazz has deep roots and Cuban musicians are creative interpreters. Havana jazz venues are all in Vedado. The genre is at its most exciting when the best Cuban and international jazz musicians gather in the capital for the Havana International Jazz Festival in

December (see Festivals, page 357).

The national **opera** company is based at the Gran Teatro, off the Parque Central. Performances are posted on notices outside, or call the theater, tel: (7) 861-3077.

With fantastic acoustics, the church of **San Francisco de Asís** in Plaza San Francisco is a great venue for classical music. Tickets are available from the venue and recitals are usually at 5pm or 6pm. The main venue for concerts in Havana, however, is the Teatro Amadeo Roldán, in Vedado, tel: (7) 832-1168, the base for the Orquesta Sinfónica Nacional and where visiting symphony orchestras play. The Sala Hubert de Blanck, in Vedado, tel: (7) 833-5962, specializes in classical concerts as well as contemporary dance. You can also find something going on at the Teatro Nacional de Cuba, on Paseo with 39, tel: (7) 879-3558.

Dance

Cubans dance from the moment they can walk and, to Westerners, it seems they all have an innate rhythm, impeccable footwork, and the endless energy expected of a pro. Perhaps that is why Cuba's professional groups are so good, and have become internationally recognized.

Afro-Cuban Dance

Now internationally renowned, **Clave y Guaguancó** was founded to keep Afro-Cuban dance, drumming, and music alive, concentrating mainly on rumba, *son*, and *danzón*. They play Yambú, Guaguancó, Columbias, and carnival music as well as African music from the Yoruba, Arará, Abakuá, Congo, or Bantú. They sometimes perform in Callejón de Hamel (Centro Habana) on Sunday noon–3pm, and give open-air performances alternate Wednesdays from 5pm, at the Hurón Azul, UNEAC, calles 17 and H, Vedado.

The **Conjunto Folklórico Nacional de Cuba** (Calle 4, 103, between Calzada and 5ta, Vedado, tel: (07) 830-3939, 830-3060, 831-3467) hosts rumba performances on the patio outside the Gran Palenque Bar, Calle 4, between Calzada and 5, every Saturday. Box office opens at 2pm on Saturday before the 3pm performance; there is often a line, so be there early. You can also book a course of dance lessons here (same numbers as above, or go in person).

Tango

Tango is not indigenous to Cuba, but can be found here. The best place for classes and excellent performances is Casa del Tango Edmundo Daubar, Neptuno, 309, between Aguila and Italia, tel: (07) 863-0097. It's a cross between a music venue and a museum with tango memorabilia dating from the 1940s.

Ballet

The **National Ballet of Cuba**, directed since its creation in 1961 by Alicia Alonso, is world-famous for its fluid grace and technique. The company is often on tour, but when they are at home they perform at the **Gran Teatro**, Paseo de Martí, 458, corner San Rafael (Parque Central), tel: (07) 861-3077/78; or the **Teatro Nacional de Cuba**, Paseo and Calle 39 (Plaza de la Revolución), tel: (07) 879-3558. The company's ballet school is based at the Gran Teatro, and during the day you can see the young students rehearsing (also see Festivals below).

The **Museo De La Danza** covers all aspects of the history of dance with special emphasis on ballet. It is at Línea, 365 and G, Vedado, tel: (7) 831-2198, housed in an elegant building that is worth a visit in itself. Open Tue–Sat 10am–6pm.

Modern Dance

Cuba's impressive **Contemporary Dance Company** (Danza Contemporánea de Cuba) performs avant-garde and other forms of modern dance. Its base is the **Teatro Nacional de Cuba**, Calle Paseo and 39 (Plaza de la Revolución), but they also perform at the Sala Hubert de Blanck (see page 356) or the Teatro Mella, Línea, 657, between A and B, tel: (7) 833-5651.

Theater

Teatro Bertolt Brecht, Línea and Calle 13. Renovated and now capable of staging a wide range of shows, from musical comedy to political satire, dance, and music.

Teatro El Sótano, Calle K between calles 25 and 27, tel: (7) 832-0630, is home to the Rita Montaner company and a place to find contemporary drama and fringe theater events.

Teatro Guiñol, calles M and 19, Vedado, tel: (7) 832-6262, stages contemporary youth theatre and drama classes.

Teatro Nacional de Cuba, Paseo and Calle 39 (Plaza de la Revolución), tel: (7) 879-3558. Three auditoria, where experimental and children's theater is staged, as well as ballet performances and concerts.

Festivals

All Cuban provinces celebrate a **Culture Week** (Semana Cultural) once a year, with music, dance, arts and crafts, and local food.

The **Havana International Jazz Festival** in December, running since 1978, is organized by Chucho Valdés. The festival is based in the Teatro Nacional de Cuba but venues include the Teatro Amadeo Roldán and Teatro Karl Marx, where major performances take place, and there are impromptu performances along the Malecón. Other festivals include the **Havana Contemporary Music Festival** held at UNEAC and Havana theaters in October, and the **International Electrical Acoustic Music Festival** in March. Outside Havana are the **International Son Festival** (October) and the **International Trova Festival** (March) in Santiago, and the **Cuculambeana Festival** of folk music in Las Tunas (June).

The **International Ballet Festival** in October, running since 1986, draws companies from Cuba and abroad. Most performances are in the Gran Teatro or the Teatro Nacional but there are various other venues. **Cubadanza** is a contemporary festival held twice a year (January and August), organized by the Danza Contemporánea de Cuba, with workshops and classes as well as performances.

The **Havana Theater Festival** is held in October with performances of contemporary international and Cuban drama in various theaters or in the open air in plazas, as well as workshops and seminars.

Havana now holds its **carnival** in August – dates have changed over

the years. The venue is the Malecón, where flamboyant parades are held throughout the day and night.

Santiago de Cuba holds a lively carnival in late July. Again, not the traditional pre-Lent celebration, but one that grew out of traditional summer festivals. Varadero has a less spirited festival, with tourist participation, in January and February.

At all these events, popular bands often play for free, and there are fairgrounds and attractions. For most Cubans the food fairs at which basic staples like rice and bananas are sold from the back of trucks at very low prices are the main attraction.

The *comparsas* or street dances of Cuba's carnivals are as colorful and symbolic as the floats. In Havana and Santiago, neighborhood groups have rehearsals at least once a week during the year, and you may be lucky enough to come across one.

A less well-known festival, **Las Parrandas**, takes place in certain towns and villages of Villa Clara province, in the week between Christmas and New Year – most famously at Remedios. For a description of this wild and colorful event, see page 242.

NIGHTLIFE

Every hotel in Cuba has one or more bars and many have programmed entertainment, often focused around the pool. Most large hotels have their own disco and cabaret. If you want to be more adventurous, ask around for the best local *peña*, disco, or cabaret, where you will be able to drink rum and dance alongside local people. Local discos are obviously at their liveliest at weekends, but don't get going until 11pm or even later.

The beach resort of Varadero has abundant discos and night-time shows and cabarets, but the best and most varied nightlife is in Havana.

1830
Malecón, 1252, right by the Miramar tunnel
Tel: (7) 838-3090
Expensive restaurant open from noon, outdoor dancing to live music at 10pm, cabaret shows and live bands. Best on Friday.

Atelier
Calle 17, corner of Calle 6, Vedado
Tel: (7) 830-6808
Basement club with small dance floor. Daily 10pm–4am. Shows start at 11.30pm, followed by a disco where styles include salsa and rap.

Cinema

Movies are often put on only at weekends or on selected evenings – other than in the main cinemas in Havana, such as those in Vedado, including the Yara, opposite the Habana Libre, and the Charles Chaplin, farther along Calle 23. These same cinemas tend to show the pick of the films during the annual International Festival of **New Latin American Cinema**, www.habanafilmfestival.com, held in the first two weeks of December drawing stars, directors, critics, and movie buffs from around the world. The Teatro Karl Marx is the venue for some high-profile screenings. In April there is also a film festival held in Gibara for low-budget movies, the **Festival Internacional de Cine Pobre de Humberto Solás**, named for the late Cuban director (1941–2008).

Casa de la Amistad
Paseo 406, between 17 and 19, Vedado
Tel: (7) 830-3114
Best nights are Tue and Sat, when there is a cover charge. Mon–Fri 11am–midnight, Sat till 2am, Sun till 6pm.
Cabaret Parisién
Hotel Nacional, calles 21 and O
Tel: (7) 873-3564
Cheaper than the Tropicana, this show in the Nacional lasts longer and is equally good. 9pm–2.30am; show starts at 10pm; reservations required.
Café Cantante Mi Habana
Teatro Nacional, Paseo and 39, Plaza de la Revolución
Tel: (7) 878-4275
The program varies: sometimes disco, live music of all kinds (usually at the weekend), or stand-up (in rapid Spanish). Afternoon and evening performances. It's a small, lively basement venue and quickly fills up. Open daily 5pm–3am.
Café de Paris
Calle San Ignacio, 202, corner of

Obispo
Live and lively music every night.
Café Taberna "Amigos del Benny"
Calle Mercaderes, 531 and Teniente Rey (Brasil)
Tel: (7) 861-1637
Restaurant and bar, live music from 8pm – good-quality son and mambo.
Casa de la Cultura de La Habana Vieja
Calle Aguiar, 509, between Amargura and Brasil (Teniente Rey)
Tel: (7) 863-4860
Starting around 8pm, nightly performances held either in the lovely theater or outdoors in the churchyard. Large crowds, mostly local people – the atmosphere is enchanting.
Casa de la Música Galiano
Avenida de Italia (Galiano), 255, between Neptuno and Concordia, Centro Habana
Tel: (7) 862-4165
Salsa, songo, and rock bands; matinee slots from 4pm for up-and-coming bands and prime evening slots from around 11pm for the big guns, when you can pay CUC$20 or more for a ticket (but usually it's far less). Also a music shop and restaurant.
La Cecilia
Avenida 5 and Calle 110, Miramar
Tel: (7) 204-1562
Music and dancing to a salsa orchestra. Thur–Sun 9.30pm till late.
Pico Blanco
Hotel St John's, Calle O, 206, between 23 and 25, Vedado
Tel: (7) 833-3740
Live bolero till 1am followed by a disco. Fantastic views over Vedado. Open every night 9am–3am.
El Delirio Habanero
Teatro Nacional, Paseo and 39, Plaza de la Revolución
Tel: (7) 878-4275
Piano bar and salsa. Cooler and quieter than the Café Cantante Mi Habana downstairs. Great views over the Plaza de La Revolución. Open Tue–Sun 6pm till late.
Jazz Café
Galerías del Paseo, Paseo, corner of Avenida 1era, Vedado

Tel: (7) 838-3556
Famous jazz club, frequented by Chuchó Valdés. Live music (two sets, 8pm and 11pm). New groups and lots of improvisation. Good food.
El Gato Tuerto
Calle O, 14, between 17 and 19, Vedado
Tel: (7) 838-2696.
A refurbished club near the Hotel Nacional. Major artists, mostly bolero. Open daily till 3am.
Club Habana
Avenida 5, between 188 and 192, Reparto Flores, Miramar
Tel: (7) 204-5700
Social and sailing club with café-bar, piano bar, and live music and dancing. Fri and Sat karaoke 10.30pm–1am.
Hurón Azul (UNEAC)
Calle 17, 351, between Avenida de los Presidentes and H, Vedado
Tel: (7) 832-4571
Headquarters of the Cuban Union of Artists and Writers, and mainly a Cuban hang-out. Boleros on Saturday night, Trova sin Traba and Peña del Ambia alternate, Wed (5–8pm), and son on Sun (5–8pm).
Club Imágenes
Calzada 602, corner of C, Vedado
Tel: (7) 833-3606
Live bolero, son, and traditional music, plus soft piano sounds. Matinées Mon–Fri 3.30–8pm, daily 9.30pm till about 3am.
Club Karachi
Calle K, between calles 15 and 17, Vedado
Tel: (7) 832-3485
Mostly Cuban clientele. Recorded and live music; a show at midnight. Open Tue–Sat till 3am and Sun afternoon.
Opus Bar
Calzada and Calle D, Vedado
Tel: (7) 832-4521
Housed in the elegant and old School of Music. Live music, cocktails, and snacks. Open 3pm–3am.
El Polvorín
Avenida Monumental, La Cabaña
Tel: (7) 860-9990, 863-8295
By the Twelve Apostles restaurant at the foot of El Morro, this is a funky disco bar and reggaeton venue with an excellent outdoor terrace. You can sip cuba libres among the big guns that face out over the bay. Popular with hip young Cubans and tourists. Open daily 9pm–3am.
La Red
Calle 19, 151, corner of Calle L, Vedado
Tel: (7) 832-5415
A mainly Cuban club serving mostly Western music, sometimes reggae, even excellent Cuban rap, open from 10pm but doesn't get going until

midnight, especially at weekends.

Salón Rosado Benny Moré, La Tropical
Avenida 41 and 46, Miramar
Tel: (7) 206-1282
The best live salsa venue in Cuba. A big, no-frills outdoor arena. The best (and lesser-known) artists play here Sat–Sun 11pm–2am. Cabaret Wed from 8pm, *peña* Thur, recorded music Fri, dance matinee Sun 3–7pm.

Tikoa
Calle 23, 177, between calles N and O, Vedado
Tel: (7) 830-9973
Salsa rules at weekends in this lively disco favored by Cubans but Mon–Thur there is usually a singer. Open daily 10pm–2am.

Tropicana
Calle 72, 4504, between 43 and 45, Marianao
Tel: (7) 267-1717
The most elaborate and impressive of Cuba's cabarets *(see page 188)*. Any hotel tourism bureau will book seats for you, but the show is expensive: CUC$70–90, depending on your seat and the age of your rum. Open air, it is canceled if it rains. Open till 2am.

El Turquino
Hotel Habana Libre, calles 23 and L, Vedado
Tel: (7) 834-6100
Disco on the 25th floor, with occasional live salsa from top groups. The roof opens and you can dance in the open air. Open daily 10.30pm–3am, cabaret 11pm and 1am.

La Zorra y el Cuervo
Calle 23, between N and O, Vedado
Tel: (7) 833-2402
Famous jazz club in a La Rampa basement (look for UK-style red phone box at entrance). Live music from 11pm. Open daily 10pm–2am.

Nightlife Outside Havana

Just about every Cuban town has a **Casa de la Trova** (traditional Cuban-style music hall), and/or a Casa de la Música. Cultural events and concerts take place in a Casa de la Cultura and there is usually a Patio de ARTex, a bar/café with an open-air space where you can hear contemporary, regional music, and comedy.

Santiago

Casa de la Trova
Calle Heredia, 208, between San Pedro and San Félix
Tel: (22) 623-943
One of the best known *casas* in Cuba. Famous musicians play here and you can hear *trova, son,* and *boleros.*

There is always something going on, and most of it is excellent. Open Tue–Sun, afternoon and evening.

Casa de las Tradiciones
Rabí, 154, entre José de Diego and García
Tel: (22) 653-892
Smaller and more intimate than the Casa de la Trova, and very much a local venue. Open 3–11.30pm, with live *trova, son,* and *boleros* from 8pm.

Patio de ARTex
Calle Heredia, 304 between Carnicería and Calvario
Tel: (22) 654-814
In the patio behind the ARTex store, there is often excellent music, with late-afternoon and evening sets. Dance, or just have a drink and enjoy the music.

Tropicana Santiago
Autopista Nacional, Km 1.5
Tel: (22) 642-579
Santiago puts its stamp on this glitzy show, with local touches to distinguish it from its Havana namesake. Open 8pm–3am, with disco after the show; tickets cost around CUC$30, but packages are available which include transport and drinks.

Trinidad

Casa de la Música
On the steps by the Plaza Mayor
Tel: (41) 996-622
Music and dancing till the early hours. There's a restaurant, show, piano bar, and music shop, very popular with local people and tourists.

Casa de la Trova
Calle Echerrri, 29
Can be great or average. When it's good, it's very good. Live music day and night, popular with Cubans and tourists of all ages.

Palenque de los Congos Reales
Calle Echerri, corner Menéndez
Tel: (41) 994-512
Son and salsa nightly on a small patio; has a lively following. During the day there are often live bands and an Afro-Cuban show.

Las Ruínas de Brunet
Calle Maceo, between Colón and Zerquera
Afro-Caribbean touristy dance show in a ruined colonial courtyard at 9pm, also daytime activities including *trova,* dance, and percussion classes.

Cienfuegos

Disco El Benny
Avenida 54 between 29 and 31
Tel: (43) 451-105
This is the best place in town for dancing. The bar is 1950s style, there is a show every night at 11pm, and

What's On

Havana's nightlife scene is constantly changing. It is well worth asking in music stores, and your hotel or *casa particular*, for venues. The weekly magazine *Cartelera* (free in most hotels), www.cartelera.com, has a reliable "what's on" section. *Guía La Habana* (also free) is a monthly publication that may also be useful.

the disco stays open until 5am; popular with Cubans and tourists, there is a great atmosphere and very few *jineteras.*

Holguín

UNEAC
Calle Libertad, between Luz Caballero and Martí
Restored colonial building, very elegant and hosting all the major cultural events in the city. There is also a good Casa de la Trova and Casa de la Música in town for a range of music and dance options.

Baracoa

Casa de la Trova
Calle Maceo, 149, between Ciro Frías and Pelayo Cuervo
Tiny, traditional place with great entertainment. Plenty of local people. Tourists welcome and women never short of a partner. Open Tue–Sun from 9pm.

El Ranchón
Loma Paraíso above Calle Calixto García
Tel: (21) 643-268
Open-air disco on the hill with a lovely view, popular with the young after other places close; live and recorded music, gets going after midnight.

Santa Clara

Club Mejunje
Marta Abreu, 107, between Alemán and Juan Bruno Zayas
Tel: (42) 282-572
There is always something going on here, an open-air venue in a ruin with trees and graffiti-covered walls where composers, artistes, and audience mingle for a drink and chat over good music. A different theme every night, from 1950s music, *trova,* and Afro-Cuban folkloric music to a gay disco with transvestite show.

Bayamo

Cabaret Bayamo
Opposite Hotel Sierra Maestra
Tel: (23) 421-698

There is a restaurant where you can have a meal before the 9pm show, everything in *pesos Cubanos* so very cheap.

Los Beatles
Calle Juan Clemente Zenea, corner Saco
You can not miss the statues of John, Paul, George, and Ringo at the door, looking as though they are waiting to go in. Live and taped music, mostly golden oldies, popular for dancing.

SHOPPING

What to Buy

Nobody goes to Cuba for the shopping. In fact, one of the most striking things for most visitors is the lack of consumer goods – along with the lack of advertising. However, two of the things that Cuba is most famous for – Cigars and rum – are easy to find and make the best gifts. Most countries have import limits on both, which travelers should check beforehand: the standard limit is 50 cigars and two liters of rum. Both items can be purchased in the big hotels or tourist stores, or directly from the cigar factories and rum distilleries that offer tours.

Some recommended places to buy cigars are listed below, and rum can be bought just about everywhere. Habana Club is the best: the cheapest variety is the three-year-old white rum; the most expensive (and this only means about cuc$12) are the *añejo siete años*; in between come the *añejo cinco años* and the *añejo reserva* – these three are all dark rums of different ages. Cuban coffee is well worth purchasing, too; Cubita, Turquina, and Hola are the best brands. Try the **Casa del Café** on Calle Baratillo, between Obispo and Jústiz.

If you love chocolate, go to the **Museo del Chocolate** on Calle Mercaderes (really just a café and store) where excellent pure chocolate can be purchased.

If you fall under the spell of Cuban music, as most people do, you will want to splash out on a few **CDs**. Many hotels have a reasonable selection, but keep an eye open for **ARTex** stores, which have a better-than-average choice *(opposite)*. Many of the groups that serenade you in Old Havana and elsewhere have their own CDs for sale. The recording quality is not the best, and the music may not sound quite as good once you get it

home, but they can make good, nostalgic mementoes.

Handicrafts tend to be of mixed quality in the state-run stores, but the legalization of private enterprise has meant that many Cubans have started painting pictures and making jewelry, embroidery, ceramics, leather goods, and musical instruments.

Foreign interest in Santería and other Afro-Cuban religions has also spawned the proliferation of souvenirs related to these cults, from the colorful necklaces associated with Santería to sculpted figures of the gods *(orishas)*.

Second-hand **books** and fascinating **newspapers** and **magazines** from the pre- and early revolutionary era are worth looking out for, too. Across Cuba you will find people selling books in the street or from the front of their houses. The biggest collection is to be found in the market in the Plaza de Armas in Old Havana (Wed–Sat 9am–6pm).

Many **peso book stores** are depressingly empty of new titles, but books of obvious interest to tourists are being published for sale in cuc stores. The range of titles is improving, but stock is often dominated by illustrated books about Cuba, expensive reprints of Cuban revolutionary volumes (the speeches of Che Guevara or the works of José Martí, etc.), and a limited number of novels in Spanish by "safe" authors (García Márquez is a favorite).

Export Procedures

Visitors who wish to buy Cuban art should note that they need an export permit. State-run stores and galleries will issue this automatically. You also need a permit if you buy a work from a street market or artist – no matter how inexpensive. Sometimes, the artist will issue a permit, but otherwise you must go to the **Registro Nacional de Blenes Culturales** (National Registry of Cultural Goods) at Calle 17, 1009, between calles 10 and 12, Vedado, and allow a minimum of three or four days for processing. Permits cost around cuc$20 and are good for up to five artworks. It is important to get one, otherwise your purchases will be confiscated at the airport. This is also true for antiques and antiquarian books, over 50 years old.

You can take up to 20 loose cigars and up to 50 cigars in their original, sealed packaging, with the official hologram, out of the country without an official receipt. For more than 50

cigars, keep both copies of your official receipt from an authorized state store (one will be retained by customs on your departure) and keep the cigars in their sealed boxes. Anything else will be confiscated. Always keep cigars in your hand luggage when you leave the country.

Buying Cigars

Cigars can be bought on any visit to a factory, such as the **Fábrica de Tabaco Partagás** just behind the Capitolio in Havana *(see page 173)*. Outside Havana, there's the shop opposite the **Fábrica de Tabaco Francisco Donatién** in Pinar del Río; numerous opportunities on *vegas* (tobacco plantations) in and around Viñales; and the **Fábrica de Tabaco Cesár Escalante** in Santiago, and many other places. Hotel cigar stores all have large humidors and usually well-informed staff, and their cigars are often cheaper than in factory stores. If you have left it until the last minute, you can buy cigars at the airport, but the selection is smaller. Some recommended stores are listed below:

In **Old Havana**, the **Casa del Habano**, attached to Hostal Conde de Villanueva, Calle Mercaderes, 202, between Lamparilla and Amargura, is an excellent cigar store. **Casa del Ron y el Tabaco**, Monserrate corner of Obispo, sells both rum and cigars; **Tabacos Habana** in the Manzana de Gómez, Zulueta with Neptuno, is open every day 9am–5.30pm. **Habanos** in the Hostal Valencia, Oficios 53 between Lamparilla and Obrapía, is open daily 10am–9pm, and **Palacio de la Artesanía**, Cuba 84 between Cuarteles and Chacón, has a cigar store.

In **Centro**, there's **Romeo y Julieta**, Calle Belascoaín, 852, between Peñalver and Desagüe; and **El Palacio del Tabaco**, Reál Fábrica de Tabacos La Corona, Calle Agramonte (Zulueta), 106, between Refugio and Colón, sells fine Corona cigars from the factory.

In Vedado, **Hotel Nacional de Cuba** and **Hotel Meliá Cohiba** both have stores.

In **Miramar**, **La Escogida**, a fine cigar store, is housed in the **Hotel Comodoro**, on Avenida 3ra, corner of 84; and **Casa del Habano**, Avenida 5ta, 1407, corner of 16, is a small but good cigar store.

Don't be tempted to buy cigars from hustlers on the street: most of them are fakes made from cheap tobacco or even banana leaves, whatever the labels say.

General Shopping

The shopping scene in Havana was transformed in the 1990s. The main commercial streets of the pre-revolutionary era are now gradually coming to life, with new and more up-market stores opening all the time. Habana Vieja tends to have smart, expensive stores, geared specifically at tourists, in the renovated streets.

Old Havana

Habana 1791, Calle Mercaderes, 156, between Obrapía and Lamparilla, sells its own brands of colognes in gorgeous old-world bottles of heavy glass and sealing wax, beautifully packaged in pure linen bags. One interesting fragrance for men is a woody cologne made from tobacco. They mix bespoke fragrances at prices well below what you would pay in Europe or the US. **La Casa del Perfume**, Calle Teniente Rey between Oficios and Mercaderes, also sells perfumes and colognes and will mix personalized fragrances.

One interesting development is the reopening of once famous department stores such as **Harris Brothers** on Avenida de Bélgica, 305, between O'Reilly and Progreso (open daily 9am–9pm), for clothes, food, and more. The **Palacio de la Artesanía**, Cuba 64, tel: (7) 866-8072, sells clothing, perfume, music, and souvenirs and is open Mon–Sat 10am–7pm, Sun 10am–1pm. There are several boutiques, aimed at up-market consumers, all open Mon–Sat 10am–6pm, Sun 10am–1pm, including **Plaza Vieja**, on the corner of Mercaderes and Teniente Rey; **Paul and Shark**, Muralla between Mercaderes and San Ignacio on Plaza Vieja; **La Bella Cubana**, Oficios, corner Lamparilla, near Plaza San Francisco; and **Vía Uno**, also on Oficios, corner Lamparilla.

Other interesting places are the **Betania market**, on Amargura, corner San Ignacio (open Mon–Sat 10am–7pm), where you can buy expensive organic products; and the small and specialized cultural market at the **Casa de los Arabes**, Oficios, between Obispo and Obrapía.

Centro Habana

The main shopping streets of Centro Habana are **San Rafael**, **Neptuno**, and **San Miguel**, where you will see many familiar names over the store fronts. **La Época** department store, Avenida de Italia (Galiano) and Neptuno, is good for children's and women's fashion. **La Vajilla**, on Avenida de Italia (Galiano) and Zanja, is a state-run antiques store (prices in pesos). You have to root about a bit, but there's often a gem or two to be found (open Mon–Sat 10am–5pm).

Plaza de Carlos III, on Avenida Salvador Allende between Arbol Seco and Retiro, is one of the biggest stores in Havana, with restaurants, cafés, banks, and other services.

Vedado

Calle 23, particularly **La Rampa** – the section that runs from the Hotel Habana Libre down to the Malecón – was once the hub of Havana's life; the street itself is inlaid with colored panels by famous Cuban artists.

Where to Buy Crafts, Books, and Music in Havana

Arts and Crafts

One of the best places for crafts in Cuba is the **Feria de Artesanía**, in Almacenes San José, on San Pedro (Avenida del Puerto), just beyond the ferry for Regla. You will find jewelry, leather goods, carved wooden items, and more. You are expected to haggle. There are smaller, cheaper versions of this market on Calle Simón Bolívar, just off Parque de la Fraternidad (near the Capitolio); opposite the Pabellón Cuba on La Rampa in Vedado, and the Feria del Malecón on the Malecón and corner of Calle D, a few blocks east of the Hotel Riviera.

The **Palacio de la Artesanía**, an attractive colonial building on Calle Cuba 64, Old Havana, has a good selection of crafts, CDs, and other items that make good souvenirs and mementoes.

In Centro, arts and crafts can be found at **ArteHabana**, on San Rafael 110 corner Industria, open Mon–Sat 10am–6pm, with a café open until 7pm, while another option worth checking out is **Fin de Siglo**, on the pedestrian part of San Rafael, open Mon–Sat 10am–5pm. **Sala Contemporánea** – a gallery selling Cuban arts and crafts – is at Calle 3 and G, Vedado (open Mon–Fri 10am–5pm).

Books

Stalls sell second-hand and antiquarian books, including many with revolutionary and political themes, at a market on the Plaza de Armas (Wed–Sat). Prices are fairly high, but there is a good choice. If you are looking for something specific, it's always worth asking around; even if a vendor does not have the book to hand, they may well be able to track down a copy for you if you can wait a day or two.

The bookstores worth checking out include the following:

● **La Librería Anticuaria El Navío**, Calle Obispo, 119, between Oficios and Mercaderes, is one of many very fine, decidedly up-market stores that are springing up all over the restored old town. Selling expensive rare books, first editions, and old postcards, the prices are steep, but it's great for a browse. If you buy, remember that export procedures apply to books over 50 years old.

● **La Moderna Poesía**, Obispo, 527, corner Bernaza, just off Parque Central. This was the most famous peso bookstore in Havana, but became a dollar, now a CUC, store.

● Palacio del Segundo Cabo (Instituto del Libro), Plaza de Armas. There are three bookshops here: **La Bella Habana** sells foreign editions of books and art in CUCs, while a second shop sells stationery, encyclopedias, dictionaries, and Cuban publications in CUCs, and a third sells books published in Cuba in *moneda nacional*.

Music

Cassettes and CDs are available all over town. Most hotels have a good selection, as do ARTex stores throughout Cuba. In Old Havana, the music store in the **Palacio de la Artesanía** at Calle Cuba 64 in Old Havana is good. The **Museo Nacional de la Música**, on Avenida de las Misiones, currently closed for renovation, has a store with knowledgable staff selling an excellent selection of CDs. **Tienda Longina**, Obispo 360 between Habana and Compostela, sells musical instruments as well as CDs and musical souvenirs. The **Centro Wifredo Lam**, San Ignacio 22, corner Empedrado, is another good place for CDs and souvenirs. In Centro, head for the **Casa de la Música**, on Galiano and Neptuno, or **ArteHabana** (see above). In Vedado, one of the best places is the **ARTex** store, La Habana Sí, on Calle 23 and L (opposite the Habana Libre); in Miramar, try the **Casa de la Música** de Miramar, Calle 35, corner 20.

The **International Press Center**, on the corner of La Rampa and Calle O, hosts exhibitions by Cuban artists, and has a store where you can buy newspapers, magazines, and books (particularly political titles), and a photo center.

On the Malecón and Prado (opposite the Hotel Meliá Cohiba) is a glass-fronted shopping mall, **Galería Paseo**, where the first-floor supermarket sells Cuban cheeses, unusual cuts of meat, and breads that are often hard to find.

Pan de Paris, is a French-owned patisserie selling the best bread in Cuba, using imported French flour. Their shops can be found at Línea, between Paseo and A, Vedado; 106 and 51, Marianao; Vento and 100, Boyeros; and at the entrance to Tarará, Playas del Este. There is also a nice shop called **Sylvaín**, selling cakes, pastries, and sweets in CUCs, at Línea and 8 (next to Cine Línea).

The **Galerías Amazonas**, Calle 12, between 23 and 25, Vedado, is a small mall of stores selling wines, liquors, and handmade chocolates, and good bread.

Miramar

Behind the Russian Embassy, rows of advertising billboards herald the former **Diplotienda** on Avenida 3ra and Calle 70. The store is now open to anyone who has CUCs and can afford to shop there; in fact, most buyers are Cubans, not foreigners. The range of food is not as good as it was, but it is still dreadfully expensive.

Havana's *haute-couture* **Maison** on Calle 16 and Avenida 7 has a

BELOW: Cuba has ideal conditions for windsurfing.

series of smart boutiques selling Cuban fashions and antiques. There are also regular fashion shows, which are very entertaining.

Le Select, Avenida 5ta and 30, is an up-market department store, with an amazing foyer with marble statues and chandeliers, and there's even a swimming pool. Closed Sunday.

SPECTATOR SPORTS

Anyone interested in attending sports events should contact their nearest Cuban tourist office or check the websites of the Buró de Convenciones, www.cubameeting.travel/, which lists all forthcoming events with contact details of organizers, or Cubadeportes, www.cubadeportes.cu.
Estadio Latinamericano
Calle Pedro Pérez 302, Cerro
Tel: (7) 870-6576.
Baseball, Cuba's favorite game, is played here five days a week. Your hotel should be able to give exact details. The stadium accommodates 55,000 spectators, and is about a 10-minute taxi ride from Old Havana.
Estadio Panamericano
Vía Monumental, Km 4.5, Habana del Este
Tel: (7) 766-6030
Built for the 1991 Pan-American Games, the stadium was upgraded in 2008 with a new synthetic surface with eight lanes for athletics. Soccer matches are also held here. It has a capacity for 34,000 spectators.
Estadio Ramón Fonst
Avenida Independencia and Bruzón, Plaza de la Revolución
Tel: (7) 881-4196
Basketball matches are held here.
Sala Polivalente Kid Chocolate
Paseo de Martí and Brasil, Old Havana
Tel: (7) 861-1547
The main centre for boxing matches, this sports center also stages competitions for judo, weightlifting, handball, tennis, and badminton.
Ciudad Deportiva
Avenida Boyeros and Vía Blanca
Tel: (7) 881-6979
A state-of-the-art indoor facility when it opened in 1958, but it is showing its age. Seats 18,000 under a domed roof and hosts local and international matches for volleyball, basketball, table tennis, and martial arts.
Velódromo Nacional Reinaldo Paseiro
Vía Monumental, Km 4.5, Habana del Este
Tel: (7) 766-3776

The other side of the road from the Estadio Panamericano but part of the same complex. Cycling is highly competitive in Cuba and world-class cyclists train and compete here.

ACTIVE SPORTS

Beach resorts usually have facilities and qualified instructors for a wide range of land and water sports. Some hotels also rent out bicycles and mopeds, but supplies vary.

There are many specialized sports tours available: cycling, fishing, birding, etc. that can be arranged via an agency in your home country, or online. Cuba is especially well organized for scuba, snorkeling, and sailing, and these are best arranged through a dedicated travel agency.

Cubanacán's UK subsidiary has a series of package tours that include scuba diving, deep-sea fishing, birding, hiking, horseback riding, kayaking, cycling, and mountain biking. Cubanacán UK Ltd, Unit 49, Skylines Village, Limeharbour, Docklands, London E14 9TS, tel: 020-7536 8175, http://cubanacan.co.uk.

In Canada, Cubanacán can be contacted at 372 Bay Street, Toronto, Ontario, M5H 2W9, tel: (416) 601-0343; and 1255 Rue University, Suite 211, Montreal, Quebec H3B 3B2, tel: (514) 861-4444.

Birding

Birding is good all over the island but tours tend to concentrate on the Zapata peninsula where thousands of migratory birds nest each winter *(see page 231)*. There are also 170 species of Cuban birds here, including most of the endemics, and the best place for seeing rare birds is around Santo Tomás. Other good spots are the Sierra Maestra mountain range, the Península de Guanahacabibes in the far west, Cayo Coco, the mountains around Baracoa in the east of the island, and the Sierra Najasa region of Camagüey.

Tours can be arranged in the UK by Cuba Welcome, tel: 020-7731 6871, www.cubawelcome.com, or Cubanacán UK Ltd, Unit 49, Skylines Village, Limeharbour, London E14 9TS, tel: 020-7536 8175, http://cubanacan.co.uk.

Cycling

There are numerous opportunities for a Cycle Cuba vacation, often organized as a means of fundraising for various charities, Just type "Cycle Cuba" into your search engine and you will be spoiled for choice.

Fishing

Deep-sea fishing can be arranged with **Marlin Náutica y Marinas** (www.nauticamarlin.com) around the island at Marina Hemingway, Marina Tarará, Base Náutica Chapelín, Cayo Guillermo, Cayo Coco, Cayo Paredón Grande, Santa Lucía, Guardalavaca, Marina Santiago de Cuba, Marina Trinidad, Marina Cienfuegos, Jardines de la Reina, Isla de la Juventud, and Cayo Largo del Sur. Good, safe fishing boats can be hired for half a day from CUC$250–300. Fish are shark, 225kg (500lb) marlin, swordfish, tarpon as large as 70kg (150lb), sawfish, yellowfin tuna, dorado, and wahoo, among others.

International sport fishing competitions are held mostly at the Marina Hemingway in Havana. The main tournaments include the International Ernest Hemingway White Marlin Fishing Tournament in June, the International Blue Marlin Fishing Tournament in September, and the International Tournament of Wahoo Fishing in November.

There are also great opportunities for fly-fishing in the Jardines de la Reina off the south coast, off Cayo Largo del Sur and in the **Zapata peninsula**. The salt flats at Las Salinas have recently been opened to fly-fishermen, but numbers are limited and access is controlled by the National Park Headquarters at Playa Larga, tel: (45) 987-249.

Good freshwater fishing can also be found in the lakes and reservoirs, mainly for large-mouth bass (trucha). Good places include Maspotón in Pinar del Río, Laguna del Tesoro in the Zapata peninsula, Zaza reservoir in Sancti Spíritus, and Redonda Lake in Ciego de Avila province.

Golf

Cuba has two professional golf courses open to foreign visitors. The **Havana Golf Club** (tel: 7-649-8918), also known as the "DiploClub", in Boyeros, is 30 minutes from the city center. The course is currently 9 holes but it's hoped to increase to the full 18 holes. The clubhouse has a pool, bowling alley, two bars, and a restaurant. Hire of clubs, personal caddies, trainers, and balls are all available at day rates. Closed Monday. The **Varadero Golf Club** (tel: 45-668-482, www.varaderogolfclub.com),

an 18-hole course covering a narrow 3.5km (2-mile) strip of land, is the venue for international events. The course, by Varadero beach, was designed in 1927 for millionaire Irenee Dupont, and the clubhouse is next to the former Dupont mansion (Mansión Xanadú). Clubs, caddies, trainers, and balls can be hired.

Horseback Riding

Viñales and Trinidad are the main sites for horseback riding. In the former, treks can be arranged through hotels Los Jazmines and La Ermita (see page 344–5). In Trinidad, you can tour the Valle de los Ingenios (see page 263) on horseback. All state tour operators offer the same deals. Private guides are now illegal, although they still operate clandestinely, offering cheaper deals than state agencies. Their horses and saddles will be in poorer condition and, if guides are caught, will be impounded.

Environmental Issues

Cuba has a good record for environmental awareness and has done much to protect and preserve the island's natural attributes. But there is, inevitably, a conflict between conservation and providing the facilities needed for the tourist industry – which is the country's main source of income. For example, hotels in certain areas must be allowed to spray against mosquitoes, even though this kills many insects that feed the indigenous and migratory birds.

"Ecotourism" is an expression bandied about a great deal, and one that is difficult to define, as it is used to cover a wide range of activities and intentions, from wilderness adventures to volunteering for activities that promote economic opportunities for local communities. And it is sometimes misused simply to promote vacations in places of natural beauty.

The infrastructure put in place to cater for our needs can have an adverse affect on a country's ecosystem, and anyone engaged in any kind of outdoor pursuit should behave responsibly, and be aware that their activities could potentially cause damage. Care should be taken at all levels, from avoiding touching coral when diving to staying on designated paths when hiking, or simply taking all your rubbish home with you.

Check that your horse appears fit and healthy.

Hotels in Varadero and other resorts will also be able to arrange treks. Or, if you want a full riding holiday, check www.cubastartravel.com or www.captivatingcuba.com.

Rock Climbing

This is mainly done on the limestone crags called mogotes in the Viñales valley; they offer fantastic climbing and the sport is becoming increasingly popular. Best months are October to April, when it is not too hot or too wet. The Hotel Jazmines (see page 345) is the central venue. Check the informative website www.cubaclimbing.com, which offers a quote from Castro: "The Revolution was the work of climbers and cavers."

Scuba Diving

Diving is extremely popular along Cuba's stunning coastline and all the major resorts offer diving courses and excursions. You can do it as part of an all-inclusive package or pay-as-you-go, with individual dives costing around CUC$35–40. The three marine platforms around the island, the Archipiélago del Rey to the north, the Archipiélago de la Reina to the south, and the Archipiélago de los Canarreos around Isla de la Juventud and Cayo Largo del Sur, offer a wealth of coral reefs and marine life, making diving a rewarding experience. Some of the main sites include Varadero, Santa Lucía, Cayo Largo, Isla de la Juventud, Faro de Luna, María La Gorda, and Cayo Levisa. Marlin Náutica y Marinas operates 18 dive centers and there are four hyperbaric chambers. There is also a live-aboard facility in the Jardines de la Reina in the southeast.

Trekking

There are great opportunities for trekking in Cuba. It is possible to arrange local guides but probably best to go on an organized trip that offers the kind of experience you want. Remember: guides are compulsory in all national parks, which is probably where you will want to walk. Pico Turquino in the Sierra Maestra is a favorite trekking destination. At 1,975 meters (6,749ft), it is the highest peak in Cuba. The landscape is stunning and there is good birdlife. Try a dedicated agency such as Andean Trails, www.andeantrails.co.uk. The Ramblers Association also take guided groups to Cuba, www.ramblersholidays.co.uk.

A – Z

A HANDY SUMMARY OF PRACTICAL INFORMATION, ARRANGED ALPHABETICALLY

A dmission Charge

There is an admission charge for most museums, galleries, and other places of touristic interest. It is generally CUC$1–5. In many places, you pay extra if you are going to use a camera, and quite a lot extra to use a video camera.

Age restrictions

The age of consent is 18 in Cuba. Sex tourism is rife and foreign men are often seen in the company of young girls but this is illegal and can be a blackmail trap. The minimum age for hiring a car is 21, although for some types of car the limit rises to 25.

B udgeting for Your Trip

A good hotel in Havana will cost around CUC$160 for a double room in high season (see page 340), but there are cheaper options, and almost anywhere outside Havana is cheaper. You can choose to stay in casas particulares, where you will, on average, be charged CUC$25 (less outside Havana), with breakfast

costing around CUC$3–5 and dinner around CUC$7–10, depending on your menu choice. Eating out is rarely very expensive. About CUC$25 per person in a smartish restaurant, but there are many restaurants and paladares where you can eat well for around CUC$15 or less. If you are going to drink wine, this puts the price up quite a lot. In a bar, beer costs around CUC$1.50, mojitos CUC$3–6, depending on location. If you go to a town such as Bayamo, where you can pay in pesos Cubanos, food and drink will be much cheaper. Car rental is expensive, around CUC$50 a day (see page 338). Taxi fares are reasonable: you can get to most places in Havana for CUC$5. Long-distance bus fares are reasonable; the longest journey you could make would be Havana to Santiago, currently CUC$51. As there are not many consumer goods for sale you are unlikely to spend much on shopping.

C hildren

Cubans love their own kids and take them everywhere with them, so they are fascinated by foreigners who do

the same. Your children will be pampered guests at any hotel and the employees will quickly learn their names and interests. The beach resorts all have supervised activities for them, and family rates are offered during the low season.

Climate

Cuba has a subtropical climate, with an average annual temperature of 25°C (77°F). The mean relative humidity is 77 percent during the dry season (Nov–Apr) and 82 percent during the wet season (May–Oct).

The sun seems to shine all the time in Cuba, but temperatures are most definitely higher during the rainy "summer" season than in the drier "winter" months. Those who are not accustomed to melting temperatures would do well to avoid visiting the island in July and August – when most Cubans spend every spare moment either on the beach or in the shower.

While the rain of the wet season is not often more than an inconvenience – torrential showers can be replaced by sun within the space of half an hour – the late summer is also

CLIMATE CHART

Maximum temperature
Minimum temperature
Rainfall

hurricane season. Therefore, the best time to visit Cuba is from December to April, after the hurricane season is over and before the hot, muggy summer months arrive. To avoid high-season prices and crowds, visit in November or from March–April.

Crime and Safety

Crime is undoubtedly on the increase in Cuba, but it is still low by Latin American standards. Indeed, in comparison with most of the countries from which they come, visitors will find Cuba reassuringly safe. However, bag snatching and pickpocketing are not uncommon, particularly in the poorer sections of Havana and Santiago.

The streets feel safe, but visitors should still take sensible precautions. Leave travel documents, large banknotes, and ostentatious jewelry in your hotel, and keep a firm grip on your camera and on any bag you decide to carry – bags are best worn crossed over your shoulder.

Violent crime is rare, but there have been some incidents that have landed tourists in hospital. Most of these occurred when people tried to fight off muggers – DON'T.

Although Havana is still considered to be safer than most cities, there are some areas – such as the darker streets of Old and Central Havana – that should be avoided after dark. Be sensible and take the same precautions you would in any large, unfamiliar city, and at night keep to busy and well-lit streets (or walk in the middle of the road if there is no street lighting).

There is much less crime outside the capital, but in Santiago you must take the same precautions as you would in Old or Central Havana.

Loss of Belongings

In case of theft, you should immediately report the crime to the nearest police station. Make sure you ask for the case report *(denuncia)* to back up any insurance claim on your return home. This may take time, but is essential if you intend to make a claim. The Cuban firm **Asistur** (tel: 7-866-8339 24 hours, www.asistur.cu) can help with cash advances and replacement of documents.

You should report lost or stolen passports to your embassy or consulate, which can issue emergency papers to get you home.

Customs Regulations

Tourists may bring in, duty-free, personal effects – including medicine for their own use or as gifts – cameras, tape recorders, MP3 players, personal computers, cellular phones (mobiles), sports and camping equipment. All of these items should in theory be listed on a customs declaration form on arrival. Customs inspections are random.

Visitors importing electrical items as gifts – TVs, kitchen equipment, etc. – should note that 100 percent duty is payable. Certain items, mainly video recorders, modems, and photocopying equipment and supplies, are restricted: you may bring them in only for accredited people such as journalists and approved organizations. Such items will be confiscated by customs until the necessary paperwork from the Ministries of Foreign Relations and Communications is presented.

D isabled Travelers

Travelers with disabilities may find getting around Cuba quite difficult. Most modern hotels and many refurbished hotels have facilities, but older hotels and other buildings do not. Streets and sidewalks are narrow, with storm drains, and wheelchair ramps do not exist. Public toilets (and those in restaurants and bars) are not adapted for people with disabilities. On the positive side, Cubans are extremely helpful and will come to the assistance of anyone who appears to need it.

E lectricity

Both 220 and 110 volts are used, but 220 is more common. Electric outlets usually take plugs with two flat prongs, but you may find some that take round prongs. It's best to come

prepared with adaptors and transformers so as not to be caught out – they are inexpensive and can be bought at the airport before you travel. Power cuts are less frequent than they were, but not uncommon.

Embassies and Consulates

Havana
Canada: Calle 30, 518, corner of 7ma, Miramar, tel: (7) 204-2516.
Germany: Calle 13, 652, corner of B, Vedado, tel: (7) 833-2539, 833-2569.
UK: Calle 34, 702, corner of 7, Miramar, Havana, tel: (7) 204-1771.
Italy: Avenida 5, 402, corner of 4, Miramar, tel: (7) 204-5616.
Spain: Cárcel 51, corner Zulueta, Habana Vieja, tel: (7) 868-6868.
United States: (Interests Section of the Swiss Embassy): Calzada, between L and M, Vedado, tel: (7) 833-3551–9, also toll-free: 1-866-374-1769.

Etiquette

Cuba is hot and many women wear skimpy tops, but bathing suits are for the beach and should not be worn around town. Dress decently to go into a church or temple. At the Basilica El Cobre outside Santiago you will even be asked to cover your shoulders if they are bare. There are often dress codes at nightclubs: Cubans dress smartly to go out at night and men are expected to wear long trousers and shirts.

G ay and Lesbian Travelers

The hardline Cuban policy on homosexuals has lessened in recent years (sex between consenting adults

Emergencies

The general numbers to dial for emergencies are **106**, for police, **105** for fire, or **104** for ambulance. However, this is a relatively new system that does not function in all parts of the country, and where it does, you may not get through to an English-speaking person. There is an extensive list of alternative numbers at the beginning of the telephone directory. **Asistur** is often a visitor's best bet. The Havana office is at Prado 208, tel: (7) 866-8339, and there are branches in tourist centers all over the island. Hotels are also able to help with medical emergencies.

TRANSPORTATION
ACCOMMODATIONS
ACTIVITIES
A – Z
LANGUAGE

was legalized in 1979) and there is generally a more tolerant attitude *(see page 23)*. It is still not the most gay-friendly place to visit, however, although there is a growing number of openly gay people – mostly in the capital and in some small, laid-back places such as Viñales and Baracoa.

H ealth and Medical Care

No health certificate is required of visitors unless they are arriving from areas where cholera, smallpox, or yellow fever exist, in which case they must show a certificate of vaccination against those diseases. However, it's a good idea to be up to date with tetanus, typhoid, and hepatitis A vaccinations. There are no malarial areas in Cuba, but dengue fever, although it has been virtually eradicted through determined fumigation measures, may still occur. There is no vaccination, so do all you can to prevent mosquito bites – use a DEET-based repellent, and cover up in areas where mosquitoes are prevalent. The fever is spread by the *Aedes aegypti* mosquito which, unusually, tends to bite during the day rather than at night. The illness presents with flu-like symptoms and, while usually mild, can be serious.

On the whole, biting and stinging insects, and bugs in general, are not a great problem in Cuba.

Common medicines – such as aspirin and basic stomach remedies – can be bought in hotels, but it's sensible to bring a small supply with you. More specialized items can usually be bought over the counter without prescription from CUC pharmacies, but you should bring all your own prescription drugs with you. In Havana, the **Farmacia Internacional** is at Avenida 41, corner 20, Playa, tel: (7) 204-2051, and at the **Hotel Habana Libre**, corner L and 23, Vedado, tel: (7) 838-4593. There are other good pharmacies at the **Camilo Cienfuegos Hospital** on Línea and Calle 13, Vedado, tel: (7) 833-3599, and at the **Clínica Central Cira García**, Avenida 20, 4101, corner Calle 41, Playa, tel: (7) 204-2880, open 24 hours. Outside Havana, try the international clinics in resort areas or any high-street pharmacy in urban areas.

To avoid upset stomachs and diarrhea – the two main complaints suffered by tourists – drink bottled water – and plenty of it – and eat lightly. Be sensible about over exposure to the sun.

Medical Services

All hotels have a first-aid post of sorts, and the larger hotels will have a resident doctor or nurse, plus transportation to take a patient to the nearest clinic or hospital. Unless you fall ill in a remote rural area, as a foreign visitor you will be treated in a CUC-only hospital or a special tourist clinic (run by Servimed, www.servimedcuba.com).

Most doctors and some nurses speak at least a little English, but hardly anybody is multilingual. The Cuban health-care system is free and readily available to all Cubans, but medicines are in short supply except in facilities that cater to CUC-paying foreigners.

I nternet

Many of the large tourist hotels have internet access and in some (the Inglaterra and the Nacional in Havana, for example) it is available to non-guests on presentation of a passport. This can be expensive, with the business centers in the top hotels charging up to CUC$15 per hour. Wi-fi is rarely available except in some of the business hotels, such as the executive floor of the Hotel Nacional or the lobby of the Hotel Parque Central. Most towns have a branch of ETECSA (the telephone and communications company), also called Telepunto, which offers internet facilities. Internet user cards, which can be used in any ETECSA or other center, cost CUC$6 and give only one hour's access, although this does not have to be used in one sitting. Be aware that telephone lines can be slow and unreliable, so it's always worth writing long emails on Word and saving them to a pen drive/memory stick in case the connection breaks. Lines may also be down completely and access unavailable.

L anguage Courses

The University of Havana, the University of Santiago de Cuba, and the Central University in Santa Clara offer intensive Spanish-language programs for foreigners and a range of specialized courses and seminars for Spanish-speaking foreigners. Low-cost lodgings and meals as well as field trips are usually part of a student package. Language courses are also offered by some tour operators, together with music and dance classes, eg Càlédöñiä Languages, based in Scotland, tel: +44-131 621-7721, www.caledonialanguages.com.

M aps

The best road map of Cuba is Guía de Carreteras by the Directorio Turístico de Cuba (on sale in Cuba for CUC$6). Freytag and Berndt's Kuba/Cuba (1:250,000) is less up to date but has useful city plans. Individual city-centre maps of larger cities cost around CUC$1–2. Hotels and bookstores in Havana and Santiago sell reasonable maps; however, they may not always be in stock when you want them.

Media

Newspapers and Magazines

The printed media of Cuba is extremely limited due to paper shortages and governmental control. Newspapers are posted on kiosks for the general population to read, and you sometimes see vendors wandering the street with copies to sell. The only daily paper is the Communist Party organ, *Granma*, which mainly offers an update on solidarity, trade and agriculture, and provides interesting rather than scintillating reading. It is published weekly in Spanish, English, French, German, and Portuguese. Tourists are more likely to find the international edition in hotel stores, but street sellers often have English-language versions.

The long-established magazine *Bohemia* offers general features, and there are other Cuban publications on sale at CUC news-stands in hotels and airports. Four- and five-star hotels (particularly in Havana) often carry foreign publications from *Time* to *Cosmopolitan*.

Insurance

From May 1, 2010, health insurance has been mandatory for all visitors to Cuba. Tourists and all non-resident Cubans must hold a medical insurance policy that has been issued by one of the specific companies approved by the Cuban government. This is in fact a list of umbrella companies that provide medical and specialized assistance (repatriation) on behalf of individual insurance companies. Check with your insurance company whether they are on the approved list (they may not know and will have to find out for you). If you do not have the correct papers, you will be forced to buy an approved insurance policy on arrival at the airport in Cuba.

TRANSPORTATION

ACCOMMODATIONS

ACTIVITIES

A – Z

LANGUAGE

Banks

Banco Financiero Internacional
Open Mon–Fri 8.30am–3pm.
You can get cash on a credit card here, if it's not from a US bank. In **Havana**, there are branches inside the Hotel Habana Libre; at the corner of Línea and O, Vedado (near Hotel Nacional), also open on Sat 8.30am–noon; at the Plaza de la Revolución; in Old Havana at Oficios, corner Brasil (near Plaza de San Francisco); and at Calle 18, 111. In **Santiago de Cuba**, there is a branch on Avenida Las Américas, corner J Sueño. There are other branches in all major towns and holiday resorts.

Banco Metropolitano SA
Head office is on O'Reilly, 402, in Old Havana, but there are many branches throughout the capital. They deal in foreign currencies (cash on credit cards, traveler's checks, etc.), and have shorter lines than the Banco Financiero).

Television
Cuban national television is broadcast on five state-owned national channels (Cubavisión, Tele Rebelde, Multivisión, Canal Educativo, and Canal Educativo 2). National and international **news** is reported on two half-hour programs. **Sports** events – especially baseball, boxing, and soccer – are often covered live. Other shows include officials and specialists speaking at length and **music** of all kinds in concerts or videos. Foreign **movies** (usually American), seven a week, are shown on Thursday, Friday, Saturday, and Sunday. Action movies are most popular, but a recent crackdown on violence and sex has resulted in an increase of "family" movies. **Soaps**, usually Brazilian, Mexican, or Cuban, are extremely popular. North American soaps and series are also screened.

Tourist hotels all have satellite TV with more than 20 channels.

Radio
Just about everybody in Cuba has a radio, and loud music is a constant background sound wherever you go. Apart from local stations, radios pick up waves from Miami, Jamaica, and the American Forces Network at Guantánamo Base. There are six state-owned national radio stations and each province has its own station as well. Reception varies and you can't pick up the signal for all of them everywhere.

Radio Reloj (Clock Radio) gives round-the-clock news on AM, to the infuriating background noise of a ticking clock; **Radio Havana Cuba** broadcasts news and features on short wave, where the BBC also comes through, though the reception is poor (early morning on 6195, 8–10am on 15220, 10am–1pm on 17840, and mid-afternoon till late in the evening on 5975).

Voice of America broadcasts from 6pm on 7070, short wave.

Radio Martí, Voice of America's Spanish-language propaganda service, broadcasts from Miami, and often changes its frequencies to avoid jamming, but without much success.

Money Matters

Cuba has two currencies: the *peso Cubano* (CUP or *moneda nacional*) divided into 100 centavos, and the *peso convertible* (CUC). Foreigners are expected to use CUC most of the time and will be charged in CUC for all accommodations, most food and transport. Euros can be used in the large resorts: Varadero, Cayo Largo, Cayo Coco, and Santa Lucía.

Some people find it useful to change a small amount of foreign currency into Cuban pesos (the exchange rate is CUC$1 = CUP24) for use on local buses (fares on most urban routes cost between 40 centavos and one peso), in cinemas, when shopping for fresh fruit at farmers' markets, when buying food and drink from street vendors, and in some off-the-beaten, track restaurants. You can make domestic phone calls using the peso phones, saving yourself a lot of money, so you may also want to have a few 20-centavo coins for call boxes. However, many old peso phones have been replaced with new phones which take only cards.

Changing Money
You can change foreign currency into *pesos convertibles* at government-licensed CADECA booths and some large banks *(see box above)*, and it is wise not to attempt to do so elsewhere. There is no black market. Branches of CADECA are fairly widely scattered. In Old Havana, they can be found on Calle Obispo and Calle Oficios and elsewhere, and in Vedado there is one on La Rampa (Calle 23) and one on the corner of the Malecón

and Calle D. Every sizable town has at least one – ask at your hotel. CADECAs change traveler's checks but you must produce the original purchase receipt as well as your passport. American Express traveler's checks or any others issued by a US bank are not accepted. British banks will not even sell you traveler's checks for use in Cuba for that reason.

Change foreign currency into convertible pesos at the CADECA booth at the airport when you arrive. Bring sterling or euros if possible, as a 10 percent tax is charged on US dollars. Make sure your notes are clean, with no writing on them, as any blemished foreign currency will be rejected. Remember to keep enough convertible pesos to pay the CUC$25 departure tax, but don't take them home with you except as souvenirs, since they are not, in fact, convertible currency, despite the name. You can exchange them back into another currency at the airport in Havana, but it is unwise to count on this as there may be delays and the exchange desk, although theoretically open 24 hours, may not be.

The exchange rate fluctuates slightly, but is approximately CUC$1 = US$1.08 (before tax), CAN$1.10, €0.80, £0.72.

Credit Cards
Access/MasterCard, Visa, and other credit cards are welcome at most hotels, and some restaurants and stores, provided they have been issued outside the US by non-US banks, so American Express is no use. Check your card, as some store cards are issued by MBNA or other US bank and will be rejected.

Credit-card operations in Cuba do not always run smoothly. The centralized computer system often fails, going down for hours at a time; this affects every credit-card machine in the land, and you will not be able to use your card at all while the system failure lasts.

A credit card can also be a useful backup if you need cash in an emergency: cash can be withdrawn against a credit card at branches of the Banco Financiero Internacional, and at CADECA, but an 11 percent commission rate is currently being charged, which makes it an expensive transaction. Added to this, all purchases of cash or goods on a credit card will be converted from CUCs to US dollars, incurring the 10 percent exchange tax, before conversion to your own currency by your credit card company, which may charge you further fees and commissions. There is also an increasing number of ATMs in Havana – for example, at the CADECA office in Calle Obispo, available when the office itself is closed – each site should give the location of others in the area. Be warned that there are almost no opportunities to withdraw cash against Cirrus or Switch cards, and that these transactions are best done in Havana and Santiago.

Cash

While traveler's checks are a safe way to carry money, you should always try to have a good supply of cash with you, particularly if you head out of the city. Not all provincial hotels will be able to cash traveler's checks for you.

Getting change from big bills is often difficult, so it is worthwhile keeping a stock of 10s, 5s, and single notes in your wallet. Try to get as many small-denomination bills as possible when you change foreign currency, and always try to break big bills when you are staying at city hotels, where they are more likely to have a better supply in their tills. If your hotel can't help, you may have to go to a bank; most banks will change big bills for you. You will normally have to show your passport if you produce a 50- or 100-CUC bill in a Cuban store.

The UK Foreign Office warns that the wider use of the convertible peso (CUC) has meant an increase in the number of forged CUC banknotes of all denominations but in particular 100-CUC notes.

Be careful, too, when you pay for something, that the change you are given is in CUCs not *pesos cubanos* – the notes look extremely similar.

Opening Hours

Most **banks** open Mon–Fri 8.30am–3pm. Most Cuban **offices** open around 8.30am–5 or 6pm, often with a break at lunch time. But it is not rare for offices, even those serving the public, to close early because of blackouts, shortages, and transportation problems.

Farmers' markets open early, from around 7am or even earlier, and close when traders decide to leave – usually between 4 and 6pm.

CUC retail stores (often referred to as dollar stores) are all over Cuba; most open Mon–Sat 10am–5pm but may stay open later.

CUC supermarkets usually open Mon–Sat 9am–6pm and Sun 9am–1pm. Tourists may be asked to show

their passport at the *diplomercado*, near the Russian Embassy in Havana's Miramar suburb *(see page 362)*. One of the city's original dollar supermarkets (before the embargo on the US$), popular with expats, the "diplo" sells fresh meat and vegetables, and household supplies. It is open Mon–Sat 9am–7pm. Many of the bigger stores open 9am–9pm.

Postal Services

Every rural town has a post office, and major cities have a central post office with municipal branches. You can buy stamps *(sellos)* here for pesos. In hotels, you will be charged the same price, but in CUCs. Some stamps are not glued, so you have to ask for a dab of glue at a post office.

Postcards and letters to Europe cost 75 cents. Domestic delivery is slow, but usually faster from city to city than within the same city. Postcards and letters to Europe and the Americas sometimes only take a fortnight but may take a month or more, even via airmail.

Mother's Day (second Sunday in May) is the one day of the year when cards and telegrams are delivered on time all over Cuba. For a week or so ahead of the mailing deadline, cardboard boxes labeled by province are stacked in the lobby of the larger post offices so senders can drop in their addressed and stamped cards. The boxes are flown to the provincial

Public Holidays

January 1 Liberation Day, commemorating the guerrillas' triumph over Batista.
May 1 Labor Day, celebrated with workers' parades.
July 25–27 A three-day holiday celebrating July 26, 1953, the date of the attack on the Moncada Garrison in Santiago, recognized as the start of the revolution.
October 10 Celebrating the start of the War of Independence against Spain in 1868.
In addition to these official public holidays, there are innumerable other important dates which are commemorated, including:
● **January 28** The birth of José Martí (1853).
● **April 19** The victory at the Bay of Pigs (1962).
● **Second Sunday in May** Mother's Day
● **October 8** Death of Che Guevara.

capital to be sorted and then dispatched – and they are sure to reach mother on her day.

R eligious Services

The government blunted the influence of the Catholic Church in the early 1960s, but never cracked down on it completely. Since the Pope's visit to Cuba in 1998 there has been a resurgence of Catholic practice – and a seeming relaxation of hostility from the government. Mass is still said in churches throughout the island. Your hotel tourism bureau can direct you to the church of your choice, but service times vary.

In Havana, times of Mass in the **cathedral** in Old Havana are posted at the entrance. The **Jewish synagogue** at Línea and Calle M holds services and has a library. The **Methodist church**, a block away from the Habana Libre Hotel at calles 25 and K, lays on social activities as well as services, and has a small guesthouse. **Catholic churches** are open all over the island and anyone can walk in at any time to have a look or attend Mass.

S tudent Travelers

There are no official discounts or special deals for student travelers in Cuba, but discounts on accommodations, museum entrance fees, etc. are offered in some places to holders of ISIC cards (International Student Identity Cards). Check their website: www.isic.org.

T elecommunications

The Cuban **local telephone service** has undergone a complete overhaul and it is now possible to make crackle-free calls right across the island (sometimes). The state telecommunications company is ETECSA, also known as Telepunto in some places. ETECSA offers a full range of services, including phone rental, internet, and international calls. There are usually lines, so allow plenty of time.

Local and international phone calls can be made through the operator from your hotel room (or sometimes hotel reception), but calls can be made far more cheaply from public phones. There are still some public phones which take coins, either 20-*centavo* or 1-*peso cubano* coins. Most have now been converted to pre-paid phonecards *(tarjetas)*. There are two types of card on offer: "chip" and "propia," which cost the same but the latter has cheaper rates at night and can be used to make calls from a private phone as well as a public call box. The best and cheapest cards to get are the **Propia** cards priced in *pesos cubanos*, but these are supposed to be reserved for Cubans and are difficult for tourists to get hold of. Foreigners are supposed to buy those priced in CUCs, which are extremely expensive. Propia cards give you a personal code which you input before using a phone. They can be bought at branches of ETECSA and cost 5 or 10 *pesos cubanos*.

Peso convertible cards, for local or international calls, can also be bought at ETECSA offices and at hotel reception desks, and come in denominations of 5, 10, 15, or 25 CUCs. Local calls cost about 5 *centavos* a minute, calls to other provinces cost about 35 *centavos* a minute. International calls with a Propia card are expensive: CUC$1.95 a minute to the US and Canada; CUC$3.65 a minute to Europe and the rest of the world (and even more if you call from a hotel), but there are reductions for calls between 6pm and 6am.

Collect calls (reverse charge/*cobro revertido*) can be made from a regular Cuban line (as found in most homes) to the US, Canada, the UK, Mexico, Puerto Rico, Portugal, Spain, and Italy, but they are prohibitively expensive. You cannot make a collect call from a hotel or a public phone.

It is possible to hire cell phones (mobiles) at **Cubacel**. There is an office of Cubacel at Telepunto, Calle Habana, 406, between Obispo and Obrapía, in Old Havana, or they can be found in ETECSA offices around the country. The head office is at Centro de Negocios Miramar, Edificio Santa Clara, corner calles 3 and 78, tel: (7) 5264-2266; www.cubacel.com; and there is an office at Havana airport. Phones cost around CUC$5 a day to hire. Call charges are high, about 70 cents a minute for local calls, rising steeply for calls outside Cuba. As with your own cell phone if used abroad, you pay for incoming as well as outgoing calls, although an incoming call from abroad is free. The bill must be paid by cash or credit card. A deposit is refunded when the phone is returned and the bill has been paid. You can use your own cell phone in Cuba (where there is a signal) and sending a short text message home can be quicker and easier than struggling with the internet at ETECSA. Tariffs depend on your own service provider.

Telephone Codes

Telephone services have been extensively modernized and many numbers have changed, but the system has now settled down. Telephone numbers are usually six digits, except in Havana, where they are seven digits, and cell phones, which have eight digits (beginning with a 5).

If you're phoning from outside Cuba, dial the country code (**53**), then the area code, and then the number. Area codes are: Havana city 7, Havana province 47, Cienfuegos 43, Las Tunas 31, Pinar del Río 48, Villa Clara 42, Holguín 24, Sancti Spíritus 41 (except Condado, El Pedrero, Topes de Collantes 42), Granma 23, Isla de la Juventud 46, Cayo Largo del Sur 45, Ciego de Avila 33, Santiago de Cuba 22, Matanzas 45, Camagüey 32, and Guantánamo 21. No area code is needed if you are dialling a cell/mobile phone.

Inside Cuba, to call another city from Havana you must dial 0 before the area code (eg Santa Clara from Havana 042-); to call Havana from another city you must dial 0 before the area code (07-); to call any city from another (eg Santa Clara from Cienfuegos) you must dial 01 before the area code (0142-). The 0 and 01 still apply if you are calling a cell/mobile phone; the initial 5 acts as an area code.

In general, don't use the area code when phoning within a province.

In listings in this guide we have not included the international code (53), and we have kept to the general rules outlined above, but be aware that there may be differences and changes. If you're stuck, ask for help in a hotel or in an office of ETECSA, the Cuban state telephone company, although in the latter you will need to speak Spanish.

To make an international call, first dial the access code **119**, then the country code, area code, and phone number. International operators speak English.

Time Zone

Cuba is on Eastern Standard Time (Daylight Saving applies during summer), which is GMT -5. When it's noon in Havana, it's 5pm in London, 6pm in Madrid and Rome, and 2pm in Buenos Aires.

Tipping

Taxi drivers, waiters, and hotel staff should be tipped in CUCs – this is the only access to convertible currency that they get. Ten percent is usual for taxi drivers and restaurant staff. You should leave CUC$1 a day for a hotel chambermaid.

Toilets

The first thing to remember about toilets is that Cuban plumbing is dodgy so you must always throw paper in the bin provided, not into the bowl – even in hotels with smart new facilities. The second thing is to take your own toilet paper with you (this doesn't apply to hotels). There are very few public restrooms and those that do exist (at bus stations, for example) are best avoided, if possible. Restrooms in bars and restaurants are usually fairly decent, and in most places they don't question whether or not you are a customer, especially as you are expected to tip the attendant who sits outside and (sometimes) proffers toilet paper.

Tourist Information

All hotels have a **tourism bureau**, where restaurant reservations can be made, sightseeing tours booked, etc. More complicated queries should be addressed to your guide (if you have one) or to your hotel public-relations manager (if they have one).

General tourist information offices do not really exist in Cuba. **Infotur** is the only tourist-information service, with kiosks at José Martí Airport, Terminal 3 (tel: 7-642-6101; in Old Havana at Calle Obispo 521, between Bernaza and Villegas (tel: 7-866-3333), and out in Playas del Este at Avenida Las Terrazas between calles 11 and 12, Santa María del Mar (tel: 7-797-1261).

Tour Agencies & Operators

There is a whole range of state tourism enterprises whose services sometimes overlap and which concentrate on offering packages or other specific services, but they can give assistance in all areas, and most of them have improved greatly in recent years in both helpfulness and efficiency.

Amistur Cuba specializes in political tours for people wishing to see the revolutionary side of Cuba. They can be found on Paseo 406, between 17 and 19, Vedado, tel: (7) 830-1220, (7) 833-4544; www.cubasolidarity.net/amistur.

Cubanacán administrates numerous hotels, promotes and arranges

TRANSPORTATION
ACCOMMODATIONS
ACTIVITIES
A – Z
LANGUAGE

conventions, and organizes tours of all kinds, including health tourism, nature tourism, and water sports activities. Its main office is in Havana, at Calle 23 (La Rampa), 156 between O and P, Vedado, tel: (7) 204-1658; www.cubanacan.cu. In the UK, tel: 020-7537-7909.

Cubamar specializes in ecotourism, youth activities, bicycle tours, and other general sports. It also rents self-drive RVs and motor homes. The main office is at Calle 3, between 12 and Malecón, Vedado, Havana, tel: (7) 833-2523–4; www.cubamarviajes.cu.

Cubatur was for many years the only commercial subsidiary of the Ministry of Tourism (MINTUR), the state umbrella organization for tourism. Now, Cubatur sells excursions through the tourism bureaux in most of Cuba's hotels and in their own offices, which can be found in most towns and resorts. Cubatur's headquarters and its tourism office in Havana are at Calle F, 157, between calles 9 and Calzada, Vedado, tel: (7) 833-3569; www.cubatur.cu.

Gaviota books hotel accommodations, organizes excursions, car rental, dive packages, and more. The main office is at Edificio La Marina, 3rd floor, Avenida del Puerto, 102, Old Havana, tel: (7) 204-7683; www.gaviota-grupo.com.

Gran Caribe runs most of the island's luxury hotels, including the Hotel Nacional in Havana. Tel: (7) 204-9202; www.gran-caribe.com.

Habaguanex is part of the Havana City Historian's office. The company runs and promotes enterprises in Old Havana, and has a number of experienced multilingual guides attached to its own travel agency, called San Cristóbal, at Calle Oficios 110 bajos, between Lamparilla and Amargura, Old Havana, tel: (7) 861-9171; www.habaguanex.com.

Havanatur arranges hotel accommodations, as well as excursions of all kinds. It has its own fleet of buses and a car rental agency, Havanautos. Its headquarters are in the Edificio Sierra Maestra, Calle 1a, between 2 and O, Miramar, tel: (7) 830-8227; www.havanatur.cu.

Tour Agencies in the UK

A growing number of UK operators offer Cuba in their brochures:

Càlédöñià Languages,
The Clockhouse, 72 Newhaven Road, Edinburgh EH6 5QG
tel: 0131 621 7721
www.caledonialanguages.com
Language courses and activity holidays, including salsa and music, trekking, diving, and cultural tours.

Cox and Kings Travel,
6th floor, 30 Millbank, London SW1P 4EE.
tel: 020-7873 5000
www.coxandkings.co.uk
Cultural tours to Havana and tailor-made vacations.

Interchange
Interchange House, 27 Stafford Road, Croydon, Surrey, CR0 9NG
Tel: 020-8681 3612
www.interchangeworldwide.com
Group tours to Havana, Varadero, and western Cuba plus tailor-made itineraries.

Journey Latin America,
12–13 Heathfield Terrace, Chiswick, London W4 4JE.
tel: 020-8747 8315
www.journeylatinamerica.co.uk
Cultural tours, tailor-made tours, and twin-center vacations with other Latin American countries.

Kuoni Travel,
Kuoni House, Deepdene Avenue, Dorking,
Surrey RH5 4AZ
tel: 01306-747002
www.kuoni.co.uk
Offices throughout the UK.

Tours include Havana, Santiago, and Camagüey. Packages to Varadero, Guardalavaca, Cayo Ensenachos, and Cayo Coco.

Saga Holidays
The Saga Building, Enbrook Park, Folkestone, Kent CT20 3SE
tel: 0800-096 0078
www.saga.co.uk
Organizes cultural and general-interest tours.

South American Experience,
W&O Travel, Welby House, 96 Wilton Road, London SW1V 1DW
tel: 0845-277 3366
www.southamericanexperience.co.uk
Cultural tours and itineraries tailor-made to meet individual requirements.

Visas and Passports

All visitors entering Cuba must show a passport valid for at least six months beyond the date of arrival in Cuba. In addition, visitors must have a **tourist card** (*tarjeta de turista*), issued by the Cuban Consulate directly or, more commonly, through a travel agent. This will be valid for the length of your planned visit, but can be extended (once) up to the date shown on your return airplane ticket – as long as the total time you are in the country does not exceed 60 days. Immigration officials stamp your tourist card, not your passport. Do not lose it – you must show it when you leave the country.

Those planning to stay with a Cuban family (other than a licensed *casa particular*) must apply some time in advance for a **tourist visa**, while any commercial travelers must obtain a **business visa**. Regulations stipulate that travelers to Cuba must spend a minimum of three nights in a pre-booked hotel, but a *casa particular* is sufficient. Ask at the local Cuban Consulate (or check with your travel agent) for more information.

Visas for US Citizens

These are handled by the Cuban Interests Section in Washington, DC. United States Treasury Department regulations prohibit US citizens from spending money in Cuba unless they qualify as journalists, researchers, businesspeople in specifically licensed sectors, or relatives of Cubans living on the island.

Americans who oppose their government's trade and travel blockade against Cuba regularly

A Dilemma

In many Cuban towns you will be approached by people asking you for soap, moisturising cream, or pens. These are articles that are in short supply and/or can only be bought with *pesos convertibles*. It is difficult to know what the response should be. On one hand, it is cheap and easy to bring a small supply of these things with you and dole them out to people who have very little. On the other, it does encourage a culture in which Cubans look on tourists simply as suppliers of unobtainable goodies and pester them accordingly. Perhaps the best way to deal with this situation, if you would like to give things that could be useful but don't want to add to the problem, is to deliver things like pens and notebooks and soap directly to schools, where teachers can distribute them – or refuse them, if they choose.

evade or purposely violate these restrictions, and some do so just out of curiosity: many fly in via Canada, Mexico, or Jamaica. Although they could theoretically be prosecuted, they generally aren't.

W ebsites

www.cubagov.cu – official government site, general information in Spanish and English.
www.cubasi.cu – news, culture, and general information about Cuba in Spanish and English.
www.cubatravel.cu – Ministry of Tourism site. Information on accommodations, events, activities, etc. in Spanish and English.
www.casaparticularcuba.org – useful site for booking *casas particulares*, in English.

What to Bring

Clothes

Casual, comfortable clothes are appropriate anywhere on the island, especially light cotton garments that can be put on and taken off in layers as the temperature changes. As far as many Cubans are concerned, the less you wear the better.

Shorts and bathing suits are accepted at all seaside resorts, though more coverage is expected for dining out or visiting museums and galleries. Unless you're coming here for business you won't have

much use for a suit and tie or a formal dress. You also don't want to stand out by looking too smart and "dressed up."

A waterproof jacket is optional – you can usually wait out a tropical shower, and if there is a real downpour, a waterproof jacket will be of minimal use – although an umbrella might be. Cubans often carry umbrellas for protection from the sun, and also whip them open at the first drop of rain.

Take comfortable walking shoes, and dark glasses for protection against harsh tropical sunlight. Straw and cloth sunhats can be bought in any tourist store if you forget to bring one. If you are going to be traveling on long-distance buses bring a fleece or warm jersey. The air conditioning usually has only one setting in Cuba – high.

Camera Film

You can buy color film in many tourist hotel stores, though it's tricky to track down slide film. Most types of video tape are also available. As a general rule, supplies of anything to do with cameras are variable, and prices are almost always higher than those at home. It is safer to bring important items with you. And, of course, most visitors now use digital cameras.

Transformers and Adaptors

As already mentioned *(see Electricity)* you cannot be sure of the voltage or the socket type you will encounter, so it is as well to come prepared.

Medical Supplies and Toiletries

Travelers to Cuba should bring their own medicines, diarroea remedies, vitamins, adhesive bandages, contraceptives, toothpaste, insect repellent, and sunscreen. It's not a bad idea to bring a supply of toilet paper and tissues as well, if you are going to be traveling around.

Most of the larger hotels sell basic medicines at European prices. A wider range of drugs can be obtained from pharmacies *(see page 366)*.

Emergency treatment is free, while follow-up treatment and medicines are payable in CUCs. Foreigners will be treated in a CUC-only hospital, and health costs at these hospitals are as high as in the US. You are strongly advised to take out **health insurance** before leaving home. Cuba is now making insurance compulsory and you are likely to be sold a policy at the airport if you don't already have one *(see box, page 366)*.

Weights and Measures

Officially, Cuba uses the metric system, but you will find that goods at places that deal mostly with Cuban shoppers, such as farmers' markets, use imperial pounds *(libras)* – a hangover from the days when the USA provided almost all of Cuba's imports.

Women Travelers

Foreign women traveling alone may opt to visit Cuba on a package beach vacation, or a cultural tour, with Cuban specialists guiding and initiating most of the action. However, Cuba is not a difficult or dangerous place in which to travel as a single woman. Cubans out in the hinterland may regard a foreign woman traveling alone as unusual, but they will normally be friendly and helpful. Women are generally safer in Cuba than in most places in the world. Although rape is uncommon in Cuba, foreign women should be aware that the Cuban definition of "rape" is not the same as in many other places; a woman who takes a man up to her hotel room or indulges in public heavy petting will not be taken seriously if she later claims rape.

Women can expect a lot of male attention: this may be in the form of whistling, hissing (this is not perceived as rude in Cuba), or comments whispered or shouted in the street. This can be annoying but it is rarely aggressive, and is just something a woman is expected to get used to in such a macho country – Cuban women receive similar attention. Ignore the perpetrators and they will normally leave you alone. Any kind of acknowledgment is likely to be taken as a come-on.

Conversion Chart

Metric to Imperial

1cm	=	0.39 inch
1 meter	=	3ft 28ins
1km	=	0.62 miles
1 gram	=	0.035oz
1kg	=	2lbs 21oz
1 liter	=	0.22 Imp. gallons
1 liter	=	0.26 US gallons

Imperial to Metric

1 inch	=	2.54cm
1ft	=	0.30 meters
1 mile	=	1.61km
1oz	=	28.35 grams
1lb	=	0.45kg
1 Imp. gallon	=	4.55 liters
1 US gallon	=	3.79 liters

LANGUAGE

UNDERSTANDING THE LANGUAGE

BASIC RULES

Spanish is the language of Cuba. It is a phonetic language: words are pronounced exactly as they are spelled. Spanish distinguishes between the two genders, masculine and feminine, and the subjunctive verb form is an endless source of headaches for students. As a general rule, the accent falls on the second-to-last syllable, unless it is otherwise marked with an accent (´) or the word ends in D, L, R, or Z.

Vowels in Spanish are always pronounced the same way. The double L (LL) is pronounced like the y in "yes," the double R is rolled. The H is silent in Spanish, whereas J (and G when it precedes an E or I) is pronounced like a guttural H (similar to the end sound of Scottish *loch*).

When addressing someone you are not familiar with, use the formal "usted." The informal "tú" is reserved for relatives and friends. It is worth trying to master a few words and phrases. It will be much appreciated, and will also make your stay more enjoyable, as the majority of Cubans do not speak English – except for staff in the smarter hotels, who are sometimes fluent; and waiters, who know enough English to understand what you want and tell you how much it will cost. The younger generation now learns English in school, but the older generation had Russian as their second language – and they are not finding this very useful now.

The following brief lexicon is Spanish as spoken in Spain, with a few Cuban amendments. A list of "Cubanisms" follows.

WORDS & PHRASES

Hello *Hola*
How are you? *¿Cómo está usted?*
What is your name? *¿Cómo se llama usted?*
My name is... *Yo me llamo...*
Do you speak English? *¿Habla inglés?*
I am British/American *Yo soy británico(a)/norteamericano(a)*
I don't understand *No comprendo*
Can you help me? *¿Me puede ayudar?*
I am looking for... *Estoy buscando*
Where is...? *¿Dónde está...?*
I'm sorry *Lo siento/Perdone*
I don't know *No lo sé*
No problem *No hay problema*
There isn't any *No hay*
Have a good day *Que tenga un buen día*
Let's go *Vámonos*
See you tomorrow *Hasta mañana*
See you soon *Hasta pronto*
At what time? *¿A qué hora?*
When? *¿Cuándo?*
What time is it? *¿Qué hora es?*
yes/no *sí/no*
please *por favor*
thank you (very much) *(muchas) gracias*
you're welcome *de nada*
goodbye *adiós*
good evening/night *buenas tardes/noches*
today *hoy*
yesterday *ayer*
tomorrow *mañana (note: mañana also means "morning")*
tomorrow morning *mañana por la mañana*
pasado mañana *the day after tomorrow*

now *ahora*
later *después*
this afternoon/evening *esta tarde*
tonight *esta noche*
next week *la semana que viene*

Getting Around

I want to get off at... *Quiero bajarme en...*
Is there a bus to ..? *¿Hay un omnibús a ....?*
I'd like a taxi *Quisiera un taxi.*
Please take me to... *Por favor, lléveme a...*
How much will it cost? *¿Cuánto va a costar el viaje?*
Keep the change *Guarde el cambio.*
What street is this? *¿Qué calle es ésta?*
How far is...? *¿A qué distancia está...?*
airport *aeropuerto*
customs *aduana*
train station *estación de tren*
bus station *estación de omnibuses/terminal de guaguas*
bus stop *parada de omnibús*
platform *andén*
ticket *tickete/boleto*
return ticket *boleto de ida y vuelta*
hitchhiking *autostop/la botella*
toilets *baños*
This is the hotel address *Ésta es la dirección del hotel*

At the Hotel

I'd like a (single/double) room *Quiero una habitación (sencilla/doble)*
... with bathroom *con baño*
... with a view *con vista*
Does that include breakfast? *¿Incluye desayuno?*
May I see the room? *¿Puedo ver la habitación?*

washbasin *lavabo*
bed *cama*
key *llave*
elevator/lift *ascensor*
air conditioning *aire acondicionado*
swimming pool *piscina*
to book *reservar*

Emergencies

Help! *¡Socorro!*
Stop! *¡Pare!/¡Alto!*
Go away! *¡Vayase!*
Call a doctor *Llame a un médico*
Where is the nearest hospital?
¿Dónde está el hospital más cercana?
I am sick *Estoy enfermo*
I have lost my passport/purse (bag)
He perdido mi pasaporte/bolsa
I want to report... *Quiero denunciar..*

On the Road

Where is the nearest garage?
¿Dónde está el taller más próximo?
Our car has broken down *Nuestro coche se ha averiado*
I want to have my car repaired

Numbers

0 *cero*
1 *uno*
2 *dos*
3 *tres*
4 *cuatro*
5 *cinco*
6 *seis*
7 *siete*
8 *ocho*
9 *nueve*
10 *diez*
11 *once*
12 *doce*
13 *trece*
14 *catorce*
15 *quince*
16 *dieciseis*
17 *diecisiete*
18 *dieciocho*
19 *diecinueve*
20 *veinte*
21 *veintiuno*
30 *treinta*
40 *cuarenta*
50 *cincuenta*
60 *sesenta*
70 *setenta*
80 *ochenta*
90 *noventa*
100 *cien*
200 *doscientos*
500 *quinientos*
1,000 *mil*
10,000 *diez mil*
1,000,000 *un millón*

Quiero que reparen mi coche
It's not your right of way *Usted no tiene prioridad*
the road to... *la carretera a...*
left *izquierda*
right *derecha*
straight on *derecho/todo recto*
near *cerca*
far *lejos*
opposite *frente a*
beside *al lado de*
parking lot *aparcamiento/parqueo*
at the end *al final*
on foot *a pie*
by car *en carro/auto*
street *calle*
square *plaza*
give way *ceda el paso*
exit *salida*
dead end *calle sin salida*
wrong way *dirección prohibida*
no parking *prohibido aparcar*
highway *autopista*
toll *peaje*
one-way street *una sola vía*
road closed *camino cerrado*
diversion *desvío*
speed limit *límite de velocidad*
gas *gasolina*/gas station *gasolinera*
unleaded *sin plomo*/diesel *gasoil*
water *agua*
oil *aceite*/air *aire*
puncture *pinchazo*
bulb *bombilla*

On the Telephone

I would like a phonecard
Quisiera una tarjeta de teléfono
I want to make an international (local) call *Quiero hacer una llamada internacional (local).*
What is the code for...? *¿Cuál es el código para...?*
Hello? *¿Dígame?*
Who's calling? *¿Quién llama?*
Hold on, please
Un momento, por favor
I can't hear you *No le oigo*
Can you hear me? *¿Me oye?*
I would like to speak to... *Quisiera hablar con...*
He/she is not here *No está aquí.*
Speak more slowly, please
¿Podría hablar más despacio?
Could you repeat that, please?
¿Me lo repite, por favor?

Banking

Where is the nearest bank? *¿Dónde está el banco más cercano?*
Can I withdraw money on my credit card here?
¿Puedo retirar dinero con mi tarjeta de crédito aqui?
Where are the ATMs? *¿Dónde están los cajeros automáticos?*

Dates and Seasons

Days of the Week
Monday *lunes*
Tuesday *martes*
Wednesday *miércoles*
Thursday *jueves*
Friday *viernes*
Saturday *sábado*
Sunday *domingo*

Months
January *enero*
February *febrero*
March *marzo*
April *abril*
May *mayo*
June *junio*
July *julio*
August *agosto*
September *septiembre*
October *octubre*
November *noviembre*
December *diciembre*

Seasons
Spring *primavera*
Summer *verano*
Autumn *otoño*
Winter *invierno*

Shopping

I'd like to buy... *Quiero comprar...*
How much is it? *¿Cuánto es?*
Do you accept credit cards?
¿Aceptan tarjetas?
I'm just looking
Sólo estoy mirando
Have you got...? *¿Tiene...?*
I'll take this one/that one *Me llevo éste/ese*
What size is it? *¿Qué talla es?*
small *pequeño*
large *grande*
cheap *barato*/expensive *caro*
enough *suficiente/bastante*
too much *demasiado*
a piece *un trozo*
each *cada una/la pieza/ la unidad*
bill *la factura* (store), *la cuenta* (restaurant)
bookstore *librería*
pharmacy *farmacia*
post office *correos*
bakery *panadería*
butcher's *carnicería*
cake store *pastelería*
grocery *ultramarinos/bodega*

Sightseeing

mountain *montaña/sierra*
hill *colina/loma*
valley *valle*
river *río*

lake *lago*
lookout *mirador*
old town/quarter *casco antiguo*
cathedral *catedral*
church *iglesia*
town hall *ayuntamiento*
staircase *escalera*
tower *torre*
castle *castillo*
fortress *fortaleza*
museum *museo*
art gallery *galería de arte*
tourist information office *oficina de turismo*
free *gratis*
open/closed *abierto/cerrado*
every day *diario/todos los días*
all day *todo el día*

Eating Out

menu *la carta*
breakfast *desayuno*
lunch/meal *comida*
dinner/supper *cena*
first course *primer plato*
main course *plato principal*
dessert *postre*
drink included *bebida incluida*
the bill *la cuenta*
fork *tenedor*
knife *cuchillo*
spoon *cuchara*
plate *plato*
glass *vaso*
wine glass *copa*
napkin *servilleta*
ashtray *cenicero*

Drinks

coffee *café*
  black *sólo*
  with milk *con leche/cortado*
  decaffeinated *descafeinado*
sugar *azúcar*
tea *té*/herbal tea *infusión*
milk *leche*
mineral water *agua mineral*
  fizzy *con gas*/still *sin gas*
juice (fresh) *zumo/jugo (natural)*
cold *frío*/hot *caliente*
beer *cerveza*
  bottled *en botella*
  on tap *de barril*
rum *ron*
soft drink *refresco*
with ice *con hielo*
wine *vino*
  red *tinto*
  white *blanco*
  rosé *rosado*
  dry *seco*
  sweet *dulce*
house wine *vino de la casa*
half liter *medio litro*
quarter liter *cuarto de litro*
cheers! *¡salud!*

Cuban Expressions

Cuban Expressions

Asere/chama friend
Consorte/yunta close friend
Jevo/a boyfriend/girlfriend/ young woman
Mango young, sexy man
Chama/ambia partner/friend
Cundango/loca/pájaro gay
mamey mummy (used casually to women of any age)

Greetings

Qué bola, asere! What's up, man?
Qué onda/hubo Hi there!
Cuál es la vuelta? How's it going?
Bárbaro/enpingao/encojonao/ escapao cool/great!
Di tú! Tell me about it!
Aquí, en la lucha You know how it is
No es fácil Things aren't easy
Chao pesca'o Bye, bye!
Bueno, voy en pira Right, I'm going now
Eres un mangón You're looking really good
Fula/verde Hard currency
Gao house/home
Pincha work
Ser un luchador to try any means to make money

Menu Decoder

Breakfast and Snacks

pan bread
mantequilla butter
mermelada/confitura jam
sal salt/*pimienta* pepper
huevos eggs
  cocidos boiled, cooked
  fritos fried
  revueltos scrambled
  tortilla omelet
sandwich sandwich
tostada toast
queso cheese

Meat/Carne/Lomo

carne picada minced meat
cerdo pork
cabrito kid/goat
chuleta chop
conejo rabbit
cordero lamb/mutton
costilla rib
jamón ham
res beef
salchichón sausage
solomillo sirloin steak
ternera veal/young beef
a la brasa charcoal grilled
al horno roast

a la plancha grilled
asado roast
bien hecho well done
en salsa in sauce
en su punto medium
estofado stew
frito fried
pinchito skewered meat
poco hecho rare
relleno stuffed
pollo chicken

Fish/Pescado

anchoas salted anchovies
atún tuna
bacalao salt cod
calamar squid
cangrejo crab
gambas shrimps/prawns
langosta lobster
langostino large prawn
róbalo sea bass
mariscos shellfish
merluza hake
pez espada swordfish
pulpo octopus
trucha trout

Vegetables, Cereals, and Salads

verduras vegetables
aguacate avocado
ajo garlic
arroz rice
berenjena eggplant/aubergine
calabaza squash
cebolla onion
champiñón/hongo mushroom
col cabbage
ensalada salad
espárrago asparagus
espinaca spinach
frijoles beans
haba broad bean
judía green bean
lechuga lettuce
lenteja lentil
maíz corn/maize
patata potato
pepino cucumber
pimiento pepper
tomate tomato
trigo wheat

Fruit and Desserts/Fruta y Postre

ciruela plum
guayaba guava
limón lemon/lime
manzana apple
melocotón peach
melón melon
naranja orange
papaya paw paw
piña pineapple
plátano banana (plantain)
sandía watermelon
uva grape
pastel cake
helado ice cream

FURTHER READING

General

Before Night Falls: A Memoir by Reinaldo Arenas, Viking, New York (1993).
A Continent of Islands: Searching for the Caribbean Destiny by Mark Kurlansky, Addison-Wesley, New York (1992).
Cuba: A Journey by Jacobo Timerman, Picador, London (1994).
Cuba in Focus by Emily Hatchwell and Simon Calder, Latin America Bureau, London (1995).
Cuba: The Land, The History, The People, The Culture by Stephen Williams, Michael Friedman, New York (1994).
The Cubans: Voices of Change by Lynn Geldof, Bloomsbury Press, London (1992).
Driving Through Cuba: An East–West Journey by Carlos Gebler, Hamish Hamilton, London (1988).
The Early Diary of Anaïs Nin by Anaïs Nin, Harcourt Brace & Co., New York (1978–85).
Falling off the Map: Some Lonely Places of the World by Pico Iyer, Knopf, New York (1993).
Havana, A Cultural and Literary History by Claudia Lightfoot, Signal Books (2001).
Walker Evans: Havana – 1933 Pantheon, New York (1989).
Hemingway in Cuba by Norberto Fuentes and Lyle Stuart, Secaucus and L. Stuart, New Jersey (1984).
Into Cuba by Barry Lewis and Peter Marshall, Alfred van der Marck Editions, New York (1985).
Mea Cuba by Guillermo Cabrera Infante, Faber and Faber, London (1994).
Memories of a Cuban Kitchen by Mary Urrutia Randleman and Joan Schwartz, Macmillan, New York (1992).
A Taste of Cuba by Linette Creen, Dutton, New York (1991).
To Cuba and Back by Richard Henry Dana, Southern Illinois University Press, Carbondale (1966).
Trading with the Enemy: A Yankee Travels Through Castro's Cuba by Tom Miller, Atheneum, New York (1992).
When It's Cocktail Time in Cuba by Basil Woon, Horace Liveright, New York (1928).
With Hemingway: A Year in Key West and Cuba by Arnold Samuelson, Random House, New York (1984).
I Wonder as I Wander: An Autobiographical Journey by Langston Hughes, Rinehart, New York (1956).

Fiction

Cecilia Valdés or **Angel Hill** by Cirilo Villaverde, translated by Helen Lane. OUP, New York. 19th-century novel about the children of white colonizers and their black slaves.
Cuba and the Night by Pico Iyer, Knopf, New York (1995). The protagonist is Cuba itself.
Dirty Havana Trilogy by Pedro Juan Gutiérrez, translated by Natasha Wimmer, Faber and Faber (2001). The protagonist, Pedro Juan, explores himself and Havana through sex, drugs, rum, music, and other self-indulgences.
Tropical Animal by Pedro Juan Gutiérrez, Faber and Faber (2003).
Our GG in Havana by Pedro Juan Gutiérrez, Faber and Faber (2010). His reworking of Graham Greene's *Our Man in Havana*.
Dreaming in Cuban by Cristina García, Knopf (1992). A story of families divided across three generations.
Havana Bay by Martin Cruz Smith, Pan Books, UK (1999). The fourth in the Arkady Renko series of thrillers by the author best known for *Gorky Park*.
Havana Quartet: Havana Red, Havana Black, Havana Blue, Havana Gold by Leonardo Padura Fuentes, translated by Peter Bush, Bitter Lemon Press (2005, 2006, 2007, 2008). Prize-winning detective novels featuring the life, work, and friends of a Havana policeman. **Havana Fever** (2009) is a follow-up after his retirement.
The Old Man and the Sea by Ernest Hemingway, Scribner, New York (1952).
Our Man in Havana by Graham Greene, Viking, New York (1958).
The Mambo Kings Play Songs of Love by Oscar Hijuelos, Farrar, Straus & Giroux, New York (1989).
Patria o Muerte! The Great Zoo and Other Poems by Nicolás Guillén, Monthly Review Press, New York (1972).
Tres Tristes Tigres by Guillermo Cabrera Infante (1967) translated as **Three Trapped Tigers**, Faber & Faber (1989). A portrait of Havana's nightlife under Batista, written with humor and insight after the author left Cuba.
The Voice of the Turtle ed. by Peter Bush (1998). An entertaining collection of Cuban short stories translated into English.
Versos Sencillos by José Martí (1891). Poems written by the national hero while in exile in New York.

Culture

Afrocuba by Pedro P. Sarduy and Jean Stubbs, Latin America Bureau, London (1993).
Cuban Music by Maya Roy, Latin American Bureau (2002).
Machos, Maricones and Gays, Cuba and Homosexuality by Ian Lumsden, Temple University Press (1996) and in London by Latin American Bureau.
Los Negros Curros by Fernando Ortíz, Editorial de Ciencias Sociales, Havana (1986).
Rumba, Dance and Social Change in Contemporary Cuba by Yvonne Daniel, Indiana University Press (1995).
Salsa: Havana Heat, Bronx Beat by Hernando Calvo Ospina, Latin America Bureau, London (1995).
Santería from Africa to the New World by G. Brandon, Indiana University Press, Bloomington (1993).

Fidel Castro

Castro, the Blacks and Africa by Carlos Moore, Center for Afro-American Studies UCLA, Los Angeles (1988).
In Defense of Socialism by Fidel Castro, Pathfinder Press, New York (1989).
Executive Action: 638 ways to kill Fidel Castro (Secret War) by Fabian Escalante, Ocean Press (2007).
Fidel Castro Handbook by George Galloway, MQ Publications Ltd (2006).
Fidel Castro y la Revolución Cubana by Carlos Alberto Montaner, Plaza and Janes, Barcelona (1984).
Fidel Castro: Rebel Liberator or Dictator? by Jules Dubois, Bobbs-Merril, Indianapolis (1959).
History Will Absolve Me by Fidel Castro, L. Stuart, New York (1961).
My Life by Fidel Castro (author), Ignacio Ramonet (editor) and Andrew Hurley (translator), Allen Lane (2007).
Papa and Fidel by Karl Alexander, Tom Doherty Associates, New York (1989).
Revolutionary Struggle 1947– 1958: Selected Works of Fidel Castro by Fidel Castro, The MIT Press, Cambridge (1972).
The Autobiography of Fidel Castro by Norberto Fuentes, translated by Anna Kushner, W.W. Norton & Co (2010).

Politics and History

Baseball: The People's Game by Harold Seymore, Oxford University Press, New York (1990).

Baseball and the Cold War by Howard Senzel, Harcourt Brace Jovanovich, New York (1977).
Che: A Memoir by Fidel Castro, Ocean Press, Melbourne (1994).
Children of Che by Karen Wald, Ramparts Press, Palo Alto (1978).
Children of the Revolution by Jonathan Kozol, Delacorte Press, New York (1978).
Cuba Confidential: The Extraordinary History of Cuba, Its History and Its Exiles, by Ann Louise Bardach, Penguin Books, London (2004).
Cuba: A Short History, edited by Leslie Bethell, Cambridge University Press, Cambridge (1993).
Cuba from Columbus to Castro by Jaime Suchlicki, Charles Scribner's Sons, New York (1974).
Cuba on the Brink by James G. Blight, Bruce J. Allyn and David A. Welch, Pantheon, New York (1993).
Cuba: Or the Pursuit of Freedom by Hugh Thomas, Eyre & Spottiswoode, London (2002, first published 1971).
Cuba: Order and Revolution by Jorge Dominguez, Harvard University Press, Cambridge (1978).
The Cuban Revolution by Jaime Suchlicki, University of Miami Press, Coral Gables (1968).
Cuba vs the CIA by Robert E. Light and Carl Marzani, Marzani and

Send Us Your Thoughts

We do our best to ensure the information in our books is as accurate and up to date as possible. The books are updated on a regular basis using local contacts, who painstakingly add, amend, and correct as required. However, some details (such as telephone numbers and opening times) are liable to change, and we are ultimately reliant on our readers to put us in the picture.
We welcome your feedback, especially your experience of using the book "on the road." Maybe we recommended a hotel that you liked (or another that you didn't), or you came across a great bar or new attraction we missed.
We will acknowledge all contri-butions, and we'll offer an Insight Guide to the best letters received.

Please write to us at:
Insight Guides
PO Box 7910
London SE1 1WE
Or email us at:
insight@apaguide.co.uk

Munsell, New York (1961).
In Cuba by Ernesto Cardenal, New Directions, New York (1974).
The Cuban Story by Herbert L. Matthews, George Braziller, New York (1961).
The Death of Che Guevara by Jay Cantor, Knopf, New York (1983).
Diary of the Cuban Revolution by Carlos Franqui, Viking, New York (1980).
The Historical Dictionary of Cuba by Suchlicki Jaime, Scarecrow Press, Metuchen (1988).
José Martí: Cuban Patriot by Richard Butler Gray, University of Florida Press, Gainesville (1962).
No Free Lunch: Food and Revolution in Cuba by M. Benjamin, J. Collins and M. Scott, Institute for Food and Development Policy, San Francisco (1984).
One Thousand Fearful Words for Fidel Castro by Lawrence Ferlinghetti, City Lights, San Francisco (1961).
Selected Works of Ernesto Guevara, edited by Rolando E. Bonachea and Nelson P. Valdes, The MIT Press, Cambridge (1969).

Foreign Relations

Breaking with Moscow by Arkady Shevchenko, Knopf, New York (1985).
The Closest of Enemies by Wayne S. Smith, W.W. Norton, New York (1987).
Cuba in Transition: Options for US Policy by Gillian Gunn, Twentieth Century Fund Press, New York (1993).
The History of Guantánamo Bay by Marion Emerson Murphy, US Naval Base, Guantánamo Bay (1953).
Inside the Monster: Writings on the United States and American Imperialism by José Martí, Monthly Review Press, New York (1975).
The Soviet Union and Cuba Raymond W. Duncan, Praeger, New York (1985).
Thirteen Days: A Memoir of the Cuban Missile Crisis by Robert F. Kennedy, Norton, New York (1969).
Los Gusanos by John Sayles, HarperCollins, New York (1991).
The Missile Crisis by Elie Abel, Lippincott, Philadelphia (1966).

Other Insight Guides

Other Insight Guides covering the region include: *Insight Guide: Caribbean, Insight Guide: Guatemala, Belize, & Yucatán, Compact Guide: St Lucia*, and *Compact Guide: Antigua & Barbuda.*

ART AND PHOTO CREDITS

INDEX

Estrecho

Miramar, Playa, Siboney

Malecón
Monumento a Calixto García
PARQUE JOSE MARTI (SPORTS GROUND)
Swiss Embassy US Interests' Section

Casa de las Américas

Calle 5

Calle 7

Hotel Presidente

Calle 9

(Calzada)

Calle 11

Calle 13

Avenida Washington

Linea

Museo de la Danza

Calle 15

Edificio Focsa

Monumento al Maine

Avenida N

Avenida O

Hotel Nacional

Calle 11

Calle 13

Calle 15

Avenida de Los Presidentes (G)

Avenida K

Avenida J

Calle 17

Hotel Victoria

Avenida M

Avenida L

Hotel Capri

Calle 23

Malecón

Humboldt

Museo de Artes Decorativas

Avenida H

Calle 17

Calle 19

Avenida F

Avenida E

Calle 21

COPPELIA Ice Cream Park

Hotel St John

Museo Casa de Abel Santamaría

Príncipe

Vapor

Torreón de San Lázaro

Hornos

Parque John Lennon

Calle 17

Hotel Habana Libre

Calle 25

Hotel Vedado

Calle 27

San Lázaro

Jovellar

Concordia

Hamel

Oquendo

Avenida D

(Rampa)

Calle 23

Calle 21

VEDADO

Calle 23

Universidad de La Habana

Julio Antonio Mella

Calzada de Infanta

Neptuno

San Miguel

Aramburu

San Rafael

San Martín (San José)

Mariana Grajales

Calle 25

Avenida B

Calle 27

Museo Antropológico Montané

Museo Napoleónico

San Francisco

Espada

Hospital

Valle

CENTRO (CENTRA)

La Tropicana

Avenida A

Calle 29

Estadio Juan Abrahantes

Zanja

Salud

Jesús Peregrino

Allende

Castillo

Soledad

Castillo del Príncipe

Quinta de los Molinos ★

Pócito

Calzada de Zapata

Avenida Salvador Allende (Carlos III)

Casa de Cultura de Centro Habana

Calle 31

Calle 32

Paseo

Lugareño

Enrique Barnet (Estrella)

Xifré

Retiro

Árbol Seco

Subirana

Franco

Oquendo

Marqués González

San Carlos

Bruzón

ESTADIO RAMON FONST

Plasencia

Peñalver

Desagüe

Calle 35

Teatro Nacional

Ministerio del Interior

Terminal de Omnibuses Astro

Desagüe

Benjumeda

Calle 2

Calle 37

Calle 39

Aranguren

19 de Mayo

Benjumeda

Santo Tomás

Calzada de Infanta

Plaza de la Revolución

Clavel

Calle 41

Paseo

Legado Cultural Hispánico

Santa Marta

Calle 6

Monumento José Martí

P. Vidal

Arroyo (Avenida Manglar)

Avenida de Colón

(Zaldo)

San Martín

Pedroso

Palacio de la Revolución

San Pedro

Marino

Avenida Carlos M. de Céspedes

Avenida Rancho Boyeros

Ermita

Territorial

Calzada de Ayestarán

Panchito Gómez

Masón

Ave. 20 de Mayo

M. Abreu

Amenidad

Pedroso

Estévez

Santa Rosa

Fernandina

Romay

San Pedro

San Pedro

3ra

2da

1ra

San Pablo

Auditor

General E. Núñez

CERRO

Pedroso

Pedro Pérez

Universidad Campos

Estévez

Cádiz

Zequeira

San Joaquín

Maxir

Avenida de la Independencia

Lombillo

Ermita

Ayuntamiento

Tulipán

Clavel

San Pedro

Mariano

Pje. Vista Hermosa

Patria

Estadio Latinoamericano

José Martí Airport

Unión y Ahorro

Borrego